RHYMING REASON: THE POETRY OF ROMANTIC-ERA PSYCHOLOGISTS

T0347420

THE ENLIGHTENMENT WORLD: POLITICAL AND INTELLECTUAL HISTORY OF THE LONG EIGHTEENTH CENTURY

Series Editor:	*Michael T. Davis*
Series Co-Editors:	*Jack Fruchtman, Jr*
	Iain McCalman
	Paul Pickering
Advisory Editor:	*Hideo Tanaka*

TITLES IN THIS SERIES

FORTHCOMING TITLES

John Thelwall: Radical Romantic and Acquitted Felon
Steve Poole (ed.)

William Wickham, Master Spy: The Secret War against the French Revolution
Michael Durey

Enlightenment and Modernity: The English Deists and Reform
Wayne Hudson

The Edinburgh Review in the Literary Culture of Romantic Britain:
Mammoth and Megalonyx
William Christie

Montesquieu and England: Enlightened Exchanges 1689–1755
Ursula Haskins Gonthier

British Visions of America, 1775–1820: Republican Realities
Emma Vincent Mcleod

RHYMING REASON: THE POETRY OF ROMANTIC-ERA PSYCHOLOGISTS

BY
Michelle Faubert

Routledge
Taylor & Francis Group

LONDON AND NEW YORK

First published 2009 by Pickering & Chatto (Publishers) Limited

Published 2016 by Routledge
2 Park Square, Milton Park, Abingdon, Oxfordshire OX14 4RN
711 Third Avenue, New York, NY 10017, USA

First issued in paperback 2015

Routledge is an imprint of the Taylor & Francis Group, an informa business

BRITISH LIBRARY CATALOGUING IN PUBLICATION DATA

Faubert, Michelle
Rhyming reason: the poetry of Romantic-era psychologists. – (The Enlightenment world) 1. Scottish poetry – 19th century – History and criticism 2. English poetry – Scottish authors – History and criticism 3. Romanticism 4. Scottish literature – Psychological aspects
I. Title
821.7'099411

ISBN-13: 978-1-138-66368-8 (pbk)
ISBN-13: 978-1-85196-955-5 (hbk)

Typeset by Pickering & Chatto (Publishers) Limited

CONTENTS

In the memory of my beloved father, Leo Faubert.

ACKNOWLEDGEMENTS

Essays closely related to this project have appeared in *Romantic Border Crossings* (edited by J. Cass and L. Peer (Burlington: Ashgate Press), pp. 113–22) and *(Re)creating Science in Nineteenth-Century Britain* (ed. and intro. A. M. Caleb (Newcastle: Cambridge Scholars Publishing, 2007), pp. 169–87). I would like to thank the editors of these volumes for their helpful comments on those essays, the opportunity to work out my ideas about various aspects of this larger project and, above all, the encouragement they gave me through their positive responses to my work. I would also like to thank Peter Logan of Temple University for his helpful insights into a draft of the latter essay.

Financial support for this study was generously provided by the Social Sciences and Humanities Council of Canada in the form of a Postdoctoral Fellowship at the University of Western Ontario. The University Research Grants Program at the University of Manitoba also provided financial aid. I conducted a good deal of research at the University of Toronto, Wellcome Library, British Library, Scottish National Library, and Library of Northumbria University. I would like to thank all of the above institutions and their staff.

I am fortunate to have several mentors and friends who have helped me immeasurably with this project. Joel Faflak was my postdoctoral supervisor at the University of Western Ontario. When I presented the concept of this project to him as a mere seedling, he responded with such enthusiasm that I began to believe in it myself. As it began to grow, he pushed me to question my comfortable approach to the topic in ways that never would have occurred to me without the spur of his sharp and curious insights, and he continued to take an interest in the project as it matured. Also, Tom Schmid of the University of Texas, El Paso, read late drafts of some these chapters. Joel, Tom: I thank you sincerely. Most of all, I would like to thank Allan Ingram, from Northumbria University, who read late drafts of this study; his keen eye and incisive commentary were indispensable to its completion. Moreover, thanks to funding from the Leverhulme Trust, which funds the larger 'Before Depression' project that Allan directs, I was able to participate in the 'Before Depression' Conference at Northumbria University in June 2008, which helped me to refine my ideas about insanity in eighteenth-century British literature. Allan has been a mentor, inspiration, and true friend to me for several years. He is a model of intellectual rigour and academic generosity. To him I offer my humble and sincere gratitude.

I would like to thank my mom for being a true friend and great support. I still feel my dad's undying faith in me, thanks to her. Finally, I thank Javier, my love and great joy. Javi, it's all for you.

PREFACE: PSYCHOLOGIST-POETS, DISCIPLINARY POWER AND THE MODERN SUBJECT

In this study, I introduce a hitherto virtually unknown body of work – the poetry of Romantic-era psychologists – and argue that the poets can be viewed as a distinct group because of their common intellectual interests, poetic themes and ideas about their own cultural roles as doctors of the mind. In their anthology of psychological texts, *Three Hundred Years of Psychiatry*, Richard Hunter and Ida Macalpine note, 'It is a curious fact how many psychiatric physicians of the eighteenth and nineteenth centuries devoted leisure to writing verse, most of it minor and long forgotten'.[1] I argue that this verse is much more than a curiosity and that its status as 'minor poetry' does not do justice to its significance for Romanticism, the history of psychology and the broad field of literary criticism that explores the intersection of psychology and literature of any period. The verse of early psychologists affords many important insights into the relationship between science and poetry in the Romantic era, a relationship that inevitably shapes our thinking about disciplinarity. In my exploration of the fields' reciprocal influences, I will show how psychologists used literary methods to develop their professional identities and psychological theories, how features of the broader psycho-medical culture of the Scottish Enlightenment are reflected in Romantic-era literature, and, as I will explain in this preface, how this interrogation leads us to far-ranging new insights about Romantic-era subjectivity and the relation of disciplinary power to literature.

My study of the poetry of Romantic-era psychologists traces a general pattern from egalitarianism to authoritarianism, but the real story is more complex than that. I will show that English psychology was influenced by the democratic and knowledge-sharing tradition of the Scottish Enlightenment and that this tradition was tied directly to the decision of many psychologists to write poetry, making the poetry itself an expression of their liberal politics. However, as will become clear, even this poetry illustrates the subjectifying nature of disciplinary power in the end. My conclusion is not that the earliest psychologist-poets were insincere in their stated desire to spread knowledge about psychology through verse or that later figures betrayed the original motivations of their forebears, but that this pattern illustrates the inescapable nature of disciplinary power as subjectifying.

At the risk of sounding like I am providing an apologia for my theoretical choices, I wish to outline briefly why I use a Foucauldian approach in this project. A study of the psychologist-poets of the late eighteenth and early nineteenth centuries virtually demands a Foucauldian approach for several reasons. First, this study focuses on a little-known group of writers and such efforts at canon-expansion are unavoidably influenced by Foucauldian theory. In describing the formation of psychology immediately after the 'Classical period', moreover, as Foucault calls the period from 1650-1789, I study both a discipline and a time that anyone familiar with Foucault's writings in even a cursory way will recognize as suggestive of his work, particularly his most famous work, *Madness and Civilization*, in which he locates the development of our modern notions of madness in the formation of psychology after the Classical period, which overlaps with my study in obvious ways. Finally, in later works like *The History of Sexuality* and *The Order of Things*, Foucault expands his treatment of psychology by singling out the discipline as one of the academic fields of knowledge through which modern power was developed through its creation of the subject. The 'power/knowledge' dynamic that derives from his thinking about disciplinary power and the creation of the modern subject is the lynchpin upon which all of Foucault's later theory rests, as Robert Strozier argues in *Foucault, Subjectivity and Identity: Historical Constructions of Subject and Self*.[2] In this volume, Strozier uses Foucault's notion of the historicized subject as the backdrop for his enlightening discussion of how the Sophist notion of the 'originating Subject' has ruled throughout the history of Western philosophy. In so doing, Strozier confirms that Foucault's entire *oeuvre* is oriented towards an understanding of the subject, even when he did not engage directly with the subject in his earlier works about the formation of ideas about madness and the discipline of psychology. I agree with Strozier because I believe that to study the roots of psychology, as Foucault does (and I do), is to study the early days of the modern subject. Foucault's work is a well-known and helpful foil that demonstrates the wider cultural significance of an unfamiliar body of work: Romantic-era psychologists' verse.

Psychology is always bound up with self-reflexivity and subjectivity. Arnold Davidson summarizes Foucault's work in a way that confirms this link:

> Foucault claimed that he had undertaken to study the history of subjectivity by studying the divisions carried out in society in the name of madness, illness, and delinquency and by studying the effects of these divisions on the constitution of the subject. In addition, his history of subjectivity attempted to locate the "modes of objectivation" of the subject in scientific knowledge.[3]

The science of the study of madness and the topic of subjectivity in the scientific realm are dual signifiers for the discipline of psychology, which is a language – or, eventually, a series of languages when different psychological approaches were defined – through which we are encouraged to speak and understand our subjectivity (amongst other disciplinary models, including literary ones). We deceive ourselves if we attempt to argue that psychology is about 'the mind', as though we are studying an object removed from our own personal experiences. Since we all have minds, we study our own minds when we study psychology; thus, psychology is the systematization of subjectivity, a concept that I will develop in Chapter One. Early psychologists announced their new field as the science of self-reflexivity: Thomas Brown wrote in 1798 that anyone in the mental sciences 'should "be capable of abstracting his own mind from himself, and placing it before him, as it were, so as to examine it with the freedom and with the impartiality of a natural historian"'.[4] In *Lectures on the Philosophy of the Human Mind*, Brown contends, 'The belief of the identity of self, then, as the one permanent subject of the transient feelings remembered by us, arises from a law of thought, which is essential to the very constitution of the mind'.[5] On one hand, Brown contends that the study of psychology entails self-reflexivity; in the next quotation, Brown makes self-reflexivity attendant upon consciousness itself and thereby performs the function of all psychological writing: to make the reader reflect upon her own mind in a particular way.

Other psychologists devised their own 'particular ways' for the reader to understand themselves, which we know as psychological approaches. They are, in this study, moral philosophy, nerve theory, moral management, association-ism and phrenology.[6] These psychological approaches are some of the languages of disciplinary power through which we understand ourselves as subjects. Bernbauer and Mahon sum up Foucault's approach to the self in terms that are helpful here: 'These practices [of self-reflexivity in the confessional] produced a unique form of subjectivization in the human being. The self is constituted as a hermeneutical reality, as an obscure text requiring permanent decipherment'.[7] The priest and, later, modern power in its manifestation as psychology, do not only enforce the moral imperative of self-reflection on the subject; the discipline of psychology also provides the context for this act and the language with which to express its findings.

Studying the intersection between early psychology and Romantic literature entails some important philosophical questions that I think the poetry of early Romantic psychologists can help to answer. The most important of these questions concerns the function of Romantic subjectivity. It is a critical commonplace to define Romantic writers as intrepid explorers into subjectivity, the self, the mind and ways of seeing our own identities.[8] The most common explanation for this interest has been historical and philosophical: as the old story goes, by retreating into and celebrating subjectivity as the source of all truth, the Romantics rebelled against eighteenth-century empirical notions of the objective world as the source of knowledge and the normalizing forces of a government bent on crushing revolution. Many critics have shown that the Romantics, in their infinite curiosity and erudition, learned a great deal about the new discipline of psychology and even neuroscience.[9] I argue that these circumstances were related and had a much wider-ranging existential significance than has been previously argued. I will even suggest that the Romantics' knowledge about subjectivity and psychology are not only signs of their rebellion and intrepid erudition, but also of self-preservation, in a sense. The result was a kind of Georgian catch-22: in a culture that was increasingly defined by its relationship to the disciplines, to remain ignorant about the content of these disciplines was to reject existential completeness, while to learn the language of these disciplines was to become a subject of power.

Both with reference to the dominant philosophy and psychology of the time, which were identifiable in moral philosophy, Romantic subjectivity carried great existential weight. One could not *be* without being self-reflexive after Descartes' cogito: 'I think therefore I am'. Descartes asserts that we know we *are* and can be sure that we exist only when we think about thinking, cogitate on our own mental processes, an activity that we would come to identify as falling within the purview of psychology by the turn of the nineteenth century.[10] Strozier describes the move from Cartesian reflexivity to disciplinary power and the rise of psychology:

> In Descartes and for some time after him, at least until the end of the nineteenth century, there was compatibility between the interiority of the individual as self-reflexively produced and the emerging scientific disciplines and discourses. These discourses are constituted by the information drawn from individual self-inquiry in a variety of venues and in turn constitute or subjectivate – that is, as subjects – in terms of the now-systematized particularities of their thoughts, feelings, and intentions.[11]

In other words, the systematization of the mind's processes, as it was introduced by Descartes and developed in Europe until the end of the nineteenth century, was the creation of the modern subject and disciplinary power.

Nor was it possible to simply opt out of this power dynamic by refusing to engage with the esoteric realm of philosophy and leaving it to the intellectuals to become subjected to power, for psychology made self-reflexivity a concern for Everyman. In early psychological writing, proper self-reflexivity is defined over and again as the very definition of sanity and therefore a concern for all. It was clear that everyone should know how to maintain her own subjective health, as it were, but early psychologists were challenged by the dilemma of how to make academic (read esoteric) knowledge about the mind – psychological discoveries – popular.[12] The issue of subjectivity in this age is not just a sophistical exercise with little effect on one's existential concerns; nor was writing about psychological themes just a way to perform one's erudition or reify the discipline by presenting it textually, although these results were certainly valuable. When Foucault says that modern power "'categorizes the individual, marks him by his own individuality, attaches him to his own identity, imposes a law of truth on him, which he must recognize", and that "makes individuals subjects"',[13] one of the key words here is 'must': the individual is compelled to become a subject. Denying this exigency is to venture into the twin-realm of madness and non-existence.[14] As I will show, the poetry of early psychologists sought to save the lay person from this fate by introducing the new field of psychology to him.

Like other disciplines, which developed along with it, psychology provided to those who studied its language a way to speak their subjectivity into being, to become a subject; having no language for subjectivity – no psychological approach to one's own subjectivity – was to be essentially non-existent. With reference to Foucault's delineation of the changes that occurred in Europe at the end of the eighteenth-century, Strozier explains,

> monarchy has given way in the modern age to a power-knowledge network of discourses (for example, medicine) and disciplines (for example, pedagogy) to which the modern individual is necessarily submitted in order to be produced as a cultural subject. The individual is nothing more than material prior to being produced as a "discursive subject."[15]

With the rise of the field of psychology, each individual must learn to be self-reflexive in the specific terms set out by the discipline in order to be properly constituted and healthy. Thus, we may understand Romantic writers' interest in psychology, as well as Romantic subjectivity, the focus on the self – even the Romantic lyric – as products, at least in part, of disciplinary power, rather than only as a rebellion against the normalizing forces of industry and government. Meanwhile, the poetry of Romantic-era psychologists can help us to identify how some Romantic ideals – like rural living, poverty and democracy, topics that echo throughout the poetry of Romantic psychologists – functioned as markers of psychological knowledge and a healthy mental state in the period. This recognition entails another that is yet more disturbing: that literature can serve disciplinary power, even when its authors' apparent motivations are anti-authoritarian and democratic.

I will take this final contention a step further to argue that poetry was, in fact, integral to the establishment of disciplinary power, or the creation of the modern subject, which is a linguistic process because it is bound up with the creation and deployment of specific discourses. In this assertion, I do more than encourage a reevaluation of the role of literary productions with regard to the creation of disciplinary power; I also suggest a resolution to a gap in Foucault's wider historical narrative. One of the questions that haunts Foucault's work is a very practical one: how does disciplinary power create subjects in wider society if the language through which it creates subjects is known mostly only to academics and in relatively esoteric realms? We must expect Foucault's theory to explain broader culture and the way that the unknown citizens of history experienced modern power because he, more than anyone, charges us to search for and listen to the silences of history that surround the disinherited, even going so far as to dedicate an entire volume to the previously unknown parricide Pierre Rivière and hold up a nameless, simple pederast from Lapcourt as the poster-boy for bucolic pleasures lost to the strictures of the modern police state.[16] If we must study the lives of these fringe figures to understand the episteme of modernity, surely we must also ask how the average citizen became a subject of power after the Classical period.

Foucault's explanation of how the average citizen became a subject of pastoral power before the Enlightenment is clear and satisfying: in his delineation of the subject created through the Catholic confessional (the subject as a product of language and self-reflection that preceded the modern, secular subject), Foucault claims that the practice that was once reserved for monks simply permeated wider society in the sixteenth century.[17] Since European society was mostly Catholic at the time, the assumption that most people were exposed to the linguistic demands of the confessional through church attendance and community expectations is reasonable. However, it is more difficult to imagine such a social permeation with regard to disciplinary power at the end of the eighteenth century, when the language of power, as of psychology, became increasingly esoteric as the discipline developed over the years and the field of knowledge grew to the point that even scholars specializing in it abandoned hope of mastering it.[18] The fact that Wordsworth, Coleridge and Shelley, amongst many other literary geniuses, were familiar with early psychology tells us nothing about how the discipline created the modern subject in wider society because they were the highly educated and brilliant exceptions in their society, rather than the norm. Indeed, the modern subject must be something closer to an Everyman if he is to represent the experience of an episteme. Thus, Foucault's conception of the history of disciplinary power leaves us asking, How did the modern subject learn the language of psychology that helped to create him as a subject? My project offers an answer to this question: The wider public learned the language of psychology and the way to discover and speak into being their own subjectivity partly through the accessible and entertaining verse of the Romantic-era psychologist-poets.

The psychologist-poets' oft-repeated wishes to spread psychological knowledge through their works of 'pop-psychology' surely echo their decision to appeal to their audience through poetry, much of which includes psychological theory.

Even when the psychologist-poets do not discuss their therapeutic approaches and theories about the mind directly, they, nevertheless, perform an important function in the creation of modern disciplinary power because, as psychologists, they position the subject – their audience, the reader[19] – in a particular context, often with reference to themselves and the distinct literary identity they present through any given work or collection. In practical terms, the modern subject of psychology was created in part through the poetry of early doctors of the mind because these forms of publication made the language of subjectivity accessible to a wide audience, to Everyman, and released it from the esoteric realm of academia within which had been formed. The Romantic-era psychologist-poets' verse was not incidental to, but a necessary part of, the formation of disciplinary power because we cannot be subjects if we do not know the language that posits us as such and provides the means of expressing our subjectivity. Even when the individual volumes of poetry were not popular enough to have a wide-ranging effect, the very fact that so many of the most famous early psychologists in Britain wrote poetry suggests its vast cultural importance. The poetry of the Romantic-era psychologists was integral to the creation of the modern subject as created linguistically through the discipline of psychology.

In such ways, my study encourages a reevaluation of Foucault's approach to this period and theorization of the disciplines, and it sometimes challenges Foucault's claims as much as it builds upon their strengths. The argument that poetry worked in the same manner as did Romantic-era pop-psychology – to aid the establishment of disciplinary power by making it accessible to a wide audience, thereafter modern subjects – entails questions about the relation of literary technique to the technologies of power, questions that contradict some of Foucault's statements about the cultural role of the literary writer. In 'What is an Author?', Foucault writes that it was 'toward the end of the eighteenth and beginning of the nineteenth century' that

> the transgressive properties always intrinsic to the act of writing became the forceful imperative of literature. It is as if the author, at the moment he was accepted into the social order of property which governs our culture, was compensating for his new status by reviving the older bipolar field of discourse in a systematic practice of transgression and by restoring the danger of writing which, on another side, had been conferred the benefits of property.[20]

According to Foucault, literary writers were revolutionary during the Romantic period and bucked against the establishment in which doctors of the mind played an increasingly crucial role. However, the notion that, during the same period, the creators of disciplinary power (such as psychologists) used literature to define their field raises some disturbing questions about the specific ways that literature can create modern subjects, such as through generic technique, topics associated with certain types of poems and rhyme itself. Yet, in other statements, Foucault himself allows that literature may be a mode of dispersing disciplinary power; he says, in an interview with J. J. Brochier called 'Prison Talk', that

> Knowledge and power are integrated with one another, and there is no point in dreaming of a time when knowledge will cease to depend on power; this is just a way of reviving humanism in a utopian guise. It is not possible for power to be exercised without knowledge, it is impossible for knowledge not to engender power.[21]

Since some literature, like that of the Romantic-era psychologists, is didactic and provides knowledge, it can, ergo, 'engender power'. Since early British psychology was dispersed, at least in part, through poetry, we must explore the potential effects of verse upon the formation of psychology as a discipline and the kind of subject formed through these means.

Moreover, since the creation of the reader as a subject is linked to the delineation of the 'author-function' in any given text, we must question how these psychologist-poets' 'author-functions' worked. Foucault says that 'these aspects of an individual, which we designate as an author (or which comprise an individual as an author), are projections, in terms always more or less psychological, of our way of handling texts: in the comparisons we make, the traits we extract as pertinent, the continuities we assign, or the exclusions we practice ... A "philosopher" and a "poet" are not constructed in the same manner'.[22] However, these psychologist-poets encouraged their readers to do just that: construct their 'author-functions' as psychologists and poets in the same way. Yet, because the fields of literature and science were not as neatly separated in the Romantic period as they are today, as I will explain in the introduction, I suggest that the psychologist-poets did not so much challenge their readers to reconsider their conceptions of the author-function of the scientific writer versus that of the literary writer. Rather, I argue, post-Classical period readers simply learned to understand psychology in a literary context. In other words, Foucault's delineation between the various author-functions for scientists and poets is somewhat anachronistic for the Romantic-era.

Our critical need to distinguish between the two author-functions raises important questions because it suggests that each type of author performs a distinct communicative task and fulfills a certain psychological need for the reader. If it is the case that scientific and literary author-functions are one, we must ask what psychological need in the reader is fulfilled by such a unique manifestation of the author-function? And how might we describe this author-function?[23] Determining the nature of these needs requires more information about what we perceive to be the nature of various author-functions. Foucault hints at the distinguishing features of the scientific writer and the literary writer when he claims that the eighteenth century presented the truth-value of scientific writing as reliant upon the links between a given text and other accepted texts of a similar nature, rather than social themes that permeate the person of the scientist, while the same century attached particular importance to the identity of the literary writer:

> every text of poetry or fiction was obliged to state its author and the date, place, and circumstance of its writing. The meaning and value attributed to the text depended on this information. If by accident or design a text was presented anonymously, every effort was made to locate its author. Literary anonymity was of interest only as a puzzle to be solved.[24]

The truth-value of scientific writing, in other words, derived from the facts it could impart and these were judged in the context of other factual texts of a similar nature, but the truth-value of a literary text was bound up with the identity of the author, suggesting that the reader related to that author on a personal, even social, level. As such, the psychologist-poet might be said to offer facts through his personal relation to the reader, a concept that I will explore in my delineation of the various literary identities of these writers and the significance of these identities for their wider scientific projects. The nature of these facts are, of course, psychological. Put simply, the author-function of the psychologist-poet fulfilled the need of the reader to define his subjectivity by presenting himself and the language he shared through his poetry as the means by which the reader might become a subject. This concept is basic to the argument I will advance regarding the social orientation of all early psychology and the social themes that permeate in the poetry of Romantic-era psychologists.

This study will also flesh out, so to speak, the non-sexual contexts in which modern subjects were formed. Foucault asserts that the modern subject is formed in specifically sexual terms. I do not dispute the legitimacy of his argument, but I suggest that the discourse of subjectivity was originally broader in scope. More attention to the early years of psychology in Britain will shed light on other, non-sexual contexts through which the modern subject was created – contexts that, I argue, we have identified as characteristic of Romantic ideology. By exploring the many ways in which the psychologist-poets implore the reader to be self-reflexive, the contexts in which they present the sick or healthy self and the literary identity they present, I will paint a broader picture of the language that the psychologist-poet offers to the reader to speak his subjectivity into being.

By studying the versified manifestations of the earliest forms of psychology while approaching psychology as a whole as one of the most powerful promulgators of disciplinary power, I examine the changing face of the subject of modern power and suggest what cultural concerns the psychologist hoped to address by defining himself – and the subject – in particular ways. Interrogating the wider significance of the poetry of Romantic-era psychologists in relation to specific psychological approaches, from moral philosophy to phrenology, allows me to focus on the specific cultural functions of each of these early psychological approaches. As such, this study is also an examination of how these early forms of psychology created disciplinary power and its subject in ways that answered specific cultural concerns. Because the expressive freedom of verse allows the psychologist-poet to cover a wide variety of themes, emotions, and subjects, this poetry reveals in bold strokes the changing face of psychology and the always-related identity of the subject.

Notes:

1. R. Hunter and I. Macalpine (eds), *Three Hundred Years of Psychiatry 1535-1860* (London: Oxford University Press, 1963), p. 710.
2. R. Strozier, *Foucault, Subjectivity and Identity: Historical Constructions of Subject and Self* (Detroit, MI: Wayne State University Press, 2002).
3. A. I. Davidson, 'Ethics as Aesthetics: Foucault, the History of Ethics, and Ancient Thought', in G. Gutting (ed.), *The Cambridge Companion to Foucault*, 2nd edn (Cambridge: Cambridge University Press, 2005), pp. 123-48, on p. 126.
4. Quoted in E. Faas, *Retreat into the Mind: Victorian Poetry and the Rise of Psychiatry* (Princeton, NJ: Princeton University Press, 1988), p. 36.
5. T. Brown, *Lectures on the Philosophy of the Human Mind* (1820) (Edinburgh: William Tait, 1828), p. 81.
6. Although many of the writers I study do not identify themselves as representatives of particular psychological approaches, I categorize them in the schools listed above according to chronological and ideal boundaries in order to aid my consideration of their cultural context and significance.
7. J. Bernauer and M. Mahon, 'Michel Foucault's Ethical Imagination', in G. Gutting (ed.), *The Cambridge Companion to Foucault*, 2nd edn (Cambridge: Cambridge University Press, 2005), pp. 149–75, on p. 154.
8. In keeping with my Foucauldian approach, I will use the word 'subject' and its variants to refer to the concept that might otherwise be called the 'self'. 'Subject' carries with it associations of one's 'subjection' to authority's understanding of the self-reflexive person and one's submission to a definition not delineated by themselves. This power relationship is important to an understanding of how the democratic, power-sharing principles of early psychology as it developed out of the Scottish Enlightenment became subsumed by later manifestations psychology – not through any tyrannical or deviously authoritarian motivations of later psychologists, necessarily, but through the very structure of discipline.
9. I discuss these critics' works in the introduction to this study.
10. Richard Rorty claims that the 'mind' as we think of it was 'invented/produced' by Descartes, which, given Descartes' dates (1596–1650), suggests that the ontology of psychology as a field may be traced to seventeenth-century France (cited in Strozier, *Foucault, Subjectivity and Identity*, p. 237; R. Rorty, *Philosophy and the Mirror of Nature* (Princeton, NJ: Princeton University, 1979)). I argue that British psychology as it

developed in the Romantic period derived from the tradition of moral philosophy in the Scottish Enlightenment, which was a branch of the rationalist tradition Cartesian philosophy and grew partly in sympathy with and partly in opposition to David Hume's challenges to the valorization of subjectivity.

11. Strozier, *Foucault, Subjectivity and Identity*, p. 19.

12. Edward Shorter defines 'Romantic psychiatry' with reference to the role subjectivity played in assessments of sanity at the time: 'Reil understood psychology as the study of the "anomalies of self-consciousness or subjectivity", as for example doubting the real-ness of one's own personality "or confusing our ego ... with that of another person"' (E. Shorter, *A Historical Dictionary of Psychiatry* (Oxford: Oxford University Press, 2005), p. 117). Meanwhile, in England, Francis Willis (grandson to King George III's doctor, the Reverend Dr Francis Willis) 'maintained that "no man ... can be considered sane, until he freely and voluntarily confess his delusions"', or, as Hunter and Macalpine put it, until he had 'insight and understanding of his illness' (*Three Hundred Years of Psychiatry*, p. 759). The influential English psychologist Alexander Crichton agreed that proper self-reflection was the key to sanity; according to Eckbert Faas, Crichton's psychological approach in *Inquiry into the Nature and Origin of Mental Derangement* (1798) was based on 'specific techniques of self-objectification and a return to childhood' (*Retreat into the Mind*, p. 59). The British tradition of defining (or recreating) sanity with reference to proper self-reflection may be traced to Robert Burton's *The Anatomy of Melancholy*, in which he equates madness with animality and notes that the major difference between humans and 'brutes' is that the latter 'cannot reflect upon themselves' (R. Burton, *The Anatomy of Melancholy* (1621) (London: T. Tegg, 1845), pp. 40, 105). Yet, one of the earliest definitions of sanity that involves subjectivity is attributed to Erasmus, who defined the rational self 'as a self that can seize itself as an object of reflection in irony' (A. Thiher, *Revels in Madness: Insanity in Medicine and Literature* (Ann Arbor, MI: The University of Michigan Press, 1999), p. 53).

13. Quoted in Bernauer and Mahon, 'Michel Foucault's Ethical Imagination', p. 155.

14. Many portrayals of madness in early nineteenth-century English literature, both medical and fictional, reveal that madness was popularly understood to be a state of non-exist-ence. One of the pioneers of moral management, Samuel Tuke, referred to madmen as '"automata"' (quoted in Hunter and Macalpine, *Three Hundred Years of Psychiatry*, p. 687), thereby positing madness as a soul-stealing condition that leaves its victims with an inhuman existence, while, in *Essays on Hypochondriacal ... Affections* (1823), John Reid discusses madhouses and madmen in a revealing way: '"Diseased members [i.e. madmen] have been amputated from the trunk of society, before they have become so incurable or unsound as absolutely to require separation. Many of the depots for the captivity of intellectual invalids may be regarded only as nurseries for and manufactories of madness; magazines or reservoirs of lunacy"' (quoted in Hunter and Macalpine, *Three Hundred Years of Psychiatry*, p. 723). Even while he argues for the better treatment of the insane, Reid uses language that could only perpetuate the popular understanding about madmen as faceless 'diseased members', incomplete humans who are 'amputated from the trunk of society', childish residents of 'nurseries', and the inhuman products of 'manufactories'. Of the fictional works of the period, one of the most striking examples of this belief occurs in the original ending of William Godwin's *Caleb Williams*. In the manuscript version of the novel, Caleb Williams goes insane while unjustly imprisoned and his final words aptly illustrate the extent of his mental distress: 'True happiness lies in being like a stone – nobody can complain of me – all day long I do nothing – am a

stone – a GRAVE STONE! – an obelisk to tell you, HERE LIES WHAT WAS ONCE A MAN!' (Godwin, W. *Caleb Williams, or, Things as They Are*, ed. and intro. D. M. McCracken (Oxford: Oxford University Press, 1970), p. 334).

15. Strozier, *Foucault, Subjectivity and Identity*, p. 12. Strozier confirms elsewhere that, in translations of Foucault's work, the word 'individual' denotes 'a state prior to discursive subjectivity', or, in other words, refers to a person who has yet to be inducted into modern subjectivity through language (Strozier, *Foucault, Subjectivity and Identity*, p. 144).

16. M. Foucault, *I, Pierre Rivière, Having Slaughtered My Mother, My Sister and My Brother: A Case of Parricide in the Nineteenth Century* (New York: Pantheon Books, 1975); M. Foucault, *The History of Sexuality*, 3 vols (New York: Vintage Books, 1980), trans. R. Hurley, vol. 1, p. 31.

17. Bernauer and Mahon, 'Michel Foucault's Ethical Imagination', p. 153; Foucault, *The History of Sexuality*, p. 20.

18. R. M. Veatch, *Disrupted Dialogue: Medical Ethics and the Collapse of Physician-Humanist Communication (1770–1980)* (Oxford: Oxford University Press, 2004), p. 41.

19. I want to emphasize here that I use the terms 'reader' and 'subject' interchangeably in this study because I contend that the reader is defined as a subject by being a member of the lay audience who learns of the language and identity of the psychologist by reading his works. This situation also puts her in a position very like that of the patient of psychology, who is, similarly, called upon to accept the psychologist's definition of the mind – readily categorized as the patient's mind in the therapeutic relationship, and more subtly identifiable with the reader's mind in psychologist's writing. Incidentally, this mind is also the psychologist's own, but, since he is the definer of it, he is not subjectified by this construction in the same way as is the reader/subject/patient.

20. M. Foucault, 'What is an Author?', in V. B. Leitch (ed.), *The Norton Anthology of Theory and Criticism* (New York: W. W. Norton, 2001), pp. 1622–36, on p. 1622.

21. M. Foucault and J. J. Brochier, 'Prison Talk', in C. Gordon (ed.), *Power/Knowledge: Selected Interviews and Other Writings, 1972-1977*, trans. C. Gordon, L. Marshall, J. Mepham and K. Soper (New York: Pantheon Books, 1972), pp. 37-54.

22. Foucault, 'What Is an Author?', p. 1629.

23. Significantly, my approach works on the assumption that the audience of the psychologist-poets' verse knew that it was written by doctors of the mind. It may be countered that the readers may not have been aware of the poet's main occupation because they did not always announce themselves as doctors on their title pages or make reference to their line of work in their prefaces. However, because the readers always had access to these facts and because the psychologist-poets often made specific reference to their professions, we may assume that the reader understood that the poets were also psychologists.

24. Foucault, 'What Is an Author?', p. 1629.

INTRODUCTION: ROMANTIC-ERA PSYCHOLOGIST-POETS AND THE HISTORICAL CONTEXT OF EARLY BRITISH PSYCHOLOGY

I. The Enlightenment Ideal of Disseminating Knowledge

In this study I will illustrate that many Romantic-era psychologists wrote poems to disseminate information about their profession to a broad audience. So much is evident in Thomas Bakewell's 'Lines, On Being Told that the Volitions of the Mind Would Overcome the Sense of Bodily Pain'. In this poem, Bakewell (1761–1835) – an asylum owner and author of *The Domestic Guide, In Cases of Insanity*, a self-help guide on madness[1] – explores current medical debates about psychosomatic symptoms and the power of the mind in a way that is humorous, appealing and illustrative of Bakewell's contention that poetry is essential to his vocation. He uses verse to popularize and debate psychological issues and, as the poem reveals, he even uses poetry to carry out psychological experiments on himself:

> Avaunt, thou stoic sophistry,
> So falsely call'd philosophy,
> That would pretend the mind may gain,
> Such power o'er corporeal pain,
> That when we mentally are pleas'd,
> The body may from pain be eas'd.
>   Of late, in a most painful hour,
> Thinks I, I'll try this mental pow'r;
> First, poetry to aid me came,
> A fav'rite laughter[-]loving dame;
> But soon I fouud [sic] her influ'nce gone;
> That inspirations she had none:
> 'Tis true, I rhym'd to a deep groan,
> By utt'ring a most piteous moan.
>
> . . . .
>
> In other cases shall we find,
> That an impression on the mind,

> Shall overcome corporeal pain,
> And sense of feeling quite restrain.
> It is a morbid state, most sure,
> If we keen suff'rings can endure,
> Without our feeling what they are;
> As sometimes maniacs will declare.
> But while our intellects are clear,
> This anguish must be cause of fear;
> And as a truth, we may maintain
> A diff'rence betwixt ease and pain.[2]

Quite aside from Bakewell's final reference to madness as the scale by which he judges the soundness of the theory in question, he makes reference to his profession as an asylum owner and psychologist in the most powerful way at the poem's commencement. The first method that Bakewell (who I assume is identifiable with the speaker here, given their mutual interest in psychology) uses to carry out his psychological research is poetic: he tries to distract himself from his bodily pain through verse. Although the test fails and leaves him only 'groan[ing]' rhythmically, it is notable that he turns to poetry first to carry out his psychological experiment. In this poem, Bakewell expresses succinctly what almost all of the other psychologist-poets show in various ways: poetry is a valuable tool for psychology. At a point in history when psychology was only beginning to be defined as a discipline, Bakewell and many other psychologists (I will examine eleven in total here) chose verse as a means of disseminating knowledge about their field, delivering psychological therapy, or guiding the reader in accordance with psychological principles.

The birth of psychology as a field in England has been traced to the period 1790-1850. Once scorned as the lowly practice of physicians who could attract no better class of patients, the treatment of the mad garnered the respectful attention of eminent doctors during this period, partly in response to the madness of King George III, who had four attacks of mental derangement beginning in 1788 and ending in 1810, after which the Regency was declared. Other famous cases of madness had a measurable effect on changing attitudes towards the treatment of the insane, such as James Hadfield's attempt on the life of King George III in 1800, after which English legal policy was altered with the passing of the *Act for the Safe Keeping of Insane Persons Charged with Offences* (1800).[3] Shortly thereafter, government officials showed their interest in the treatment of the mad by passing the Act that first enabled the establishment of public lunatic asylums in 1808, and by appointing the first major parliamentary inquiries into madhouses in 1807 and 1815. The furious press and pamphlet war that attended these parliamentary inquiries brought the issues involved in psychological treatment to the wider public, while the *First Report Minutes of Evidence Taken Before the Select Committee of the House of Commons* reveals the shocking evidence of mistreatment in asylums that the governmental committees collected, and which would change the face of psychological treatment in England forever by inspiring widespread concern for the better treatment of the insane.[4] Additionally, the fear that madness was on the rise was prevalent in Georgian-era England. Some of the most famous psychologists of the day, such as Thomas Arnold and John Haslam, highlighted this subject in their texts about madness. The page heading of the second section of Arnold's *Observations on the Nature, Kinds, Causes and Prevention of Insanity* reads, 'Insanity why common in England', while Haslam begins his preface to *Observations on Madness and Melancholy: Including Practical Remarks on those Diseases* with the following comment: 'The alarming increase in Insanity, as might naturally be expected, has incited many persons to an investigation of this disease'.[5] Thus, it becomes clear why knowledge about the human mind was deemed to be essential for any representative of culture, not the least of whom were the Romantic-era poets.

In recent years, the body of criticism outlining the Romantic poets' knowledge about psychological subjects has grown. This field of criticism is an offshoot of an earlier critical field, which focuses more specifically on madness in Romantic literature, and both interrogate the wider cultural influences of the theme of subjectivity that characterizes Romantic literature. Some of the most notable critical works in these fields are Philip W. Martin's *Mad Women in Romantic Writing* and Frederick Burwick's *Poetic Madness and the Romantic Imagination*.[6] More recently, Alan Richardson's important work, *British Romanticism and the Science of the Mind*, amongst other works of a similar nature, has shown that Romantic poetry concerned itself not only with madness, but with the exploration of how the human mind works and fails on physical and metaphysical levels.[7] Aside from Beverly Taylor's *The Cast of Consciousness: Concepts of the Mind in British and American Romanticism*, most other recent critical works that describe Romantic writers' knowledge of psychology are dedicated to individual writers; amongst these are Jeremy Tambling's *Blake's Night Thoughts*, William Brewer's *The Mental Anatomies of William Godwin and Mary Shelley* and Neil Vickers's *Coleridge and the Doctors*.[8] In *Romantic Psychoanalysis: The Burden of the Mystery*, Joel Faflak reveals that Romantic writers were proto-psychoanalysts.[9] Critics writing on this subject recognize that the inclusion of scientific subjects in Romantic poetry was itself new and suggest that many of the most famous poets of the time originated the concept of developing psychological subjects in verse after having read the medical prose of eminent doctors. However, I suggest that these poets may have been responding to a broader cultural phenomenon that understood literature and medicine as fields connected in scope and ideology, rather than as opposed, as we see them today. Many facets of this fascinating Enlightenment and early Romantic-era phenomenon are highlighted in the poetry of Romantic-era psychologists. From the poetry of asylum-keeper Nathaniel Cotton, whose hugely popular *Visions in Verse* reached eleven editions by the year of his death in 1788, to that of Thomas Forster, a well-known phrenologist whose last collection of verse appeared in 1850, this previously unexplored field reveals valuable and original insights about the intersection of psychology and poetry in the Romantic era.[10]

Politically democratic and ideologically egalitarian, for the most part, these representatives of the emerging profession of psychology regarded their roles as public in a way that necessitated the use of an appealing form of writing, specifically poetry, in order to communicate psychological ideas, as well as cultural and moral concepts that reflect the religious and political milieu of their psychological training – and which would be echoed by so many canonical Romantic poets that centuries of criticism would identify them as distinct features of Romantic literature. Many of the psychologist-poets include references to their vocations as psychologists in their verse and use the inherent characteristics of poetry – such as the lyric's potential to represent the speaker's mind and the mnemonic qualities of rhyme – to teach their readers about psychology. In fact, these poets sometimes even provide psychological therapy to their readers through their poetry, which suggests that the field of psychology required, to some extent, the poetic medium for communicating ideas, just as statisticians need graphs, gangs need graffiti or academics need essays. In other words, for the psychologist-poets, medicine is not framed by poetry, as is commonly implied in literary criticism that presents verse as the distillation and peak of scientific expression. Rather, poetry is framed by medicine. By presenting their professional identities in this context and emphasizing certain poetic themes, the psychologist-poets helped to develop early psychology as a field. In so doing, they also contributed to the formation of disciplinary power, the discourse of subjectivity and its relationship to literary writing in heretofore unrecognized ways.

These psychologist-poets' common intellectual interests, poetic themes and ideas about their own cultural roles show the influence of the Scottish Enlightenment and its signature subject, moral philosophy, out of which modern psychology grew. Almost all of the psychologist-poets studied medicine in Scotland, which was as widely renowned in the eighteenth century for its medical schools as the schools were for their Whiggish character. The psychologist-poets' literary interests may be traced to the liberal character of the Scottish medical schools of the eighteenth century because Scottish Whigs encouraged a diversity of interests and areas of expertise as insurance against intellectual tyranny and conservatism. Their liberality also demanded that education be available to students from a wide range of social classes, and the psychologist-poets responded in kind: they attempted to erase class boundaries through the accessible medium of verse and the celebration of low-class, rustic life in order to appeal to a wide range of readers about psychology and liberal politics. Besides the desire to disseminate knowledge, this poetic effort was also motivated by the concern for self-promotion, for this poetry helped to define the professional identity of the psychologist as a cultural sage with broad interests and a particular facility to communicate in various ways and with a wide variety of social groups. These new doctors of the mind, who were just beginning to recognize their fellowship in an emerging profession, defined their professional identities in recognizable and consistent ways through poetry. They sought to present the image of the psychologist as more than a scientist. The psychologist was also a man of letters, an arbiter of morals, a shaper of culture, and, above all, an expert in communicating with all classes and types of people.

The specific themes and literary techniques that these writers use tell us much about how psychology related to literature during the Romantic period and how the delineation of the modern subject is bound up with all types of writing. While it becomes clear that some of the major characteristics of this poetry reflect the writers' specific cultural milieu – for example, the egalitarian impulse of the Scottish Enlightenment shines through the common thematic emphases on sympathy, social concern and the celebration of simple, rural living, while the literary techniques of using humour and the epistolary form may be said to illustrate the psychologist-poet's democratic desire to present an accessible and friendly professional identity – any student of Romanticism will also recognize these themes and techniques as common to the more popular works of the period. I argue that these common themes and techniques reflect the development of modern disciplinary power on a broad scale that encompasses both the literary and psychological fields and, in effect, treats them as identifiable during this period. The discipline of psychology and the attendant discourse of subjectivity were deployed in a literary context, forming the readers of this literature into the subjects of modern power.

As much as this exploration of early psychology and its poetry contributes to the now-familiar Foucauldian contention that the discipline is authoritarian, thereby subjectifying the modern subject, it also complicates this narrative by arguing – just as strenuously, I hope – that early psychologists' poetry and the culture out of which it grew points to the originally egalitarian and democratic roots of psychology. In *Madness and Civilization*, Foucault identifies the psychologist in the Romantic era as the 'apotheosi[zed] ... *medical personage* ... peculiar to the world of the asylum as it was constituted at the end of the eighteenth century', a figure who gained his power through the relative ignorance of his patient: 'it was in the esotericism of his knowledge, in some almost daemonic secret of knowledge, that the doctor had found the power to unravel insanity; and increasingly the patient would accept this self-surrender to a doctor both divine and satanic, beyond human measure'.[11] I will argue, though, that this 'demonic' identity was, from the beginning, only one aspect of a deeply complex character and developed as an inevitable consequence of the growth of psychology as a field. This authoritarian identity is intimately and inevitably united with the changing discourse of subjectivity that is psychology itself. That is to say, the mere fact that psychologists systematize subjectivity, define the private experience of self-reflection or the mind, and improvise a language not created by the subject that is, yet, intended to speak his identity into being, makes them masters of subjectivity and contributes to their authoritarian identity. Nor does this aspect of psychology entail a negation of its stated principles, as though tyranny were the sole goal of discipline. Indeed, as Foucault notes in a lecture he presented on 14 January 1976, 'We are subjected to the production of truth through power and we cannot exercise power except through the production of truth'.[12] Simply by searching for the truth of the human mind, early psychology established a network of power and subjectivity – and subjectedness. In the following pages, I will introduce eleven psychologist-poets of the Romantic period, outline in greater detail the features of the tradition to which they contributed, provide a brief history of the role of psychology and literature in eighteenth-century Scotland and suggest specific areas of overlap between their work and that of better-known Romantic poets. Through these means, I will not only frame the evolution of early psychology in a literary context but, more to the point, I will work towards defining the cultural role of the psychologist-poet in Romantic-era Britain with specific reference to the formation of the modern subject.

We have not probed adequately the deeper cultural significance of the common assertion that interest in subjectivity in literature arose in relation – and perhaps in response – to the increased attention to subjectivity in psychology during the Romantic period. If these movements are parallel, they must, at some level, deploy similar cultural effects. Romantic criticism has, for the most part, accepted the narrative that attention to subjectivity in Romanticism was part of its rebellion against the more socially oriented Augustan movement in literature, as well as that it represented the Romantics' insistence upon laying claim to a private, ungovernable space that the government could not control during this time of heavy censorship and fear of revolution. Romantic literature, in short, has almost uniformly been counted on the side of protest and anti-establishment sentiment. Yet if it is true, as many well-regarded critics have claimed, that Romantic literature was heavily influenced by psychological writings, then these assertions about the defiant nature of Romantic literature must, at least, be called into question since psychology is basically the systematization of subjectivity, as I will argue in Chapter 1. When literature uses a psychological approach to subjectivity, it is complicit in making subjectivity socially mediated and a product of the state; it replaces private identity with the authorized version of the self as defined in the increasingly reified and influential discipline of psychology. Although almost all of the psychologist-poets I study here claim a democratic political stance, as did so many of the best-known Romantic writers, they all contributed to the systematization of the last bastion of privacy, namely subjectivity, regardless of whether they were aware of doing so. Despite the personal politics of early psychologists and literary writers (who are often one and the same), the programme of psychology governs the private and makes it social. This concept underpins all of my arguments in the following chapters. In attempting to establish this contention with reference to the verse of Romantic-era psychologists, I am encouraging a reconsideration of the wider cultural meaning of literature that is influenced by psychology.

The unique subject matter of this project also offers the means of reconsidering other familiar histories. In the process of narrating the development of the psychologist-poets' tradition, I also offer the means of reframing the history of psychology through its literary expression. This focus leads to some new conclusions about the formation of the modern subject out of a discipline that originated in a Whiggish environment and, in many ways, was born of egalitarian impulses, but that morphed into its opposite and contributed to disciplinary power by dint of its very essence. My focus on the literature of early doctors of the mind also leads to some original conclusions regarding the confluence of literature and psychology in the Romantic period. For example, I trouble the accepted critical narrative about the literary expression of nerve theory in the culture of sensibility by suggesting that moral managers borrowed some of the tropes and genres most intimately associated with nerve theory. I also argue that the Romantic period heralded a new kind of nerve theorist, one that established his difference from nerve doctors of the Cheynian stamp by championing the lower classes and associating nervous illness with insanity, both of which assertions threatened the aristocratic basis of the culture of sensibility. While the field of Romantic-era psychologists' poetry is new to the critical scene, it provides insight into some of the most familiar areas of inquiry.

II. The Tradition of Psychologist-Poets' Verse

In approximate birth order and with brief reference to their claims to psychological fame, the poets whom I study are Nathaniel Cotton (b. *c.* 1705 d. 1788), owner of a private madhouse called the *Collegium Insanorum*; James Beattie (1735–1803), Professor of Moral Philosophy and author of the *Elements of Moral Science*, which includes a lengthy section on 'psychology'; William Perfect (1737–1809), owner of a private madhouse and author of *Select Cases in the Different Species of Insanity, Lunacy, or Madness*; Andrew Duncan Sr (1744–1828), author of *Observations on the Structure of Hospitals for the Treatment of Lunatics*;

Thomas Beddoes (1760–1808), author of *Hygëia; or, Essays Moral and Medical on the Causes Aff ecting the Personal State of Our Middling and Affl uent Classes* (and father of the famous Romantic poet and playwright, Thomas Lovell Beddoes); Thomas Trotter (1760–1832), author of *An Essay, Medical, Philosophical, and Chemical, on Drunkenness, and Its Effects on the Human Body*, which was the first text to present alcoholism as a psychological ailment; John Ferriar (1761–1815), physician at Manchester Infirmary Lunatic Hospital and author of *An Essay Towards a Theory of Apparitions*, which was the first text to propose a psychological explanation for ghosts; Thomas Bakewell (1761–1835), asylum owner and author of *The Domestic Guide, In Cases of Insanity*; Thomas Brown (1778–1820), Professor of Moral Philosophy and author of *Lectures on the Philosophy of the Human Mind*; and, finally, Thomas Forster (1789-1860), author of *Observations on the Casual and Periodical Influence of Particular States of the Atmosphere on Human Health and Diseases, Particularly Insanity*.[13] I also touch on the more familiar verse of Erasmus Darwin (1731–1802) in the first chapter to introduce the tradition of which he is the most famous member. Many Romantic-era doctors wrote poetry,[14] but these doctors of the mind are particularly important for the study of Romanticism because its distinctly psychological character suggests that the poetry and the figure of the psychologist-poet may have affected its formation.

Before I move any further into a description of this project, I must clarify my terminology. The issue of the proper terminology for early doctors of the mind is highly contentious. Roy Porter explains that the word 'psychiatry' was used by the late eighteenth century and Allen Thiher confirms that the German Dr J. C. Reil (1759–1813) gave us the word 'psychiatry' – although it seems rather unlikely that the German document in which this information appeared would so immediately become known to, and its contents and terminology so quickly adopted by, Romantic-era British medical professionals.[15] Edward Shorter confirms that the term only originated in 1808 with Reil's work and adds that 'The use of the new term spread rather slowly', even in Germany.[16] We can safely assume, then, that Romantic-era doctors of the mind were not called 'psychiatrists' in England. Yet, in their seminal work, *Three Hundred Years of Psychiatry 1535–1860*, Hunter and Macalpine use 'psychiatry' and its variants to refer to all doctors of the mind, including those who practised before the nineteenth century. They embrace in this vast compendium of major figures throughout 'three-hundred years of psychiatry' such figures as Thomas Beddoes the elder, a doctor who never consulted with the insane; Thomas Bakewell, an asylum owner who was not a doctor and, in fact, had no formal education; and Thomas Brown, a doctor, professor and moral philosopher who neither met with patients nor wrote about mental illness. In short, Hunter and Macalpine see as relevant to the history of psychiatry even those figures who were not doctors, did not meet with mental patients and did not write specifically about mental ailments. Because the field and its attendant terminology was not yet closely regulated, such inclusiveness makes sense, as does Hunter's and Macalpine's use of an umbrella term ('psychiatry') to refer, simply, to the study of the mind.

I have been similarly inclusive in my identification of early doctors of the mind and have followed Hunter's and Macalpine's authoritative lead by choosing an inexact term to refer to these figures' subject of study. However, I use the term 'psychology' and its variants to refer to matters of the mind because it was current in the period I study. Gladys Bryson claims that Dugald Stewart was one of the first to use the term in the late eighteenth century.[17] In fact, David Hartley had used the term in the 1750s, as did others before him according to the *Oxford English Dictionary* (hereafter *OED*) entry for 'psychology', but it is arguable that the word was only employed to signify the concepts with which we now associate it near the end of the eighteenth century in the work of Dugald Stewart and James Beattie.[18] Indeed, Part 1 of Beattie's *Elements of Moral Science* is entitled 'Psychology' and contains section titles that refer to such now-familiar psychological concepts as 'Perception, or External Sensation', 'Consciousness, or Reflection', 'Dreaming' and 'Sympathy'. In the Romantic period, 'psychiatry' and 'psychology' were not yet distinguished from one another as referring, in the former case, to the practice of doctors who treat mental ailments with physical interventions and, in the latter case, to the practice of doctors who treat such matters in non-surgical and non-chemical ways, such as through talk-therapy. However, 'psychiatry' did entail the sense of ailment and need for treatment, while 'psychology' referred more generally to matters of the mind. Since several of the figures I study contributed to our knowledge of the workings of the human mind in general, if not so much the sick mind, and since several influential figures used the term in the Romantic period, I have chosen 'psychology' and its variants to refer to the psychologist-poets' area of expertise.

No concrete evidence exists to suggest that these psychologist-poets worked within a recognized tradition, but a few key pieces of evidence from the Romantic period indicate that the psychologist-poets knew of one another, even if they did not regard themselves as part of a definable 'school' of psychologist-poets. For example, these psychologists often make reference to one another's prose work. Reference to Darwin's work appears in Trotter's and Beddoes's prose and probably elsewhere. Perhaps the most famous of such allusions is Brown's *Observations on the Zoönomia of Erasmus Darwin, MD*, in which Brown, at age nineteen, attacks the comparatively Goliath-like Darwin in a thoroughgoing critique of the established doctor's most comprehensive work. Moreover, Beddoes (not to mention Coleridge) knew Ferriar's prose, as Vickers reveals in 'Coleridge, Thomas Beddoes and Brunonian Medicine', while, in *Facts and Enquiries Respecting the Source of Epidemia, with an Historical Catalogue of the Numerous Visitations of Plague, Pestilence, and Famine*, Forster quotes from Ferriar's *An Essay Towards a Theory of Apparitions*.[19] Arguably, if these psychologists were familiar with each other's prose, they were also familiar with each other's poetry.

Perhaps the most compelling evidence of these doctors' connections is poetic, though. Bakewell compares himself to another psychologist-poet in his verse. In the theatrical final poem of *The Moorland Bard*, called 'The Author's Dream', Bakewell subtly claims his right to a literary identity by hinting that the field of psychologist-poets is already established, even as he humorously excuses himself from the contest:

> At the shop door, in steps a bold stranger,
> And stalks up to me like any free ranger.
> "If you are the poet", says he, "you must go
> "Before the Reviewers:" – I answer'd, "O no!"
> My hands they did shake, and my legs they did totter,
> I trembled as much as that poor honest Trotter.[20]

In these lines, Bakewell certainly refers to Thomas Trotter, another psychologist-poet whom I study; according to my research, no other writer by the name of Trotter published poetry at this time. Moreover, a connection exists between Trotter and another poet with whom Bakewell seems preoccupied in these volumes. In 'The Weaver's Request' and 'Epistle to a Neighbouring Gentleman', the first and third poems of *The Moorland Bard*, Bakewell makes pointed references to the so-called 'cobbler-poet', Robert Bloomfield (1766–1823), references that indicate his familiarity with and interest in Bloomfield's poetry. Bloomfield's volume, *The Farmer's Boy: A Rural Poem*, probably attracted Bakewell's notice because of its stupendous success: it went into nine editions by 1806, a year before Trotter's *The Moorland Bard* was published.[21] This surprisingly popular book of poems further establishes the probability that Bakewell refers to our own Thomas Trotter in 'The Author's Dream' because, if Bakewell was familiar with *The Farmer's Boy*, he may well have been familiar with 'The Snowstorm', a poem by Trotter that appeared in the Bloomfield volume. In his reference to another psychologist-poet, Bakewell may indicate that he wrote within, or in response to, a tradition of poetry in the Romantic period hitherto unrecognized by critics today.

At least one other psychologist-poet gestures to the possible existence of this genre of poetry. Beddoes indicates that he writes in conscious awareness of and perhaps in response to other psychologist-poets in his preface to his long poem, *Alexander's Expedition*.[22] Beddoes compares his verse to that of Erasmus Darwin by insisting repeatedly that he did not copy the former poet's work and praising the asylum-owner and 'author of the Botanic Garden' for having a 'store of images and a command of language, sufficient to constitute a poet'.[23] I will discuss Beddoes's relationship with Darwin in greater detail in Chapter 3, but for now it suffices to say that his repeated references to the poetry of Darwin function in a manner similar to Bakewell's comparison of himself to 'that poor honest Trotter': these writers indicate that they respond to verse similar to their own, thereby suggesting the possibility that they contributed to a tradition of poetry by early psychologists.

III. The Scottish Enlightenment: Democracy, Moral Philosophy and the Medical Sage

We can speak of a tradition of verse by psychologist-poets because common themes and statements of political positions echo throughout the work. These features were likely the result of cultural and educational influences on these doctors: most of them were Scottish or had been schooled in Scotland and their distinct brand of liberalism bears the stamp of the Scottish Enlightenment. The psychologist-poets bring into focus the residual effects of the Scottish Enlightenment on Romantic-era British culture. We are accustomed to viewing the Enlightenment, as represented by such figures as the English empiricist John Locke, as oppositional to Romantic ideology, which we have tended to see as spiritual, emotional and subjective, all of which qualities are opposed to the empiricist focus on material reality, experiment and hard fact. However, I argue that many of the ideals that we now identify as distinctly Romantic reflect the influence of the Scottish Enlightenment,[24] and nowhere are these ideals expressed more poignantly than in the poetry of psychologist-poets trained in the Scottish medical tradition of the eighteenth century.

Throughout Europe in the eighteenth century, Scotland was reputed to have the most prestigious medical schools. As young scientists with great aspirations, many of the psychologist-poets took their medical degrees at Edinburgh University, including Brown, Ferriar, Duncan, Beddoes and Trotter, the last three of whom were students of the famous nosologist of nervous disorders, William Cullen, while Brown studied under Stewart, the renowned 'Common Sense Philosopher' and author of *Elements of the Philosophy of the Human Mind*.[25] The most famous psychologist-poet of all, Erasmus Darwin, studied medicine in Edinburgh from 1753 to 1756.[26] Brown eventually taught at Edinburgh University, as did Duncan after a stint at St Andrew's University, which was the *alma mater* of Perfect.[27] Meanwhile, Beattie was a Professor of Moral Philosophy and Logic at Marischal College in Aberdeen and 'held the chair until his death despite tempting and lucrative offers in the 1770s of a chair at Edinburgh University'.[28] Forster made himself an essential part of the psychological scene in Scotland when, on 15 April 1816, he 'delivered a paper to the Wernerian Society of Edinburgh. A note in the minute book observes that this was the first paper on phrenology read before a learned society in Scotland' and he seems to have been eager to claim his Scottish connections, for he wrote several poems in the Scottish dialect.[29] The only two figures in this study that have no solid connections with Scotland are Cotton and Bakewell, but it is notable that, near the end of the eighteenth-century, Cotton's poetry was published several times with that of Scotland's most popular poet in the Romantic period, Robert Burns, which may show that the editors recognized an affinity between their work or that they wanted to present this early psychologist-poet's verse in a Scottish context because audience expectations demanded a Scottish flavour to the poetry of psychologists by that time. As for Bakewell, it is arguable that the poetic identity that he formed for himself – that of 'the moorland bard' – was a direct descendant of Beattie's distinctly Scottish 'minstrel', Edwin, as I will maintain in Chapter 1. These psychologist-poets created a tradition of verse that was nurtured in a single geographical area and bound by a common view of what it meant to be a doctor and specifically a doctor of the mind. This view was a quintessential expression of the Scottish Enlightenment.

The term 'Scottish Enlightenment' recognizes that Scotland saw a resurgence in knowledge, especially scientific, in the eighteenth century that was distinct from the Enlightenment in the rest of Europe. Historian Gordon Graham asserts that the Scottish Enlightenment was based in the 'Scottish philosophical community and a distinctive tradition of inquiry. The Scottish philosophers formed a community because, unlike their counterparts in England or France, they were almost all university based, and were frequently related as teachers and students'.[30] Moreover, he adds, they shared 'a methodology (the so-called "science of the mind")',[31] an aspect of the Scottish Enlightenment that I will discuss at greater length hereafter in my discussion of moral philosophy. Significantly, historians such as David Hamilton describe the chronological boundaries of the movement with reference to Edinburgh University and literary events: 'the cultural Enlightenment' in Scotland, paralleled 'the period of growth of the medical school in Edinburgh', and he goes on to note that the Enlightenment only really ended with death of Sir Walter Scott in 1832.[32] The tradition of poetry by doctors of the mind derived from a movement that was bound by literary events and the life of the medical school in Scotland. Finally, Lisa Rosner's account of the Scottish Enlightenment is most suggestive; she writes that 'the first lesson taught by the medical societies was that medicine was a literary activity' and adds that societies like the Royal Medical Society in Edinburgh also 'had special resonance as focal points for Edinburgh literati'.[33] In other words, the intersection of the fields was recognized and valued by medical practitioners, students and literati alike.

So integral was the connection between literature and medicine in Enlightenment Scotland that there seems to have been no sharp distinction between the fields then or in Romantic-era England. Richardson draws attention to this circumstance when he maintains that the Romantic era was characterized by fluid boundaries between fields, such as between 'sciences and the humanities'.[34] With respect to this fluid boundary, it is important to note that it was a relatively recent development in Britain, not a static holdover from a kind of unified pre-Lapsarian academic paradise. According to John Christie and Sally Shuttleworth, the division between science and the humanities occurred when the English scientific movement became institutionalized with 'the foundation of the Royal Society of London' in 1660; this break happened at the same time as in France, where 'the demarcation of literary, aesthetic and scientific culture was produced through the official and bureaucratized cultural politics of the monarchy's cultural ambitions'.[35] Just as the divisions between the fields reflected the power of the monarchy in both France and Britain, so, too, I argue, did the dissolution of these boundaries echo radical, even revolutionary, sympathies in the Enlightenment era.

To be sure, the Scottish Enlightenment was almost synonymous with radical politics. Bryson lists 'Intellectual equalitarianism – a democratic temper in matters of religion, morals and taste' – as principle characteristics of the Scottish Enlightenment.[36] Certainly, this description suggests how the movement included many supporters of the French Republic. In *Philosophic Whigs: Medicine, Science, and Citizenship in Edinburgh, 1789–1848*, L. S. Jacyna confirms that Thomas Paine – perhaps the most famous of the English sympathizers with the French Revolutionary cause – was a kind of hero in Scotland.[37] Jacyna also suggests that a republican spirit was inculcated into the Scots from their schooldays, calling the educational system in eighteenth-century Scotland a 'genuinely democratic one' that allowed students to move between classes[38] partly because people of all classes could afford an education, given the low cost of tuition.[39] Additionally, some of the most influential figures of the Scottish Enlightenment were well-known Whigs. So important was the nerve theorist William Cullen that many historians of medicine say that 'the eighteenth-century "Golden Age" of Edinburgh medicine ... ended around 1789 with the retirement of William Cullen'.[40] Cullen's republican principles are evident in the major changes he effected on the Edinburgh University campus: he was the first to use English instead of Latin for his medical lectures, which showed his desire to communicate with more students than simply those who had a grammar school background (and may show his sympathy with the psychologist-poets on the topic of using accessible language to disseminate medical knowledge); he also 'started the tradition that university students should be given free medical treatment'.[41] These liberal sympathies gesture to Cullen's schooling at Glasgow University, where he earned his medical doctorate and which Jacyna calls a 'seminary of Whiggism' in the decades following his term there.[42] Additionally, Stewart was a high-profile

Whig; adherence to his psychological theories was, therefore, a claim to radical-ism, Jacyna contends.[43] His protégé, Brown, is also likely to have passed on such radical principles in his university lectures. While the above assertions indicate an elision between Whiggism and radicalism that is not familiar to students of English politics, the elision was real in late eighteenth-century Scotland, where the French Revolution set into sharper focus the divide between the reformist Whigs and the conservative Tories. In an integral way, political and social reform was married to the spirit of innovation that characterized science and especially medicine during the Scottish Enlightenment, and all kinds of 'reactionaries saw the overthrow of the *ancien régime* as confirmation of all innovation.'[44] The Enlightenment in Scotland was characterized by a radical Whiggism that it disseminated in its schools, especially its medical schools.

The radical and democratic leanings of most of the psychologist-poets I study come into clearer focus through this delineation of their exposure to the Scottish Enlightenment at medical schools in Scotland. Their literary interests were evidently a part of the cultural milieu of young doctors and medical students as well. But how were these factors tied together? Again, Jacyna provides a clear explanation of how the fields of literature and medicine were integrated:

> Scottish Whiggery was of a different character to its aristocratic English counterpart. It was more the property of professional men who gave a keen intellectual edge and a greater coherence to the eclectic Whig programme ... Their ethos eschewed ... any form of narrow specialization.[45]

These cultural leaders felt it incumbent on them to develop a wide range of literary and scientific interests. Not only did the Whigs of the Scottish Enlightenment admire creativity and fancy in its scientists, thinking that such qualities revealed individuality and a freethinking character that defied subjection to tyranny, but they even thought it a basic civic duty to cultivate both scientific and philosophical knowledge: the pursuit of all kinds knowledge was a strategy against corruption and a means of levelling the field of education.[46] I suggest that the psychologist-poets promoted reform – social, political, spiritual, but especially psychological – by writing poetry, for they could more easily teach a wide audience of readers about various political and medical issues through the attractive and popular medium of poetry than they could through academic essays. Just as Cullen lectured in English to communicate better with his students and the great Stewart taught his medical students to work towards political renewal and avoid the dangers of narrow specialization by teaching them to balance, for example, abstract metaphysics with sociology, so, too, did the psychologist-poets teach their readers directly and by example.[47] As I will show, the Romantic-era psychologist-poets' dedication to teaching was a major component of their function as cultural leaders.

Some historians of the Scottish Enlightenment maintain that developments in psychological matters characterized the entire movement of the Scottish Enlightenment. Charles Waterston points out that psychological topics were 'of interest to many Scots since, during the eighteenth century, Enlightenment philosophers had wrestled with the implications of man's understanding of himself in body and mind'.[48] This claim is supported at least in part by the simple fact that one of the greatest Enlightenment philosophers of all, David Hume, was Scottish and his work *Treatise of Human Nature* was hugely influential for psychology (both directly and negatively, as I will show in my discussion of Beattie).[49] But Graham maintains that other notable philosophers must be viewed with reference to the history of psychology, as well, when he asserts that in the Scottish 'school of Reid and [Sir William] Hamilton [there is] an almost unspoken assumption that the question of mind ... lies at the heart of philosophy'.[50] Finally, in his introduction to *Enlightened Scotland*, Philip Flynn explains that, in a sense, all science was subordinate to psychology in its manifestation of moral philosophy in eighteenth-century Scotland:

> The Scottish understanding of the phrase 'moral philosophy' came to include more subjects than Newton had intended ... [as] parts of their 'science of man'. In that large ambition, they recognized that a study of the sources, limits, and processes of human knowledge was basic to their philosophic program; and they believed that the subject known as 'pneumatology', 'the philosophy of mind', 'mental science', or 'psychology' might achieve a status similar to that achieved already in some branches of natural philosophy ... David Hume noted that natural philosophy itself, as well as mathematics and natural theology, is a product of human understanding.[51]

Indeed, psychology, or moral philosophy, was perceived as the most comprehensive of the sciences during the Scottish Enlightenment and, crucially for the present study, the cultural scene and intellectual products born of moral philosophy played a major role in forming the psychologist-poets' tradition of verse.

Other critics have noted the influence of moral philosophy on Romantic culture. In *Romanticism and the Human Sciences: Poetry, Population, and the Discourse of the Species*, Maureen McLane asserts that 'The spirit of the age, as gauged by Hazlitt's essays, seems best embodied ... by poets and moral philosophers', but she claims that the two were in contest with each other.[52] Notably, McLane limits her discussion of moral philosophy to its sociological implications, but the field included many other subjects, including psychology. Allan Bewell points out in *Wordsworth and the Enlightenment: Nature, Man, and Society in the Experimental Poetry* that Wordsworth wrote at the precise time when 'the immense field of moral philosophy ... was about to break up into the modern disciplines of anthropology, sociology, psychology, philosophical ethics, economics, history and political science', but, notably, Bewell adds that the first concern of moral philosophers was to effect 'synchronic analyses of the mind and passions'.[53] Regarding the psychological nature of moral philosophy, Beattie provides an informative description of how psychology relates to his area of expertise, moral philosophy, and explains how the mysterious field of 'Pneumatology'[54] relates to both in the following definition, taken from the introductory section of his *Elements of Moral Science*:

> Moral Philosophy ... consists, like every other branch of science [,] of a speculative and a practical part ... The speculative part of the philosophy of mind has been called Pneumatology. It inquires into the nature of those spirits of minds, whereof we may have certain knowledge, and wherewith it concerns us to be acquainted; and those are the Deity and the human mind ... Pneumatology, therefore, consists of two parts, first, Natural Theology ... and, secondly, the Philosophy of the Human Mind, which some writers have termed Psychology.[55]

Beattie identifies moral philosophy as a science and therefore an appropriate field of study for medical men. As important as Beattie's statement is for an understanding of what constituted moral philosophy in the Romantic period (and its importance will become clearer in Chapter 1, where I will outline the extent of Beattie's influence on the Romantics), he does not speak only for his time, but also for the eighteenth century as a whole. Indeed, as Roger Emerson writes in 'Science and Moral Philosophy in the Scottish Enlightenment', moral philosophy was a scientific phenomenon of the Baconian stamp as early as 1700 and, even then, its emphasis was on the human mind; he explains that analysis of 'the passions, will, reason, and the other faculties of the mind ... was essential ... for moral philosophy'.[56] Bewell and McLane have argued convincingly that the Romantics were influenced by the sociological and anthropological work being accomplished in the field of moral philosophy. Meanwhile, Edward Reed claims in *From Soul to Mind: The Emergence of Psychology from Erasmus Darwin to William James* that the terms 'moral philosophy' and 'psychology' are synonymous, but chronologically divergent.[57] The precise nature of the relationship between moral philosophy and psychology is debatable, but one thing is clear: psychology was one of the most influential fields of study in Enlightenment and Romantic-era Britain.

One need only mention that most of the psychologist-poets were influenced by or contributed to the Scottish Enlightenment to suggest that they were apprized of the teachings of moral philosophy, but, as I have mentioned, several of them also wrote and lectured about the topic. Beattie's *Elements of Moral Science*, quoted above, was an abstract of his lecture course on moral philosophy, which he taught for thirty-seven years at Marischal College, while Brown published his own series of lectures as Professor of Moral Philosophy, *Lectures on the Philosophy of the Human Mind*. One may assert with some certainty that every student of a Scottish university in the eighteenth century took a course in moral philosophy because, as Graham informs us, all five of the universities during the Scottish Enlightenment 'had persisted with the basic mediaeval curriculum in which moral philosophy ... played an important and compulsory part'.[58] If moral philosophy was an integral part of the education of a medical student in Scotland, so, too, was psychology, for the fields are at some level identifiable.

As for more recent academic attention to moral philosophy, Bryson's *Man and Society: The Scottish Inquiry of the Eighteenth Century*, published in 1945, remains the most extensive treatment of the subject. Clearly, the time is ripe for a more updated study of the topic, which I hope to accomplish, in part, with the present study, but Bryson's exploration remains valuable. She confirms that moral philosophy was a defining feature of the Scottish Enlightenment and, as Bryson notes in *Man and Society: The Scottish Inquiry of the Eighteenth Century*, this development can be attributed, in part, to Thomas Reid, who made the field essential to 'Common Sense Philosophy', of which he is regarded widely as the originator.[59] According to Bryson, Reid was responsible for both popularizing moral philosophy and giving it the psychological character that would come to define it in the eighteenth century.[60] Yet Reid was by no means the only influential Scottish philosopher who regarded psychology as an essential subject. Bryson writes, 'Ferguson was as certain as Hume that psychology, or the science of man, was the basic study for an understanding of society'; she then adds that amongst 'all of the Scottish writers ... [psychology] was regarded as the most fundamental portion of any knowledge they might have or might achieve regarding man'.[61] The importance of the Scottish school of moral philosophers for the history of psychology in England cannot be ignored.

IV. The Psychological Milieu of Romanticism

The similar interests of many of the psychologist-poets can be traced to the strongly psychological character of the Scottish Enlightenment and its unique emphasis on the doctor as a man of politics and literature, as well as of medicine. Meanwhile, their connections to the English Romantics – in terms of their interest in psychology, their political ideas and their notion of the broad cultural role of the poet – may also be located in this influential movement. Many similarities exist between the political attitudes and opinions about the necessity of accessible writing and ideas of both moral philosophers and famous Romantic writers. Even if we trace the philosophical influences upon Romanticism through another national tradition, such as through the work of the German philosopher Immanuel Kant, the Scottish Enlightenment still asserts its relevance, according to Vickers, who claims, 'It is a fact too rarely adverted to that many of the earliest accounts in English of Kant's critical philosophy came from men who had all been associated at one time or another with Edinburgh University medical school'.[62] Meanwhile, in summarizing the attitudes behind the 'rationalistic anti-intellectualism', which in turn produced moral philosophy, Bryson writes, 'Since truths of nature are universal, they must have been as well known to the earliest, least sophisticated men as to any other members of the race; what is more, early men were really in a better position to apprehend such truths than men of later periods'.[63] This sentiment echoes strongly Wordsworth's statement in the 1800 preface to the *Lyrical Ballads* about why he chose as his poetic subject 'low and rustic life':

> because in that situation the essential passions of the heart find a better soil in which they can attain their maturity ... [and] because in that situation our elementary feelings exist in a state of greater simplicity and consequently may be more accurately contemplated ... and are more durable; and lastly, because in that situation the passions of men are incorporated with the beautiful and permanent forms of nature.[64]

Bryson's explanation of the humble attitude underlying moral philosophy also recalls Jean-Jacques Rousseau's concept of the superiority of the uncivilized man over the man of the city and the related Romantic valorization of the 'rural genius', which manifested itself in the great popularity of Robert Burns, John Clare, Stephen Duck, Ann Yearsley and others. In several ways, moral philosophy and Romanticism express the same political ideals.

The establishment of the powerful connection between psychology and literature during the period before the humanities and sciences were understood as discrete and even opposed fields highlights why some famous Romantic-era passages of literary criticism use the language of psychology to judge the success of poetry. Some of the most scathing and memorable reviews of Romantic poets' work include psychological language as a kind of diagnosis of the poet's literary faults, which are figured as psychological ailments. In Francis Jeffrey's cruel review of Wordsworth's *Excursion* in *The Edinburgh Review* of November 1814, the critic treats what he considers to be Wordsworth's poetic foibles as psychological ailments, an identification that may also reflect Jeffrey's contact with Brown, a founder-member of *The Edinburgh Review* and fellow alumnus of the Edinburgh Academy of Physics (as were Francis Horner and Henry Brougham, the other two Whig founders of *The Edinburgh Review*).[65] Four years earlier, Jeffrey had shown his interest in psychology in other ways: he had published in the same journal his review of Stewart's *Philosophical Essays* – and Stewart is widely recognized for popularizing the 'science of the mind' at the start of the nineteenth century through his university lectures and the great success of his psychological treatise, *Elements of the Philosophy of the Human Mind*.[66] While the following critical passage has long been viewed in light of Jeffrey's use of the topics of mental illness and psychology as vehicles in a metaphor for the relationship between the poet and critic, I maintain that the passage may also be read quite literally. The critic treats psychology as the standard by which he judges poetry. He attributes Wordsworth's 'perversity of taste or understanding', which has produced the 'moral and devotional ravings' of the poetry itself, to an apparently mental disease:

> The case of Mr Wordsworth, we perceive, is now manifestly hopeless; and we give him up as altogether incurable, and beyond the power of criticism. We cannot indeed altogether omit taking precautions now and then against the spreading of the malady; – but for himself, though we shall watch the progress of his symptoms as a matter of professional curiosity and instruction, we really think it right not to harass him any longer with nauseous remedies, – but rather to throw in cordials and lenitives, and wait in patience for the natural termination of the disorder.[67]

Jeffrey establishes not only the poet as mad, but also the psychologist as a poetic authority. Literary criticism, he implies, can 'cure' the mental ailment that leads to bad poetry. Such is also the case in John Gibson Lockhart's infamous criticism of Keats's poetry in the August 1818 edition of *Blackwood's*. Here, 'The Scorpion' writes,

> Of all the manias of this mad age, the most incurable, as well as the most common, seems to be no other than the Metromanie ... The phrenzy of the Poems was bad enough in its way; but it did not alarm us half so seriously as the calm, settled, imperturbable drivelling idiocy of Endymion ... [However,] if Mr Keats should happen, at some interval of reason, to cast his eye upon our pages, he may perhaps be convinced of the existence of his malady, which, in some cases, is often all that is necessary to put the patient in a fair way of being cured.[68]

Lockhart also presents the critic as a psychologist with the power to cure 'Metromanie', the madness for poeticizing. These most notorious critical reviews of the Romantic period identify the figure of the psychologist as an authority on poetry. As much as they posit the writing of bad poetry as the symptom of a mental ailment, they present the ability to judge the value of poetry as psychological knowledge. Arguably, these formidable reviewers were contributing and responding to a literary atmosphere that prized psychological knowledge and indicated to poets that they must establish themselves as learned with respect to the mysteries of the human mind.[69] The inescapable nature of the discourse of psychology and the Foucauldian idea that there is no 'outside of power' when it comes to 'subjectivization', even in the literary realm, seems undeniable in light of these reviews.[70]

Besides these famous instances of the critical enforcement of psychological knowledge in Romantic poets, pre-Romantic literature supported such interests, as well. The literary precedent for poetry that probes the workings of the human mind can be found in the 'graveyard poetry' of the eighteenth century, such as the verse of Mark Akenside, Robert Blair, James Thomson, Thomas Gray, Edward Young and Thomas Parnell. Significantly, Beattie is also sometimes classified as a 'graveyard poet'. These poems helped to popularize literary self-scrutiny: their speakers wander disconsolately in graveyards and muse miserably at night, albeit with great relish. Romantic poets include as part of their focus on the mind a recognition of the pleasures of melancholy but, as Beverly Taylor and Robert Bain put it, their interest in psychology far surpasses that of their predecessors: 'This concern with consciousness suffuses Romantic writing to an extent not seen before in Western literature ... Romantic writers probed the capacities, limits, experiences, and mysteries of the mind'.[71] The most famous texts of the Romantic period support these claims. The subtitle of Wordsworth's greatest work, *The Prelude*, is 'Growth of a Poet's Mind', while Coleridge's initial prefatory note to 'Kubla Khan' christens the poem 'a psychological curiosity', as opposed to a proper work of literature to be assessed on the basis of its '*poetic* merits'.[72] As I will show in the following chapters, other aspects of Romanticism, such as its valorization of humble living and democratic principles, may also be traced to the cultural phenomenon that produced the verse of the psychologist-poets, namely the Scottish Enlightenment.

Evidence that scientific poetry was not introduced to Romantic poetry through the pioneering efforts of the best-known Romantics, but that it was accepted because the cultural demand for it was inescapable, may be found in the critical statements of the most famous first-generation Romantic poets. Intriguingly, these texts also illustrate the writers' ambivalence towards the topic of science in literature. For example, on one hand, Wordsworth confirms his fascination with psychological topics in the preface of 1800 to the *Lyrical Ballads*, where he reveals that the 'purpose' of the volume is 'to illustrate the manner in which our feelings and ideas are associated in a state of excitement ... [and] to follow the fluxes and refluxes of the mind when agitated by the simple affections of our nature'.[73] However, in the revised and expanded version of the preface, published in 1850, Wordsworth compromises his dedication to scientific poetry in his very definition of what constitutes a poet. In his extended reply to his own question, 'What is a poet?', Wordsworth explains,

> The Poet writes under one restriction only, namely, that of the necessity of giving immediate pleasure to a human Being possessed of that information which may be expected from him, not as a lawyer, a physician, a mariner, an astronomer or a natural philosopher, but as a Man.[74]

Here, Wordsworth intimates that the reader should not expect the poet to 'give pleasure', to poeticize, about anything remotely scientific, for his expertise involves only what is most basic to human existence, such as the realm of emotions. However, he expands our notion of what kinds of knowledge and writing 'gives[,] ... pleasure' in the passage that immediately follows:

> We have no knowledge, that is, no general principles drawn from the contemplation of particular facts, but what has been built up by pleasure, and exists in us by pleasure

alone. The Man of Science ... know[s] and feel[s] this ... [H]e feels that his knowledge is pleasure; and where he has no pleasure he has no knowledge.[75]

Wordsworth confirms that the knowledge of the 'Man of Science' is appropriate subject-matter for 'pleasure'-giving poetry. Yet, he envisions the conflation of science and poetry as guided by the ready-made poet, not initiated by the man of science. He describes a brave new world in which the poet

will follow the steps of the Man of science ... [, will] be at his side, carrying sensation into the midst of the objects of the science itself. The remotest discoveries of the Chemist, the Botanist, or Mineralogist, will be as proper objects of the Poet's art ... If the time should ever come when what is now called Science, thus familiarized to men, shall be ready to put on, as it were, a form of flesh and blood, the Poet will lend his divine spirit to aid the transfiguration, and will welcome the Being thus produced, as a dear and genuine inmate of the household of man.[76]

Even as Wordsworth expands the boundaries of poetry to include scientific topics, he limits the scientist's access to the realm of poetry. In '"Twin Labourers and Heirs of the Same Hopes": The Professional Rivalry of Humphrey Davy and William Wordsworth', Catherine Ross argues cogently that Wordsworth felt competitive with Davy, a scientist, because the latter's scientific interests and cultural role overlapped too closely with his own. We must also consider the possibility that Wordsworth's objections to scientific poetry reveal his opinions about the broader functions of science and poetry.

Coleridge delineates the boundaries of poetry even more rigidly, which is perhaps more surprising, given his freewheeling intellectual interests as a polymath. Coleridge's famous retort to Wordsworth's preface to the *Lyrical Ballads* in the *Biographia Literaria* presents a similarly ambivalent attitude towards the marriage of science and poetry. Because we recognize attention to the mind as a major feature of Romanticism, we are familiar and comfortable with Coleridge's assertion of his interests in psychological phenomena in chapter 14, where he asserts that his poetic task for the *Lyrical Ballads* project was to compose poems that would interest 'the affections by the dramatic truth of such emotions, as would naturally accompany ... [supernatural] situations, supposing them real. And real in *this* sense they have been to every human being who, from whatever source of delusion, has at any time believed himself under supernatural agency'.[77] Here, Coleridge confirms his attempt to display the mind's response to powerful beliefs, a worthy psychological and scientific topic. Moreover, by commending chemist and friend Davy for bringing together science and poetry in his 'Essay on the Principles of Method' in *The Friend*, Coleridge demonstrates that, on principle, he did not oppose scientists writing poetry.[78] Yet Coleridge seems to refute the possibility of a new, scientific poetry altogether when he asserts that

> A poem is that species of composition, which is opposed to works of science, by propos-
> ing for its *immediate* object pleasure, not truth; and from all other species (having *this*
> object in common with it) it is discriminated by proposing to itself such delight from
> the *whole*, as is compatible with a distinct gratification from each component *part*.[79]

According to Coleridge, poetry and science can never blend perfectly. He even
uses the above distinction to criticize Wordsworth's project in the *Lyrical Ballads*, arguing that it belongs not to poetry, but to moral philosophy (out of which
psychology developed).[80] Clearly, Wordsworth and Coleridge were ambivalent
about the appropriateness of mixing science and poetry (which, incidentally,
suggests that the fluid boundaries between the fields to which Richardson gestures were beginning to solidify).[81] Given this ambivalence, how do we explain
the popular current critical assumption that Romantic literature valorizes the
scientific study of the mind, or that, as Faflak has argued soundly in *Romantic
Psychoanalysis*, Romantic literature is itself deeply psychological? One explanation for this impasse is that Romanticism encompasses both conflicting views.
The ambivalence in these influential Romantic texts reveals the heterogeneous
nature of Romantic ideology in a way that indicates the need to understand the
period in terms of 'Romanticisms', as Arthur Lovejoy put it in 1924.[82] Or, to
put the matter back in a Foucauldian context, we may view Wordsworth's and
Coleridge's objections as glimpses of the post-Romantic future, in which the disciplines would be discrete. Importantly, such moments of contention about the
blurring of disciplinary boundaries confirms the accepted narrative about the
reification of the disciplines in the nineteenth century – and the fact that poets
are engaged with this process indicates that, indeed, the power dynamic that
is established by disciplinarity functions as a network through which power is
dispersed everywhere, instead of being a top-down form of tyranny.

V. The Cultural Role of the Psychologist-Poet: A Clerisy for the People

In his earliest manifestations, the psychologist-poet was an ethical and spiritual
teacher, who, partly through his accessible writings and partly through his very
focus on faith, distinguished himself from the snobbish celebrity nerve-doctors and ivory-tower Humean sceptics (whom I will describe in greater detail
in Chapter 1). Toward the turn of the century, he was frequently radical, sometimes even being accused of being a Jacobin. When he was not revolutionary,
he was often still involved with political movements that indicated some degree
of dissent with the establishment, such as the anti-slavery movement, and his
identification with the powerless, such as downtrodden workers, the colonized
or even animals. This leftist position is tied in some cases to the liberal nature
of the Scottish education system of which almost all of the doctors I study

were products, as I have indicated, while the madhouse-owners who were not part of this system showed their broad social sympathy in their very choice of livelihood: as Michael Donnelly notes, for most of the eighteenth century, the apothecaries and 'mad-doctors' had little respect because of their 'humble work in a lowly branch of medicine', with which less liberal doctors refused to become involved.[83] As a student of the Scottish Enlightenment, the psychologist-poet consciously delineated the cultural role of the sage, the teacher, the wise leader who attempted to disperse through poetry his knowledge about the human mind in order to benefit a wide range of readers.

The idea of the poet as a cultural leader reveals another commonality between the goals of the psychologist-poets and the major Romantics. William Blake argues in his prophecies that the divisions between the spiritual and material worlds, subject and object, the sources of all conflict – social and otherwise – condemn us to the fallen state of Ulro, but these conflicts may be mended by the imagination, which is the particular office of the poet. Thus, the poet is a cultural leader. In what Harold Bloom calls the 'Dedicatory Quatrains' of Blake's *Milton*, the Bard swears, 'I will not cease from Mental Fight,/ Nor shall my Sword sleep in my hand:/ Till we have built Jerusalem,/ In Englands [sic] green & pleasant Land'.[84] Wordsworth, meanwhile, also sees himself as having a social function, as he illustrates in his address to Coleridge at the conclusion of *The Prelude*:

> though, too weak to tread the ways of truth,
> This Age fall back to old idolatry,
> Though men return to servitude as fast
> As the tide ebbs, to ignominy and shame
> By Nations sink together, we shall still
> Find solace in the knowledge which we have,
> Bless'd with true happiness if we may be
> United helpers forward of a day
> Of firmer trust, joint-labourers in a work
>
> . . . .
>
> Of their redemption, surely yet to come.[85]

Wordsworth's use of the phrase 'joint-labourers' echoes the psychologist-poets' attitudes towards poetic authority by establishing a sense of democratic, working-class effort. More to the point, the poet's wish that his and Coleridge's verse might redeem their community illustrates Wordsworth's view that poetry is 'social work', and that the poet performs an important function as a cultural leader.

Shelley makes the function of the poet as a social leader a major part of his argument in *A Defence of Poetry* when he dramatically concludes the essay with the statement, 'Poets are the unacknowledged legislators of the World'.[86] Significantly for this study, Shelley bases his powerful declaration about the social function of poets on their integral relationship to what he calls 'ethical science', or moral philosophy, which I have argued was the basis for the field of psychology as it grew out of the Scottish Enlightenment: 'Poetry', Shelley claims, 'acts to produce the moral improvement of man. Ethical science arranges the elements which poetry has created, and propounds schemes and proposes examples of civil and domestic life'.[87] According to Shelley, moral philosophy depends upon poetry for the creation of the materials that it studies. He is not arguing that human morals are somehow derived from poetry, but that poetry provides a kind of language that enables us to comprehend moral principles. We may approach this concept in terms of another claim that Shelley makes in *A Defence*, specifically that 'We want the creative faculty to imagine that which we know'.[88] Poetry, the product of the creative faculty, enables us to 'imagine', or comprehend, those moral principles of which we are already aware. We must remember that an ethical 'legislator' would not present the products of his craft in an objective and detached way, though. In order to legislate, he must somehow recommend an ethical imperative. Shelley explains that the poet teaches good morals in a 'three-step program', so to speak, that involves an appeal to the reader's imagination: 'The great secret of morals is Love ... The great instrument of moral good is the imagination ... Poetry enlarges the circumference of the imagination'; or, viewed from the opposite perspective, poetry improves the reader's imagination, which intensifies her power to love, which, in turn, improves her morals.[89] In so far as the poet performs a social function by means of his imagination, Shelley's notion of the poet as a cultural leader echoes Blake's, and both poets show their agreement with Wordsworth and Coleridge, writing in the preface to the *Lyrical Ballads* and *Biographia Litararia*, respectively. All of them indicate that the poet's purpose derives first and foremost from his heightened imaginative powers and only secondly from his more practical – scientific or social – knowledge. However, a letter that Shelley wrote to Thomas Love Peacock from Naples in 1819 suggests, to the contrary, that Shelley prizes above all the latter, more scientific kinds of knowledge, the domain of the psychologist: '"I consider poetry very subordinate to moral ... science, and if I were well, certainly I would aspire to the latter"'.[90] In this statement, Shelley all but refutes Wordsworth's and Coleridge's implied claims about science and poetry. Rather than presenting the scientific domain as subordinate to poetry and dependent upon the born 'Poet' to make it relevant to the average person, Shelley seems to consider poetry as a pale imitation and servant of moral science. Between Shelley's interest in moral science and the poet as a social legislator, he seems more than any other major Romantic poet to be declaring his support for the project of the psychologist-poets.

Yet, to further complicate Coleridge's already complex position on the matter as I have outlined it, his description of what he calls 'the clerisy' may be understood in much the same way. In chapter 5 of *On the Constitution of the Church and State*, Coleridge outlines the structure of a historical social order that he clearly means to propose as a model for his own society. He describes the duties of a 'small number' of 'guide[s], guardian[s], and instructor[s]' as being part of 'permanent class or order', of which 'A certain smaller number were to remain at the fountain heads of the humanities, in cultivating and enlarging the knowledge already possessed, and in watching over the interests of physical and moral science'.[91] Not only are these guides, guardians and instructors of society experts in physical science – just as doctors are – they maintain the interests of 'moral science', the specific study of psychologists. Moreover, these leaders are to 'remain at the fountain heads of the humanities', perhaps, we may surmise, as poets. These guardians sound very like and may be identifiable with 'the Clerisy', a class of leaders that Coleridge describes a few passages later:

> The CLERISY of the nation, or national church, in its primary acceptation and original intention comprehended the learned of all denominations; – the sages and professors of the law and jurisprudence; of medicine and physiology; of music; of military and civil architecture; of the physical sciences; with the mathematical as the common organ of the preceding; in short, all the so called liberal arts and sciences, the possession and application of which constitute the civilization of a country.[92]

These 'sages' of 'medicine', 'physical sciences' and 'liberal arts' had the most important cultural role of all, for they were responsible for maintaining the civilization of a country.[93] Coleridge discusses these fields as though they each have a separate representative, but his own legendary knowledge about almost all of them demonstrates that one person could represent several fields, such as medicine and literature. Elsewhere in the essay, Coleridge shows that, at this late point in the development of moral science, or moral philosophy, the field had finally become so separated from the religious realm from whence it grew that he was compelled to identify it as a type of 'science', and that religious-minded intellectuals like Coleridge in 1830 could only forecast hopefully the reunification of moral philosophy and religion.[94] In the following passage, Coleridge also indicates that he conflates moral science with psychology by noting that it focuses on what separates humankind from animals, which was a common means of describing the purview of psychology:[95]

> in all ages, individuals who have directed their meditations and their studies to the nobler characters of our nature, to the cultivation of those powers and instincts which constitute the man, at least separate him from the animal part of his own being, will be led by the supernatural in themselves to the contemplation of a power which is likewise superhuman; that science, and especially moral science, will lead to religion, and remain blended with it – this, I say, will, in all ages, be the course of things.[96]

The spiritually and socially renovating field of which Coleridge writes here is none other than the moral philosophy of the Scottish Enlightenment, which was, according to Emerson, a scientific movement that had 'gone a long way towards breaking the ties between morals and religion'.[97] Yet, the clearest connection between the overlapping interests of Coleridge and the psychologist-poets may be suggested by his plan for an unfinished project. Coleridge wrote of this project in a letter to Davy on 9 October 1800: "'its title would be *An Essay on the Elements of Poetry* – it would be in reality a disguised system of morals and politics"', which McLane calls 'moral philosophy'.[98] Whether it be through the medium of the imagination, morals, or psychology, many of the major Romantic poets saw their role as one of social leadership, as did the psychologist-poets.[99]

In the foregoing discussion of features of the verse of psychologist-poets and their relation to the better-known verse of the Romantic period and the Scottish Enlightenment (including its focus on moral philosophy), I have been working towards a definition of who the psychologist-poet was as a cultural figure. He was a doctor of the social stamp, one who attempted to communicate psychological ideas to a wide readership in a familiar and entertaining way: through the attractive form of verse. His frequent references to the necessity of accessible language reveals his egalitarian impulse. The social nature of the psychologist-poet is also evident in his use of humour, which he uses to establish in his reader a sense of trust and even camaraderie, and in his celebration of the lifestyle of the lower-classes, in which he extols the benefits – mental and otherwise – of humble living. In many ways, the psychologist-poet established his cultural role as a psychologist of the masses by illustrating his social concern through the rhetorical and thematic features of his verse.

VI. The Development of the Psychologist-Poet

The psychologist-poet emphasizes his broadly social role by using the popular form of verse to communicate and create his identity in the relatively new field of psychology, which was only beginning to split off into various approaches, like the ones I explore in the following chapters: moral philosophy, moral management, nerve theory, associationism and phrenology. By popularizing psychology through accessible verse that appeals to a broad audience, he weaves the social focus of his profession into his very medium. In short, as Marshall McLuhan famously states in *Understanding Media*, 'the medium is the message'.[100] This social focus is the very basis of psychology itself and constitutes the difference between pre-disciplinary self-reflection and the subjectivity defined by psychology. Foucault recognizes the secularization of the Christian injunction to be self-reflective as connected to the increasingly social function of the psychologist in *Power/Knowledge*, where he claims that 'The doctor becomes the great advisor and expert, if not in the art of governing, at least in that of observing, correcting, and improving the social "body" and maintaining it in a permanent state of health' after the Classical period and he later mentions 'the frequent role of doctors as programmers of a well-ordered society (the doctor as social or political reformer is a frequent figure in the second half of the eighteenth century).[101] The workings of modern power/knowledge, which Foucault recognizes in a late interview as the underpinning concern of his *oeuvre* even in its earliest days, is always deployed in a social context.[102] While Foucault's attention to sexual relations between people is related to his focus on the social context in which modern power situates the subject, I will examine the other distinct ways that psychology's discourse of subjectivity is social, such as through attention to Christian values of charity and humility, sympathy, the dynamics of personal relationships and the rejection of class distinctions, among other related topics; these topics also serve as shorthand for Romantic ideology, which shows the real influence of psychology upon literature and vice versa. Ultimately, Romantic-era psychologists present varying social contexts for expressing the real goal of all psychological searching: the subject. The once-private act of faith, self-reflection or subjectivity became contextualized by the social virtue of modest living or a matter of one's relationship to the moral manager; regulated by the nerve theorist, who acted as a kind of governor; or utterly orchestrated by the associationist. The verse of Romantic-era psychologists is, at once, the manifestation of their genuine adherence to their democratic, knowledge-sharing social programme, as it was their way of communicating with a wide audience and, oddly, the surest means of subjectifying English society on a wide scale by defining a language for the private and incommunicable.

In *Disrupted Dialogue: Medical Ethics and the Collapse of Physician-Humanist Communication (1770–1980)*, Robert Veatch outlines how eighteenth-century physicians were involved with wider British culture, especially the humanities, in a way that would become unknown by the mid-nineteenth century. Veatch's study, which focuses on medical ethics, traces virtually the same relationship that mine does, beginning with his focus on the relationship between philosophy and religion with medicine and especially in his attention to the medical schools of the Scottish Enlightenment as the locus of this link. The medical historian comments, 'We see here an Enlightenment pattern – an intelligentsia being broadly and classically educated without concern about the disciplinary boundaries separating the sciences and the humanities'.[103] Veatch's wording here is suggestive, for, indeed, the reification of the disciplines throughout the Romantic period was integral to the power–subject dynamic that is so familiar to us today. In answer to his questions, 'Why the isolation after the beginning of the nineteenth century? ... What happened at the end of the eighteenth century that stopped the dialogue between the medical community and the humanists?', Veatch surmises that one of the 'unintended effects of the Enlightenment' was to create 'narrow, specialized experts' who, because of the sheer volume of information that had been amassed during the age of discovery, were simply unable to become masters of all trades, as it were.[104] Perhaps also for this reason psychology broke up into distinct approaches, from nerve theory to moral management, as so on. A doctor did not necessarily practice only one approach to patient care in the Romantic period – and figures like Beddoes, Bakewell and Perfect illustrate that he often did not do so, as I will explain – but the fact that these discrete approaches existed, and could be adopted as a doctor's sole approach to understanding madness, reveals different ideological approaches to the mind and the need to compartmentalize psychological information. This process is the reification of the disciplines, which was attended by an increasingly difficult and therefore esoteric vocabulary that became the domain of medical practitioners and the source of division between the psychologists and wider culture. This knowledge became their power, but not before the psychologist had established himself to a broad reading public as an authority on the mind, not before psychology was established, in all its various forms, as the language of subjectivity and not before the average citizen became a subject of psychological discourse – thanks, in part, to the poetry of Romantic-era psychologists.

1. ERASMUS DARWIN, JAMES BEATTIE AND NATHANIEL COTTON AS PRE-ROMANTIC PSYCHOLOGIST-POETS

I. 'To inlist Imagination under the banner of Science'

As pre-Romantic influences on the tradition of poetry by early psychologists, Erasmus Darwin, Nathaniel Cotton and James Beattie represent the various forces that contributed to the literary tradition and psychological approaches as I will discuss them in the subsequent chapters. Romanticism, I contend, was synchronous with the reification of the discipline of psychology, which saw the field fragment into various schools, like moral management, nerve theory, associationism and phrenology, all of which I will examine in the following chapters. Even though this process was not complete by the end of the Romantic period – which is evident even with respect to the few figures I study here because their writings may be said to contribute at once to several different approaches[1] – the fact that various doctors of the mind were beginning to devote their entire written *oeuvres* to single approaches is an indication that the field of psychology was beginning to splinter into the multifaceted field that we know today, in which psychologists tend to profess and practice single ways of approaching psychological health, like behaviouralism, psychoanalysis and the like. As the best-known of the psychologist-poets and the most wide-ranging in his interests, I will examine Erasmus Darwin in the first part of this chapter by way of an introduction to the psychologist-poets' tradition. Darwin's verse serves as a good introduction because he represents the Scottish Enlightenment ideal of the scientist as polymath and not only in his bridging of the scientific and literary realms: just as Darwin himself cannot be classified as only a biologist, psychologist, inventor, physician or poet, so, too, does his verse show the broad range of scientific interests for which students of the Scottish Enlightenment are celebrated. The contrast between Darwin's materialist, frankly earthy approach and the deeply religious foci of Cotton and Beattie also reveals how deep were the divisions between interpretations of the mind even in the eighteenth century.

In the second part of this chapter, I will illustrate how the poetry and spiritual psychology of Beattie and Cotton support the contention that psychology is a secularization of Christianity. Moral philosophy, the signature field of the Scottish Enlightenment, is the matrix field that fragmented into the disciplines of, for example, anthropology, sociology and, of course, psychology. Because Beattie, professor and poet of moral philosophy, was its most influential and prolific poet, his verse provides important insights into the philosophical and religious concerns that shaped psychology as a discipline. Meanwhile, Cotton establishes the religio-psychological approach that he practised in his asylum as poetic fodder in his runaway hit volume of verse about dreams as the source of Christian moral lessons, a volume that also gestures to the religious roots of psychology. By developing the themes of faith, self-reflection and dreams in their verse, Cotton and Beattie illustrate the specific ways through which subjectivity became the focus of a new science. First, an examination of Darwin's verse will reveal the contours of the psychologist-poets' tradition that he helped to establish.

Erasmus Darwin: Polymath, Democrat and Psychologist-Poet Extraordinaire

To set up the pre-Romantic scene of the psychologist-poets, gesture to its reception and ground the links between the literature and science influenced by the Scottish Enlightenment, a brief examination of the verse of Erasmus Darwin (1731–1802) is in order. Although he seems to be an odd fit with Beattie and Cotton because his materialism marked him as a radical kind of Christian – if not an outright atheist, as Coleridge, amongst others, accused him of being – his identity as a pre-Romantic psychologist-poet demands his inclusion here.[2] Darwin, a renowned physician and madhouse owner whom Reed calls the 'most important European psychologist' of his time, wrote phenomenally popular verse.[3] Darwin's remarkable success in combining his interests has been long noted, beginning with comments made in his own time. Indeed, fellow poet and collaborator Anna Seward remarked that Darwin's "'[T]he Botanic Garden forms a new class of poetry" by "adapting the past and recent discoveries in natural and scientific philosophy to the purposes of heroic verse"'.[4] Poet Anna Letitia Barbauld was equally supportive of Darwin's efforts to unite science with poetry, even though she was not, as far as we know, in love with Darwin, as was Seward.[5] In 'Essay on Akenside's Poem on the *Pleasures of Imagination*', Barbauld nevertheless gushes,

> we are delighted to find with how much dexterity the artist of verse can avoid a technical term, how neatly he can turn an uncouth word, and with how much grace embellish a scientific idea. Who does not admire the infinite art with which Dr Dar-

win has described the [industrial cotton spinning] machine of Richard Arkwright. His verse is a piece of mechanism as complete in its kind as that which he describes.[6]

Such comments as these show that Darwin achieved his poetic goal, as outlined in the 'Advertisement' of *The Botanic Garden*: 'The general design is ... to inlist Imagination under the banner of Science'.[7] Today, Darwin's poetry is the most widely discussed of the psychologist-poets' verse.

Darwin was, by far, the best-known and most influential English psychologist-poet, and his influence on the English Romantics has been outlined thoroughly by Desmond King-Hele in *Erasmus Darwin and the Romantic Poets*, as well as several other critics in smaller studies.[8] When King-Hele laments that his book-length study of Darwin's influence on the Romantics has been largely ignored by literary critics, he also points to a general dearth of critical recognition of the importance of poetry by scientists for English Romantics, which I hope to remedy in part with the present study.[9]

Certainly, the significance of Darwin's work cannot be underestimated, despite the fact that it fell out of favour by the turn of the nineteenth century and sank into near oblivion thereafter. In addition to King-Hele, Darwin's influence on the Romantics has been outlined well by such critics as Nelson Hilton, David Ullrich and Kathleen Coburn, who assert, respectively: that 'Erasmus Darwin was regarded as the greatest English poet of the time', Wordsworth plundered Darwin's prose catalogue of diseases, *Zoönomia* (1794–6), for the *Lyrical Ballads* and Shelley 'of all the Romantic poets was the most indebted to Darwin';[10] that 'We can assume that Blake read *The Loves of the Plants* ... as did nearly everyone else in 1789';[11] that there are no fewer than thirty-five references to Darwin in *The Notebooks* and *The Letters* of Coleridge;[12] and, finally, that '"one can find almost anything one is looking for ... [o]nce on the trail of Coleridge through Erasmus Darwin and especially *The Botanic Garden*"'.[13] Some critics have provided counterweights to such buoyant commentaries on Darwin's influence by noting, for example, that Wordsworth hated Darwin's poetic style by the time that he wrote *Lyrical Ballads* and aimed his barbs about poetic diction directly at Darwin's verse.[14] Nevertheless, it is undeniable that Darwin's verse and prose were influential for the Romantics and in more areas than the literary realm alone. As the founder of the wide-ranging group of intellectuals, the Lunar Society of Birmingham (or 'Lunatics', as they mischievously called themselves), Darwin took part in the development of everything from 'carriage steering mechanisms, chemistry, steam and water vapor, speaking machines, botany, shorthand, meteorology, dual-pencopying machines, air travel, rocketry, and multilens microscopes'.[15] His boundless influence is even evident today: from his reading of Antoine Lavoisier's chemical texts in French, Darwin introduced to English the words 'oxygen' and 'hydrogen', and – long before his more famous grandson

Charles Darwin published *Origin of Species* – he introduced in *Zoönomia* the ideas of 'sexual selection, protective colouring for security, and physical adaptation through food supply'.[16] It was also in this tome that Darwin 'launched a true alternative psychology ... [where he] defined ideas as the motions of fibers in our organs of sense, and the pattern of these motions'.[17] Finally, in his long poem, *The Temple of Nature*, Darwin anticipates the more recent discovery that all life on earth originated in the ocean when he writes, "'Nurs'd by warm sun-beams, in primeval caves,/ Organic Life began beneath the waves'".[18] The hard evidence of Darwin's incredible success during his lifetime – such as that he received 1,000 guineas in advance for *The Economy of Vegetation* and 900 pounds each for *The Botanic Garden* and *Zoönomia* – would lead us to the mistaken assumption that his name would remain a household word for centuries to come.[19] Darwin's disappointing reception in the years just after his death does not diminish his significance for the present study, though: he still looms large as the most notable psychologist-poet of the pre-Romantic period.

The fact that Darwin was yet another alumnus of a Scottish university further suggests that Scotland's educational system was a cradle for psychologist-poets. Darwin shared many medical and political views with his fellow psychologist-poets, who also had Scottish connections. According to McNeil, 'Darwin's nosological views were close to those of the influential Edinburgh physicians William Cullen and John Brown', the first of whom taught several of the other psychologist-poets and the second of whom developed a very popular medical approach that made free use of opium and alcohol to balance what was called the patient's 'excitability', the life-force in Brunonian theory.[20] Yet, we need not trace the connection of Darwin to other psychologist-poets, like Beddoes, through such a tenuous route. After all, the men were correspondents and Beddoes devotes a substantial portion of the preface to his long poem *Alexander's Expedition* (which I will discuss in Chapter 3) to a discussion of Darwin's poetry. Such friendly support did not go unreciprocated: the aging 'Darwin became an advocate of the new "pneumatic medicine", developed by Beddoes'.[21] Darwin's specific psychological interests also suggest his exposure to the Scottish Enlightenment, which I have argued was both psychological and literary in character. He owned a madhouse, where he put into practice his 'advanced' views about madness and its treatment, as Hunter and Macalpine describe them (even though his methods included treatments that are considered to be barbarous today, such as bleeding, purging and the circular swing).[22] Darwin also incorporated his psychological theories into his poetic practice; as Logan indicates, 'the foundation stone of ... Darwin's most significant doctrine of taste, that the language of poetry must arouse visual images', is the product of his psychological theory 'that ideas of imagination, recollection, and association are the same fibrous motions as irritative ideas' and, thus, reading poems, for example, creates effects that are the same in essence as would witnessing the events in person.[23] Again, contact with Edinburgh during the Scottish Enlightenment created a poeticizing psychologist out of an English medical student.

Darwin, like so many of his fellow students in Scotland and psychologist-poets of the Romantic period, was radical in his politics. He had radical friends who were sympathetic to the American Revolution, the abolition of slavery and the French Revolution in its early stages and his own radical sympathies are evident in his poetry.[24] For instance, Darwin originally wanted to call *The Temple of Nature* by a more political title, 'The Origin of Society'. However, his publisher, Joseph Johnson, preferred the former title, for his reputation as a radical publisher had already made him politically vulnerable (he had been tried in the Treason Trials of 1794).[25] Darwin would have been wise to follow in Johnson's careful footsteps, for he was lampooned in the *Anti-Jacobin* with a work called the 'Loves of the Triangles', which was a satire of his *Loves of the Plants*.[26] Certainly, Darwin risked his neck in allowing himself to be identified so publicly as a radical. He also thereby risked his literary reputation – and he lost. As Richardson points out, Darwin was identified as a materialist with interests in the physical nature of the brain at a time when the popular reader understood such science to be 'French-inspired', Jacobin and contemptible.[27]

During his lifetime, Darwin was linked to radical politics because of his poetry and prose, not to mention his social network, but his posthumously published prose work, *Zoönomia*, sealed his reputation as a revolutionary. To many, including Coleridge, the tome solidified Darwin's identity as a godless materialist.[28] Strangely, though, in his preface to *Zoönomia*, Darwin seems to try to shed his image as an atheist even as he underlines another radical (and, indeed, forward-looking) outlook, that all life on earth shares a common ancestor: 'The great Creator of all things has infinitely diversified the works of his hands, but has at the same time stamped a certain similitude on the features of nature, that demonstrates to us, that *the whole is one family of one parent*'.[29] Nor is Darwin's somewhat traditional reference to a 'Creator' a means of drawing attention away from his holistic theory, for he boldly makes this theory the *raison d'etre* for *Zoönomia* itself. In this massive volume, which Darwin claims he wrote over a period of twenty years, he divides and classifies the minutiae of natural life for a single grand purpose: these details, he contends, can help man defeat his only natural enemy, disease. Darwin writes, 'The purport of the following pages is an endeavour to reduce the facts belonging to Animal Life into classes, orders, genera, and species; and, by comparing them with each other, to unravel the theory of diseases'.[30] This holistic vision of the world he expressed in his long poems, such as in his gossipy commentary on the romantic lives of plants in *The Loves of the Plants*, which personifies vegetable sexuality, and in *The Temple of Nature*, where Darwin asks,

> ... [Thus] drew the enlighten'd Sage the moral plan,
> That man should ever be the friend of man;
> Should eye with tenderness all living forms,
> His brother emmets, and his sister-worms.[31]

Darwin's holistic vision of the world is also reflected in the blurring of traditional distinctions in his work between the phenomenological and the psychological, or the spiritual. L. J. Jordanova claims that Darwin tried to 'transcend the division between mind and matter by developing a unified science of life derived from a radical epistemology which underlay his whole outlook'.[32] But Darwin was eager to quell any suspicions that he was a materialist who approached the human body as if it were one of the new machines for the Industrial Revolution that he and his friends from the Lunar Society, like James Watt, had devised. In pointing out the mistakes of earlier inquirers into diseases, Darwin writes,

> instead of comparing the properties belonging to animated nature with each other, they, idly ingenious, busied themselves in attempting to explain the laws of life by those of mechanism and chemistry; they considered the body as an hydraulic machine, and the fluids as passing through a series of chemical changes, forgetting that animation was its essential characteristic.[33]

However, the finer points of Darwin's particular brand of Christianity (or natural religion, or atheism, depending on your perspective) and complex approach to the relationship between body and mind were lost on his English audience, which rejected him as a dangerous, impious radical.

The other psychologist-poets of the Romantic period were often equally rebellious, particularly with respect to the medical profession. One way in which Darwin and his fellow psychologist-poets showed their dissent from the wider body of physicians and psychologists was by asserting their sympathy with a broad audience of lay readers, which they did by disseminating their medical ideas – partly through the medium of poetry – in order to make it accessible to more than their fellow doctors, as well as by criticizing the members of their profession. For example, *Zoönomia* was not a catalogue of diseases intended for the doctor's bookshelf only. Darwin wanted to reach a popular audience so that he could save people from disease, as well as from unscrupulous quack doctors. With an Enlightenment philosopher's (and even a French Revolutionary's) kind of abhorrence of mental fallacies that keep the populace in the subjection of ignorance, as religion and its trappings were said to do, Darwin announces in his preface that he wants to help 'the public' – which has 'become superstitiously fearful of diseases' – to avoid becoming 'the daily prey of some crafty empiric' by providing them with knowledge.[34] All of these positive outcomes may be effected, he claims, through his delineation of

> A theory founded upon nature ... [that] would capacitate men of moderate abilities to practice the art of healing with real advantage to the public; it would enable every one of literary acquirements to distinguish the genuine disciples of medicine from those of boastful effrontery, or of wily address; and would teach mankind in some important situations the *knowledge of themselves*.[35]

In *Zoönomia*, Darwin tries to abolish the current superstition that diseases were only treatable by a doctor who had unique access to cures for diseases. With clear devotion to democratic principles, Darwin tries to open up the field of medicine – including psychology, a subject that forms a substantial portion of this work – to everyday people. The only prerequisite for becoming one of the class of the medically enlightened is literacy.

Nor is a high or specialized level of literacy needed to access the informational riches of *Zoönomia*. In order to reach such a wide audience with the book, Darwin uses words from the realm of philosophy in limited ways that are more comprehensible to those readers who do not have the educational background to register the nuances of the words as they have developed through the history of philosophy. Darwin explains in his preface that:

> The words idea, perception, sensation, recollection, suggestion, and association, are each of them used in this treatise in a more limited sense than in the writers of metaphysic. The author was in doubt, whether he should rather have substituted new words instead of them; but was at length of opinion, that new definitions of words already in use would be less burthensome to the memory of the reader.[36]

Just as Wordsworth uses 'the very language of men' to represent rustic scenes, Darwin is careful to make his scientific discussions relevant to the masses by using language that is familiar to them.[37] At times, Darwin seems to have chosen his subject matter on the basis of such democratic principles, as he deals with such topics of popular interest as 'why swine and dogs cry out in pain, and not sheep and horses' and 'why children cannot tickle themselves'.[38] Such egalitarian impulses directed his personal and professional life, as well. Darwin made friends with people of all classes, such as Josiah Wedgwood, who was of humble origins, and he charged medical fees on a sliding scale in order to make his medical services available to people from a wide range of economic backgrounds.[39] This kind of dedication to the destruction of class boundaries is also evident in the professional and literary output of the other psychologist-poets.

Most importantly, with respect to Darwin's similarities to the other psychologist-poets of the Romantic period, he tried to convey scientific knowledge to the public poetically. He hints at his reasons for doing so in a footnote from *The Temple of Nature*, in which he reinforces his revolutionary attitude that religion subjects its believers by lauding ignorance:

Some philosophers have believed that the acquisition of knowledge diminishes the happiness of the possessor; an opinion which seems to have been inculcated by the history of our first parents, who are said to have become miserable from eating of the tree of knowledge. But as the foresight and the power of mankind are much increased by their voluntary exertions in the acquirement of knowledge, they may undoubtedly avoid many sources of evil, and procure many sources of good.[40]

Darwin supports this radical position by trying to teach his audience through poetry, the attractive qualities of which he tries to improve upon further by injecting humour into his verse. In *The Temple of Nature*, much of Darwin's humour consists in half-ironic, unflattering comparisons of humans to plants or animals: 'Hence when a Monarch or a mushroom dies,/ Awhile extinct the organic matter lies'.[41] His extended use of prosopopoeia also imparts a light-hearted tone to his verse, as the following charming passage illustrates:

> Loud trills sweet Philomel his tender strain,
> Charms his fond bride, and wakes his infant train;
> Perch'd on the circling moss, the listening throng
> Wave their young wings, and whisper to the song.
> The Lion-King forgets his savage pride,
> And courts with playful paws his tawny bride;
> The listening Tiger hears with kindling flame
> The love-lorn night-call of his brinded dame.[42]

Darwin tries to enchant his reader into learning more about the natural world through the attractive means of poetry. Jacyna claims that it was a feature of the Scottish Enlightenment to regard the attainment of scientific and philosophical knowledge as a basic civic duty for the masses and aristocrats alike, but the same may be said of the Enlightenment in Europe as a whole.[43] What gives a truly Scottish flavour to Darwin's attempt to spread scientific knowledge is its literary, and especially its poetic, nature. In this respect, he represents well the psychologist-poets of the Romantic era, even if, as we will see, his rejection of the role of traditional spirituality in psychological matters divorced him from his fellow pre-Romantic psychologist-poets, Beattie and Cotton.

II. James Beattie and Nathaniel Cotton: Saving Subjectivity through Scientization

Beattie and Cotton marry their spiritual approaches to the mind with their poetic programmes by engaging with specific themes, like dreams and selfhood, in an appealing way that helped to make the scientization of the soul acceptable to the wider public. In response to Humean scepticism, which Beattie and others berated as threatening to all subjective experiences, including faith, the poet of *The Minstrel* developed a kind of moral philosophy and a poetics of individuality that abjured its adherents to have confidence in the reality of their subjective experiences, a move that also established Beattie as one of the earliest psychologists to relate spirituality to the scientific realm, a process that would have wide-ranging consequences for psychology and the subject it defines.[44] This scientization of faith also reveals Beattie's commonalities with a pre-Romantic psychologist-poet with whom Beattie would seem, otherwise, to have little in common: Cotton. Indeed, the elder poet was English, while Beattie was Scottish; Cotton was educated at Leiden under the materialist Hermann Boerhaave, while Beattie completed all of his schooling in Scotland, where he learned the basics of a far more spiritual field, moral philosophy; Cotton wrote no texts on psychology, while Beattie penned one of the most widely read texts of moral philosophy of the Romantic period; finally, Cotton owned an insane asylum, where he was head apothecary, while Beattie's experience of psychology was purely theoretical and his professional concern with madness was apparently negligible.[45] Yet, Cotton's verse is essential to our understanding of the reception of psychologist-poets verse in England, for it suggests a prior interest in and receptiveness to the tradition. The trope of dreams as revelatory of moral lessons in *Visions in Verse* frames this feared manifestation of subjectivity as productive and encourages self-reflection as the path to spiritual and mental health. Finally, Cotton's poetic presentation of faith in terms of the moral good of humble living, so like Beattie's, further supports the longstanding contention that psychology is a kind of reconceptualization of Christianity in social terms. Cotton and Beattie dramatize their subjective experiences of dreaming and selfhood in verse while emphasizing the Christian moral good of modest living – thereby communicating the inner life in social terms. As many (particularly post-Foucauldian) historians of psychiatry have averred, early psychology secularized Christianity. Cotton's and Beattie's verse reveals one of the avenues through which this process was popularized and made palatable to the public.

That the poetry of early psychologists is an important influence on Romanticism becomes clear upon an examination of these pre-Romantics, Cotton and Beattie, both of whom celebrated subjectivity, the much feared foe of the Augustan period and hallmark of Romanticism. Both psychologist-poets made subjective experience the focus of their poetry (and prose, in Beattie's case) in a similarly systematic, scientific way that sought to give respectability to a faculty that had previously been rejected as chaotic and destructive. These earliest psychologists may therefore be viewed as establishing the popular taste for canonical Romantic poetry, which also focuses on the positive value of subjective reflection, especially in the creation of art, but their contributions to the development of psychology as a discipline during the Romantic period are no less important. In their effort to rescue the subjective experience of faith from the empirical detractors of the Enlightenment, Cotton and Beattie systematize spiritual experience and perform, as it were, the first and last function of psychology: they translate what is private, mysterious and intensely personal (the subjective realm, our relationship with God, who, as an unseen presence, may be said to exist within us, making our relationship with him purely subjective) into something social, both by giving it linguistic expression and by recontextualizing it in terms of our relationships with each other. Indeed, Beattie and Cotton show in their professional practices that a well-constituted mind is predicated on a healthy relationship with God, which, in their poetry, is expressed through social terms: modest living, humility and the democratic good of poverty are presented as ideals. These ideals, expressed often in their verse through references to country living in a simple cottage, also reappear in Romantic verse, although they have most often been interpreted as signifying the Romantic political ideal of egalitarianism there. The presence of the trope of humble living in the verse of these Christian, pre-Romantic, early psychologists suggests that it may be more closely aligned with the popular expression of Christian morals, a process that is closely tied to the dissemination of psychology as the field developed.

The idea that the Augustans feared subjectivity is almost a critical commonplace, one that is held up by Romanticist critics who rely on it as a comfortable explanation for what constitutes the difference between the two eras and critics of eighteenth-century literature who seek to define their field in terms of the popular empirical philosophy of Locke, amongst others. At its most extreme, the eighteenth-century fear of subjectivity was a fear of insanity, or what may be identified as improperly constituted subjectivity, as two seminal critical works on Augustan madness reveal. Max Byrd claims in *Visits to Bedlam: Madness and Literature in the Eighteenth Century* that isolation was thought of as unhealthy to the Augustans, who spurned private thoughts and moments, as well as the concept of individuality.[46] As part of the continuum of this distrust, Byrd adds, Augustans viewed 'melancholy [as] ... the first stage of madness', since its symptoms of withdrawal from society echoed, for them, the madman's withdrawal from reality.[47] Michael DePorte suggests something similar in *Nightmares and Hobbyhorses: Swift, Sterne and Augustan Ideas of Madness* when he states of the period, 'Madness comes to be seen as self-concern so intense as to eclipse external reality'.[48] If it is true that extreme subjectivity was considered to be a kind of madness, then it is logical to conclude that psychology would have sought to discourage self-reflection. However, the opposite is true. Psychology encourages self-reflection in order to promote mental health. The key feature of psychological self-reflection is that it is systematized subjectivity. What the Augustans really feared may have been chaos, destructive disorder of any kind, including the subjective. Porter's restatement of Alexander Crichton's late eighteenth-century psychological theory is pertinent to this discussion: 'Voluntary imagination (i.e. that governed by will) begets ideas and art; involuntary imagination ... spews nonsense'.[49] In this way, the psychological celebration of subjectivity and self-reflection that is so closely connected to the same ideal in Romanticism may be said to have derived directly from Augustan principles of order and system, a notion that challenges directly the standard critical line about Romanticism as a rebellion against Augustan principles. After all, in *The Prelude*, Wordsworth presents the 'Growth of a Poet's Mind' as a neatly ordered, roughly chronological process divided, in its last manifestation, into an epic fourteen books.[50] This is systematized subjective reflection in high style.

The Augustans expressed their distrust of subjectivity in terms of quintessentially subjective experiences, such as the use of the imagination, dreaming and religious enthusiasm, all of which provide insight into Cotton's and Beattie's contributions to the development of literature and psychology. 'For centuries', Byrd asserts, 'Western men have thought of the primary meaning of imagination as evil, literally diabolical' and adds that some Augustans, like Dr Johnson, developed various literary means to deal with the threat, such as through publications like *The Rambler*, which Byrd describes suggestively as a kind of guide-book delineating the various ways in which the imagination 'encroaches upon reason in human conduct' and leads to madness, Johnson's personal terror.[51] The Augustan author's attempt to control the imagination through a kind of literary guidebook suggests that, even in strictly literary circles, some were beginning to develop methods of systematization as an answer to the threat of the uncontrolled imagination. Dreams were exemplary of this dangerous force: Augustans believed that they are 'actual moments of madness', while, on the other side, Thomas Tryon described madness as a waking dream at the end of the seventeenth century.[52] In *Managing the Mind: A Study of Medical Psychology in Early Nineteenth-Century Britain*, Donnelly explains that the belief that insanity was 'the dream of waking persons, the state of quasi-sleep', led some doctors of the mind to the conclusion that the most effective treatment would therefore involve waking the patient, such as through shock therapy.[53] Cotton and Beattie devised an alternate, less physical way of controlling wayward subjectivity: by appealing to their readers' dreams, faith and sense of individuality, they attempted to meet subjectivity on its own terms, but systematically. Cotton transforms dreams into neatly ordered moral lessons in *Visions in Verse, For the Entertainment and Instruction of Younger Minds*, while Beattie's poetic autobiography, *The Minstrel*, is the history of how his creative imagination developed, as the subtitle referring to the 'progress of genius' reveals. Far from avoiding subjectivity out of a fear of it, these doctors of the mind boldly establish it as the focus of their systematizing activities. As much as they challenge the empirical approach to subjectivity that is so often cited as the hallmark of Enlightenment thinking, Cotton and Beattie reveal themselves to be products of their intellectual milieus through other means: as Simon Schaffer declares in 'States of Mind: Enlightenment and Natural Philosophy', the 'enlightened mind' was thought to be 'the most important resource possessed by the researcher. Thus the mind was represented as a "laboratory", since it could be subjected to experimentation and observation, and as a "state", since it could be managed and reformed'.[54] Indeed, both Cotton and Beattie imply that their verse is a reflection of their own subjective experiences and encourage the reader to mimic their methods of systematizing self-reflection. By taming subjectivity in psychologically inflected verse, Cotton and Beattie provide a roadmap for all types of Romantic writers, artistically and scientifically inclined, to do the same.

Another greatly feared expression of uncontrolled subjective experience in the eighteenth century, fervent religiousness, was reinterpreted by Cotton and Beattie in a way that signals developments in literature and psychology on a wider scale. When religious devotion was thought to be excessive, it was called 'enthusiasm', a word that Pope and others use as synonymous with insanity.[55] Yet, enthusiasm was feared not only because it was it was excessive, but precisely because it was seen as antisocial, a response to 'inner light' or inspiration that could not be communicated to others or controlled in a social context, an interpretation that derived from Locke's comments about enthusiasm in book 4, section 19 of *Essay on Human Understanding*, where 'enthusiastic subjectivity', as Melinda Rabb suggestively calls it, appears as that which "'accepts supposed illumination without search and proof'".[56] Since faith is subjective and dependent upon one's beliefs and emotions, rather than one's logic and reasoning, it is inherently unsystematic and uncontrolled.

The cultural milieu out of which Beattie and Cotton wrote was especially focused on the issue of the private and incommunicable quality of faith. Protestantism, particularly Presbyterianism, champions the private, inward nature of the believer's relationship with God. After all, one of the major differences between it and Catholicism, from which Protestantism divorced itself, is its rejection of the pope and priests who are said to have special access to God and are blessed with unique abilities to interpret the Bible for the wider body of believers; each believer, Protestantism contends, has equal and personal access to God (a force that may also be understood as subjective because, as immaterial, it can only be perceived inwardly) through the power of the believer's subjective relationship with him, making the state of his faith a matter for which he alone is personally responsible.[57] Perhaps as a response to the increasingly socialized form of Christianity in the next century, Danish Protestant philosopher Søren Kierkegaard made the private nature of the believer's relationship with God the cornerstone of his thought, using the Old Testament story of Abraham's willingness to sacrifice his son, Isaac, as the ultimate example of properly constituted faith in *Fear and Trembling* because it shows this 'knight of faith's' rejection of society's laws in favour of God's inwardly communicated directives.[58]

'Every individual', Kierkegaard confirms in *Concluding Unscientific Postscript to the Philosophical Fragments*, his philosophical treatise on selfhood and subjectivity, 'is taught essentially only by God'.[59] Thus, faith was perceived as potentially dangerous in eighteenth-century Britain because it was by definition irrational, unsystematic and antisocial. As scientific believers and defenders of Christianity, Cotton and Beattie sought to strengthen faith in the Enlightenment period by contextualizing it in terms that were more scientific and objective, terms that gave it the ring of empirical truth. Cotton allied faith with reason by appealing to it in order to perform psychological treatment at his insane asylum, while Beattie systematized it in his lectures and prose about moral philosophy. In their poetry, they made faith objective by emphasizing the social responsibilities of the believer – in particular the Christian ideals of poverty and modest living – as expressions of healthy faith, which, as subjective, is identifiable as a healthy mind.

Cotton and Beattie made religiousness part of their psychological approach and thereby divested it of its potential as a kind of madness, not only by enlisting faith on the side of reason and organizing it into a scientific system, but also by contextualizing religious belief in terms of the believer's ethical responsibilities to the rest of society in their poetry. This social focus is the last stage in the transformation of the soul as a private, incommunicable phenomenon into the object of study called the mind, a process that would eventually see the term 'moral philosophy' replaced with 'psychology' by the end of the Romantic period. Reed notes of the early nineteenth century that 'psychology had more or less abandoned the soul and replaced it with the mind. Nevertheless ... most psychologists still expected this science of the mind to reinforce important religious beliefs'.[60] In the mid- to late eighteenth century, though, when Cotton and Beattie were practising and versifying, the soul was still very much a part of the psychologist's professional focus. Indeed, psychology transformed the 'god-relationship' – as Kierkegaard would call the private, purely subjective relationship between the individual and the immaterial reality that is the Divine – into moral terms and made the faithful person's responsibilities to the unseen presence, God, into something that could be assessed by other people. No longer was faith a matter of what lay within, while one's social responsibilities were only an addenda.

In his work on moral philosophy, the early roots of psychology, Beattie systematized morality and made it a matter of scientific study by putting discussions of it alongside sections on the mind and language. Part 1 of Beattie's *Elements of Moral Science*, which is an abstract of his lectures on moral philosophy delivered at Marischal College, Aberdeen, is entitled 'Psychology' and contains such section titles as 'Perception, or External Sensation', 'Consciousness, or Reflection', 'Dreaming' and 'Sympathy'. Throughout the text, Beattie repeatedly associates the 'mind' with the 'soul' or 'spirit' – the faculty that enables us to have a relationship with God. Although he did not explore and devise an approach to treating mental illness as we define it today (after centuries of psychology's efforts to divorce itself from its religious past), Beattie was motivated throughout his career to treating what he viewed as a spiritual illness, which must also be an affliction of the mind, since they are the same in his approach. That avoidance of enthusiasm is one of Beattie's major goals is clear in *Elements of Moral Science*, which, he asserts, will help the reader to 'guard against superstition and enthusiasm, by forming right notions of God's adorable nature and providence'.[61] N. T. Phillipson adds, in 'James Beattie and the Defence of Common Sense', that 'man, the improving agent, was capable of knowing himself, ordering his beliefs and governing his actions through the use of his will' in Beattie's philosophy.[62] Significantly, Beattie's essay *Evidences of the Christian Religion* also establishes him as a proponent of the belief that proof of God's existence is everywhere in the natural world, a theory that was commonly called 'natural religion' (although Beattie rejects the term as belonging to 'infidels').[63] In his attempts to systematize belief and establish irrefutable proof in support of it, Beattie frames the most subjective of all experiences, belief in an unseen being, in objective terms; by submitting the ineffable to the rules of objective science, Beattie makes it communicable with others in society. He thereby tames faith and removes it from the realm of the illogical whence enthusiasm springs. As in the later psychological approaches that followed Christian moral philosophy, Beattie's method was not to reject subjectivity in favour of reason, but to systematize it. In his verse, the inner and private experience of faith undergoes a process of objectification and socialization.

The same may be said about Cotton's approach. Since Cotton's only prose work is *Observations on a Particular Kind of Scarlet Fever that Lately Prevailed in and about St Alban's. In a Letter to Dr Mead*, a very short medical description, our knowledge about his psychological approach depends upon evidence in his poetry and letters written by his most famous patient, William Cowper, who resided in Cotton's madhouse during his second period of mental illness, from December 1763 to 17 June 1765.[64] Cowper describes his treatment under the psychologist-poet in a way that confirms that Cotton identified the cure of his patients' minds with the cure of their souls, their faith. In a process that seems to be a kind of spiritual talk-therapy, Cotton made himself a kind of priest for his patient, according to the account provided by Leslie Ritchie in the *Oxford Dictionary of National Biography* (hereafter *ODNB*):

> Cowper writes that he was 'closely confined' and 'narrowly watched' by servants, and that Cotton 'visited me every morning while I stayed with him ... [T]he Gospel as always the delightful theme of our conversation'. Bibles carefully placed on a garden bench and a window seat (opened to the story of Lazarus and Romans 3:25's promise of salvation) restored Cowper's faith in divine grace at critical moments.[65]

In that Cotton's methods included watching his patients 'narrowly', he seems to have been a kind of proto-moral manager, but, more importantly with respect to his similarities to Beattie, Cotton used religious instruction to treat madness. A letter that Cowper wrote on 4 July 1765 suggests the efficacy of this form of psychiatric therapy:

> I reckon it one instance of the Providence that has attended me throughout this whole event, that ... I was carried to Dr Cotton ... [for] I had so much need of a religious friend to converse with ... The doctor was as ready to administer relief to me in this article likewise [i.e. religious anxiety], and as well qualified to do it as in that which was more immediately his province. How many physicians would have thought this an irregular appetite and a symptom of remaining madness! But if it were so, my friend was as mad as myself, and it is well for me that he was so.[66]

Indeed, Cotton's psychological approach of attending to his patients' spiritual wellbeing was comforting and effective for some, but others may be surprised at Cotton's methods, given his medical tutelage in Leiden under the empiricist Boerhaave, who theorized that nerves were 'hollow pipes, filled under pressure by a fluid' that functioned like a hydraulic system.[67] Cotton's approach is far less empirical: like Beattie, his conception of the mind is identifiable with the soul and his psychological theory is therefore spiritual. According to William Hayley in *The Life of Cowper*, Cotton saw even the natural world through the eyes of faith: "He is truly a philosopher, according to my judgment of the character, every tittle of his knowledge of natural subjects being connected, in his mind, with the firm belief of an omnipotent agent".[68] For Cotton, the soul was identifiable with the mind and, because the ultimate goal in his insane asylum was psychological cure, it follows that Cotton treated his patients' souls as matters of scientific interest. Faith was, thus, systematized in his professional practice as much as that other manifestation of subjectivity, dreams, were domesticated as moral lessons in his verse.

By making our most subjective experiences – faith, imagination and dreams – themes for their poetry and the content of their systematic approaches to the mind, Cotton and Beattie translate what is private and unknowable into social terms, just as they emphasize in their poetry that one aspect of Christianity – humble living, a social good that can only be measured with reference to one's neighbours – is representative of the properly constituted Christian experience as a whole. Their chosen medium for conveying this increasingly social approach to the Christian's relationship with God is apt, for popular verse may be viewed as democratic linguistic coinage. In so doing, the poets indicate that the properly constituted subject is not just answerable to God; nor is his subjective reality unseen. Rather, the healthy subject is answerable to all and his faith is displayed in the objective terms of modest living.

The idea that psychology developed out of the socialization of Christian subjectivity – manifested in morals, faith, or the self-reflection recommended for the maintenance of both – has raised myriad battles in the history of psychiatry. Vieda Skultans expresses the view of many historians influenced by Foucault when she writes, 'Medicine, and particularly psychiatry, are the means whereby the dominant values of society are disseminated'.[69] This perspective has been interpreted by many as being identifiable with the radical view that 'there is nothing but the social construction of disease ... [and] that no such entity as mental illness exists; therefore, any history of madness' is the history of an 'unreal' category created by society, as Sander Gilman summarizes it.[70] After all, if psychology is derived from social principles, then its main focus, mental health and illness, would seem to be predicated upon the same factors. However, I contend that these concepts are not so closely related. Psychology must, perforce, approach its subject from within a social framework because one's behaviour and other means of communicating remain the only ways that others, psychologists and laypeople alike, may glimpse what passes in the mind (as opposed to the brain) of the subject. Moreover, only by comparing these behaviours with cultural norms may we define what is not normal. These assertions do not deny the anguish that attends mental illness, but they do emphasize the social and cultural specificity of our definitions of madness, a feature of them that such respected critics as Burwick and Robert Houston have noted.[71] I do not claim, with Foucault, that 'madness belonged to social failure' at 'the moment when madness was perceived on the social horizon of poverty, of incapacity for work, of inability to integrate with the group; the moment when madness began to rank among the problems of the city', since such strong terms have led to Szaszian and Laingian interpretations of psychology as a witch-hunt and insanity as illusory.[72] My focus on social power dynamics as they form the modern subject is undeniably Foucauldian, but my position is also represented well by such anti-anti-psychiatrists as Shorter when he defines 'Romantic psychiatry' as deriving from the approach that opposed the purely material and biological one gaining ground at the end of the eighteenth century, an approach that emphasized 'one's personal history and social surroundings'.[73] This social aspect of the developing field of psychology and of the context of the subject thereby defined comes into focus most clearly in the popular verse of Beattie and Cotton, which made socially accessible their psychological views of subjectivity.

Nathaniel Cotton as Eighteenth-Century Psychologist: Priest of the People

In the introductory poem to his collection, *Visions in Verse*, Cotton draws attention to the snobbish culture of medicine in eighteenth-century Britain. He writes,

> Were you diseas'd, or pres'd with Pain,
> Strait you'd apply to Warwick-Lane;
> The thoughtful Doctor feels your Pulse,
> (No matter whether Mead or Hulse)
> Writes — Arabic to you and me, –
> Then signs his Hand, and takes his Fee.
> Now, shou'd the Sage omit his Name,
> Wou'd not the Cure remain the same?
> Not but Physicians sign their Bill,
> Or when they cure, or when they kill.[74]

When Cotton jokes that his fictional doctor 'Writes – Arabic to you and me'[75] on his prescriptions, he draws attention to the famously poor penmanship of physicians (some things never change, it seems), but he is also hinting at the increasingly mysterious language of medicine that separated learned doctors from their patients, a situation that the psychologist-poets sought to remedy by communicating in the entertaining and accessible form of verse, as I have noted with reference to Darwin's prose. This was the time of the 'celebrity nerve-doctor', such as George Cheyne, 'physician to Samuel Richardson, [and who] was sought for advice by Johnson and, perhaps, David Hume'.[76] I will discuss the impact of Cheynian medicine in greater detail with reference to nerve theory in Chapter 3, but at this point it suffices to say that celebrity doctors like Cheyne received large sums for treating their eminent patients and their services were therefore unattainable for most of the population. While information about psychology was 'readily accessible to men of general education' in the eighteenth century, some publications from the time show that medicine occupied an increasingly rarefied atmosphere.[77] The medical profession as a whole was becoming increasingly specialized and doctors, seeking to protect their chosen fields from apothecaries and midwives with no formal education, as well as from 'gossips' (local women who dispensed medical advice and prescriptions for traditional cures), began lobbying for stricter rules regarding the qualifications necessary to practise medicine. Physicians made it clear that their specialized education alone warranted them to practise medicine and they reinforced this claim by expressing their knowledge in an esoteric tongue that illustrated to those who were without formal medical instruction that they were ignorant about such matters and, the implication followed, that they should leave important health matters to the knowledgeable.[78] Through these means, the eighteenth-century doctor succeeded in establishing his authority, but it was an authority that depended on his division, linguistic and otherwise, from the rest of society.

An anonymous tract from 1724 reveals just how early in the eighteenth century this divide formed. In the preface of *Pharmacopolae Justificati: or, Apothecaries Vindicated From the Imputation of Ignorance. Wherein is Shewn, That an*

Academical Education is No Way Necessary to Qualify a Man for the Practice of Physick, the anonymous author confirms that socially recognized classes of medical practitioners existed by the first quarter of the eighteenth century and that these classes were created in part through the words that the physicians wrote:

> whoever will read the Books wrote by Physicians, will find the Apothecaries charg'd generally with Ignorance, and rank'd with Circumforanians, Midwifes, Nurses, and Old Women. And it is no wonder, if Expressions utter'd against them by men of known Learning, and such as may be supposed best to judge concerning them, a rereceiv'd with a general Assent.[79]

A few pages later, the author indicates that doctors used education as a key division in setting themselves above other kinds of health practitioners: 'the *Doctor's* high Opinion of his superior Knowledge in *Languages, Anatomy, Chymistry Mathematicks, Theory of Physick,* and *Natural Philosophy* in all its Parts, (all which he has acquir'd by the Advantages of an *University Education*,) is the Foundation of his Contempt of the *Apothecary*'.[80] Indeed, the acquirement of a formal education became the basis of the physician's claim to the sole right to practice medicine. This quotation also suggests that a notable component of the education that gave the physician his superior position in the realm of health care included a non-scientific subject, specifically languages. At another point in the tract, the author hints sarcastically at how the doctor's superior linguistic skills translated into greater scientific accreditation:

> while the Disciples of the *Rationalists* were enquiring into the *Philosophy* of their Times, and the Conjectures of others concerning the *Nature and Causes of Diseases*, the Followers of the *Empiricks*, entirely neglecting *them*, were only diligently attending to the *Diseases* themselves, observing their *Symptoms*, and the *Operations* of *Medicines*. Thus both increasing their Knowledge in their Way, it was no wonder the *Empiricks* lost their Reputation in *Physick*, even while the Practice was more successful; because tho' they could cure better, they could not write so well.[81]

In other words, while the 'college boys' (and, indeed, as I note above, female healthcare workers were excluded from the academic side of the contest) were discovering philosophy, theorizing abstractly about diseases and learning to write well, the 'Empiricks' – such as the apothecaries – were gaining practical experience with the curing of ill people.[82] Yet the former group managed to wrestle control of the medical profession to their corner because they had the communicative power to convince wider society that their type of broad-based knowledge was more valuable. If this anonymous author's assertions are true – if the physician gained his position as the only acceptable type of medical authority not as a scientist alone, but as a man of broad education – then perhaps what Foucault claims about the psychologist at the turn of the nineteenth century was only a matter of course. He writes, 'the doctor's intervention is not made by virtue of medical skill or power that he possesses in himself and that would be justified by a body of objective knowledge. It is not as a scientist that *homo medicus* has authority in the asylum, but as a wise man'.[83] For the most part, the early psychologist-poets battled to bridge the gap that had already formed between physicians and their patients through the very means that doctors had used to create the division, specifically, linguistic means. The psychologist-poets escape identification with the snobbish doctors that the anonymous tract writer describes through their democratic use of language. All of them except Bakewell were university educated, but they succeeded in divorcing themselves from the image of the lofty doctor by writing more than academic treatises. They wrote poetry, an entertaining and attractive medium, and most of them included some psychological component in their verse.

Christian Tutor of the Collegium Insanorum

Cotton (b. *c.* 1705 d. 1788) may be considered to be the first of the psychologist-poets of the pre-Romantic era, for his verse, which was first published in the 1750s, enjoyed a resurgence in popularity in the 1790s. It also provides evidence of the strongly religious and didactic qualities of this tradition of poetry in its early stages and hints at the religious roots of psychology itself. Especially in his best-known work, *Visions in Verse, For the Entertainment and Instruction of Younger Minds*, Cotton teaches his reader that the most Christian way to live is also the most psychologically healthful and dramatizes his recommendation to be self-reflective through the very form of his poems, which are presented as his own dream-visions. By virtue of the fact that the lessons he derives from them are the interpretations of his subconscious activity, Cotton demonstrates that self-reflection – even on the products of the much-feared uncontrolled imagination – is a valuable moral resource.

Notably, this early English psychologist was educated and practised psychology outside of the immediate influence of the Scottish Enlightenment and its signature subject, moral philosophy. While Cotton, the son of a Levant merchant, did not publish any strictly psychological works from which we might learn about his theories, we may surmise that his methods of treatment were as educative as are his poems, for he called his private madhouse near the abbey in St Albans the '*Collegium Insanorum*', or the 'insane college'.[84] That his approach was also spiritual is certain, judging by the letters Cowper wrote while at the *Collegium Insanorum*, as quoted above. Cowper even implies that Cotton's religious approach to psychological cure surpassed both that of the priests who lacked psychological knowledge and the doctors who lacked religious knowledge in his description of a maturing boy in the poem 'Hope':

> Now see him launched into the world at large;
> If priest, supinely droning o'er his charge,
> Their fleece his pillow, and his weekly drawl,
> Though short, too long, the price he pays for all;
> If lawyer, loud whatever cause he plead,
> But proudest of the worst, if that succeed.
> Perhaps a grave physician, gath'ring fees,
> Punctually paid for length'ning out disease,
> No Cotton, whose humanity sheds rays
> That make superior skill his second praise.[85]

Yet, as Leslie Ritchie, author of the *ODNB* entry for Cotton, notes, 'Such care was not without an earthly price. In a letter to Joseph Hill dated 14 August 1765 Cowper mentions that he owes Cotton at least £140'.[86] Perhaps because the cost of treatment in the *Collegium Insanorum* would have been prohibitive for many, Cotton made his religio-psychological method of treatment available to all in his wildly popular volume of poems, *Visions in Verse*.

Visions in Verse is a collection of nine allegories about 'Slander', 'Pleasure', 'Health', 'Content', 'Happiness', 'Friendship', 'Marriage', 'Life' and 'Death'.[87] The subtitle of the volume – *For the Entertainment and Instruction of Younger Minds* – suggests that it was written in the popular tradition of moral verse for children, to which Isaac Watts made, perhaps, the most notable contribution in the eighteenth century.[88] Significantly, the Cotton-like speaker of *Visions* suggests that the dreams he presents as neatly ordered and numbered poetic lessons are his own, which appear here as organized manifestations of his subjectivity. For example, in 'Pleasure. Vision II', the speaker moves into a description of the dream after a short introduction of the lesson that should be learned from it:

> One Summer's Evening as I stray'd
> Along the Silent Moon-light Glade;
> With these Reflections in my Breast,
> Beneath an Oak I sunk to Rest;
> A gentle Slumber intervenes,
> And Fancy dres'd instructive Scenes.[89]

By emphasizing that these poems narrate the speaker's own dreams and, moreover, by calling them 'visions', Cotton underscores that the trope of subjectivity is essential to his poetic and psychological purpose in several ways. First, that they are the manifestations of his own inner life underlines their subjective nature. Moreover, that he calls these dreams – themselves the feared expression of the uncontrolled imagination – 'visions' raises the spectre of enthusiasm, for this word commonly denotes the religious hallucinations of enthusiasts.[90] Significantly, though, these subjective experiences are nothing if not ordered. Not only are they composed entirely of lines organized into perfectly rhyming duos, but each poem, constructed to represent a coherent moral lesson apiece, is numbered and moves steadily and predictably towards 'Death', a chronological advancement that establishes the sequence's literary ancestry in the line of other Christian allegorical works, like John Bunyan's *The Pilgrim's Progress*.[91] By enlisting these 'visions' as tools for the establishment of mental peace, which is associated with reason, Cotton transforms the chaotic and private realm of the subjective into that which is shareable, social. Regardless of how fantastic his personal 'visions' may seem, Cotton informs his reader throughout the poems that they are not only provided as 'entertainment', but also as 'instruction'. As will become clear, his emphasis throughout the volume on the ethico-Christian good of poverty underscores that Cotton, like Beattie, socializes Christian self-reflection, which is a good summary of what psychology as a whole would eventually do.

In addition to these myriad means of taming the subjective and familiarizing it through the social, Cotton also develops throughout his volume theme of poverty as a great moral good. This theme adds more than simple Christian piety to the poems; because the celebration of modest living is one of the most social of the Christian virtues, Cotton implies that mental and spiritual health are tied to social responsibility.[92] The healthy subject and properly constituted self, then, can only exist in the context of good social relationships. Crucially, Cotton sets the tone for the entire volume in 'An Epistle to the Reader', the introductory poem. Here, he combines all of his interests – the moral value of humility, medicine, mental health and religion – in a few lines. Near the poem's beginning, the speaker describes his own rural life as one adorned only by modest pleasures:

> I pass the silent rural Hour,
> No Slave to Wealth, no Tool to Pow'r.
> My Mansion's warm, and very neat;
> You'd say, a pretty snug Retreat.
> My Rooms no costly Paintings grace,
> The humbler Print supplies their Place.[93]

By extolling the virtues of 'humble' art, Cotton effectively advertises for his own book of poetry, the easy vocabulary and melodic rhythm of which marks it as being written for 'younger minds' and the lower classes. He implies that his humble, accessible kind of poetry is superior to art for the higher classes, just as the 'humbler Print' replaces 'costly Paintings' in the home he describes.[94] Cotton helps to define to the political role played by the psychologist-poets by aligning himself with the poor and opposing the rich, a role that grounded their intention to appeal to a wide audience through the attractive medium of poetry and underscored their connection to the egalitarian politics of the Scottish Enlightenment. This celebration of poverty throughout the volume also plays a crucial role in situating the new psychological subject as mediated through the social.

Inviting the audience to follow his example, the poems' self-reflective dreamer models a subjectivity that finds balance and wholeness in a socially responsible, modest lifestyle.

This emphasis on humility characterizes the entire volume. For example, in 'Content. Vision IV', Cotton shows how contentment – surely identical with mental health as the opposite of mania, anxiety and melancholy – shuns wealth and pomp and seeks the rural lifestyle. In classic allegorical style, Cotton personifies 'Content':

> CONTENT shuns Courts, and oft'ner dwells
> With modest Worth in humble Cells;
> There's no Complaint, tho' brown the Bread,
> Or the cold Stone sustain the Head;
> Tho' hard the Couch, and coarse the Meat,
> Still the brown Loaf and Sleep are sweet.[95]

Similar sentiments regarding the salutary effect on mental health of rural and other means of living humbly appear in almost all of the other Visions. Above all, though, Cotton's introductory poem is the most explicit about how humility is good for one's mental health. The psychologist-poet expresses this sentiment in medical terms:

> Fortune (for I'll mention all,
> And more than you dare tell) is small;
> Yet ev'ry Friend partakes my Store,
> And Want goes smiling from my Door.
>
> . . . .
>
> 'Tis true, my little Purse grows light;
> But then I sleep so sweet at Night!
> This *Grand Specific* will prevail,
> When all the Doctor's Opiates fail.[96]

In short, the Christian virtue of charity, which may make one poor and humble if practised in earnest, provides better psychological treatment than the period's favourite medicine, opium. Again, Cotton mocks the efficacy of his profession's preferred prescriptions and replaces chemicals with his own '*Grand Specific*', Christian charity and its attendant condition, humble living. Finally, near the end of this introductory poem, Cotton confirms the religious character of his verses and encourages his readers to read his poems carefully in the following lines:

> Now the Religion of your Poet —
> Does not this little Preface show it?
> My Visions if you scan with Care,
> 'Tis Ten to One you'll find it there.[97]

In this inaugural poem, Cotton sets up the theme of humility and the tone of religious instruction and psychological treatment in a medical setting for the entire volume.

Cotton abjures his readers to contemplate their actions fully for the sake of their own mental health, which he identifies as linked to their eternal salvation by the end of the volume. In so doing, he shows his belief that he may reform his readers' souls by appealing to their understanding and advocating mental health, a belief that is generated by his psychological theory that the 'mind' and 'soul' are one. For example, in 'Pleasure: Vision II', Cotton implores,

> Your Cares to *Body* are confin'd,
> Few fear Obliquity of *Mind*.
> Why not adorn the better Part!
> This is a nobler Theme for Art.
> For what is Form, or what is Face,
> But the Soul's Index, or its Case?
>   Now take a Simile at Hand,
> Compare the mental Soil to Land.
> Shall Fields be till'd with annual Care,
> And Minds lie fallow ev'ry Year?[98]

The elision in these lines between the words 'soul' and 'mind' confirms that, for Cotton, the province of psychology includes spiritual matters. He emphasizes the fact that our existences are grossly material, but he charges his readers to attend to our spiritual natures as the jewels that our bodies encase. The psychologist-poet also introduces and concludes the poem in a way that is typical of *Visions* with respect to its unique combination of psychological and spiritual commentary, which also shows Cotton's view that the mind and soul are one. The asylum-owner writes,

> Let not the unexperienc'd Boy
> . . . .
> ... say, that Dreams are vain and wild,
> Like Fairy Tales, to please a Child.
> Important Hints the Wise may reap
> From Sallies of the Soul in Sleep.
> And since there's Meaning in my Dream,
> The Moral merits your Esteem.[99]

In other words, although dreams are the product of 'fancy', as Cotton reiterates throughout the volume, they are not therefore low, as Coleridge implies the products of fancy are in comparing them to the lofty creations of the primary and secondary imagination in *Biographia Literaria*. Dreams are, Cotton claims, 'instructive' and the 'meaningful' productions of the 'Sallies of the Soul in Sleep'.

In this phrase, Cotton identifies dreams, which we often think of as connected to the mind alone, as being derived from the work of the soul, our spiritual faculty. Moreover, while many eighteenth-century writers recoiled from using the products of the uncontrolled imagination, such as the stuff of dreams, Cotton shows the confidence born of a psychologist's familiarity with the wayward mind by presenting each of his religious poems as the products of dream-visions.

The psychologist-poet underlines his spiritual focus by discussing frankly the moral purpose of his creative techniques in 'Health. Vision III'. Here he explains the poetic method that underlies the whole of *Visions*:

> But Morals, unadorn'd by Art,
> Are seldom known to reach the Heart.
> I'll therefore strive to raise my Theme,
> With all the Scenery of a Dream.
>   Soft were my Slumbers, sweet my Rest,
> Such as the Infant's on the Breast;
> When Fancy, ever on the Wing,
> And fruitful as the genial Spring,
> Presented in a Blaze of Light,
> A new Creation to my Sight.[100]

By explaining that he presents moral lessons as dreams in order to 'reach the Heart' of his reader, Cotton shows his understanding that people react negatively to 'unadorn'd' preaching, that he has considered how to work around this psychological quirk and that he has created his versified 'Art' with an eye to overcoming it; these poems are, as the subtitle tells us, for 'Entertainment and Instruction', after all.[101] It is as though Dr Cotton has studied the reader's mind as he would that of a patient and offers psychological treatment in the form of poetry, thereby performing an elision between the concept of 'reader' and 'patient' that is repeated throughout the psychologist-poets' verse. In keeping with his instructive and religious psychological methods in the *Collegium Insanorum*, Cotton's poetic treatment of his readers is heuristic, moral and informed by his specialized knowledge as a psychologist.

'Health. Vision III' further develops the concept that the purview of doctors is not only medical, but also moral. Cotton writes,

> If Folly has possess'd his Prime,
> Disease shall gather Strength in Time;
> Poison shall rage in ev'ry Vein, ----
> Nor Penitence dilute the Stain:
> And when each Hour shall urge his Fate,
> Thought, like the Doctor, comes too late.
>   The Subject of my Song is HEALTH,
> A Good superior far to Wealth.[102]

Cotton distinguishes himself from other doctors in several ways: through his wish to communicate psycho-moral lessons to a broad public; through his suggestion, critical of his colleagues, that doctors can be negligent (they 'come[ ] too late'); and in his claim that his real medical interest is psychological by mentioning 'folly', 'penitence' and 'thought' as connected to the experience of bodily disease, to which the word 'Vein' draws attention. Here Cotton assiduously tailors his image as a superior sort of doctor who treats the soul and mind together – an image that Cowper faithfully helped to develop in his lines about Cotton in 'Hope'.

By combining psychological insight with moral teachings, Cotton may have influenced the development of psychology as a field, as well as psychological poetry in the Romantic era. Some of his poems provide strong evidence for the latter contention. For example, 'Pleasure', the second Vision, presents the splendours of the high life to the poem's dreaming pilgrims in a way that strikes any student of Romantic poetry as familiar:

> Now as our Journey we pursue,
> A beauteous Fabrick rose to View;
> A stately Dome! and sweetly grac'd
> With every Ornament of Taste.
> This Structure was a Female's Claim,
> And PLEASURE was the Monarch's Name.
>   The Hall we enter'd uncontroul'd,
> And saw the Queen enthron'd on Gold;
> *Arabian* Sweets perfum'd the Ground,
> And laughing *Cupids* flutter'd round;
> A flowing Vest adorn'd the Fair,
> And flow'ry Chaplets wreath'd her Hair:
> The GRACES deck'd her with their Smiles,
> And FRAUD bestow'd her artful Wiles.[103]

Such are the temptations that present themselves to the unreflective mind, the mind that lies 'fallow', to use Cotton's agricultural comparison. This passage provides strong evidence that Coleridge – who was, reputedly, preoccupied with the notion that he did not use his mental 'talents' sufficiently – was familiar with Cotton's work. In his preface to his poetic 'psychological curiosity', Coleridge claims that 'Kubla Khan' is the transcription of a dream that he had after reading 'Purchas's Pilgrimage' and taking an 'anodyne', doubtlessly laudanum. I maintain that if we could inspect the volumes that lay at Coleridge's elbow during this most fruitful of naps, we would find Cotton's *Visions in Verse*, as well; indeed, Cotton's volume title may well have inspired Coleridge to subtitle his poem, 'A Vision in a Dream'.. Consider, first, Cotton's description of the debauched lady 'PLEASURE['s]' 'stately Dome', which the speaker 'enter'd uncontroul'd', where he was greeted by the smells of '*Arabian* Sweets [that] perfum'd the Ground'

and 'Citrons [that exhale] their balmy Sweets' and where he witnessed the sights
and sounds of 'Fountains murm'ring to the Song'.[104] The details of this rich scene
echo strongly those of Coleridge's Xanadu, where Kubla Khan 'A stately pleas-
ure-dome [did] decree', 'Where blossom[s fill] ... many an incense-bearing tree',
where a similarly evil and sensuous 'woman wail[s] for her demon lover', where
an 'Abyssinian maid' plays music and a fountain 'Burst[s]' uncontrollably and
sinks 'in a tumult'.[105] The Arabic dream-scene appears elsewhere in Romantic
poetry, too. Without borrowing so many details from Cotton's poem, Wordsworth also expresses his agreement that dreams can reveal psychological truths
in Book 5 of *The Prelude* when he describes the dream of his 'Friend' (no doubt
Coleridge himself, as he is the friend to which Wordsworth refers throughout
the long poem).[106] Wordsworth confesses that he has borrowed the idea of 'This
Arab Phantom' 'from the world of sleep' and 'to him ha[s] ... given/ A substance'
in which not only 'madness, [but also] reason did lie couched'.[107] All three poets
use dreams to draw attention to the treasures of the imagination, which are
represented as Arabian in order to signify its exotic, mysterious and potentially
dangerous quality. More specifically, in so far as Cotton and Coleridge figure
dreams as oriental, they draw upon the popular associations of the East as pleasurable, sensual and all the more threatening for the temptations it offers. They
may also gesture to another eighteenth-century poem, Mark Akenside's 'The
Pleasures of Imagination'.[108] Both poets also indicate the need to systematize the
imagination in order to make it useful: Coleridge implies as much when he states
the necessity of 'weav[ing] a circle round' the inspired poet 'thrice' in 'Kubla
Khan', an image that gestures to the need to contain and organize the imaginative
threat posed by the figure, while Cotton's speaker's neat ordering of his dreams
into instructive and coherent lessons presents the ultimate domestication of the
potentially hazardous faculty of the fancy.[109] The speaker commands the reader
to attend to such visionary activity closely at the end of the introductory poem:
'scan with Care' 'My Visions', he advises.[110] If the reader does so, Cotton implies,
she will apprehend an important psychological truth that had hitherto been as
mysterious as the Arabic world is to Englishmen, or psychological knowledge
is to laymen. Thanks to this written account of the speaker's own dreams, what
other doctors write is not 'Arabic to you and me', to refer again to 'An Epistle
to the Reader'; nor does the Arabian dream of 'Pleasure' retain its dangerous
exoticism.[111] Cotton's dispersal of psychological knowledge through a moralistic
interpretation of his dreams in *Visions in Verse* makes the exotic and threatening
unconscious realm into that which is familiar and useful. Certainly, Cotton is
more blunt about the didactic purpose of his psychological poems than were the
best-known Romantics, but passages like these suggest that the Romantics, too,
helped to divest the subjective realm of its mystery by exploring it as a theme in
their popular poetry.[112]

This familiarization of the subjective and private is identifiable with the process of contextualizing self-reflection in social terms, which I argue is key to the development of psychology as a field. That these apparently socially oriented discussions of topics like 'Slander', 'Friendship' and 'Marriage' derive their ultimate significance in terms of the subjective experience of faith – one's private relationship with God – becomes clear upon reaching the last poem, 'Death. Vision the Last', which Cotton implies is the most important by making it more than twice as long as most of the other poems in the volume and giving it pride of place as the final word.[113] Here, the psychologist-poet sums up the gist of his advice throughout the volume when he admonishes the reader to 'Study the Science of your Heart', adding, 'This nobler self with Rapture scan,/ 'Tis Mind alone, which makes the Man'.[114] The 'Science of ... [the] Heart' is none other than the kind of eighteenth-century psychology that Cotton and Beattie promoted, specifically, psychology that reveals the mind as a spiritual organ, which, in turn, is the seat of our moral and religious actions. These interests are at the root of the critical attitude towards the medical profession that Cotton illustrates throughout the volume, including 'Death'. These poems argue that medicine must explore more than the transitory body and thereby illustrate that fear of the consequences of Darwin's style of materialism began long before *Zoönomia* or *The Temple of Nature* was published. The last Vision reveals why Cotton so often broaches the topic of the inefficacy of medicine and the inability of physicians to ward off death in the volume. Death, he indicates, is an inescapable part of our earthly lives. However, Christianity teaches that 'we wake eternally', as John Donne contends in 'Death, be not proud', if we nurture our eternal souls.[115] And, significantly, Cotton identifies our souls with our minds. He asserts this view again in 'Death' when he writes, 'But whence the Soul! From Heav'n it came!/ Oh! prize this intellectual Flame'.[116] Cotton states here what he implies throughout the volume: our spiritual element is identifiable with our 'intellectual' being, the subject of his religio-psychological verse. Physicians cannot give us eternal bodily life, but, according to Cotton, his kind of versified spiritual and psychological therapy can help the reader to attain the everlasting life of the soul.

Because he is dedicated to a spiritually based psychology, Cotton is necessarily critical of the medical profession, for he believed that, despite its great claims, empirical medicine is sorely limited in its ability to help mankind. In the following description of the unfortunate 'Honorio's' fever, Cotton implies that the brain, so much the focus of the materialist physician, holds a precarious reign:

> No Drugs the kindly Wish fulfill,
> Disease eludes the Doctor's Skill.
>
> . . . .

> The Brain's an useless Organ grown,
> And REASON tumbled from his Throne.[117]

Cotton also revisits the question of how the body – which was the focus of his medical education in Leiden – relates to the mind, or soul, through the voice of 'REASON'. Even when he seems about to share secrets about how to keep the body healthy, Cotton seems to chide the reader for his curiosity about the lowly subject and encourages him to focus on his mind instead:

> With curious Eyes review thy Frame,
> This Science shall direct thy Claim.
> Dost thou indulge a double View,
> A long, long Life, and happy too?
>
> . . . .
>
> Come then, is Happiness thy Aim?
> Let mental Joys be all thy Game.
>
> . . . .
>
> And when Disease assaults the Heart,
> When sickness triumphs over Art,
> Reflections on a Life well past
> Shall prove a Cordial to the last;
> This Med'cine shall the Soul sustain,
> And soften, or suspend her Pain;
> Shall break DEATH's fell tyrannic Pow'r,
> And calm the troubled dying Hour.[118]

If death's 'Pow'r' can be broken by the 'Med'cine' of 'Reflections on a Life well past', then Cotton attempts to offer victory over death to the reader in *Visions in Verse*, for he shows us how to 'pass' our lives well – how to lead moral lives – and how to reflect on our lives. This powerful medicine is the reader's to create. In the true spirit of his strange didacticism, in which he teaches while relinquishing his authority, Cotton has taught the reader how to be her own spiritual apothecary in these poems. Like Darwin, who tailors his language and poetry to appeal to the masses with his scientific observations, and Beattie, who, as we shall see, endeavours to make moral philosophy accessible to everyone, Cotton truly democratizes his religious psychology.

Unlike the materialist Darwin, however, Cotton proposes to take power away from empirical medicine and offer more control to his reader through his spiritual, self-reflective psychology, an approach that necessitates the reader's/patient's involvement in her own treatment. The physical body may not last forever, but each reader has the power to develop what is permanent in herself, specifically, her soul and her relationship with God:

> And shall a Man arraign the Skies,
> Because Man lives, and mourns, and dies!
> Impatient Reptile! REASON cry'd;
> Arraign thy Passion and thy Pride.
> Retire, and commune with thy Heart,
> Ask, whence thou cam'st, and what thou art.
> Explore thy Body and thy Mind,
>
> . . . .
>
> Go, Man, and act a wiser Part,
> Study the Science of your Heart.[119]

The 'Science of ... [the] Heart' is the psycho-spiritual therapy that Cotton has taught throughout the volume, while the reader's 'Study' is identical with the meditations that are inspired by reading *Visions in Verse*. This poem is appropriate as the crown of the volume because it includes an explanation of its own value. It suggests to the reader that, if she has read carefully, as Cotton instructs her to do in 'An Epistle to the Reader' ('My Visions ... scan with Care') and has followed his instructions regarding marriage, life, pleasure, health and all of the other topics he explores in the poems, she will already be practised in the methods of 'Science of ... [the] Heart', for Cotton has encouraged the reader to meditate on her motivations and moral actions throughout the volume.[120]

In this way, Dr Cotton demonstrates his egalitarian attitude towards his readers, for he tries to educate them about his methods so that they will no longer need his greater authority or therapy. He positively attempts to deny his authority as a psychologist in the following lines, still spoken by 'REASON':

> Why such a Stranger to your Breast!
> Why turn so many volumes o'er,
> Till *Dodsley* can supply no more!
> Not all the Volumes on thy Shelf,
> Are worth that single Volume, Self.
> For, who this sacred Book declines,
> Howe'er in other Arts he shines;
>
> . . . .
>
> With all his Knowledge is a Fool.[121]

Notably, 'Dodsley' is Cotton's own publisher. Thus, the poet takes aim at his own authority in these lines as surely as he mocks the abilities of physicians at other points in *Visions*. The point of this volume, Cotton suggests in this summarizing final poem, is to teach the reader to learn about herself by looking within. However, by encouraging the reader to be self-reflective in a consistent way – by discussing the path to spiritual and mental health in terms of religion and modest living – Cotton provides a particular context for the self, a language through which he encourages the reader to be subjective. Even though he is egalitarian in many ways, Cotton's definition of a context through which the subject is defined in his popular poems must be understood as contributive to the language of psychology, a working out of the grammar of disciplinary power.

James Beattie: Subjectivity, Faith and Moral Philosophy

Beattie is like Cotton in that he understands mental health in similarly moral terms, but he approaches his subject from the perspective of a moral philosopher for whom psychology and religious devotion are inseparable. As his prose work shows us, he, too, uses the words 'soul' and 'mind' interchangeably and in his poetry, particularly his long poem *The Minstrel*, Beattie suggests in various places that the 'progress of genius' to which the subtitle refers is also a spiritual journey for the main character, Edwin.

The Minstrel must be viewed in light of the fact that it was written while Beattie was composing his famous rebuttal to Humean scepticism, *An Essay on the Nature and Immutability of Truth, in Opposition to Sophistry and Scepticism*, in which he reviles Hume's philosophy as damaging to Christian faith.[122] Thus, when Beattie celebrates the subjective life of Edwin, he not only shows his reader the path to mental peace by providing a particular language for self-reflection; by implying that one's subjective world cannot be held up to the standards of the objective realm, Beattie also defends the seat of faith and thereby offers mental serenity. Beattie is often classified as a 'graveyard poet' and grouped with Parnell, Young and Akenside, partly on account of 'The Hermit', which is clearly connected to *The Minstrel*, as the reclusive sage on whom the smaller poem focuses is indistinguishable from the same character who teaches Edwin near the end of the long poem. Yet, by viewing Beattie as a graveyard poet alone, we fail to recognize how his verse expresses the tenets of his moral philosophy. As he makes clear in both his psychological and poetic texts, humility means trusting in the dictates of the simple religion that is available to all – over and against the sophistical lessons of sceptical philosophy – and leading a modest lifestyle that would not lead one into the complicated, abstract intellectual arguments presented by the followers of Hume.

In his poetry, Beattie develops themes, like modest living and the value of self-reflection, that overlap with those of Cotton. We may attribute Beattie's interest in the rural lifestyle to his humble beginnings. According to Beattie's contemporary, William Forbes, 'James Beattie, LLD was born on the 25th October, 1735, at Lawrencekirk, at that time an obscure hamlet in the county of Kincardine in Scotland'.[123] His father was a retail shop owner and farmer and therefore not wealthy, but the boy was lucky enough to be Scottish, which assured him of a good education in the eighteenth century. As Forbes later confirms, thanks to the Scottish public school system, the lower classes of people in Scotland often display a superior degree of abilities through common life ... the youth, even of the peasantry, may, if so inclined, receive such a measure of instruction, as is suited to their station, or may enable them, if possessed of superior genius, to arrive at still higher attainments in literature.[124]

Beattie grew up with the notion that the lower classes should be exposed to literature and other products of 'high culture', to use an anachronistic Arnoldian term. The egalitarian Scottish system encouraged the young Beattie to take a proprietary approach to literature: 'his turn for poetry began to show itself, and among his school-fellows he went by the name of the Poet'.[125] He tackled the topic that formed the basis of his professional career, moral philosophy, with the same democratic attitude that characterized the Scottish educational system and expressed his theories of moral philosophy in verse by way of making it accessible to all.

After studying at Aberdeen on a bursary awarded to poor scholars with promise, Beattie became a schoolmaster at Fordoun in Scotland, where he learned his love of nature and became friends with James Burnett, Lord Monboddo.[126] We can surmise that Beattie's interest in language, which I will discuss with reference to *An Essay on ... Truth*, was influenced by his relationship with Monboddo, whose notorious work *Of the Origin and Progress of Language* set off a cultural debate about language (not to mention numerous jibes about Uncle Orangutan).[127] In 1760, he took a chair at Marischal College in Moral Philosophy and Logic, which he held 'until his death despite tempting and lucrative offers in the 1770s of a chair at Edinburgh and of two rich livings in the Church of England'.[128] The appointment at Marischal College was extraordinary, for Beattie had never taught moral philosophy; nor could he claim any particular expertise in the subject. According to Phillipson, the confrontational character of Beattie's rebuttal to Humean scepticism, *An Essay on ... Truth*, was tied to his odd position: Beattie's 'inability to master the very subject in which he was supposed to achieve excellence was first of all vented on the subject itself and then on Hume and his circle, who, he thought, were plotting to destroy his reputation and his peace of mind'.[129] Beattie's experiences at Aberdeen also seem to have encouraged his poetic talents and they may even have influenced the form his poetry would take. Aberdeen was the site of his election to the Aberdeen Philosophical Society, which afforded him the company of such great intellectuals as the early psychologist Reid, the physician John Gregory and Alexander Gerard, from whom he learned moral philosophy and whose chair he filled when the older scholar retired.[130] William Forbes tells us that 'This literary society ... which the vulgar and uninformed denominated the Wise Club', inspired numerous 'literary compositions, which have instructed or amused the world'.[131] The strong emphasis on both philosophy and literature in 'the Wise Club' may have inspired Beattie to marry the two realms in his verse and prose.

As the earliest form of theoretical psychology, moral philosophy was different from the psychology that Cotton and Darwin practised. The latter doctors' profession involved providing therapy for mentally unbalanced patients, while Beattie's work involved the abstract study of the healthy human mind.[132] Beattie defines his field in the first pages of *An Essay on … Truth*. He establishes the similarities between his philosophical position and that of his enemies, the sceptical philosophers, by describing both as psychological (he refers to the 'conscience', 'understanding', 'and 'information of sense'), but he does so even as he denies Humean scepticism the very title of 'philosophy', calling it 'that pretended philosophy which supposes, or which may lead us to suppose, every dictate of conscience, every impulse of understanding, and every information of sense, questionable and ambiguous'.[133] In the subsequent statement, Beattie outlines his idea of the proper purview of sceptical philosophy, only to suggest that it fails to reach its goal of teaching about psychology, or 'human nature':

> How then is this science to be learned? In what manner are we to study human nature? Doubtless by examining our own hearts and feelings, and by attending to the conduct of other men. But are not the writings of philosophers useful towards the attainment of this science? Most certainly they are … But I fear we shall not be able to improve ourselves in any one of these respects, by reading the modern systems of scepticism.[134]

Beattie asserts that he focuses on the soul when he draws attention to 'our own hearts and feelings, and … the conduct of other men'; that he means his lessons not to remain in the abstract, but to be applied practically when he expresses his concern that 'we shall not be able to improve ourselves' if we practise Humean 'scepticism'; and that his psychological methodology includes self-reflection, contemplating one's own mind, since the soul is, for him, as it is for Cotton, identifiable with the mind (he asserts later in the work that 'Every mind is conscious, that he has within him a thinking active principle called a soul or mind').[135] Here, again, is Christian self-reflection and faith undergoing the transformation into psychology.

Beattie maintains that everyone has the ability to be self-reflexive and should be confident in their own ability to comprehend the significance of what they find within, for it constitutes nothing less than the faculty that enables us to have a relationship with God. Nowhere is Beattie clearer on this point than in 'Section V: Of Consciousness, or Reflection' in *An Essay on … Truth*. First, he defines 'consciousness' as the faculty that allows us to 'attend to and perceive what passes in our own minds', which indicates that, to Beattie, the most basic state of human mental awareness involves self-reflexive thought, or thinking about thinking.[136] By encouraging readers to study 'what passes in our own minds', Beattie asserts that our subjective thoughts are of primary importance and anticipates a concern that would become central to Romantic ideology. He confirms the value of subjective perception when he writes, 'Of the things perceived by this faculty [i.e. consciousness], the chief is the mind itself. Every mind is conscious, that he has within him a thinking active principle called a soul or mind'.[137] In the last words of this bold statement, Beattie clarifies that the 'soul' that we use to experience spirituality and relate to God is, at its basis, a self-reflexive faculty. This 'soul' or 'mind' is what makes us who we are; it is the self, subjectivity, the beginning and end of our self-reflection.

While Beattie and Hume both emphasize the value of self-reflection, their views differ regarding what constitutes the proper approach to subjective phenomena. Humean psychology challenges its students to reflect on subjective phenomena, such as religious beliefs, with the uncompromising eye of an empirical scientist searching for anomalies in logic or oddities in the material world. Beattie argues that the value of beliefs must be judged by a different standard: zeal. He maintains in his prose that that if we passionately believe something to be true, it is so.[138] Thus, the fervour with which Beattie writes about moral philosophy can be interpreted as evidence of his piety.[139] He saw philosophy not just as an academic exercise, but as a spiritual task. To Beattie, properly constituted philosophy concerned no less than one's relationship with God and he wrote with a passion equal to his weighty task of aiding the faith of his audience. James Harris confirms that Beattie tried to change the actual 'habits' of his reader when he explains, 'Theoretical "psychology" is valuable only to the extent that it yields a better understanding of the grounds and rewards of virtue. Both as a teacher and a writer, inculcating correct sentiments and habits is always Beattie's aim'.[140] When he shows his broad audience how to study their own minds, Beattie – like Cotton – also teaches them how to have a closer relationship with the Divine.

Beattie's perception of his role as a kind of spiritual midwife to the masses may explain why he was so dedicated to making the language of philosophy accessible to a wide audience. In his *Elements of Moral Science*, an abstract of his lecture course in moral philosophy at Marischal College, Beattie's discussion of what he terms his 'Psychology' in the table of contents begins with an explanation and swift refutation of sceptical philosophy on the grounds of 'the constitution of our nature', which he later defines as the human propensity to believe what is not necessarily logical or empirically verifiable. He begins by conceding a point to his opponents, even as he erases its significance: 'We cannot prove by argument, that bodies exist, or that we ourselves exist; nor is it necessary that we should: for the thing is self-evident, and the constitution of our nature makes it impossible for us to entertain any doubt concerning this matter'.[141] This comment he follows up by asserting that Hume and his successors

> came at last to affirm, that the soul perceives nothing but its own ideas; and that ... the whole universe which we see around us, has no existence but in the mind that perceives it. Never were reason and language more abused than by this extravagant

theory ... We perceive outward things themselves, and believe that they exist, and are what they appear to be. This is the language of common sense, and the belief of all mankind.[142]

As a redresser of the wrongs committed against 'the language of common sense', Beattie acts as a champion of the masses in the cold war of communication between the public and those academic philosophers who debated the psychological questions that concerned everyone, but who would bar the common person's understanding of these debates through the use of difficult language and discussion of confusing concepts. Beattie encourages his reader to trust in the evidence of his own senses in his self-reflexive task and ignore the alienating language of the 'sceptics'.

He maintains his stand on accessible language in his 'Introduction' to *An Essay on ... Truth*. Here, Beattie asserts, as does Cotton in *Visions* and Darwin in *Zoönomia*, that he scorns needlessly overcomplicated language and establishes his position as an intermediary between those psychologists who would confuse or ignore the class of readers who were not educated enough to understand them. Opening the *An Essay on ... Truth* in the combative style that characterizes the whole and made it a bestseller, Beattie announces,

If I have any knowledge of my own heart, or of the subject I propose to examine, I may venture to assure the reader, that it is no part of the design of this book, to encourage verbal disputation ... [which] has been the cause of much evil, both in philosophy and in common life.[143]

In this powerful opening, Beattie confirms that his subject relates to 'common life', and he opposes angrily those who would divorce it from the experience of the ordinary reader. A page later he practically shouts, 'verbal disputant! what claim can he have to the title of philosopher! ... Let him not intrude upon the company of men of science'.[144] Just as the increasing professionalization of medicine had increased the distance between physicians and the rest of society, a distance that was manifested linguistically, so, Beattie protests, has the increasingly abstract, academic nature of philosophy alienated it from the genuine concerns of life. Beattie goes even further in his linguistic egalitarianism than do Darwin, Cotton or the author of *Pharmacopolae Justificati*, for he asserts in the above passage that such 'verbal disputants' are not scientists at all. Through such declarations – as well as statements in the body of *An Essay on ... Truth*, like 'Some philosophers of note have given the name of Common Sense to that faculty by which we perceive self-evident truth' – Beattie has come to be known as one of the principle 'Common Sense philosophers', a group that is often regarded as being led by the philosopher who inspired Beattie's text, namely Reid.[145] In fact, many of Beattie's contemporaries, as well as commentators of today, have labelled Beattie's *An Essay on ... Truth* a popularization, or even a vulgarization, of Reid's 'Common

Sense philosophy', especially as it is articulated in *Inquiry into the Human Mind on the Principles of Common Sense*.[146] However, viewed in the context of the forces that contributed to the psychologist-poets' tradition, it becomes clear that Beattie's simplification of 'Common Sense philosophy' was part of his intention to make the language of his moral philosophy – so necessary, he thought, for the integrity of his readers' psychology and faith – accessible to a broad public.

In writing of the 'Philosophical Society', or 'Wise Club', to which Beattie belonged, Everard King confirms that the members were dedicated to education, for, indeed, all but one of them were university teachers: 'As teachers, they tried to satisfy the public desire for self-improvement by adapting their courses of study, by teaching their students to write in a simple and direct style, and by cultivating their taste and feelings on all aspects and problems of human life'.[147] Thus, in recognition of Beattie's desire to share his knowledge and humble identification with the common reader, King maintains that 'he deliberately avoided the intricacies of pure thought in order to make philosophy practical and useful' to many.[148] Beattie's fervent attempt to debunk scepticism may, then, be traced to his egalitarian sense of responsibility as a writer. Phillipson, amongst others, has surmised that Beattie's energetic refutation of Hume was motivated by more personal circumstances, such as his frustration over the difficulty of learning Humean psychology; the historian also calls *An Essay on ... Truth* an attack of the Aberdeen provincial on the 'culture of the metropolis', arguing that Humean philosophy represented to Beattie the kind of Enlightenment philosophy of 'improvement' that plagued Scotland and sold it into the 1707 union with England out of a desire to modernize it and make it more urban.[149] However accurate Phillipson's explanations for Beattie's opposition to the Humeans may be, the wild popularity of Beattie's work illustrates that it fulfilled more than only his own personal needs.

If the faith of the British population was under attack by Hume's sceptical philosophy, which 'requires us to reflect coolly and sceptically on the nature of our deeply-held beliefs and to test their credibility by reflecting on their source', then it is easy to see why many, including no less than Samuel Johnson, hailed Beattie's refutation of it on the basis of self-reflexive contemplation as a confident blow delivered from the very seat of faith itself.[150] We must also consider that Beattie's sincere dedication to the humble classes partially inspired his refutation of Hume. One of Beattie's Romantic-era biographers confirms that the moral philosopher's passionate opposition to Hume's sceptical philosophy was spurred most intensely by the 'infidelity', or loss of faith, it caused amongst the 'lower classes':

> Hence his indignation was roused; and his sympathy excited for those unhappy persons, who, robbed of their religious hopes, are left abandoned to the wretchedness of

unbelief! Contemplating its pernicious effects on every order of society, he could not view it without considerable emotions.[151]

Meanwhile, Hume seems to have cared little for the humble classes. Speaking of Hume's 'rhetoric of disdain' in 'David Hume and the Common People', Harvey Chisick notes that the philosopher regarded 'the common people with contempt', for he believed they were 'superstitious, undisciplined, seditious and ignorant'.[152] 'The vulgar', as Hume called the lower classes, were 'opposed to philosophers, or those capable of a scientific and dispassionate understanding of things', and 'could not be trusted to make important decisions, even concerning themselves. More than this, he believed that they could not support, and so should not be told, the truth as it was perceived by the enlightened'.[153] In the same way that some university-trained doctors wanted to establish sole proprietorship over medical knowledge, Hume and his supporters wished to garner complete control over psychological knowledge of the theoretical kind. Chisick goes on to explain that

> A change is perceptible during the 1750s ... and discussion of people in their productive capacities during the second half of the century resulted in a positive revaluation of the lower classes. Most of Hume's works were written and published before the end of the 1750s, [though] and he seems to have been largely untouched by the new attitudes.[154]

As such, Beattie's attempt in the latter half of the eighteenth century to popularize the rebuttal to Hume offered by Common Sense philosophy in order to make it accessible to the masses establishes him as a man of his time and explains his success, to some extent. As grossly anti-intellectual as it may seem that 'Beattie was anxious to uphold the credibility of all deeply held beliefs, no matter how we had come to hold them if it would cost us unnecessary anxiety and pain to abandon them', the very fact that he nevertheless encouraged a wide range of readers from all classes to attend to their beliefs and study the workings of their own minds indicates that his purpose was not to inspire complacency and ignorance in his wide audience, but to invite them into the current philosophical discussion about the mind.[155]

Beattie's appeal to a wide readership was not limited to philosophical prose. In the following quotation, Beattie suggests that creative literature, such as poetry, may inspire the same results as properly constituted philosophy:

> facts and experiments relating to the human mind, when expressed in proper words, ought to be obvious to all. I find that those poets, historians, and novelists, who have given the most lively displays of human nature ... are the most entertaining, as well as the most useful. How then should the philosophy of the human mind be so difficult and obscure?[156]

The phrase 'the philosophy of the human mind' reminds us that his focus is, indeed, psychological and his relation of it to the work of 'poets' prepares us to search for evidence of his psychology in his verse. In a section of his massive psychological text *Elements of Moral Science* that deals with memory as one of the 'perceptive faculties', Beattie asserts,

> by most people, verse is more easily remembered than prose, because the words are related not only in sense, and measure, but also by similar sounds at the end of the lines. And, in general, elegant and harmonious language is better remembered, than what is harsh and incorrect.[157]

Finally, in a letter he wrote to one Lord Hailes, Beattie gestures to the relationship between *The Minstrel* and the subject of his academic study, which indicates that what he wanted the reader to remember through the special qualities of verse were the psychological principles he wove into the poem: "'My intention from the beginning was to give rather a philosophical or didactic than a narrative poem'".[158] Given Beattie's confidence in the ability of verse to teach the reader, his passionate denunciation of Hume's sceptical philosophy in the prose work that he wrote simultaneously with *The Minstrel* – namely *An Essay on ... Truth* – and his dedication to teaching moral philosophy as a professor of the subject, we must expect to find religio-psychological lessons in Beattie's major poem. Through his well-ordered prose, Beattie systematizes spiritual self-reflection; by identifying it as part of the psychology inherent to moral philosophy, Beattie scientizes the soul; and by popularizing these discussions in both verse and prose, he transports to the secular and social realm of communication topics that were previously, for many, entirely private.

Beattie's *The Minstrel* was hailed as utterly unique when it was first published, but it would find many echoes in the Romantic period. King notes, 'As a distinct, clearly etched character, Edwin was a revelation to eighteenth century readers ... Edwin was so lifelike, that he was often compared to real people'.[159] Beattie's method for creating such a wonderfully authentic character can be summed up in the cardinal rule of writing: write about what you know best. Beattie based Edwin, the minstrel, on himself and thereby achieved a verisimilitude that had never been seen before.[160] One of Beattie's earliest biographers writes,

> We have been credibly informed, that in *The Minstrel* the author has rendered Edwin the representative of himself. In that character, therefore, the poet has freely delineated his own history, and indulged his own feelings. In this poem the progress of taste is finely traced from its simplest emotions up to that lofty sublimity which moves and agitates the soul![161]

In *The Minstrel*, which was republished several times in the Romantic period, Beattie takes the bold step of representing himself in a long poem and, even more originally, he focuses on his subjective reaction to his environment, tracing his 'simplest emotions', as well as the agitations of his 'soul', the faculty that Beattie and his fellow psychologist-poets identified with the mind. In Beattie's preface to *The Minstrel*, he asserts that his poem will delineate the psychological development of a poet: 'The design was, to trace the progress of a Poetical Genius, born in a rude age, from the first dawning of fancy and reason, till that period at which he may be supposed capable of appearing in the world as A MINSTREL'.[162] Echoes of this short description of the poet are everywhere in the Romantic canon. In fact, Wordsworth's subtitle to *The Prelude* – 'Growth of a Poet's Mind' – seems to be a *précis* of Beattie's poem, so accurately does it describe the older poet's work.[163] The difference between the two poems is that Beattie's is the original long exploration of the poet's mind in English verse. Beattie models self-reflection for his reader and thereby dramatizes a subjectivity spoken into being by his religio-psychological approach.

Early Romantic Self-Reflection in Nature

Just as Cotton implores his reader, 'Study the Science of your Heart', Beattie teaches his reader to examine his own mind and feelings in his psychological poetry.[164] Appropriately, given his job as a teacher of moral philosophy, Beattie celebrates self-reflexivity and solitary meditation in Edwin. More particularly, he meets Hume on his own playing field and tries to reconfigure the sceptical approach to religious belief by endowing subjective perception with intrinsic value, instead of determining its worth by holding it up to standards determined in the objective realm of logic. Early in the poem, Beattie describes his proto-Romantic hero in terms of his mental attributes, particularly his propensity to focus on his inner life and reject the material world around him:

> And yet poor Edwin was no vulgar boy;
> Deep thought oft seem'd to fix his infant eye.
> Dainties he heeded not, nor gaude, nor toy,
> Save one short pipe of rudest minstrelsy.
> Silent when glad; affectionate, though shy;
> And now his look was most demurely sad,
> And now he laugh'd aloud, yet none knew why.
> The neighbours star'd and sigh'd, yet bless'd the lad:
> Some deem'd him wondrous wise, and some believ'd him mad.[165]

Beattie identifies Edwin as solitary and individual on account of his exaggerated attention to the mental realm, which makes him 'laugh' at mental scenes only he can perceive. Even though some 'believ'd him mad', Beattie indicates that Edwin's utterly individualistic characteristics exempt him from common standards of behaviour and the minstrel is celebrated for his individuality. In short, the very intensity of his selfhood – his 'inscape', as Gerard Manley Hopkins would put it, his '*Haecceitas*' or 'thisness', as the thirteenth-century Fransiscan thinker John Duns Scotus would say – is the very quality that establishes the value of his subjectivity, just as the intensity of belief establishes its truth in Beattie's moral philosophy.[166] In other words, Beattie applies the standard of zeal to judge the strength of one's individuality or subjectivity. Beattie rescues self-reflection from the clutches of chaos that would ally it with madness through this implied argument, for he alights on the very quality that would mark faith as insanity or enthusiasm – that is, intensity – and resurrects it through his verse and prose as the very mark of health and success.

Beattie makes a virtue of focusing on one's own mind and individuality and illustrates dramatically his adherence to this teaching by representing his own mental growth in this autobiographical poem. Because the poem is autobiographical, we can expect it to have a rural and humble setting, for Beattie's early years were spent in rural Scotland and his youthful home was a modest one. But Beattie does not present this lifestyle as superior simply because it is a reflection of his own.[167] Rural living and a modest lifestyle, which are almost inextricable in his verse, are virtuous because they are associated with simplicity; they are therefore opposed to the overcomplicated and faith-killing sophistries of the sceptical philosophers. From his first description of the figure of the minstrel, Beattie rejects 'learned' experience in favour of a simple one shaped by nature:

> Nor need I here describe in learned lay,
> How forth the Minstrel fared in days of yore,
> Right glad of heart, though homely in array;
> His waving locks and beard all hoary grey:
> While from his bending shoulder, decent hung
> His harp, the sole companion of his way,
> Which to the whistling wind responsive rung:
> And ever as he went some merry lay he sung.[168]

In a significant pre-Romantic reference to the aeolian harp – that metaphor for the spontaneity and natural source of inspiration at the heart of Romantic ideology – nature itself guides the minstrel's song as the 'whistling wind' blows through his harp. Shortly thereafter, Beattie admonishes his reader – whom he expects to be surprised upon meeting a poor and humble poetic figure instead of the usual aristocratic rakes and wits of Augustan literature – that the pomp of upper-class life can teach nothing important in comparison to the truths provided for all in nature:

> Fret not thyself, thou glittering child of pride,
> That a poor Villager inspires my strain;
> With thee let Pageantry and Power abide:

The gentle Muses haunt the sylvan reign;
Where through wild groves at eve the lonely swain,
Enraptured roams, to rave on Nature's charms.
They hate the sensual, and scorn the vain,
The parasite their influence never warms,
Nor him whose sordid soul the love of gold alarms.[169]

Again, Beattie's influence on Wordsworth is clear. He draws attention to his use of lowly figures as the subject for his verse long before Wordsworth did in the preface to the *Lyrical Ballads*. These similarities may also add to our knowledge of what inspired the focus on humble and rural living in Romanticism. Since Beattie was motivated by his desire to refute sceptical philosophy, which he thought was so opposed to spiritual concerns, we may venture to assert the same thing about the canonical Romantics. With regard to Beattie, in particular, the last line of this passage shows that, like Cotton, he links humility with the state of one's 'soul', the seat of belief and the synonym of mind. The 'muses' that visit the 'poor Villager', Edwin, confirm the wisdom of his humble rural life through their very presence, while they 'scorn' the 'vain', whose souls are 'sordid', both attributes that Beattie associates with sceptical philosophers. Since Beattie identifies the soul with the mind elsewhere, we may conclude that he also offers psychological advice in his implicit directive to keep the soul healthy through humble living in this passage.

Particularly when he associates one's health, mental and otherwise, with humility, Beattie shows his similarities with his fellow psychologist-poets, but he also shows his similarities to the later Romantics by making nature essential to the equation. After confirming that creative talents far surpass any luxury in worth,[170] Beattie substantiates his claim by arguing that disease is born of luxury and wealth disturbs the contemplative mental state that is so essential to the creation of verse: 'Canst thou forego the pure ethereal soul/ In each fine sense so exquisitely keen,/ On the dull couch of Luxury to loll,/ Stung with disease and stupified with spleen'.[171] 'Spleen', or melancholy, brought on by a physical life of 'luxury', dulls the soul and interferes with meditation. A few lines later he reiterates this idea while emphasizing that nature, the poor man's therapist, is essential to mental health:

These [natural] charms shall work thy soul's eternal health,
And love, and gentleness, and joy, impart.
But these thou must renounce, if lust of wealth
E'er win its way to thy corrupted heart;
For, ah! it poisons like a scorpion's dart.[172]

By warning of the dangers of wealth to one's 'soul', 'heart' or, in other words, mind, Beattie confirms what Cotton asserts in *Visions*: humility contributes to the content born of quiet contemplation (while, as George Cheyne maintained, an immodest lifestyle destroys the body's ability to defend against 'spleen', or melancholy, an influential view that I will discuss in Chapter 3). By counselling the benefits of humility, these poets do more than offer ethical advice. They offer versified psychological therapy.

Elsewhere in *The Minstrel*, Beattie expands on his celebration of humble living to include personal modesty, but nature remains essential to this equation. Beattie's most direct attack on the sceptical philosophers is attended by his characterization of Edwin as a man of nature and the philosophers as proud and inhuman:

> Thus Heaven enlarged his soul in riper years.
> For Nature gave him strength and fire, to soar
> On Fancy's wing above this vale of tears;
> Where dark cold-hearted sceptics, creeping, pore
> Through microscope of metaphysic lore:
> And much they grope for truth, but never hit.
> For why? their powers, inadequate before,
> This idle art makes more and more unfit;
> Yet deem they darkness light, and their vain blunders wit.[173]

These misguided 'sceptics' refuse the path of humility and modesty, which leads to contentment, mental and spiritual. Asserting that the sceptics 'creep' on earth and are plagued by spiritual 'darkness', Beattie implies that Edwin escapes this fate and attains spiritual enlightenment with the help of 'Nature' and by using his subjective powers of 'Fancy'. In these ways, the psychologist-poet makes his spiritual advice synonymous with his psychological advice and, by linking the ultimate health of both kinds of subjectivity to rural life and a humble lifestyle, he establishes both as properly constituted by social responsibility. The conjunction of these characteristics fully popularizes – or secularizes – Christian self-reflective activity, the very purpose of his simple and accessible prose and poetry, and a key step in the development of psychology as a discipline.

References to rural living and sceptical philosophy, which were both so much a part of Beattie's life, perform Beattie's celebration of subjectivity in another way, as well. They indicate that Edwin's self-reflexive activity in the world of the poem is a kind of recreation of Beattie's meditation on his own mind, which is carried out dramatically in the writing of the poem. In this way, Beattie again illustrates his psychological assertions in *An Essay on ... Truth* because, as I have mentioned, he defines consciousness as perceiving 'chief[ly] ... the mind itself'.[174] One of the most significant episodes that reveals Beattie thinking about his own thinking comes in his description of the sublime, a subject on which the poet would become a known expert at a time when many philosophers were inspired by Edmund Burke's *A Philosophical Enquiry into the Origin of Our Ideas of the Sublime and Beautiful*.[175] In *Elements of Moral Science*, the tome that contains Beattie's popular lectures on moral philosophy, he supplements his initial definition of the sublime as 'Things of great magnitude ... [that] fill the mind of the beholder with admiration and pleasing astonishment, with the following passage:

> Poetry is sublime; first, when it elevates the mind, and makes it, as it were, superiour to the cares and troubles of this world: secondly, when it infuses any sublime affection, as devotion, valour, universal benevolence [,] the love of virtue and of our country: thirdly, when it affects the mind with an awful and imaginary, but not unpleasing horrour: ... and fifthly, when it conveys a lively idea of any grand appearance, natural, artificial, or imaginary. That style is sublime, which makes us readily conceive any great object or sentiment in a lively manner; and this is often done when the words are very plain and simple.[176]

Not only does Beattie's definition of the sublime establish the phenomenon as a purely mental one that defines a type of perception rather than an environmental phenomenon, but it also suggests, yet again, that Beattie's thinking was a formative influence on Romantic ideology, for which the sublime was so crucial.

Beattie's commentary on the relationship between the mental phenomenon of the sublime and 'words [that] are very plain and simple' may give us additional insight into his influence on Romantic poetry, especially as it is expressed in Wordsworth's opposition to poetic diction in the *Lyrical Ballads*, which I discuss in the introduction. As King and Robinson have noted, Wordsworth read and was greatly impressed by *The Minstrel* and uses some of Beattie's ideas about the influence of nature upon the self and the possibilities of poetic autobiography in *The Prelude*, but I suggest that Wordsworth was also aware of Beattie's ideas about the sublime.[177] The following passage detailing Edwin's experience of the sublime in *The Minstrel* strongly recalls more famous passages from *The Prelude*:

> And oft the craggy cliff he lov'd to climb,
> When all in mist the world below was lost.
> What dreadful pleasure! there to stand sublime,
> Like shipwreck'd mariner on desert coast,
> And view th'enormous waste of vapour, tost
> In billows, lengthening the horizon round,
> Now scoop'd in gulphs, with mountains now emboss'd!
> And hear the voice of mirth and song rebound,
> Flocks, herds, and waterfalls, along the hoar profound![178]

Here stands Edwin on a mountain, surrounded by 'the voice' of 'waterfalls', his feet touching the 'vapour', which is 'tost/ In billows', like a tumultuous ocean. This scene surely inspired Wordsworth's description of his sublime experience at the top of Mount Snowdon in Book XIII of *The Prelude*, one of the most critically discussed scenes in Romantic literature. This episode offers the speaker redemption for the failures of insight that come before it, such as in his anticlimactic crossing of the Alps and his misplaced Revolutionary fervour. Appropriately, Wordsworth uses the simple language of sublimity prescribed by Beattie as he details how

> ... on the shore
> I found myself of a huge sea of mist,
> Which, meek and silent, rested at my feet.
> A hundred hills their dusky backs upheaved
> All over this Ocean, and beyond,
> Far, far beyond, the vapours shot themselves,
>
> . . . .
>
> [and] Mounted the roar of waters, torrents, streams
> Innumerable, roaring with one voice.[179]

To be sure, the imagery is almost identical in these two scenes: the speaker stands atop a mountain and compares the mist at his feet to an ocean. More significantly, though, both poets focus on the speakers' perception of sublimity in nature, or, in other words, their intense subjective experience of the scene. In both cases, the poet implies that a state of consciousness, rather than the objective world, is the real subject by using metaphor, which demonstrates that nature itself is significant only insofar as it provides the medium for the all-important mind to perform its creative transformations, such as imagining mist as the ocean and being impressed with a feeling of awe. With specific reference to Beattie's purpose in *The Minstrel*, his emphasis on the mystic resonances of sublime experience endows subjectivity with great meaning and inherent worth. Before the valorization of self-reflection in nature was recognized as a Romantic ideal, Beattie argued for its importance in the spiritual and psychological life of humankind. Thus, if Beattie's verse was as influential for some of the major Romantic poets as other critics have argued, then we can conclude that his influence may have extended to the specific psychological theory upon which the verse was based.

Religio-Psychological Therapy in Verse and Other Languages of Subjectivity

Cotton and Beattie express their democratic goals as early psychologists influenced by the liberal milieu of the Scottish Enlightenment by encouraging their readers to adopt for their own use some of the psychological strategies outlined in the verse.[180] This feature of the verse is reflected in the common plea of these psychologist-poets for the reader to be self-reflective, whether it be by encouraging her to 'Study the Science of [her] ... Heart' through self-reflection, as Cotton directs, to study the natural world and one's mind as a part of it, as Beattie illustrates how to do through the example of Edwin, or, as they both do, to develop mental and spiritual 'contentment' by rejecting luxurious living.[181] Indeed, a major purpose of the prose and poetry of Cotton and Beattie is increased faith through directed self-reflection. In 'Death', the final poem of *Visions in Verse*, Cotton confirms that developing a better understanding of the mind is identical with understanding better the Divine source that created it. Immediately after identifying the 'SOUL' and 'Mind' as one, the speaker of the poem asks, 'shall the Man, who knows her [the soul's] Worth, / Debase her Dignity and Birth; / Or e'er repine at Heav'n's Decree, / Who kindly gave her leave to be?'.[182] When he writes, later in the same poem, that 'Minds, tho' sprung from heav'nly Race, / Must first be tutor'd for the Place', Cotton's didactic and psychological goal is clarified: he teaches us to understand our minds better so that we may prepare them better to return to their divine homes, where they will be finally judged.[183] The object is not to put the readers in charge of their own fates, but their own minds by reminding them that they are answerable to God for their mental and spiritual development and health. Similarly, Beattie states directly that his psychological philosophy leads back to God in his poem entitled 'The Hermit', which focuses on a reclusive sage that seems to be the very one who teaches Edwin in *The Minstrel*. Beattie resumes the attack on 'false Science' that he began in the longer poem:

> 'O pity, great Father of light', then I cry'd,
> 'Thy creature who fain would not wander from Thee!
> Lo, humbled in dust, I relinquish my pride:
> From doubt and from darkness thou only canst free'.[184]

The phrase 'dust to dust', which forms part of the Christian funeral rite from the Book of Common Prayer, emphasizes that death is, indeed, the great leveller that humbles equally the ignorant peasant and the educated aristocrat. What Beattie would call the arrogance of sceptical philosophy – which proudly accepts no belief, including religious belief, at face value – can only lead to 'infidelity', the rejection of God, which this moral philosopher equates with mental confusion ('false Science ... bewilder[s], and dazzles').[185] His philosophical prescription for mental health is also humble subjection before God.

The Christian element of Cotton and Beattie's psychological approaches was nothing new – spiritual advice guides had been around for centuries.[186] What was unique about their approach is that they put the familiar focus on faith and Christian self-reflection in the context of developing ideas about the mind. This crucial detail, presented through the medium of poetry and with a strong focus on the social theme of humility, does more than underscore the influence of the principles of the Scottish Enlightenment on the medical community of Britain. It also presents early and specific evidence of how psychology may be said to be a secularized, socialized manifestation of Christian principles. These doctors of the mind champion democratic ideals by rejecting luxurious living, valorizing nature and the rural lifestyle (which all may enjoy) and, especially, teaching the reader to be self-reflexive and gain greater insight into her mind through the accessible means of poetry. In so doing, they also help mould the modern subject for her relationship with disciplinary power as it would be reified throughout the nineteenth century. In short, Cotton and Beattie teach the Christian subject to be self-reflexive in increasingly socialized terms, in terms that they outline, are mediated through the popular form of verse, and establish her mental health as relative to public issues like the democratic good of humble living. As we will see in the coming chapters, later psychologist-poets would focus on different aspects of the subject's social life, but they all devise a psychological discourse that posits mental health and social responsibility as parts of the same continuum.

Unlike Cotton and Beattie, however, Erasmus Darwin was accused of atheism and was a staunch materialist. This deep difference between the thinkers reflects the developing distinctions between various approaches to psychology as early as the eighteenth century – and even amongst those who shared intellectual and political roots in the Scottish Enlightenment and took the unusual approach of writing poetry to disseminate their ideas. Nevertheless, the fact that Darwin wanted to call *The Temple of Nature* by the title 'The Origin of Society', as I have mentioned, suggests his similarity to his fellow psychologist-poets: in more ways than one, psychology defined a social context for the mind.[187] As the discipline of psychology developed during the Romantic period, differences between various psychological approaches became more defined and complex. As I will show, nerve theory, moral management, associationism and phrenology all began to lay down distinct ways of understanding the mind, thereby providing specific languages for self-reflection and modalities of for the dispersal of modern power. One thing remains constant between all of the approaches, though: they all contextualize the subject through social means – in addition to the social means of language itself – and realize an external frame for the self.

2. THE HUMAN TOUCH: THOMAS BAKEWELL, ANDREW DUNCAN SR, JOHN FERRIAR AND MORAL MANAGEMENT

I. The Popularization of Moral Management in England

While most histories of the development of psychology in England focus on the French roots of moral management, I argue that an essential aspect of the widespread acceptance of this type of psychology was the popularization of its principles in the verse and prose of such psychologist-poets as Thomas Bakewell, John Ferriar and Andrew Duncan Sr. Moral management's great contribution to the understanding and treatment of mental illness was born of its focus on the social life of the patient; for example, social interaction was used as a reward or punishment for good or bad behaviour. All of the psychologist-poets' work that I explore in this chapter shows this new kind of doctor's social concern, his contribution to an established relationship between the realm of psychology (specifically nerve theory) and literature that helps to expand the current critical narrative about it and the subtle means by which he helped to establish disciplinary power, even as he attempted to share knowledge about psychology in a democratic way.

The apparent goal of all of the moral managers I discuss in this chapter was to present the literary identity of the socially concerned psychologist; Bakewell, Duncan and Ferriar cleverly use the form of the epistle to define this literary identity. Through the epistle's associations with the literature of sentiment and sensibility's associations with humanitarianism and charity, these psychologist-poets clothe their new cultural identities with the garments of social concern, so vital to their presentation of the field of moral management. Bakewell establishes his desire to provide psychological advice to a broad audience in his popular self-help guide, *The Domestic Guide, in Cases of Insanity*, where he details for home-use the gentle methods he used to treat patients in his asylum. The success of this volume encouraged the moral manager to write *The Moorland Bard; or, Poetical Recollections of a Weaver, in the Moorlands of Staffordshire*, in which he dispenses versified advice about avoiding melancholy and other forms of mental disturbance through a humorous tone and the persona of a lowly weaver (which Bakewell was, by trade), which emphasizes the ideal of sympathizing with the humble classes.[1] Many of Bakewell's poems are literary epistles to depressed ladies that mention the role of nerves to their mental health, which firmly establishes his literary persona as deriving from the literature of sentiment and shows the wide-ranging concerns of the moral manager. Meanwhile, Duncan shows beneficent interest in the mental health of people from all classes in *A Short Account of the Rise, Progress, and Present State of the Lunatic Asylum at Edinburgh*, in which he argues that the health of the most poverty-stricken affects the health of the rich.[2] He also published versified and friendly admonitions to his wide readership about how to maintain mental and bodily health in popular magazines and a collection called *Miscellaneous Poems, Extracted from the Records of the Circulation Club at Edinburgh*.[3] Using the epistolary form, as does Bakewell, Duncan capitalizes on the link between nerve theory and literature to popularize his field, moral management. He emphasizes the sentimental concerns of sympathy and social concern to concretize the association, as well as to characterize moral management as humanitarian. Moreover, by aligning himself with the literature of sensibility and the humble classes, Duncan, like Bakewell, reconfigures the connection between the literary and the psychological. Both moral managers present the culture of sensibility as anti-classist and thereby make way for the literary expression of a non-aristocratic nerve theorist, embodied in Perfect, Trotter and Beddoes, as I will explain in Chapter 3. Finally, Ferriar illustrates the relationship between literature and mental health in his humorous epistolary poem about obsessive book-collecting, *The Bibliomania, An Epistle, to Richard Heber, Esq.*, through which he teaches psychological lessons in an attractive way that encourages the reader's acceptance of them.[4] I conclude that the social function of the epistle was not only an apt expression of the moral management approach through its humanitarian and personable associations, but, with respect to broader issues regarding modern power, the epistle presented a discourse of self-reflection for the reading subject's that was predicated upon the personal identity of the moral manager as a fictional correspondent.

Moral managers were faced with a particular challenge regarding how the public viewed them. The most familiar face of psychology was that of the snobbish celebrity nerve-doctor of the eighteenth century who courted the rich. However, the turn of the nineteenth century brought media attention to the field of the study of the mind that was even more negative, for it framed the asylum-keeper as a sadist who preyed on some of the most helpless members of society. The first major parliamentary inquiries into madhouses were undertaken in 1807 and 1815, while the Act first enabling the establishment of public lunatic asylums passed in 1808, but whether such official measures informed or reflected public attitude is a matter of debate.[5] What is certain is that the public became increasingly aware of the appalling treatment of the insane in public asylums and their attitudes towards the authorities responsible registered their disgust. Indeed, when the report called *The Select Committee of the House of Commons Appointed to Consider of Provision Being Made for the Better Regulation of Mad-houses, 1815* published a sketch of William Norris, an inmate of Bethlem who had been chained by his neck and feet into the same position for ten years, the public reaction was swift and intense.[6] The apothecary to Bethlem, John Haslam, was fired the next year as a direct result of the commission.[7] Since neither snob-bishness nor cruelty complemented the image of the moral manager, whose very difference from his predecessors lay in his personal approach and his endeavours to cure his charges, rather than simply to control them through physical means, the Romantic-era moral manager was forced to perform damage control with respect to his public image. Bakewell, Duncan and Ferriar hit upon an effective means of doing so. They wrote verse that formed a completely different identity for themselves: that of the socially concerned man of culture and, through the epistolary form, even friend and confidant.

The history of moral management in France hints at how different this approach to madness was from previous methods, especially with respect to the doctor's relationship with his patients and the public. In October of 1793, Philippe Pinel freed the patients at Bicêtre, the hospital for the insane in Paris and he did so for reasons that appealed to the liberal hearts of the psycholo-gist-poets. As Hunter and Macalpine note, 'Pinel's message to free the insane from oppression and brutality found an echo in the minds and hearts of all who were concerned with social and humanitarian reforms and there were many in early nineteenth-century England'.[8] Moral management appealed to reformers and humanitarian types because it advocated treating patients gently and fairly at a time when the appalling conditions of mental institutions across Britain were becoming a matter of great public concern. Shorter asserts, 'Pinel rec-ommended gaining the confidence of patients by talking to them and treating them fairly, organizing fixed daily schedules of asylum life, involving patients in work of various kinds, giving them timely and appetizing meals, and other steps directed toward a well-run and orderly mental hospital'; reasoning that the mad had damaged mental faculties, a 'psychological approach rather than sheer physical confinement seemed the best way of imposing "energetic and long-last-ing impressions on all of their external senses"'.[9] In other words, Pinel advocated appealing to the minds of the mad and trying to cure them, rather than using corporal punishment as a response to their symptoms and attempting to control their bodies alone.

The way that Pinel's principles were disseminated in England are various. The most immediate method was through the translation (by D. D. Davis) and publication of his text, *A Treatise on Insanity*, in 1806. Another way that English psychologists became aware of Pinel's ideas about moral management was through the success of asylums that practised his therapeutic principles, such as The Retreat at York, a Quaker Asylum founded and managed by William Tuke in 1796. This famous asylum was later described by his grandson, Samuel Tuke, in the highly influential text, *A Description of The Retreat*.[10] Tuke confirms that The Retreat was managed in conscious accordance with Pinel's principles. Indeed, he states that 'The superintendent, who is also the apothecary of The Retreat ... fully unites with the intelligent Dr Pinel, in his comparative estimate of moral and medical means' and he shows that these therapeutic means reflect a shared understanding of the nature of insanity when he adds, 'we must consider moral treatment, or management, of very high importance. If we adopt the opinion, that the disease originates in the mind, applications made immediately to it, are obviously most natural; and the most likely to be attended with success'.[11] Tuke recognizes Pinel as the most notable moral manager with respect to the therapeutic approach at The Retreat, and, to be sure, later English commentators on the rise of moral management in England trace its source almost exclusively to Pinel.[12] For example, Robert Gardiner Hill's *Total Abolition of Personal Restraint in the Treatment of the Insane* is almost a paean to Pinel, so eager is the psychologist to praise his predecessor. He admits that he envisions himself as an heir to Pinel, proclaiming, *'I wish to complete that which Pinel began'*.[13] However, it is reasonable to assume that William Tuke began his own form of moral management before he learned about Pinel's methods. Although Pinel liberated the patients in France in 1793 and Tuke opened The Retreat in 1796, the Frenchman's attitude to the insane was not organized into a psychological approach nor communicated in writing until 1801, when the French version of *A Treatise on Insanity* was published. Moreover, ideas in England about the efficacy of gentle, non-physical treatment of the insane existed before the appearance in English of Pinel's text in 1806, which, nevertheless, helped to systematize and popularize the approach. As I will show, some specifically British social factors contributed to the establishment of the 'moral', psychological – and non-physical – approach in late eighteenth-century England.

II. The Political and Philosophical Links Between the Psychologist-Poets' Tradition and Moral Management

The same social and political movements that attended the creation of the psychologist-poets tradition of poetry also influenced the rise of moral management in England. Hunter and Macalpine attest that '"Management" meant humane treatment and reflected the spirit of philanthropy and awakened social conscience of the period which sponsored not only more and better hospitals, but was concerned also with the welfare of the poor, prison reforms, abolition of the slave trade etc'.[14] Certainly, reforms for the treatment of the insane in asylums were necessary and required the attention of humane types, even well into the nineteenth century. In Hill's *Total Abolition of Personal Restraint*, the author quotes 'an able Journalist' to describe the care for the insane previous to the time at which he writes:

> Lunatics were regarded rather in the light of wild beasts, than of human beings, and the mode of managing them corresponded with this brutal and unworthy notion. In fact, neither medical men, nor the public at large, had any hope of a cure of the insane … And to what period, think you, does this description apply? It is scarcely twenty years since nearly every word of it might be said with truth of the receptacles of the insane in Britain! It was only at that period that a better spirit spread abroad on the subject of Insanity. Asylums began to be regarded as places for the cure, not for the living burial, of Lunatics.[15]

Importantly, Hill notes that the gentle treatment of the mad entailed not just beneficent feelings for them, but also a novel understanding of what madness was and how doctors should approach it. Hill recognizes that madness could be cured, a perspective that was engendered along with the notion that madness could develop and be treated through means other than physical ones. As Porter notes in *Mind-Forg'd Manacles* of this shift in thinking, 'In so far as madness could be cured, it would not be through medicine, but through management, directed to the mind and character of the sufferer, engaging his attention, gaining his respect, breaking evil habits and associations'.[16] Mild treatment of the insane reflected a new understanding of them as fellow, thinking human beings and not wild beasts dominated by physical impulses.

Previous treatment for insanity was based on the assumption that it originated in the body and that addressing the disease through corporal treatments – or what seem to us today to be tortures – was therefore necessary. Bleeding, purging, swing chairs (which could spin the patient up to one hundred times a minute), vomits, whipping and shackling were all common practices in eighteenth-century madhouses. Even well into the nineteenth century, Thomas Monro, the last member of the family that reigned for several generations over the world's oldest asylum, Bethlem,[17] could report about the treatment of the patients, '"after they have been bled they take vomits once a week for a certain number of weeks, after that we purge the patients; that has been the practice invariably for years, long before my time; it was handed down to me by my father and I do not know any better practice"'.[18] This statement, given for the *First Report Minutes of Evidence taken before the Select Committee of the House of Commons*, which was commissioned to improve the lot of the insane, shows that Monro and other traditional mad-doctors continued to regard madness as body-based and physical treatment as the only proper approach. However, as

Samuel Tuke reveals in *A Description of The Retreat*, moral managers believed that the mad did not lose their reason and become purely physical beings, but that they only reasoned wrongly: 'Insane persons generally possess a degree of control over their wayward propensities. Their intellectual, active, and moral powers, are usually rather perverted than obliterated'.[19] Tuke emphasizes that madmen have the same powers of the mind as their sane counterparts do, which underlines the commonalities shared by the psychologist and his patient. This concept of a common ground was linked to the egalitarian character of the many reformers who were moral managers, including Duncan, Bakewell and Ferriar. Before I move on to a discussion of these psychologist-poets as moral managers, though, I must clarify Tuke's use of the word 'moral' in the above statement and Romantic-era psychology in general.

The word 'moral' is problematic in all discussions of early nineteenth-century psychology, but it is even more so in the present study because of the role that the field called 'moral philosophy' plays here. Moral management is not, as one might suppose, the practical arm of moral philosophy. Some historians of psychiatry have stated unequivocally that we misunderstand the word 'moral' as it appears in the phrase 'moral management' when we assume that it refers to ethical and religious concerns: in *A History of Psychiatry*, Shorter notes that the phrase 'moral therapy' comes from 'Pinel's 1801 phrase "*le traitment moral*" (a word which in this French context means "mental" not "moral")' and Marlene Arieno claims that 'Moral management in the nineteenth century generally meant mildly humane treatment, in contrast to previous inhumane treatment of the insane. Moral, at the time, meant psychological or psychosomatic rather than physical cause'.[20] Lynn Gamwell and Nancy Tomes add, 'In the eighteenth and nineteenth centuries, the term "moral" referred to emotional and spiritual experiences, as opposed to sensory experience of the "material" world'.[21] Such historians assert that the term 'moral' in such phrases as 'moral management', 'moral treatment' and 'moral therapy' mean something quite different from our usual understanding of the word as roughly the equivalent of 'ethical'.

However, other historians of psychiatry discuss the term 'moral management' in ways that suggest it has plenty in common with our common understanding of the word 'moral'. For example, Vieda Skultans writes that moral managers 'held that insanity was independent of physical disease and was to be located in the relationship between the emotions and the will', which seems to refer to the ethical realm.[22] In *The English Malady*, Elaine Showalter describes the term in a similarly familiar way and, unlike many other commentators on the subject, she even suggests that moral management and 'moral insanity' were terms tied to the same type of treatment of and approach to mental illness: '"moral insanity" redefined madness, not as a loss of reason, but as deviance from socially accepted behaviour. "Moral management" substituted close supervision and paternal concern for physical restraint and harsh treatment, in an effort to re-educate the insane in habits of industry, self-control, moderation, and perseverance'.[23] Showalter's reference to 'socially accepted behaviour' and 'self-control, moderation, and perseverance' suggest that the term 'moral' is not just an antiquated word for 'metaphysical', but that it implies social judgment of one's actions as the expression of one's inner impulses, as our contemporary use of the word 'moral' does.

I contend that the word 'moral' in the phrase 'moral management' did carry a sense of social judgment and appropriateness of behaviour and retained its religious overtones. After all, the phrase was being used in an English – not just a French – context and its connotations in English were as powerful then as they are now. Historical evidence shows that word 'moral' had a denotation familiar to us today; at the end of the eighteenth century, the influential American psychologist, Benjamin Rush (1746–1813), defined 'disorders of the moral faculty' as illnesses of 'the power of distinguishing good from evil'.[24] Such evidence suggests a connection between moral management and moral philosophy as these movements developed in Britain: they both reflect the Protestant tradition of intense self-scrutiny and meditation. Tracing the development of moral management in England to Pinel alone can lead one to the mistaken assumption that psychology in early nineteenth-century England was entirely secular; as the reasoning goes, if Pinel was inspired to develop a new understanding of and treatment for the insane in accordance with the principles of the French Revolution, it would follow that the resulting psychology was opposed to religion in the way that the Revolutionaries were. Yet, even if one does trace moral management in England to Pinel alone, one is not left with an amoral space, as Foucault has shown. Foucault allows that Pinel's form of moral management was non-religious, but he explains that it was, nevertheless, moral, and he uses this word in its familiar, religious and social sense: describing the asylum as Pinel helped to establish it, Foucault writes that it is 'a religious domain without religion, a domain of pure morality, of ethical uniformity'.[25] Yet, Pinel was not the only influence upon Romantic-era moral management in Britain. In terms of attention to the patient's inner life, moral management in England shows the strong influence of the Quakers, who pioneered the most successful experiment in moral management in the form of The Retreat.

As Samuel Tuke notes about The Retreat, religious observance and Bible study formed an essential component of the treatment of the insane in the asylum because the attention and serious comportment demanded by such activities helped the patient to learn to control herself – and these goals are the very essence of moral management.[26] The entire second section of Tuke's text is devoted to this subject and is called 'Of the Means of Assisting the Patient to Control Himself'. Just as Cotton and Beattie recommended the practice of solitary self-reflection for improved mental health and a closer relationship with God, later moral managers insisted that the patient must be taught to look inside herself, to recognize the impulses that manifest symptoms of madness in her actions and to control her response to these impulses so that she may behave in accordance with social expectations. Significantly, the initial decision of William Tuke to open a Quaker asylum stemmed from religious concerns that also shaped moral management in ways other than strictly religious ones. Samuel Tuke reveals that the Quakers living around York decided to open The Retreat after a Quaker woman died in the York Asylum:

> it was conceived that peculiar advantage would be derived to the Society of Friends, by having an Institution of this kind under their own care ... It was thought, very justly, that the indiscriminate mixture, which must occur in large public establishments, of persons of oppositional religious sentiments and practices ... was calculated to check the progress of returning reason.[27]

The Quakers were inspired to open their own asylum in accordance with their understanding that the insane would benefit from better organization and increased distinctions between them. Distinguishing between the insane according to their particular characteristics – not only in terms of their religious beliefs, but also the severity and tenor of their madness – became an essential feature of moral management and, as I have argued elsewhere, it developed into one of moral management's most influential contributions to the field of psychology: the focus on taxonomy as essential to psychological treatment.[28] The influence of religious meditation and reformist principles on psychological approaches like moral management shows that the link between religion and psychology was strong well into the nineteenth century and also reveals the development of modern power and subjectivity out of religious roots other than the Catholic confessional in which Foucault locates it.

To be sure, early, religious psychologists like Cotton and Beattie have much in common with the moral managers. Bakewell shows his similarity to Cotton when he asserts that the same man who is dedicated to his society's spiritual development may also ensure its mental health in *The Domestic Guide, In Cases of Insanity. Pointing out the Causes, Means of Preventing, and Proper Treatment, of that Disorder. Recommended to Private Families, and the Notice of the Clergy*: 'If I cannot venture to recommend myself to the notice of medical men, I must beg leave to solicit the attention of the clergy, in the most earnest manner. To them, particularly, belong complaints of the mind'.[29] Duncan shows his appreciation of the distinctly religious approach of the Quakers in *A Short Account of the Rise, Progress, and Present State of the Lunatic Asylum at Edinburgh* in an encomium that was so pleasing to Samuel Tuke that he included it as one of the appendices to *A Description of The Retreat*.[30] By way of recommending the Quaker's approach to moral management as the basis for care in the Edinburgh asylum, Duncan writes that

> The fraternity denominated Quakers have demonstrated, beyond contradiction, the very great advantage resulting from a mode of treatment in cases of Insanity, much more mild than was before introduced into almost any Lunatic Asylum, either at home or abroad. That fraternity, who have been long and justly celebrated for charity and humanity, have established in the neighbourhood of the city of York, *The Retreat*, as they term it.[31]

There is, moreover, evidence that the moral managers were widely recognized as religious. For instance, Coleridge was familiar with Ferriar's work and, in a letter to John Thelwall in 1796, he notes the psychologist's traditional religiosity: "'Ferriar believes in a soul, like an orthodox churchman'".[32] Yet, moral management was not as religious as Cotton's and Beattie's psychological approaches. As I will explain at the end of this chapter, God-the-father was replaced by the doctor-father and, instead of encouraging self-reflection in terms of a Divine Other, the reader was encouraged to establish his subjectivity in relation to the moral manager, who established a personal dynamic with the subject through his poetry, amongst other means.

III. Communication, Community and Cure

One of the most notable aspects of the writing of Bakewell, Duncan and Ferriar is that they, like the psychologist-poets who came before them, emphasize the importance of communication with their audience. Their contention that the mad were fellow human beings, complete with the faculty that Pinel identified as our distinguishing feature – namely reason – entailed the recognition that the psychologist and the patient could and should communicate. No longer did the psychologist confirm his distance from his patient by establishing a physical relationship with him that was devoid of interaction, in which the doctor acted upon the patient's body and the patient, forced into submission, merely bore his actions. Since the moral manager focused on the mind, a certain degree of interaction became necessary. The psychologist could not assess the patient without the establishment of a communicative relationship between them. The accessible persona of the moral manager in England may be traced to its development in accordance with Quaker tradition, for the Quaker community is based on principles of friendship and society (their alternate name is the 'Society of Friends'). As Porter puts it, part of the Quaker creed is 'the value of a spiritually close community or "meeting"', and, thus, the 'atmosphere [of The Retreat] was domestic, and it was run along paternal lines ... and a spiritual bond was sought between staff and patients'; Porter also confirms that this kind of 'new intensification of personal contact between physician and patient' was characteristic of all moral management.[33] Finally, by locating madness in the mind and arguing that it was curable, psychologists recognized that the madman's mind was not foreign or monstrous, but simply human and damaged. The egalitarian spirit that fuelled the reform movement on so many fronts also helped to reform psychology, which, through its focus on the similarities between the mad and the sane, created a therapeutics based on human sympathy and the power of linguistic exchange.

This basic characteristic of focusing on communication, which formed one of the major differences between moral management and previous forms of asylum management, indicates how the democratic and linguistically-oriented psychologist-poets contributed to the development of psychology. Even some moral managers who did not write poetry considered it necessary to open the field of psychology to a broad audience. Samuel Tuke complains that those "'who have devoted their whole attention to its [insanity's] treatment, have either been negligent, or cautious of giving information respecting it'", a comment that summarizes well the jealous guardianship over medical knowledge that Cotton mocks in his introductory epistle to *Visions in Verse* and about which the author of *Pharmacopolae Justificati* complains, as I show in Chapter 1.[34] Tuke also reveals that the humane treatment of the insane must be attended by the communication of psychological knowledge when he writes,

> It is much to be regretted, that we possess so few accounts of the mode of treatment, and the success of establishments, for the relief of insanity. The want of facts relative to this subject, and our disposition to hasty generalization, have led to many conclusions, equally unfriendly to the progress of knowledge, and the comfort of the patients. The interests of humanity and science, alike, call upon us to communicate freely the discoveries we make.[35]

Tuke reminds us here that the moral manager desired a communicative relationship with a wide reading audience, for he gestures to the importance of communicating not only scientific truths, which would appeal to fellow doctors of the mind, but also humane truths, which appeal to all. This expansive attitude had its limits in moral management – for example, Porter claims that moral management developed into 'a regime in which physician and patient refused to communicate with each other in normal speech' – but the fact that Tuke transcribes in his text two long poems by inmates of The Retreat indicates, I believe, that the founding spirit of moral management was oriented to open communication, however much this attitude may have changed as the field developed.[36]

Such social interaction relied upon the moral manager's presentation of himself as a figure to whom the patient must relate in an interpersonal way in order to effect a cure. The moral managers Bakewell, Ferriar and Duncan show their dedication to this principle by writing prose texts on psychological subjects that are the equivalent of today's books of pop-psychology. These books about care for the insane are tailored to the comprehension of a wide audience (e.g. Bakewell's *Domestic Guide*) and address the need to involve the entire community in decisions regarding the erection of a public lunatic asylum (e.g. Duncan's *A Short Account of the Rise, Progress, and Present State of the Lunatic Asylum at Edinburgh* and Ferriar's *Medical Histories and Reflections*).[37] Meanwhile, the verse reveals a wish to appeal to their readers through an entertaining medium. The same humane and egalitarian attitudes by which they understood the madman as a 'fellow-creature' with whom they could communicate through the shared medium of language also led these moral managers to present themselves as accessible figures, often through the use of humour, and even intimate correspondents in their verse.[38]

IV. A Sentimental Moral Management?

Bakewell, Duncan and Ferriar adopt the epistolary form in their poetry in an attempt to create the literary identity of the personable psychologist and capitalize on the established link between psychology and the culture of sensibility. Bakewell's poetry shows the most similarities with literary sensibility through its additional focus on a feminine audience, discussion of bad nerves and recommendation of sympathy for others and charity for the poor, but Duncan and Ferriar also nod at the eighteenth-century culture of sensibility by using the epistolary form, which, by the nineteenth century, had become identifiable with the literature of sentiment.[39] Through their poetry, Bakewell, Duncan and Ferriar may be said to frame the newly developed practice of moral management in the literary context occupied by nerve-theory. Their reason for adopting this literary role is doubtlessly connected with their desire, shared with many nerve-theorists and other doctors of the mind, to present themselves as valuable contributors to broader English culture, but the literary form of the epistle proved to be particularly amenable to the persona they wished to present to the public because it suggested the possibility of a relationship between the speaker of the poem – who may be identified as the poets in Bakewell's, Duncan's and Ferriar's poems – and the reader, who stands in metonymically for wider society and symbolically for the potential patient of the doctor's care. By reconfiguring the bond of sympathy suggested in earlier works of sentiment into the connection between the moral manager and his public, these doctors of the mind forge a literary identity for themselves that is in keeping with the socially concerned identity of the Scottish Enlightenment doctor and establish the reader as a new kind of subject.

These psychologist-poets' utilization of the epistolary form for their poems may be viewed as their attempt to capitalize on a cultural link between literature and psychology that was already widely recognized by the late eighteenth century. The most famous novels of sentiment, such as Samuel Richardson's *Pamela* and *Clarissa* – not to mention Henry Fielding's mocking response to *Pamela*, *Shamela* – were written in epistolary form. Moreover, such notable literary critics as G. S. Rousseau and G. J. Barker-Benfield have delineated the connection between the eighteenth-century literature of sensibility and nerve theory.[40] In *The Culture of Sensibility*, Barker-Benfield draws a direct link between nerve theory and the literature of sentiment through the two main figures that represented each field, namely Cheyne and Richardson. After establishing the existence of a correspondence between the two, Barker-Benfield concludes, 'Cheyne seems to have been Richardson's primary source for the version of the nerve paradigm injected into his novels, and thereby into the mainstream of sentimental fiction'.[41] Nerve theory, it seems, played no small part in the creation of sentimental fiction, a conclusion at which G. S. Rousseau also arrives in 'Nerves, Spirits, and Fibres: Towards Defining the Origins of Sensibility'. According to Rousseau, a main focus of the study of 'nerves, and their subsidiaries – fibres and animal spirits', was their link to the brain, which, through this research, was newly posited as the seat of love and the soul.[42] In turn, love and the soul are two of the main concerns of sentimental fiction.[43] In short, literary sentiment, the eighteenth-century literary fashion that 'encouraged a sensitivity to – and spontaneous display of – virtuous feelings, especially those of pity, sympathy, benevolence, of the open heart as opposed to the prudent mind', found its origins in nerve theory.[44]

Nerve theory established itself as socially concerned partly by delineating extreme sympathy as a symptom of the afflicted. Jonathan Andrews and Andrew Scull show how the social concern expressed by such moral managers as Duncan and Bakewell would ally them with the literature of sentiment in *Undertaker of the Mind* when they state that 'as part of a new cult of sensibility, men and women of feeling allowed more scope for being emotionally overcome ... by worldly suffering and pathos' and add that 'the moving (if sometimes artificial) tears of sensible souls, became especially popular means of engagement with this world and the next, and signs and signals of a self-consciously superior politeness, civility, and humanity'.[45] The critics' use of the phrase 'sometimes artificial' to describe the tears of sensibility points to an anomaly in its principles: people of sensibility claimed, at once, to sympathize with the lower classes and to be more aristocratic, educated and, in a word, finer, on account of its sensitivity. Indeed, as I explain in Chapter 3, to be called 'nervous' under the Cheynian model – which both Mullan and Barker-Benfield link to novels of sentiment – was a kind of compliment. In 'The Nervous Patient in Eighteenth- and Nineteenth-Century England: The Psychiatric Origins of British Neurology', W. F. Bynum states bluntly, 'Cheyne flattered his patients', adding that Cheyne called nerves troublesome to 'as many as one-third of all people *of quality* in England'.[46]

Shorter confirms in *A History of Psychiatry* that nerve-doctors of eighteenth-century England 'cater[ed] ... to the neurotic illnesses of a patrician population that wished to steer wide of "madness"' by calling themselves 'nervous' and, simultaneously, to lay claim to the '"fashionable" status' afforded to the nervous.[47] As I will show, Bakewell, for his part, may be said to erase this hypocrisy in the history of the literature of sensibility by referring to his own lowborn status, thereby showing a true alliance with the poverty-stricken. He also encourages us to rethink the connections between literary sensibility and psychology by using it to develop an identity for moral management and not nerve theory.

V. Thomas Bakewell: From Tape-Weaver to Pop-Psychologist

In accordance with the moral management principles of benevolence, interpersonal communication and the valorization of knowledge-sharing, Bakewell (1761–1835) presents himself as personable in his largely epistolary poems, especially those in which he communicates psychological advice. He also uses humour, often of a self-deprecating nature, which communicates to the reader a literary identity characterized by friendly gregariousness. Bakewell continues the tradition of sympathizing with the lower classes in yet another way in his poetry: he identifies himself first and foremost as a lowly 'weaver' in *The Moorland Bard*. Given Bakewell's place as an early champion of moral management, it is appropriate that he attends to the social effects of his writing by emphasizing the importance of open communication, appearing accessible and challenging class stratification.

Even though Thomas Bakewell had no formal medical education, his knowledge of the insane was vast. One of the only psychologists in this study who did not have a direct connection to Scotland, Bakewell was born in Staffordshire, to which he moved the family's established asylum in 1802, having learned the trade of mad-doctoring from his maternal grandfather, who ran a private asylum.[48] Before taking over the family madhouse practice in 1793, he was apprenticed in 1774 as a tape-weaver, a position at which he seems to have excelled, for he 'progressed eventually to become foreman over 300 men'.[49] His experience as a labourer and the homely way by which he obtained his knowledge about madness surely influenced his later decision to share his knowledge with the public freely, so that the average Briton might learn about this important topic in the same informal way, as well as his choice to practice mad-doctoring in an equally familiar fashion. Bakewell certainly fits the description that Leonard Smith gives him in the *ODNB* when he calls him a 'prototype popular psychiatrist'.[50]

In his endeavour to develop a relationship between lay people and psychologists, Bakewell 'delivered lectures in towns around the midlands and north ...

[and] became a frequent contributor to literary journals, first the *Monthly Magazine* and then the *Imperial Magazine*.[51] He also published several monographs that were designed to inform as wide a public as possible about the insane. For example, in *A Letter Addressed to the Chairman*, which he published after being invited to present information to the governmental committee, Bakewell claims that he wrote the book in order to break down the prejudices against the mad that had led to the unprotected and tormented state in which the committee discovered them.[52] The author declares that it is not 'a small evil that it [i.e. madness] shall have excited so much the feelings of horror, odium and disgust, in those owning no kindred ties'.[53] In order to demolish these negative impressions, he intends to impress upon the public the idea that the mad are not Other to them and that human decency demands that the insane be approached in a gentle, sympathetic way. In the text that was published along with the *Letter*, called *Remarks on the Nature, Causes, and Cure of Mental Derangement*, Bakewell declares that 'it is only the balance of rational conceptions that constitutes the difference betwixt those who are called Sane, and those who are called Insane', and he tells an entertaining and pertinent anecdote about an interview he held with a 'raving lunatic' who had yelled for days on end:

> I said, 'Pray, my good man, what is the matter with you?' His answer was, 'Why, Sir, the folks say that I am mad, for I cannot help saying whatever comes into my head'. Now were I to say all that ever comes into my head, the folks would soon say that I was mad, and my readers may confess the same.[54]

Essentially, Bakewell argues here that the difference between the sane and the mad is not qualitative but quantitative. In his most popular prose work, *The Domestic Guide*, he sums up this idea succinctly when he suggests that 'perhaps every human being possesses the seeds of this disease, and that it is possible to excite it in every individual'.[55] This democratic attitude suggests that Bakewell adopted and recommended the mild and social methods of moral management because humaneness demanded it, given our commonalities with the insane. His attitude also indicates why he thought all members of society were capable of and responsible for knowing more about mental illness, knowledge that Bakewell hoped to provide through his poetry and prose.

Such egalitarian impulses also moved Bakewell to tailor his language and writing style to appeal to the less educated and less serious reader. In a description of his prose style that may reflect upon his choice to write in verse, he confides in the preface of his household guide that he 'took some pains too, to soften down the asperity of the subject, so as to render the book not absolutely insupportable to those who read only for amusement'.[56] As attractive as some may have found his intentionally accessible writing style in *The Domestic Guide*, others would have thought that it reflected a lack of authority, as Bakewell was well aware.

Indeed, he indicates that he appealed to the masses at the expense of his acceptance amongst other psychologists when he writes:

> The writer trusts that he has kept the promise implied in the title-page, by adapting his language to common capacities; though in doing this he may have subjected himself to the severe criticism of more learned readers ... These pages, most assuredly, will not labour under the disadvantage of being learnedly obscure ... The reader has my full liberty to call me illiterate, provided he does not pronounce me ignorant.[57]

Bakewell admits that his simple writing style and desire to appeal to the masses reflects his humble background, but he also claims that he writes in an intentionally accessible fashion for reasons connected to his particular psychological approach:

> What is Insanity? I have gone over the pages of all, or the greater part of what is presented to the mere English reader upon mental Derangement, and have felt myself greatly disappointed by learned distinctions, and scientific definitions. It is true, that I may not be able, from the want of education, to appreciate the merits of the respective writers; be that as it may, I confess that I am an empiric, whose opinions are entirely the result of assiduous observation.[58]

In other words, Bakewell garnered his knowledge about the insane not from books and classes, but by living with them, developing relationships with them and spending much time in their society. He rejects the complex terminology of the snobbish psychologists that have come before him and wears his lack of education proudly, for it represents his connection with his broad audience and personal involvement with his patients.[59] Bakewell made himself an essential part of their cure by inviting them into social intercourse with him, noting, 'I never sit at table without a number of Lunatics on each side of me; I treat them exactly as I should do if they were not afflicted with that disease, and, in return, they almost uniformly behave as if nothing was the matter with them'.[60] He made his own friendly company essential to his endeavour to re-socialize the patient into normal interpersonal behaviour. By writing in an accessible way and creating a personable literary identity in both his prose and his poetry, Bakewell duplicates the therapeutic scene in his writing and emphasizes the dedication to social ties that can be expected of a moral manager.

VI. A Low-Class Sage and Accessible Authority

Bakewell frames *The Moorland Bard* with poems that present him as our confidant and attentive correspondent. Although the last poem in the collection, 'The Author's Dream: Addressed to the Reviewers', is not written in epistolary form, it complements such poems in several ways: it is addressed to a particular party, the reader is afforded a glimpse into a personal exchange and it shares with the epistolary poems the same kind of self-deprecatory humour that manifests Bakewell's humility.[61] In this poem, Bakewell recalls a dream in which he was challenged by reviewers who judge him for both his poetry and his psychological writing. The cruel reviewer demands,

> How came you on medicine vainly to write?
> In poetry too, you did verses indite:
> I would have you to know, that you're a great calf,
> And torture for you, Sir, is too good by half.[62]

Having made no secret of his lack of formal education in the preface to this collection of poetry, Bakewell jokingly condemns himself here for his presumption in writing about the subject of psychology in *The Domestic Guide* and poetry in this collection, a humble attitude that makes him appear accessible and likeable to the reader.[63]

Besides using the literary themes and forms associated with the literature of sensibility, as I will detail momentarily, another method that Bakewell uses to make his literary persona accessible to a wide audience is to stress his lowly status as a weaver. In fact, in 'The Author's Dream', he even identifies this kind of labour as his 'proper employ', which suggests that he has a rightful claim to neither writing poetry nor asylum-keeping.[64] By the end of the poem, the dreaming poet begs the reviewers to 'Have pity ... upon a poor weaver', promising, 'I swear by my shuttle, I'll do so [write poetry] no more'.[65] Bakewell also introduces *The Moorland Bard* with a reference to his status as a weaver. In the first poem of the collection, 'The Weaver's Request, that the Public Will Hear his Song', he identifies his place in a particular community of poets when he writes:

> You have heard the tuneful Plowman,
> Who sung so 'blithe and free',
>
> . . . .
>
> You've heard a tuneful Shoemaker,
> Who still divinely sings:
>
> . . . .
>
> And now an untaught Weaver begs
> You'll hear his Moorland song.[66]

Here he claims the status of the 'rural genius', the untaught poet of the countryside who, supposedly, composed verse out of a fund of natural inspiration and knowledge, untouched by the bastardizing influences of the city. His poetic persona is consistent with the medical persona he portrays in *Remarks*, where he distinguishes himself from the learned doctors who have imbibed their knowledge within the walls of the academy. Bakewell asserts that, in contrast to them, he has arrived at his understanding of insanity through more practical and less sophisticated means: 'I have lived for a number of years amongst Lunatics; I have been in their company almost constantly, from morning till night, and not unfrequently from night till morning'.[67] He implies that his medical abilities are superior to those of college-educated mad-doctors because he has imbibed his knowledge through direct contact with the mentally ill. In like fashion, he presents himself as a rural poet to suggest that his ability as a versifier is natural, unforced and, therefore, of a high quality.

Bakewell also presents himself as a bard of the countryside in these verses. Arguably the figure of the rural genius was introduced by Beattie in his representation of the shepherd-bard Edwin in *The Minstrel*, but the most famous real-life poet who embodied these qualities was Robert Burns, whom Bakewell mentions first in his poem ('The Tuneful Plowman'); he also makes reference to Robert Bloomfield ('a Tuneful Shoemaker'). These references to other rural geniuses can be understood as an advertising gimmick: Bakewell may have been trying to sell more copies of *The Moorland Bard* by introducing it as the product of the popular cult of rural, or natural, genius. He admits as much when he states in the preface that it would be 'a great injury' to his work if he would conceal 'it from the world, that he was in an humble situation in life; for such is the indulgence of the public, so completely is the field of letters open, that the knowledge of this has proved an advantage in more than one instance'.[68] The motivation behind identifying himself first and foremost as a weaver demonstrates a characteristic in Bakewell that we have seen in other poems: his desire to appeal to a broad audience.

Simplicity and accessibility to a wide range of readers are two of the major attractions of the rural genius tradition of poetry. Another poem that appears early in the first volume of the collection, 'Epistle to a Neighbouring Gentleman, Complaining of the Want of Poetic Fame', emphasizes these characteristics and suggests how his choice of the epistolary form is connected to them. Bakewell asserts his status as a weaver with an eye to its lowliness, humorously pointing out the difference between him and the higher classes for the length of the poem, while the letter-form of the poem invites the reader into an imaginative relationship with him. He jokingly complains to his correspondent of the injustice in not being recognized for the great poet that he is, for he

> Can spout like any man of letters,
> And sing of love just like my betters;
>
> . . . .
>
> So like a gentleman behave.
> Should I not leave my loom and shuttle,
> And do naught else but sing and guttle?[69]

Bakewell's reason for underlining his low-class status as a weaver becomes clear upon consideration of his comments in the preface about the poems' accessible subject matter and his desire to reach a broad audience through simple, even colloquial, language. In a passage reminiscent of Wordsworth's attack on poetic diction in the preface to the *Lyrical Ballads*, Bakewell writes, 'Amidst numbers of poets, who write so as to be comprehended by none but those who possess poetical knowledge, and taste, a work may perhaps find acceptance with the public, which is ... plain and simple enough to be understood by all that can read'.[70] In keeping with his psychological approach as a moral manager who endeavoured to forge interpersonal relationships with his patients, this psychologist-poet tries to present himself as lowly enough to be personally accessible to many readers in his verse. For the same reason, he appeals to his audience through a particular style of poetry that is designed to establish the sense of a social relationship between them that is mediated by his psychological expertise, as the following lines confirm:

> When piercing heart-felt griefs invade,
> My muse oft lends her cheering aid;
> She can my woe-fraught thoughts engage,
> And mental anguish well assuage
>
> ....
>
> Should I with sudden passion rage,
> If trifles gloomily engage
> My thoughts: my muse will step between –
> An Epigram can cure the spleen.[71]

Here, Bakewell establishes not only that his verse has a therapeutic psychological function by claiming its ability to cure melancholy ('griefs') or 'the spleen' but, by asserting that it can cure both ailments in himself, he further establishes a link of common humanity between himself and his reader. In several ways, then, Bakewell performs his identity as a moral manager.

VII. Versified Love Letters to Languishing Ladies

In a sure bid to capitalize on the link between nerve theory and the culture of sensibility that was forged in numerous epistolary novels of the eighteenth century, many of the poems in *The Moorland Bard* are written as letters. Just as he addressed *The Domestic Guide* to the general public and tailored the language within it to reach a wide audience and just as he endeavoured to form interpersonal relationships with his patients in the asylum by socializing with them, so, too, does Bakewell use the form of the letter in many of his poems in *The Moorland Bard* in order to dramatize the idea that his speaker and reader are friends, or potential friends, having a lively discussion about a personal subject. In order to create the impression that the poems are one side of a friendly written exchange, Bakewell personalizes them by signing many of them 'T. B.' and gesturing to private information in the preface, where he confesses that the poems 'were composed as a means of diverting the thoughts, when under the pressure of severe domestic calamity, while the hands and eyes were employed in their proper vocation', in a sure reference to his stressful profession of mad-doctoring and probably also to the death of either his first or second wife.[72] In the poems themselves, Bakewell invites his reader to regard him on a personal level by providing a surprising amount of information about his personal life in the form of an open letter to the public. For example, 'The Author's Advertisement for a Wife' is, essentially, a versified personal ad, in which the psychologist-poet describes humorously and charmingly the qualities he desires in a wife. By way of explanation for his appeal to the public on this intimate matter, Bakewell ends the poem with the following lines:

> A tear of affection I still have in store,
> And the charms of dear woman, I still can adore.
> Any lady desiring the writer to see,
> May leave with the printer a line for T. B.[73]

Sadly, the poem is followed by the note, 'Several copies of the above have been long distributed, without producing any advantage to the poor author'.[74] Such information inspires in the reader feelings of affection for the author, which adds to our sense of having met him personally after reading this appeal to our sympathy and, if the reader happens to be a single woman, even our love.

This inclusion of the subject of love in the versified epistles further emphasizes that Bakewell presents his poems in the context of the literature of sentiment, the plots of which are usually romantic. Moreover, by presenting himself as one half as the love-relationship, Bakewell encourages his reader to consider him in a personal light that served his purposes as a moral manager well, for he thereby drew attention to the therapeutic focus on the person of the moral manager. He implies that the moral manager is as important to the issue of the mental health of the patient – and, speaking in broader terms, the constitution of the subject in the new terms set out by psychology – as a lover is to romance. Bakewell makes not only his words essential to the definition of the reader's comprehension of her own mind, or subjectivity, he also makes himself an integral part of this process.

The fact that three other poetic epistles in *The Moorland Bard* are addressed to ladies suggests that the dynamic of appealing to women suited well Bakewell's poetic intentions to present himself in a personal light. In 'Lines Written on a Blank Leaf of my *Domestic Guide*, and Presented to a Young Lady', Bakewell highlights his professional identity as a psychologist by drawing specifically upon his success as the author of a text about caring for the insane and he chooses a woman as the recipient of his caring advice by way of presenting himself as a guardian over the weaker, delicate female, to whom he preaches ladylike restraint:

> O may that pow'r that guards thy life,
> Still keep thy mind from hate and strife;
> From all extremes of passion wild,
> That erst mankind have oft beguiled.
>
> . . . .
>
> So shall insanity ne'er dare,
> To rack thy brain with frenzy'd care.[75]

In this passage, Bakewell may illustrate an impulse of early asylum keepers that Andrews and Scull have delineated with reference to John Monro's treatment of female patients in the eighteenth century. In *Customers and Patrons of the Mad-Trade*, the authors note that Monro 'set down particularly long histories of ... unsuccessful engagements and love affairs, implying that he, along with their families, may have shared a special empathy with these unfortunate women'.[76] Doubtlessly, Monro was responding, in part, to the idealized image of the weak, lovelorn madwoman that was so popular in the literature of sensibility.[77] In this poem, Bakewell devises a scene strongly reminiscent of those from novels of sensibility, in which he stars as the dashing protector of a swooning lady – or, rather, the knowledgeable doctor who saves her from madness by preaching ladylike restraint as the surest preventative against the ravages of a 'passion wild'. Bakewell certainly believed that women were particularly in need of his professional attentions; as he notes in *The Domestic Guide*, 'Women, most assuredly, are more liable to insanity than men' because they must endure childbirth, which, he claims, often leads to insanity.[78] By stressing the importance of interpersonal relationships for the maintenance of mental health, Bakewell uses verse to offer aid to women and serve the cause of moral management.

Similarly, the longest poem in these two volumes, 'Epistle to a Lady, who had Requested Some Maxims of Health', introduces the speaker as a healer of sick minds whose treatment methods are distinctly interpersonal in nature. Bakewell repeats almost verbatim the general advice he doles out to the lady in the above poem when he writes:

> Yet be not too intense in care;
> Of great anxiety beware;
> Be lively, temperate, and mild;
> Pray don't indulge those passions wild.[79]

Bakewell's advice to the lady to curb her 'passions wild' suggests that, as is the case in 'Lines Written on a Blank Leaf', he is trying to save the supposed female recipient of this epistle from being mentally ruined by unrequited romantic devotion, a fate that had befallen legions of women before her – at least in the world of Monro's casebooks, early Romantic poetry and, especially, sentimental novels. As such, this passage provides psychological advice that is, again, social in nature. Yet, how Bakewell fits into this social scene is not clear until we come across his foremost gem of advice. Here, it becomes clear that Bakewell does not counsel the female reader to be celibate, but to choose the object of her love wisely and, as Bakewell sees it, wisdom consists in choosing himself for a mate:

> The first thing I prescribe, will be,
> A loving husband, just like me;
> Who shall your tender health repair,
> And guard it with most anxious care.[80]

Notably, Bakewell does not just advise his female addressee to land a husband, but to find one who is 'just like' him. Bakewell's offer of himself as the choicest social company for those who wish to avoid 'mental affliction' is more than a humorous exaggeration of the personal relationship between the moral manager and his patient, or the implied relationship between the poet and reader. By simultaneously presenting to the reader a new language to give expression to and form her subjectivity, Bakewell makes the definitions of psychology and the psychologist himself the context for the delineation of selfhood. Healthy subjectivity is, therefore, mediated through the narrow social context of the person of the moral manager in these poems, just as he was at The Retreat.

Bakewell's efforts confirm the socially oriented nature of early psychology. Elsewhere in 'Epistle to a Lady', Bakewell's advice for maintaining a healthy mind includes developing close friendships. Nowhere in his psychological prose is he as explicit about how to avoid depression as he is in this poem. In *A Letter Addressed to the Chairman*, Bakewell hints at the kind of society that is dangerous to depressed patients when he writes, 'Country Asylums [improperly keep] in close confinement, criminal Lunatics, dangerous Idiots, pauper Lunatics, curable and incurable, those under the most violent paroxysms of madness, and those under the depressions of melancholy'.[81] Yet, Bakewell's reader must turn to 'Epistle to a Lady' for his most direct commentary on the link between depression and social interaction. His poetic advice to ward off melancholy demands the presence of others and attention to their social and economic status:

> Should you be prone to discontent,
> Or pine at what your lot has sent;
> Then look around upon the poor,
> Enter the wretched cottage door;
>
> . . . .
>
> Let thoughts of these your bosom fill,
> Let all your discontents be still.[82]

Just as the moral manager encourages his charges to observe and mingle with others as part of their cure, such as during the famous tea-parties at The Retreat,[83] Bakewell encourages the lady to whom he addresses these lines to chase away depression by reflecting upon her own situation in relation to that of others. He advises her to develop strong friendships for a similar reason:

> And oft at early dawn to walk,
> With those you love, and freely talk,
> Will greatly mend your health, you'll find,
> Your relax'd system gently bind.
> And as o'er flow'ry banks you stray,
> Then social converse by the way,
> On all around you see and hear,
> May well your pensive bosom cheer.[84]

Again, the message is that social ties based on free communication make one mentally healthy. Put otherwise, properly constituted subjectivity has a strongly social context. Having made this point, the psychologist-poet cannot resist putting himself forward as a good candidate for such a relationship and he ends the poem in a way that is typical of Dr Don Juan:

> A letter sure so long as this,
> May well deserve a friendly kiss;
> I'll claim it when I next you see,
> Till then, I'm truly Yours, T. B.[85]

Regardless of how ripe with the potential for misconduct is the situation he describes, Bakewell certainly presents himself as a psychologist in a personal context here and he thereby reinforces one of the mandates of moral management. Or perhaps he was unable to refrain from flirting – a strong possibility, given that he produced twenty-four children.

Finally, in 'Epistle to a Lady; Occasioned by her Advertisement, in a London Paper, for Country Lodgings in a Family where there were None but Females, Complaining at the Same Time of Frequent Depression of Spirits', the intrepid reader who makes it beyond the end of the cumbersome title is rewarded with a delightful disputation on the mental benefits of socializing with the opposite sex. Claiming that social interaction is the key to mental health, Bakewell writes:

> I heal disease of the mind
> With me you would constantly find,
> A balm for the vapours and spleen,
> If e'er in my presence they're seen.
>
> ....
>
> With ladies, I never am dull,
> Wit and mirth then so flow to my scull;

> For anecdote, laughter, and whim,
> No widow, or old maiden prim,
> Could so your attention engage,
> Or mental affliction asuage [sic].[86]

Bakewell's projected liaison with the (doubtlessly fictional) recipient of this versified epistle is a version of the kind of personal relationship into which the Tukes invited their patients at The Retreat. Tuke himself describes the principles of The Retreat as being social in nature and working on 'the *desire of esteem*', which he argues can cure the madman by teaching him to restrain his propensities as he endeavours to avoid lowering 'his character in the eyes of his companions and attendants'.[87] Essential to the patient's cure, in the eyes of the moral manager, was the intense personal relationship between the psychologist and the patient. Bakewell's sentimental presentation of himself as a candidate for a relationship with the reader of these letters emphasize several important features of this moral manager's literary and professional identity: his personable and accessible nature, his humanitarian and charitable temperament (via the associations with the literature of sentiment) and his personal importance to the mental health of the addressee/subject/patient of these letters.

In the preface to *The Domestic Guide*, Bakewell asserts that he writes 'from the honest impulse of wishing to be found useful to his fellow creatures, and from a full conviction that such a work is wanting'.[88] He supports this claim to beneficence by selling the text 'at a price within the reach of the poorest family', even though, he points out later in the preface, in what may be a reference to the huge and well-known advances offered to Erasmus Darwin, 'it is not many years since a more fortunate person than myself, refused a thousand guineas for the disclosure of what these pages contain'.[89] In this last comment, Bakewell hints that Foucault's 'divine and satanic' doctor, who jealously guarded his professional domain, blighted the field of psychology long before the nineteenth century. He confirms this suggestion when he writes in *A Letter*:

> The reason we know so little of the particulars of treating Insanity by the Antients is, no doubt, owing to those who undertook it as a profession, purposely concealing their methods, under the appearances of mystery, for the sake of giving them consequence, while at the same time their practice might be simple and easy.[90]

In his poetry, Bakewell's stated purpose for addressing the reader in a way that includes references to his private life and the adoption of the epistolary form involves his wish to expand upon the volume of prose pop-psychology that immediately preceded it by further familiarizing the reader with the figure of the moral manager and his psychological approach. These efforts are in keeping with the principles of his psychological forebears in the Scottish Enlightenment. Although he was probably unaware of the broad and lasting cultural effects of his poetry, it, nevertheless, also functioned to present the person of the doctor and the discipline that he represents and creates through this very writing as the context within which the modern subject is formed.

VIII. 'No Man is an Island': Andrew Duncan and Madness as a Social Problem

Because moral management was so closely tied with issues of social relationships, charity and even class, we can understand the appearance of these issues in the poetry of Romantic-era moral managers as illustrations of their psychological approach and as important means of building a particular literary and cultural identity for the new discipline of moral management as a whole. Duncan's verse illustrates this function of the poetry. His mostly lighthearted and occasional verse is the perfect accompaniment to his psychological prose: while the former indicates the moral manager's desire to establish the literary identity of the kindly, jovial doctor-of-the-people, the latter work shows how this desire is connected to his specific psychological approach. Duncan shows how the verse of psychologist-poets is essential to the public image that was so vital to these socially-oriented doctors of the mind and how it may have been essential in the formation of the modern subject.

Duncan's dedication to sociability is evident in many aspects of his professional life, such as in his performance of his duties as a professor at University of Edinburgh. Andrew Duncan, the elder (1744–1828), was born near St Andrews in Scotland.[91] After having obtained an MA degree at St Andrews University in 1762, he became a medical student at Edinburgh University, where was taught by such notables as Cullen, John Gregory, Monro *Secundus* and William Black. When he became a teacher himself, he fulfilled his duties in a particularly amiable way – such that his biographers report that 'He was both generous and hospitable to his pupils, and was much loved for the geniality and benevolence of his character' – while his prose works reveal the broad social implications of his contributions to psychology, which focused on the establishment of public institutions for the insane.[92] G. T. Bettany and L. Rosner, authors of the *ODNB* entry for Duncan, reveal that the representatives of Scottish society recognized Duncan for his efforts to improve the lot of the mad in their midst: in 1808 the freedom of Edinburgh was conferred on him for the foundation of the asylum and a public dispensary and in 1821 he became first physician to the King in Scotland.[93]

Duncan's place as an influential early moral manager is born out, in part, in his prose history of the public asylum in Edinburgh, *A Short Account of the Rise, Progress, and Present State of the Lunatic Asylum at Edinburgh*. Indeed, his very advertisement orients the work in a social realm. Claiming in the prefatory matter that his account of the asylum is intended for 'the serious attention of the opulent and of the benevolent', Duncan hopes to attract funding for the completion of the asylum by impressing upon the rich members of Scottish society the idea that the mental illness of some members of society affects everyone within it.[94] He goes into greater detail about this subject in the first pages of the text when he attests that madness reduces the unfortunate sufferer

> to a state endangering both his own life and that of others, particularly of his best friends. The removal of insanity, therefore, should certainly call forth the united exertions of all ... It has accordingly been a common observation, that among the different enlightened States of Europe, in proportion to the degree of civilization at which they have arrived, means have been furnished for the accommodation and cure of those subjected to mental derangement.[95]

According to Duncan, insanity is a social concern, both locally and broadly considered; it affects those who are close to the insane, for they may be harmed by the sufferer, and it also reflects the state of civilization of the whole society that surrounds him, for the stability and degree of development of the community are intricately connected to how madness is treated. Duncan also shows, in these words, the truth of Foucault's statement that the psychologist after the Classical period was 'the great advisor and expert ... [in the art] of observing, correcting, and improving the social "body" and maintaining it in a permanent state of health'.[96] The subject that is formed by this discourse is a product of his social relationships – especially, as we shall see in Duncan's poetry, with the moral manager himself.

Duncan also illustrates that his approach to treatment was social in nature with respect to the division of the patients. Moral managers' practice of classifying and dividing their patients was an essential feature of how the approach became the basis for modern psychology, for it was through these means that psychologists began to identify and treat with greater accuracy various manifestations of mental illness.[97] In short, such classification was an essential aspect of psychology's basic goal: to systematize subjectivity. Duncan's text illustrates that moral management included classifying the patients according to their respective class, in addition to their symptoms. Explaining that the asylum he proposes would offer all means of recovery, 'both physical and moral, for the various aspects of mental derangement', Duncan points out that it is

> intended to afford an opportunity for a division of patients, not only according to the accommodation for which they could pay, and according to their sex, as being rich or poor, male or female, but also according to the conditions of their disease, as being furious, melancholic, curable or incurable.[98]

Duncan's insistence that patients be organized according to their symptoms, as well as their social class and economic status, reflects yet another aspect of moral management. Duncan's push towards ordering the patients echoes his belief in the importance of what he calls 'regimen': 'there is a good chance to hope, that it will afford demonstrative evidence of the singular benefit which may be derived from what may justly be called the moral part of the cure of Insanity; that is, the cure depending on *regimen*, in the most extensive sense of the term'.[99] By noting that classification according to class and symptom was essential to the 'moral part of the cure of insanity', Duncan confirms his adherence to an important tenet of moral management: that it should treat the mind, rather than the body alone.[100] This move away from harsh physical treatment demands a complex response from today's reader. On one hand, we must view this move as positive because it was apparently motivated by humanitarian intentions and entailed gentler physical treatment of the mad. Viewed in context of a broad historical framework, however, it becomes clear that the new focus on the mind in early psychology is inextricable from the formation of the modern subject and disciplinary power by externalizing and controlling the internal and private through the definition of it.

Besides championing the poor and lower classes in his prose, Duncan also shows his political sympathy with other moral managers like Bakewell by using verse to engage his readers. Just as Duncan attempts to convince the wealthy members of his society that the lot of the mad is intricately connected to their own situation at the beginning of this psychological text, he maintains in a May-day poem written from the top of Arthur's Seat that the rich must care for the poor in order to protect their own destinies. In 'Advice Given to the Rich and Great, by a Physician, Who has Very Nearly Arrived at the Eightieth Year of his Age ... 1st of May, 1822', Duncan confirms his role as a sage of the people by both teaching the wealthy and representing the interests of the poor:

> Ye Rich and Great, who wealth and honours prize,
> Know, these are blessings only to the Wise.
>
> . . . .
>
> Partake the joys of pure benevolence.
> Like him, from these sweet paths who never rov'd,
> Of man a lover, and by man belov'd
> That road to bliss with steady steps pursue,
> The peace of others ever keep in view.[101]

Here, Duncan illustrates his feelings of kinship with the lower classes and confirms his community with the other psychologist-poets who wrote in a similarly democratic and edifying way. He also firmly positions himself as a social governor and thereby confirms the new identity of the moral manager that he and others hoped to establish.

IX. Meet, Drink and Be Merry: Andrew Duncan and the Culture of Social Clubs

Duncan's advisory poetry about charity and social wellness brings together his professional and personal experiences. The moral manager's biographers state at the end of their short account of Duncan's life that 'For more than half a century he walked to the top of Arthur's Seat on May day morning, accomplishing this for the last time on 1 May 1827', but a discussion of his poetry must begin with this fact, for he composed many of his verses during his annual visit to this famous natural vista in Edinburgh.[102] These poems reveal Duncan as a true sage of the people: he took his inspiration from a scene that may be enjoyed by all, he addressed his poetic meditation to society at large in the epistolary form that Bakewell also used, he wrote about events that touched everyone, and he published his poems in popular venues that would disseminate his ideas to the largest possible audience. The volume in which some of these poems appear, *Observations on the Office of Faithful Teacher, and On the Duty of an Attentive Student of Medicine, Delivered as an Introductory Lecture to the Institute of Medicine in the University of Edinburgh*, includes an anonymous appendix that explains their background:

> For many years past, it has been a practice with him, to walk to the top of that hill, on the morning of May-day, when the English Villagers are, with great joy, hopping about the May-pole. On these occasions he has sometimes written there short poetical addresses, on remarkable occurrences which have taken place in the course of the year. These addresses have appeared in different newspapers and have conveyed, with regard to Dr Duncan's state, both of mind and body, intelligence very agreeable to many of his friends at a distance.[103]

That the writer of this note describes these poems as 'addresses' through which Duncan informs his 'friends at a distance' about himself speaks to their epistolary nature.[104] Some of the poems written from Arthur's Seat were about the royalty: in one case Duncan celebrates the Queen's recovery from a dangerous illness, in another he celebrates the approaching marriage of Princess Charlotte and in yet another he mourns the Princess's death after childbirth. Many others were simple responses to his own passing years. Through all of these accessible topics, Duncan endeavours to communicate to his broad audience on an accessible level and, like Bakewell, Duncan introduces his own biography into the poems to suggest the imaginative possibility of a relationship between him and his reading audience, which was essential to the establishment of the particular cultural identity of the moral manager.

Duncan's Scottish education taught him to view his cultural role as a doctor as deeply social for, as historian James Harris attests, the social clubs to which he was introduced as a student played a prominent role the young doctors' training:

> A central part of eighteenth-century Scottish intellectual life was the literary or
> philosophical club. It is difficult, in fact, to overemphasize the importance to the
> "Scottish Enlightenment" of these informal, privately-organized ... societies, which
> met to discuss every kind of contemporary question, from the most abstract issues in
> Newtonian science to problems in agriculture and husbandry.[105]

These societies and clubs may provide the most convincing argument regarding
the motivations to publish poetry and the connections between the psychologist-poets, in fact, for the members contributed literary criticism – such as
Ferriar's 'Comments on Sterne' – and poetry as readily as they did scientific
essays. As for the company these society members kept, the list of members of
the Manchester Literary and Philosophical Society alone includes several of the
psychologist-poets: Beattie was an honorary member (defined under the laws of
the society to be any member who presents a paper at a distance from Manchester), as were Ferriar and Erasmus Darwin, not to mention Watt, Lavoisier, and
Rush, all of whom contributed to the Enlightenment and radical scene I explore
in this study. The medical societies to which Duncan and Ferriar belonged (not
to mention almost all of the other psychologist-poets) were formative influences
in defining the new role of the psychologist as an enthusiastic member of his
community who shared his medical knowledge with others in an informal fashion and made his mark on other aspects of culture in a way that made him seem
less esoteric than he was in the early decades of the eighteenth century.[106] For
Duncan, in particular, the medical societies that he established later, such as the
Aesculapian Club and the Harveian Club, were also great inspirations for his
poetry, much of which is addressed to these societies.[107]

Even when Duncan was writing poetry for a more exclusive group of readers,
such as the members of one of the many medical societies to which he belonged,
he continued to show his dedication to the development of broad social ties. For
example, in *Miscellaneous Poems, Extracted from the Records of the Circulation
Club at Edinburgh*, the poem entitled 'Diploma of Doctor of Mirth, Solemnly
Conferred on Alexander Wood, Esq. April 12, 1813' is evidently directed to a
select and highly educated audience because many of the lines are in Latin.[108] Yet,
its jovial tone and many references to the pleasures of sharing drinks with friends
emphasize the fact that its purpose is to celebrate community, rather than to dis-
criminate against those who cannot understand the poem. Duncan writes,

> O honour mirth,
> From which true circulation takes its birth;
> It gives the aid of mind to rouse the heart,
> And send the living stream to every part.
> On earth, I often felt its generous power,
> Enjoy'd its influence to my latest hour.[109]

The sentiment in these lines echoes throughout many of poems in the volume that extol the benefits of drinking with friends. Moreover, Duncan notes that 'the mind' is roused with 'the heart', which indicates that, quite unlike Beddoes and Trotter, whom I will discuss in the next chapter, Duncan believed, with the famous John Brown, that intoxicants can actually aid the mind and are salutary.[110]

However scientific was Duncan's approach to alcohol, the humorous way in which he versifies about it shows that he did not lose sight of the enjoyment it offers. For example, 'Fragment of the Life of the *Scriba Praetorious* ... Written by Himself in Hudibrastic Rhyme' reveals Duncan's lighthearted approach to alcohol:

> From business and from sickness free,
> Aged precisely Sixty-three,
> I have resolv'd on this my birth-day,
> With generous wine to moisten stiff clay.[111]

Given Duncan's opinions about the pleasures of drinking, it is easy to see why other members of the Circulation Club refer to him as the 'Dr of Merriment' in some of the poems in this volume. Meanwhile, in Duncan's 'Appendix', it becomes evident that such societies as the Circulation Club were, by and large, drinking clubs:

> the social meetings among the Medical Men at Edinburgh, by no means include all the eminent practitioners of the city ... Dr Gregory ... has declared that he belonged to no medical club ... holding the exhilarating power of Wine in great contempt ... Dr Gregory observes: "Though much has been said, and with some truth, of the good effects of wine in producing rapidity and vivacity of thought, it has scarcely every been pretended that it favoured the exercise of discrimination and judgment".[112]

Through his scoffing paraphrase of Gregory's argument, Duncan's own medical opinion about the powers of alcohol are further clarified: he thought that it could help one think clearly and creatively and, in that sense, he believed that alcohol was beneficial for one's mental health.[113] However, Duncan's dedication to the mental benefits of alcohol was also linked inextricably to his belief in the importance of social relationships for mental health, as he discusses the matter in his psychological prose. After all, the members of the Circulation Club drank together, not in isolation.

In other addresses, Duncan presents himself as essential to the subjectivity of the reader by defining how she should understand her own mind. In the verse written on 1 May 1818 about 'a late melancholy event, the Death of Her Royal Highness the Princess Charlotte of Wales', as the short epigraph tells us, Duncan gives basic advice that is reflective of his psychological interests and universalizes the significance of his specific subject to give it meaning for his broad audience.

Although the poem is written about Princess Charlotte's death and from the imagined perspective of her grieving husband – topics that were relevant to Duncan's audience in any case, given that they were all subjects of the royal couple – Duncan tailors the message of the poem to make the life of every reader the focus of the final meditation:

> In sphere of Bliss, the good shall ever find,
> Freedom from pain, of Body, and of Mind.
> Let me then strive, thro' life's remaining days,
> To join my Wife, by Virtue's pleasing ways.
> For Virtue only is our Bliss below,
> And all our knowledge is, – ourselves to know.[114]

He abjures the reader to be virtuous and further defines how she might be so by clinging to her marriage partner, as he does; he then suggests that such reflection on one's (sexual) morality is linked with knowledge of herself, with properly constituted subjectivity. By signing many of these poems in the manner of a correspondent (Duncan signs himself 'Medicus Septuagenarius' here), he welcomes his audience into a kind of relationship with him, much in the manner of his fellow moral manager, Bakewell and, like Cotton and Beattie, he advises self-reflection. In this way, Duncan helps to form a discourse of subjectivity that is not only social, but that also situates his own person as the social Other to whom the properly constituted subject must relate.

Duncan's evaluation of the last lines of this poem as essential to his poetic and professional programme is confirmed by his repetition of them in another poem written after his visit to Arthur's Seat on 1 May 1821, which ends:

> Earnest I pray, that life's last day may find
> Good health of Body join'd to peace of Mind;
> And, that my race, thro' life's uncertain span,
> May prize the wisest lessons taught to man –
> "That Virtue only is our bliss below;
> "And all our knowledge is, Ourselves to know".[115]

Besides echoing himself – and, of course, Socrates, whose abjuration 'Know thyself' clearly influenced Duncan's thinking in these lines – the psychologist-poet also echoes the words of others in this study, such as Cotton, who reminds his reader in 'Death. Vision the Last' that 'Not all the Volumes on thy Shelf,/ Are worth that single Volume, Self'.[116] Through such lines, the psychologist-poet teaches the reader to be self-reflective and understand the self in the particular terms that he sets out, making his words and psychological approach essential to the reader's subjectivity.

X. The Diverting Science and Practical Aesthetics of John Ferriar

Ferriar (1761–1815) indicates his commonalities with his fellow psychologist-poets by blurring the boundary between psychological writing and literary discussion in a way that illustrates his contribution to the image of the psychologist as a sage of the people and cultural commentator. Ferriar was born in Roxburghshire, studied medicine at Edinburgh University, where he took his MD degree in 1781, and later established himself as one of the premier physicians in Manchester.[117] Ferriar gained considerable fame as an author of both literary and medical texts that challenge the reader to see psychological texts as entertaining and literary texts as psychological. This challenge is an expression of his identity as a moral manager, for Ferriar, like Duncan and Bakewell, wanted to present an image of the psychologist as one who was involved in and knowledgeable about the social and cultural life of his patients.

By writing about his beneficent interests in his psychological and literary works, Ferriar demonstrates two characteristics that we expect of him as a product of the Scottish Enlightenment: social concern and the belief that the psychologist must use attractive literary means to communicate his ideas. To begin with, in *Medical Histories and Reflections*, Ferriar describes what he calls the 'management of mind' in a way that confirms his beneficent concern for his patients: 'It was formerly supposed that lunatics could only be worked upon by terror; shackles and whips, therefore, became part of the medical apparatus', he reveals, adding that he approved of the 'system of mildness and conciliation [that] is now generally adopted'.[118] His biographer in the *ODNB* further underlines his moral management approach, noting that he was appointed 'in 1789 to a new post of assistant physician in the Manchester Infirmary', where he

> advocated the management of the mind by a system of mild but exact discipline, using encouragements and rewards or else punishment through seclusion, solitude, and deprivation of light and food. His purpose in disciplining was to instil self-restraint, and he believed that mechanical means should be avoided if possible but that a sense of imposed restraint was important and thus that removal from home quickened recovery.[119]

Ferriar's use of reward and punishment to encourage the patients to develop self-restraint and his avoidance of physical methods of treatment make him an exemplar of moral management, while his use of such methods as 'seclusion, solitude' and 'removal from home' confirm that the approach was primarily social in nature.

Ferriar also illustrates the broader social concerns that reflect his beneficent principles as a moral manager and appear in his literary works when he discusses the needs of the pauper insane. His theory in *Medical Histories and Reflections* that insanity is a broader social issue that affects more than the mad individual constitutes his most significant contribution to Romantic-era psychology. Indeed, in a manner similar to Duncan, Ferriar argues that the wealthy and sane members of society must concern themselves with the plight of the pauper insane not only out of humanitarian interest for the unfortunate, but also because their own health and safety depends on it. Arguing that melancholy is at the root of epidemics that could eventually infect and destroy the health of the wealthy, Ferriar explains that the poor are particularly prone to melancholy because of their adverse social and economic situations: 'the mortifying sense of their condition [i.e. the poor], produces a continual depression of spirits', which can result in epidemics by producing 'animal poisons'.[120] He concludes the essay by maintaining that everyone must be vigilant in

> disarming the virulence of animal poisons, by increasing the happiness of our fellow creatures ... [C]loser attention to the comfort of the poor, than is commonly practised, is a desirable object of attainment; and it may excite the benevolence of some men, if they can be convinced, that acts of charity will not only serve them in another life, but promise them a longer enjoyment of the present.[121]

Here, Ferriar illustrates well the humanitarian and broadly social interests that also motivated his fellow moral managers, Duncan and Bakewell, and he provides original insight into how social conditions may be directly associated with mental illness by arguing that poverty can lead to depression.[122] Indeed, in several places in the text, Ferriar contends that society as a whole is measurably – and physically – affected by the problem of insanity:

> While innumerable methods are proposed for supporting the poor of this nation, with the least possible expence it has not been sufficiently explained to the public, that their present situation is extremely dangerous, and often destructive to health and life, to the middle and higher ranks of society.[123]

Through these passages in his psychological prose, Ferriar demonstrates why his profession as a moral manager necessitates his knowledge of and interest in social problems. He also implicitly advances moral management's definition of a healthy mind – or properly constituted subjectivity – as socially mediated.

In yet another way that allies him with Duncan, Ferriar manifested his belief in the inextricable link between being a physician and being involved in the social life of his community: he, too, was an active member of social clubs. Indeed, as a young doctor, Ferriar joined the 'Manchester Literary and Philosophical Society for which he wrote a number of papers covering poetry, drama, and archaeology, such as one on the work of Laurence Sterne'; through this club he also met 'the physician Thomas Percival and other local cultural leaders'.[124] Such social clubs facilitated the acquirement and dispersal of medical knowledge and helped to define the doctor as a cultural leader in a broad way, for the members of these societies were encouraged to present their researches into a wide variety of topics, amongst which literature was foremost. Ferriar, for his part, established himself as an expert in literature almost as definitively as he did in the realm of psychology.

Ferriar's presentation on Sterne for the Manchester Literary and Philosophical Society was integral to his reputation as an expert on both literature and psychology. He expanded this lecture into a significant monograph called *Illustrations of Sterne, With Other Essays and Verses*, in which he traces the influence of early French romances on *Tristram Shandy*.[125] Notably, Ferriar traces Sterne's sources to Robert Burton's *Anatomy of Melancholy* at several points in the study.[126] This detail, coupled with the fact that Ferriar signs himself 'John Ferriar, MD' on the title page, suggests that Ferriar endeavoured consciously to apply his psychological knowledge to the literary realm and thereby mould his image as an expert in both. Other essays in the text also show his desire to blend both kinds of knowledge. For example, in the essay 'Of Genius', he applies his knowledge as an expert on the mind to our broader cultural idea of what constitutes genius, particularly of the literary sort:

> When we speak of a man who has ... written a fine poem, or a very good novel, we call him a man of genius, without understanding our own meaning ...[A]uthors have agreed in the same error, of considering genius as a distinct power of the mind, while in reality, it originally denoted something totally independent of it.[127]

Later in the same essay, Ferriar goes into great detail about how madness has often been mistaken for genius, thereby further illustrating his creative use of his medical knowledge and his desire to make the debate concerning such knowledge accessible to all.[128]

Ferriar complains in another essay of a problem that is, presumably, only known to medical professionals. In 'Of Certain Varieties of Man, Described by Authors', he bemoans the plethora of facts and the lack of experts in medicine: 'How many collections of pretended facts are daily offered to medical men, in which it is happy for mankind if the author's [stylistic] weakness be sufficiently evident, to destroy, at first sight, the credit of his observations!'.[129] By presenting this assessment of medical prose in a volume dominated by literary criticism and suggesting that the same aesthetic expectations may be applied to both kinds of writing, Ferriar further blurs the boundaries of medicine and literature. The psychologist concludes this section with a comment that suggests the philosophical attitude that underlines his holistic approach: 'every man who is in quest of real knowledge must lament, that so few books are written with a design to instruct, and so very many only to surprise or amuse'.[130] Here, Ferriar reintroduces a debate with which many other psychologist-poets were engaged and which was first presented by Horace's formulation about the purpose of poetry in *Ars Poetica*, specifically, that poetry should be both '*dulce et utile*', or 'pleasing and useful'.[131] In *Illustrations of Sterne, with Other Essays and Verses*, Ferriar unites issues from a realm that is often perceived as only 'pleasing' – literature – with a realm that is often regarded as simply 'useful' – medicine – and challenges his reader to find a Horatian balance between them by considering the point at which they overlap.

Throughout his psychological and literary works, Ferriar offers this challenge, but one lengthy poem expresses his goal best. The longest of all the versified letters written by the moral managers, *The Bibliomania, an Epistle, to Richard Heber, Esq.*, presents the practice of obsessive book-collecting as a mental disease, of which later commentators have suggested Ferriar himself was a sufferer, even though he dedicated the poem to one Richard Heber, whom Marc Vaulbert de Chantilly calls the greatest bibliomaniac of all in consideration of his library of 150,000 volumes.[132] Once again, the letter format of the poem gives the reader the impression of an exchange between friends, which presents the poet in an accessible light, while the content of the verse highlights his profession as a psychologist. In this humorous epistle, full of erudite references to collectible texts, myth, saints and history, Ferriar illustrates cogently how the practice of psychology may provide insight into our experience of the realm of literature. The poem begins,

> What wild desires, what restless torments seize
> The hapless man, who feels the book-disease,
> If niggard Fortune cramp his gen'rous mind,
> And Prudence quench the Spark by heaven assign'ed!
> With wistful glance his aching eyes behold
> The Princeps-copy, clad in blue and gold.[133]

However, the bibliomaniac's passion does not reveal a love of learning, as one might assume. Ferriar asserts that this obsessed collector chooses his texts for aesthetic and social reasons: he loves the appearance of rare books and wants those around him to admire his collection. Ferriar intones,

> But devious oft' from ev'ry classic Muse,
> The keen Collector meaner paths will choose:
> And first the Margin's breadth his soul employs,
> Pure, snowy, broad, the type of nobler joys.
> In vain might Homer roll the tide of song,
> Or Horace smile, or Tully charm the throng;
> If crost by Pallas' ire, the trenchant blade
> Or too oblique, or near, the edge invade,
> The Bibliomane exclaims, with haggard eye,
> "No Margin!" turns in haste, and scorns to buy.

> . . . .

> And who can say, what books, matur'd by age,
> May tempt, in future days, the reader's rage?
> How, flush'd with joy, the Bibliomane may shew
> His Carrs *uncut* and Cottles, fair in row;
> May point, with conscious pride, to env'ying throngs
> His Holcroft's dramas, and his Dimond's songs?[134]

The subtlety and perspicacity of Ferriar's insight that bibliomania is not a desire for the books themselves, but a desire to appear superior to other people, reveals what is suggested by the very title of the poem: Ferriar's poem blends perfectly the realms of psychology and literature, for it is a versified psychological meditation on a literary topic.

In the last lines and parting advice of this epistolary exploration of a literary mania, Ferriar hints most strongly at the truly psychological nature of this poem. Even as he implies that *The Bibliomania* pleads nothing more than the old *cliché* that one should 'not judge a book by its cover', Ferriar states that his message will remain unheeded because of a psychological quirk of his subject:

> The cheapest page of wit, or genuine sense
> Outweighs the uncut copy's wild expence.
> What coxcomb would avow th' absurd excess,
> To choose his friends, not for their parts, but dress?[135]

Ferriar's claim about the 'coxcomb's' inability to admit to the shallowness of his preferences suggests that the psychological problem with the bibliomane and his fellow aesthetes is their self-deception about their real motivations or inability to admit reason as their guide. In these crucial last lines, Ferriar may suggest the proto-Freudian idea that one's id may overrule the inclinations of the superego. He suggests that, even though the bibliomane may know, thanks to his superego, that a book's real worth is in the ideas it relates rather than its appearance, his id may, nevertheless, urge him to buy up those 'Cottles, fair in a row'.

This interpretation is supported by Ferriar's psychological prose: four years before *The Bibliomania* was published, he produced a remarkably proto-Freudian text – *The Theory of Dreams in Which an Inquiry is Made into the Powers and Faculties of the Human Mind, As They are Illustrated in the Most Remarkable Dreams Recorded in Sacred and Profane History* – that develops the idea of different levels of consciousness and the discreet motivations that rule each. Ferriar writes that 'if vice peeps out' when we are awake,

> it accommodates itself to the opinion of men, and is abashed; and veiling its passions, it does not entirely give itself to its impulse, but restrains and contends with it, but in sleep flying beyond opinions and laws, and transgressing all modesty and shame, it excites every lust and stirs up evil propensities.[136]

Or, to use psychoanalytic discourse, the superego rules our waking actions, but our dreams are guided by the id. Ferriar may despair of healing the bibliomane of his mania – for he, like the 'coxcomb' will not, he implies, 'avow' that he chooses books for their aesthetic value – but Ferriar succeeds in relaying psychological information to his reader. By suggesting that the bibliomane would do well to take an honest look at his own motivations, Ferriar preaches self-reflexivity to his reader; by submitting that one may behave in an erroneous or 'manic' manner even in the presence of self-reflection, Ferriar implies the need for an interpreter of subjectivity, specifically, the psychologist. Later in *The Theory of Dreams*, Ferriar makes a similar claim regarding the mysteries of the mind and psychology's ability to unravel them. In this remarkably proto-Freudian text, the first definition of 'dream' that Ferriar provides is from 'Macrobius, an ancient author', who regards the phenomenon 'as a figurative and mysterious representation that requires to be interpreted'.[137] The methods and language for this interpretation comprise the discourse of psychology.

In several ways in his poetry and prose, Ferriar teaches the discourse of moral management and entices the reader to learn his lessons. For example, his humorous tone in *The Bibliomania* suggests that literature and psychology share the ability to entertain. Like Duncan, Ferriar treats his psychological topic – here, the phenomenon of mania, or obsession – in a lighthearted way that emphasizes the accessibility of his ideas to a wide audience, to society as a whole, the real addressee of this verse epistle. Similarly, Ferriar focuses on the entertainment value of psychology in *An Essay Towards a Theory of Apparitions*. He introduces the subject of hallucinations in the context of Gothic literature and the Romantic reader's fascination with ghosts. However, rather than attempting to show the seriousness of such ghostly apparitions by arguing that they are the fearful symptoms of mental illness, as we expect him to do, Ferriar suggests that we may divert ourselves with hallucinations and even provides the literary means of doing so in this text. He claims that many hallucinations have resulted from reading ghost stories and other works that stimulate our sense of the supernatural and then he proceeds to fill his text with impressive tales of phantoms, which, presumably, will help his reader to hallucinate about their own ghosts.[138] He even seems to advertise his text as a kind of aid to seeing ghosts, arguing that a 'great convenience will be found in my system; apparitions may be evoked, in open day ... Nay, a person rightly prepared may see ghosts, while seated comfortably by his library-fire, in as much perfection, as amidst broken tombs, nodding ruins, and awe-inspiring ivy'.[139] Here, Ferriar does not present his scientific explanation of ghosts as tedious reading for the scientifically minded reader. Quite the contrary, he presents his psychological treatise on 'spectral delusions' as entertainment in itself: 'Take courage, then, good reader, and knock at the portal of my enchanted castle, which will be opened to you, not by a grinning demon, but by a very civil person, in a black velvet cap, with whom you may pass an hour not disagreeably'.[140] Dour though his dress is, Ferrier presents the scientist of the mind in his brightest colours as an accessible, amusing writer, figuratively speaking. In all of these ways, Ferrier hawks his particular brand of self-reflection. Dreams, he writes, 'must be considered as the work of the mind, sketches of the fancy';[141] a mania, as in bibliomania, is a mental delusion; apparitions are creations of the mind – and all of these subjective realities afford pleasure, either through their diverting capabilities, or as the subject matter of humorous poetry. Again, the personable literary identity of the moral manager helps to establish the discourse of psychology, which is also a specific language of subjectivity.

XI. The Democrat's Eye and the Visible Mind

The dualistic identity of the moral manager as at once egalitarian and a master of disciplinary power is reflected not only in his writings, but also in his practice. The moral manager's democratic stance was undermined in part by his efforts to maintain his authority over his patient. Showalter and Porter have described in detail the paternalistic character of moral management, while Smith notes that Bakewell, for his part, 'sought to foster a supportive milieu that resembled a large family' in his asylum.[142] In *A Letter Addressed to the Chairman of the Select Committee of the House of Commons, Appointed to Enquire into the State of Mad-Houses*, Bakewell recommends that the insane person be considered a 'Child of the State' and goes a step further in his *Domestic Guide*, where he reveals that he was not above whipping his charges when he felt the establishment of his authority demanded it.[143] Similarly, Samuel Tuke compares the treatment of madness to raising children in *A Description of The Retreat* and, significantly, he connects the fatherly role of the moral manager to the all-important issue of the control he wielded over his charges: 'The principle of fear, which is rarely decreased by insanity, is considered as of great importance in the management of patients. But it is not allowed to be excited, beyond that degree which naturally arises from the necessary regulations of the family'.[144] As Tuke notes in a section of the text entitled 'Of the Means of Assisting the Patient to Control Himself', 'the management of patients' relied, to a great degree, upon the fear that the psychologist could inspire in them.[145] Even though the moral manager held the egalitarian view that the patient was not different in kind from himself, but could obtain a state of normalcy again, he regarded his own greater authority over his charge as an essential aspect of his ability to treat him effectively. This discrepancy in the attitude of the moral manager towards his patient is just one aspect of an underlying conflict in this kind of psychology that has earned the figure of the moral manager his Janus-faced reputation as a liberator and democrat, on one hand, and a tyrant, on the other.

The moral manager's attention to the mind of the patient as the source of his madness and locale of his potential cure was related to his democratic attitude, for he fought tradition by refusing to afford significance to one's 'outside'. In like manner, Ferriar argues that that 'Mind *has no* colour' in his poetic prologue to his anti-slavery, *Oroonoko*-inspired drama *The Prince of Angola*, Duncan illustrates the connection between the wealthy and the poor in *Short Account* and Bakewell, the humble Moorland Bard, declares that he can 'spout like any man of letters, / And sing of love just like my betters'.[146] Neither race, nor economic status, nor class makes the mind – or the self – what it is; only what is inside of us matters. By identifying madness as a mental phenomenon that required the moral manager for interpretation and treatment, this new kind of psychologist posited the mind as abstract and invisible to the untrained eye and himself as essential to its health and very being. The moral manager needed not just sight, but insight, to identify madness, and not just brute physical force, but the ability to establish his greater mental strength over the patient to treat him. The emphasis on the mind that confirmed the moral manager as utterly egalitarian also had the opposite effect of establishing him as uniquely knowledgeable and absolutely necessary to the formation of the properly constituted subjectivity, the healthy mind. For these reasons, the moral manager, who was so democratic in some ways, has been identified by Foucault and later historians of psychiatry as the prototype 'satanic' doctor and esoteric tyrant.

As egalitarian and accessible as he was in his poetry and prose, the moral manager also presented himself as a special being. He claimed to have the unique, almost magical ability to detect madness and the myriad subtle characteristics, upon the articulation of which a cure relied. James Cowles Pritchard maintained that insanity could be 'invisible to the untrained or lay eye, though quite conspicuous to the expert psychiatrist'; Porter confirms that 'early nineteenth century psychiatrists vaunted their ability to seize upon the slightest clue which, dexterously unravelled, would reveal an entire delusional system'.[147] The moral manager's power to perceive madness was not a passive mode of observation. Rather, his insight forced madness to reveal itself and posited the psychologist as the controller of both the disease and the afflicted, according to Foucault, who writes that all moral management practice 'was designed to make the medical personage the "master of madness": the one who makes it appear in its truth ... and the one who dominates it'.[148] Even though the moral manager's identification of insanity as a mental phenomenon grew out of his awareness that the insane mind had enough in common with the sane mind to be recognizable and accessible to the psychologist, locating madness within the patient's subjective reality established the disease as abstract, invisible and, therefore, more mystifying to the subject herself, while the psychologist's ability to detect and control it appeared, consequently, more awe-inspiring.

Strikingly, in Romantic-era texts, the moral manager's power of metaphysical insight into the subjectivity of his patient is symbolized by his eyes, which become the repository of his power and the source of his command over the patient. I argue that his eyes were only symbolic of his real power because their true function – to see the physical world – had little to do with this power. The moral manager's eyes conveyed more than they perceived of material reality and saw what is invisible to simple ocular organs. Andrew Cooper claims, 'the moral managers used eye-contact to establish their authority on the assumption that this was the first step in recalling the patient to a normative awareness of moral and social values', while Porter confirms that moral managers were seen in increasingly heroic terms around the turn of the nineteenth century with respect to their ability to control the insane patient, as though they were priests wrestling with demons.[149] Most famously, Francis Willis, who treated King George III during his madness, was reported to have overpowered his royal charge 'by the eye', a talent that Porter identifies as characterizing Willis as 'a true proto-Romantic contemporary of [Johann Caspar] Lavater and [Franz] Mesmer'.[150] Willis also gained fame for practicing this dramatic style of moral management at his own insane asylum in Lincolnshire, as the words of an anonymous visitor in late 1795 or early 1796 reveal:

> His usually friendly and smiling expression changed its character when he first met a patient. He suddenly became a different figure commanding the respect even of maniacs. His piercing eye seemed to read their hearts and divine their thoughts as they formed. In this way he gained control over them which he used as a means of cure.[151]

Nor were the gentle Quakers above vaunting this ability of the moral manager. In *A Description of The Retreat*, Tuke describes a scene in which the superintendent of The Retreat was threatened by a 'maniac' with a large stone; he dramatically concludes the story thus: 'The superintendent, in no degree ruffled, fixed his eye upon the patient, and in a resolute tone of voice ... commanded him to lay down the stone'.[152] The endowment of the moral manager with special powers of domination that he wielded with the help of his basilisk-like eyes made a super-being out of him, superior to his fellows in mental and physical attributes and a far cry from the humble, jovial sage-of-the-people that is his literary persona. This presentation of the moral manager was accurate in spirit, though, being inspired by his own methods of treatment: the goal of such tyrannical behaviour was to cure the patients and not simply to master them in order to prove the psychologists' authority. Yet, this very method posited an essential difference between psychologists and patients that contrasts with the egalitarian politics which moral managers professed in other arenas.

William Pargeter's moral management approach manifested both of these aspects of the field. Hunter and Macalpine state that 'His aim was to make immediate contact with patients and this he achieved without words simply by catching their eye'; they also attest to the fact that Pargeter's goal was, ultimately, curative, not simply autocratic: 'He showed how the physician's manner could not only soothe and check developing excitement and render the furious madman tranquil, but even halt incipient madness'.[153] Pargeter himself expresses this goal most powerfully in *Observations on Maniacal Disorders*:

> The chief reliance in the cure of insanity must be rather on *management* than medicine ... As maniacs are extremely subdolous, the physician's first visit should be by surprize. He must employ every moment of his time by mildness or menaces, as circumstances direct, to gain an ascendancy over them, and to obtain their favour and prepossession ... [by use of his] discerning and penetrating eye.[154]

Pargeter assigns particular roles, with seemingly unchanging characteristics, to the madman and the moral manager in a way that emphasizes their oppositional relationship in this therapeutic confrontation. The 'maniac' is 'subdolous', clever, deceptive, but the psychologist is 'discerning and penetrating' – characteristics that are manifested in his eyes – and altogether too astute for the maniac's tricks. Moral managers may have adopted this approach to madness out of their egalitarian and sympathetic feelings for the less fortunate and desire to cure them, but the specific methods that developed out of the view of insanity as a mental phenomenon created what Foucault calls 'master[s] of madness' out of democratic physicians.[155]

This focus on the moral manager's ability to hold the mad patient 'by the eye' and the subsequent mythical status he gained in the popular imagination during the Romantic era suggests his personal power in the therapeutic relationship, as well as in the imaginative relationship with the reader that he establishes through his poetry. Through the form of the epistle, all of these moral managers suggest that they are personally vital to the formation of the subjectivity of the reader, who is encouraged to relate to the moral manager one-on-one – *tête-a-tête* or, better yet, eye-to-eye – in order to understand herself. On the level of discourse, the reader is encouraged to study her mind and discover her subjectivity through the promptings and definitions of his poetry, which provides the context and language through which moral management's particular approach to the reader's subjectivity is spoken into being. Importantly, the very accessibility of this poetry is vital to the formation of the discipline of psychology, since the reader is thereby attracted to learn the language upon which her very subjectivity is predicated.

The epistolary form functions in a complex and essential way in the formation of subjectivity through modern power. The form of the letter not only posits the poet in a hypothetical relationship with the reader, it also suggests the possibility of a reply that, prompted by the original, would adopt its definitions. This response exists only as an implication and potentiality, but it is inevitably suggested and may be understood as setting out the terms of the reader's very subjectivity, which is, as Foucault notes, a function of language – here the language of verse. In the versified presentation of psychology, particularly the epistolary verse of the moral managers, the psychologist-poet appeals to the reader to be self-reflective and implies the possibility of a corresponding letter of response, which would thereby present the subject as textually framed by the original letter. As I have noted, the moral manager's attention to the mind, and not the body, as the source of his illness and locale of his cure entailed a relationship between the doctor and patient that was based on verbal interaction, since the moral manager could neither assess the patient without the latter's adoption of the active role of communicator, nor deliver therapy without communicating it. The epistolary form, with its implied – and, for Bakewell, sometimes direct – entreaty for a response, dramatically illustrates this relationship. Viewing the poems in this way also suggests how the psychologist could be simultaneously personable and tyrannical: the very accessibility of his literary identity as a moral manager and his psychological knowledge is key to the reader's newfound subjectivity, or, in other words, the creation of the modern subject through the discipline of psychology. These poems make subjects of and subjectify the reader, while, as early contributions to the expression of psychology, they posit the poet as master of modern power.

3. THOMAS TROTTER, WILLIAM PERFECT AND THOMAS BEDDOES: NERVOUS ILLNESS AND SOCIAL HYGIENE

Perfect, Beddoes and Trotter expand our notions of the role of the psychologist in Romantic-era culture just as surely as do Bakewell, Ferriar and Duncan. In the foregoing chapter, I describe the poetry of moral managers in terms of the literature of sensibility, which is so often associated with nerve theory, and I suggest that Bakewell, Ferriar and Duncan used some of sensibility's literary techniques and forms in order to popularize their field and build their cultural identities in accordance with the characteristics already associated with the nerve doctor. In the present chapter, I will trouble further the accepted critical narrative about nerve theory by arguing that other kinds of nerve doctors existed in the Romantic period, ones who, politically speaking, had more in common with the Whiggish moral philosophers and moral managers I have described thus far than they did with the 'doctor of society', such as Cheyne and Francis Willis, because they did not so strenuously court the upper-classes. Moreover, their specific approaches cannot be said to be reflected in the 'culture of sensibility', as Barker-Benfield has called it, partly because two of them rejected these upper-class associations, and because all of them present nervous illness as madness, not sensibility.[1] Perfect, Beddoes and Trotter show their indebtedness to the distinctly democratic culture of the Scottish Enlightenment – one of several that characterized the period, as my discussion in Chapter 1 of the classicist attitudes of Hume indicates – by addressing in poetry and prose the concerns of the wider population and less wealthy members of British society, like sailors, slaves and colonized populations, in addition to the 'middling and affluent classes', as the complete title to Beddoes's *Hygëia* states. One might call this new breed of nerve doctor a rebel because he risked offending both potential wealthy patients and their well-established doctors by associating nerves with insanity and, for Trotter and Perfect, identifying nervous illness as a problem for all classes of society, not just the rich. By reinterpreting the social significance and causes of nervous illness, these psychologist-poets also redefined their positions as nerve theorists

– and, in so doing, they redefined the contours of the modern subject, who was delineated, in many ways, through the negative spaces created as the psychologist defined his cultural identity and field of knowledge.

Perfect, Beddoes and Trotter were hardly the first to register their frustrations with the "'fashionable status'" of the "'Vapours, Hippo, and Spleen'"; amongst others, the anonymous author of *A Treatise of the Dismal Effects of Low-Spiritedness* had done so before them.[2] They also followed their eighteenth-century forbears by linking nervous illness to the excesses of a successful society, such as gluttony and overindulgence in alcohol. However, Trotter and Perfect maintain that these vices are shared by the lower classes (and Beddoes implies as much), while all three identify nervous illness as madness in no uncertain terms. By refusing to define nervous illness in a way that made it a sign of refinement and a sure mark of wealth, these nerve doctors distinguished themselves from their Cheynian forbears and recreated nerve theory's relationship with literature and wider culture. If nervousness was truly a mark of madness, it was to be strenuously avoided; if the lower orders may be afflicted with it, it was no longer *de rigueur*; and if the nerve theorist was no longer the patsy of the patient, but, rather, passed down rules for better health that must be obeyed, the relationship between the nerve doctor and the patient had entered into a new phase of disciplinary power. Trotter, Beddoes and Perfect present a new identity for the nerve theorist: the hygienist who governs the mental and physical health of the nation by appealing to the individual to adopt rules of maintenance. While the subjectivity defined by the earliest psychologists was social in Christian terms and that of the moral managers was filtered through the narrow social avenue of the theorist himself, the subjectivity created by nerve theory – aristocratic and democratic – was socially mediated in a much broader way.

I. Nerve Theorist, Governor, Hygienist

Unlike the moral managers I describe in the previous chapter, the nerve theorists that I study in this chapter do not invite the reader/subject into a personal relationship with themselves, even imaginatively speaking. Rather, they present themselves as commentators on wider social ills, which they trace to the nervous and psychological state of the individual, thereby delineating their roles both as part of society's governance and contributors to the discourse of psychology. By establishing a theory of nerves that presents luxury and excess as social ills of modern civilization and the health of the body politic as closely related to that of the individual, these early nerve doctors define a subjectivity that depends upon the proper governance of personal and social excess. Through their dedication to the increasingly popular concept of hygiene – which emphasized the importance of self-regulation according to proscribed rules for health, the maintenance of personal health for the good of society as a whole and the rejection of dangerous external factors in the preservation of health – Perfect, Beddoes and Trotter define healthy subjectivity in a unique and utterly social way.

Several influential writers on Romantic-era medicine have commented on the social role of the doctor, but the relevance of his poetry has not been explored in detail. The study most pertinent to the present exploration is Porter's *Doctor of Society: Thomas Beddoes and the Sick Trade in Late-Enlightenment England*, in which the critic comments briefly upon Beddoes's long poem, *Alexander's Expedition*, relating it to a wider investigation of his role as a medical therapist of a range of social ills. Regarding Beddoes's view of the medicine's cultural role in the Romantic period, Porter comments, 'The doctor's duty was to instruct the people in the lessons of living ... [T]he Beddoesian doctor would be the humanist physician become priest and preceptor to humanity'.[3] In short, the doctor's role was broadly social and his governing role was not only physical, but also moral or metaphysical. These statements echo those of Foucault in 'The Politics of Health in the Eighteenth Century', in which he describes the figure of the late eighteenth-century doctor in the following terms:

> The doctor becomes the great advisor and expert, if not in the art of governing, at least in that of observing, correcting, and improving the social "body" and maintaining it in a permanent state of health. And it is the doctor's function as hygienist, rather than his prestige as a therapist, that assures him this politically privileged position in the eighteenth century, prior to his accumulation of economic and social privileges in the nineteenth century.[4]

Here, Foucault makes several claims that are reflected in the writings of Romantic-era nerve theorists. To begin with he reminds us that their treatment of the individual body parallels their social role. By defining a holistic approach that treated the body and mind as inseparable, the nerve theorist transformed himself from mere physician to ethical guide.

If the mind, identified in the period as the seat of the soul, affects the health of the body and vice versa, it stands to reason that the doctor of one must care for the other.[5] The case of Beddoes reveals as much, for he advanced 'numerous clinical demonstrations of psychosomatic and somatopsychic complaints', showing that there was no 'rigid ontological differentiation between the physical and the moral'.[6] Indeed, all of the nerve theorists I study in this chapter indicate their belief in such a reciprocal relationship, as I will show, for a holistic approach was definitive of nerve theory in general: the 'advent of new theories about "nervous disease"' began to shape psychosomatic symptoms, Shorter writes in *From Paralysis to Fatigue: A History of Psychosomatic Illness in the Modern Era*, a development that put the two in the same category.[7] When Shorter expands upon this theme in *A Historical Dictionary of Psychiatry* by adding, 'everybody understood that nerves meant psychiatry', he leaves no doubt that the Romantic-era nerve theorist was a doctor of the mind, as much as he was a physician.[8] Although the focus on nerves would seem to us today to indicate that these doctors devised a strictly materialistic, body-based approach to health, the understanding in the period of what nerves were helps to illustrate the truly psychological nature of nerve theory. Janet Oppenheim remarks in *'Shattered Nerves': Doctors, Patients, and Depression in Victorian England,* 'Increasingly, during the course of the eighteenth century, the idea of a nervous fluid conveyed the sense, not of an actual liquid, as denoted in the previous century, but of a so-called etherial or imponderable fluid', and this immaterial fluid was said to move through what Porter calls 'superfine, light, delicate fibers'.[9] Nerves and their contents were intangible physical realities, material enough to give the stamp of empirical proof to statements made about their metaphysical effects and spiritual enough to provide an escape route into more conservative, religious perspectives on the body for the vitalists.[10] The spiritual nature of nerves, their workings and their supposed connection with the soul established nerve theorists as ethical and moral guides for the individual and society as a whole.[11]

That nerve theory is a social construct is clear from the ethical duties it performed and demanded, so much so that the Cheynian 'body is a moral body', according to John Mullan.[12] Nerve theory proposed to govern relations between people. Yet, it is also social in epistemological terms. Shorter maintains that all psychosomatic illness, of which nervous illness is the historical exemplar,[13] is distinctly social in nature because patients understood and expressed their symptoms in ways that they thought would escape the medical practitioner's ridicule. Bynum argues in 'The Nervous Patient in Eighteenth- and Nineteenth-Century England: The Psychiatric Origins of British Neurology' that contemporary aetiologies of nervous illness continue to discover its social origins:

> nervous diseases were a class in which physical symptoms predominated but for which the evidence for structural derangement was lacking. Historians have been particularly intrigued by these "functional diseases", as they have come to be called, for they seem to show most clearly the cultural, social, and ideological factors which influence definitions and perceptions of disease, and constrain the behaviour of both patients and their doctors.[14]

This social configuration of nerve theory and nervous illness does not indicate its irrelevance to the more personal matters of the individual's self-understanding, though. As is the case with all psychological theory, it remains a discourse through which the modern subject perceives her self and expresses her self-reflexivity.

Although all of the nerve theorists in this chapter proclaim their democratic, egalitarian politics – such as by addressing their works to the lower classes as well as the high, or, in the case of Beddoes and Trotter, offering treatment for venereal disease when so many contemporary doctors avoided doing so out of fear of staining their reputations by association with ailments that were regarded as shameful – they also establish their contributions to disciplinary power in decisive ways. In *Nerves and Narratives*, Peter Melville Logan comments upon an aspect of nerve theory that demonstrates how the nerve theorist's work is integral to the formation of modern power:

> Thus, to be empirically effective, medicine must rely on more ephemeral qualities in the physician, qualities that few possess and that exceed the quantitative sum of rational knowledge: "Nature has endowed so few minds with that superior intelligence of being equal to this task, that we cannot be surprized when told, that medicine is still in many respects ' conjectural art'.[15]

The parallels between the nerve doctor's almost magical ability to perceive and treat illness and the moral manager's basilisk-like eye (which he could use to both control the patient and divine the truth of his illness) illustrate the connectedness of all psychological endeavour, especially in terms of the formation of disciplinary power. With regard to nerve theory, in particular, the establishment of both the subject's body and mind as mysterious by attributing their functions to the superfine fluids that no one could see, but which the nerve theorist claimed to understand and even control, helped to confirm the psychologist's mastery – and the subject's subjectedness.

Despite such delimitations, the general programme of nerve theory was unifying: it presented a broad social context for the delineation of one's innermost self or subjectivity (which, of course, ceased to be truly private through the external perspective and socially mediated discourse of psychology) and linked the physical body and the immaterial mind or soul, understood interchangeably as the seat of ethical, socially acceptable behaviour. The above quotation from Foucault encourages a reconsideration of the Romantic-era doctor as a hygienist ('it is the doctor's function as hygienist, rather than his prestige as a therapist, that assures him this politically privileged position in the eighteenth century'). Approaching the Romantic-era manifestation of British nerve theory, such as that of Perfect, Trotter and Beddoes, with reference to Foucault's idea of the doctor as hygienist is helpful because, arguably, their dedication to hygiene – or their delineation of a socio-psychological approach defined in terms of the developing idea of hygiene – distinguishes them from their forebears and contributes to our idea of a distinctly Romantic-era nerve theory. Significantly, two of the three announced their interests in this theme by writing poems and prose texts in praise of Hygeia when the related concept of hygiene was only beginning to gain currency. As I will show, all of these early psychologists devise an approach to mental health that reflects hygiene as an organizing principle through, for example, an emphasis on health maintenance (as opposed to production and cure), the avoidance of dangerous external elements, the need for regulation and the nerve theorist's role in social governance.

References to the Greek goddess of health, Hygeia, may be found throughout medical literature, but Darwin's invocation of her in *The Botanic Garden* was doubtlessly the inspiration for the increased interest in her for these psychologist-poets. (Beddoes, in particular, was a personal friend of Darwin and admitted the more famous poet as an influence on his poetry; he called his seminal text on nervous illness *Hygëia*). Until the end of the eighteenth century, the figure of Hygeia suggested simply the great value of good health by presenting the concept as a deity, but a close examination of the etymology of the words that derive from 'hygeia' reveal that they acquired during the Romantic period the more specific suggestions of governance, maintenance and rules for health through moderation. The following definition of 'hygiene' in the *OED* establishes it as a form of social governance as much as it is a distinct approach to health: 'That department of knowledge or practice which relates to the maintenance of health; a system of principles or rules for preserving or promoting health; sanitary science'. The earliest uses of the word in medical literature show that 'hygiene' referred to the preservation of health: according to the *OED*, the author known only by the initials 'A. M.' writes in his 1597 text on French surgery that 'Hygiena, [is that] ... which instructeth how we shoulde continuallye preserve our presente health', while, in *Lexicon Technicum, or An Universal English Dictionary of Arts and Sciences* (1704–10), John Harris defines 'Hygieina' as 'the Art of preserving Health'.[16] However, Robert Southey admits in 1796, 'I do not understand this word [i.e. 'Higiene'; Southey's spelling]; perhaps it means the doctrine of health' (quoted in *OED* online entry for 'hygiene').[17] Southey's admission that he does 'not understand this word' indicates that it had not yet passed into popular parlance, but the nerve theorists' texts show that it was gaining currency.

That 'hygiene' entailed not just the abstract study of health, but devised practices devoted to the maintenance of health is clear from a quotation from 1811, in which the word is defined as 'that division of therapia which treats of the diet of the sick'.[18] This Romantic-era use of 'hygiene' is most suggestive, as it links the concept firmly to nerve-theory, which, from Cheyne to Beddoes, Perfect and Trotter, had identified improper eating habits as a major source of nervous illness, a concept that I will develop below. For now, suffice it to say that food is only one of the external dangers that the nerve theorist attempts to regulate for the patient, or, rather, which he teaches the subject to regulate in her own experience in order to preserve health. Meanwhile, the first definition of 'hygienic' in the *OED* presents the related word as denoting a system of maintenance: 'Of or pertaining to the conditions affecting health, esp. with reference to cleanliness and precautions against infection and other deleterious influences; pertaining to or concerned with sanitation. Also occas. of conditions or surroundings: Free from deleterious influences'.[19] The last phrase of this definition regarding the need for vigilance against 'deleterious influences' in hygienic practice speaks volumes. The task of the hygienist is to counsel against external dangers of the physical and metaphysical sort, deleterious influences that may be edible or not. In today's common parlance, we focus on sanitation with reference to hygiene. For the good of society, to which we are inextricably tied, we must regulate our own cleanliness, we are told. We must also guard against the personal dangers presented by contamination in external society, which may undermine our very existences, threaten our selves, because, again, we are inextricably tied to society. Another way of looking at the Romantic-era hygienist's task of providing strictures for social and mental health is to say that, in part, it was devised to guard society against change and difference. In this sense, the nerve theorist-cum-hygienist was a master of the *status quo* and, with respect to Trotter, even a lover of primitivism. Perfect, Beddoes and Trotter show this aspect of their hygienic roles in their prose and verse paeans to country life, pre-civilized England and heroic ancient times.[20] It is a strange enough position for an otherwise radical trio and more evidence, perhaps, that the nerve theorist's literary identity was as Janus-faced as that of the moral manager.

With these definitions in mind, the links between the concept of hygiene and psychology become clear. Rather than helping the individual produce a new subjectivity, psychology claims to enable the individual to render the raw psychic materials already in existence into a clearly delineated, understood, communicable subjectivity. Because psychology purports to help you become more 'yourself' – to understand yourself, express yourself and be a more mentally (and existentially) sound you – it is deeply implicated in the practices of maintenance, or, in other words, mental hygiene. The three psychologist-poets in this chapter encourage their readers to understand them as hygienists by focusing on bodily and mental maintenance, prevention of deleterious influences and social governance. Beddoes announces himself as a hygienist in no uncertain terms in his most famous book of scientific prose, *Hygëia*, but his anti-colonial[21] poem *Alexander's Expedition* may also be regarded as contributory to his hygienic project in its underlying message about the dangers of external influences and the responsibility of literature to impart proper morals to readers. Perfect celebrates the goddess Hygeia in his verse alongside poems that preach a return to the rural English lifestyle, the health benefits of simple food and, especially, the value of gaining 'content', a word that represents the goal of all such self-regulation in his poetry. By comparing his poetry to his prose texts about nervous illness and related psychological conditions, such as *Cases of Insanity, the Epilepsy, Hypochondriacal Affection, Hysteric Passion, and Nervous Disorders, Successfully Treated*, the truly psychological tenor of Perfect's approach becomes clear.[22] Trotter does not mention hygiene, specifically, but his text *A View of the Nervous Temperament* leaves no doubt regarding to his commitment to disease prevention and the avoidance of harmful external factors. His long and longing prose passages about the former heartiness and vigour of the ancestors of pre-civilized England, as well as his poems – conventional in form and largely about the beauties of simplicity and the ancient English country lifestyle – confirm his dedication to maintaining the *status quo*. In each case, the ultimate goal of the nerve theorist is to govern the health of wider society and the socially oriented subject by encouraging the internalization of rules for its maintenance and danger-avoidance. Romantic-era nerve theory teaches self-regulation partly through raising awareness of the subject's social context and the need to control it.

The hygienic subject of nerve theory is defined by her relation to wider society. Her self-reflection focuses upon her ability to resist the deleterious influences of civilization, such as excessive drinking and eating – especially food that is not native to England – amongst other luxuries available in rich colonial countries, while the maintenance of personal health, in turn, affects the health of the body politic. In the new era of 'noso-political' power that developed out of eighteenth-century medicine, which was dominated by nerve theory, 'Doctors ... have the task of teaching individuals the basic rules of hygiene which they must respect for the sake of their own health and that of others'.[23] Truly, the hygienist's role was to govern on a personal and broadly social scale by devising rules for the maintenance of health and the avoidance of negative influences, while the subject's role was to develop a self-reflexivity – or, as Foucault would say, 'care of the self' – that echoed the nerve theorist's socially regulating approach. By viewing Romantic-era nerve theory in relation to the concept of hygiene and how it is deployed in the prose and poetry of Perfect, Trotter and Beddoes, we gain insight into the broader social programme of psychology at the time and the development of distinct cultures relative to the practice of nerve theory. All nerve doctors blamed luxury and wealth as the culprits for the nervous problems of the English nation, but the nerve theorists that I study in this chapter develop a therapeutic answer to the problem of luxury that illustrates their adherence to the Scottish Enlightenment principles that they imbibed with their medical education, since hygiene promotes moderation and the avoidance of excess through a return to simplicity. The critical commonplace explored in the previous chapter – that Cheynian nerve theory finds expression in the literature of sentiment – is sufficient evidence of its excesses and its opposition to moderation and regulation, for novels of sensibility celebrate aristocratic heroines dying for love, awash in tears, fainting with emotion and other histrionic absurdities. Moreover, the clear link between Cheynian nerve theory and elitism confirms that its cultural significance is distinct from the professedly democratic nerve theory of Perfect,

Beddoes and Trotter. Besides these Romantic-era nerve theorists' illustration of their desire to communicate to a wide audience through their poetry, they maintain that their nervous patients may come from every class of society. Moreover, their recommendations for avoiding nervousness uniformly include a return to simple, rural living, while, by contrast, the patients of Cheynian nerve theory revel in their superiority and, with guilty pleasure, their luxurious lifestyle.

II. William Perfect: Humility as Cure

Perfect's poetic emphasis on the moral goodness of a rural lifestyle and humble living echoes closely Beattie's and Cotton's sentiments on the subject – not to mention those of some of the most notable Romantic poets[24] – and this emphasis is related to his medical education in the Scottish Enlightenment and his particular role as a nerve theorist and hygienist. In his psychological prose, Perfect (1737–1809) argues that nervous illness springs from overindulgence in luxuries like rich and foreign food and a lack of quiet isolation and self-reflection. He uses his poetry to model a healthier lifestyle: he celebrates rural life and the calm, simple pleasures associated with it, thereby making his verse a dramatic illustration of the therapeutic technique he practised at his asylum in West Malling and an extension of his advice regarding how to avoid nervous illness. Perfect's earnest counsel that the reader reject the luxuries of society is not the only way that he shows his opposition to the aristocratic and literary culture of sensibility associated with Cheyne in the eighteenth century: by classifying nervous illness as a kind of insanity, Perfect posits the disease as undesirable, demonstrates his refusal to hone his diagnoses to flatter his rich patients and makes himself – rather than the patient – the ultimate authority.

A commentary about Perfect published within his lifetime describes his identity as a psychologist. This announcement, which seems to be more of an advertisement, appeared in a publication called *Seymour's New Survey of Kent*, which is reprinted on the page facing the title page in *Cases of Insanity, the Epilepsy, Hypochondriacal Affection, Hysteric Passion, and Nervous Disorders, Successfully Treated*. The description is worth quoting at length:

> Mr Perfect, a skilful and experienced Surgeon of this town, (West Malling) has fitted up divers convenient apartments, for the reception of all persons insane or immersed in the desponding abyss of melancholy; they are attended at his house with the affection of a parent, and the abilities of a man, who has, from study and observation, reduced into a practical science, the method of restoring the most wild and fixed madness, to cool sense and rational judgment: this Gentleman, actuated by a noble principle of universal benevolence, and a tender concern for the mental infirmities of his fellow creatures, has so far succeeded in the arduous task of curing demented individuals, as to deserve a singular favour and countenance from the legislature.[25]

In a few sentences, the author of this passage summarizes not only Perfect's medical character, but also several of the organizing principles behind his poetry. The 'skilful … Surgeon' shines through his references to medicine, his 'parent[al]' concern for his patients appears in his directives to live humbly and his 'benevolence' emerges in his disarming humour (such as in his poem, 'A Parody from Hamlet, Wrote when Indisposed and in Doubt about Bleeding', which includes the clever and revelatory echo, 'Thus Doctors do make Patients of us all').[26] Yet, perhaps most notable is the mention of Perfect's 'experience', his 'observation', his 'practical science'. Perfect was no detached theorist, but an actively engaged practitioner of mental medicine who wished to further connect himself to the wider public through his accessible verse, which may be understood as another mark of his education in the Scottish Enlightenment.

Indeed, even after he earned his MD in 1783 at St Andrews, Perfect was far from the proud and impractical 'college-boy' of whom the anonymous author of *Pharmacopolae Justificati* complains.[27] At the time that he wrote most of his poetry, Perfect belonged to several of the parties that the anonymous tract author tries to defend against the snobbish antics of physicians. As Shirley Burgoyne Black reports in her short biography of the psychologist-poet, Perfect started his medical career in 1757 as a 'man-midwife' – which was still quite novel, since men only started practising midwifery after 1730 – and he was also a surgeon and apothecary.[28] In the very year that he earned his medical degree, he published the second volume of *Cases in Midwifery* and continued to act as an asylum-owner after he received his medical degree in Scotland, which suggests that his formal education alienated him from neither his fellow 'lowly' midwives nor his unfortunate charges in any of his several asylums.[29] Our psychologist-poet had intense, personal contact with his numerous mental patients in his asylums, contact that many doctors in the eighteenth century would have perceived as beneath their dignity. This experience alone could be said to constitute his personal claim to humility, the moral and psychological good that he lauds throughout his poetry, but Perfect showed his concern for the downtrodden of society in other ways, as well. As Black points out, Perfect offered treatment to the poor, even if they could not pay; upon the presentation of a note from their parishes recognizing their straitened circumstances, the good doctor would give them a course of medicine for free.[30] Clearly, the emphasis on the moral directives for humility and generosity that characterizes his poetry also characterized his own medical practice.

In *Address to the Public*, Perfect underlines his egalitarian approach to psychological knowledge. He describes the deplorable state of madhouses, protesting that many impoverished patients have suffered at the hands of keepers who "have punished with the hand of relentless severity their cries and lamentations, which evinced the sense of all their woes and injuries, as the clamorous ravings of madness and phrenzy, and often anticipated by these nefarious acts of implacable rigour and sordid knavery, the very evils which they should have endeavoured to redress and prevent".[31]

Perfect takes the part of the helpless insane against their keepers, the asylum authorities with whom he would have been identified as an asylum-owner himself and he subtly accuses the keepers of acting in a way that makes them indistinguishable from their charges, thereby levelling the playing field between those who controlled the insane and the insane themselves.[32] He effects a similarly democratic move in *Cases of Insanity, the Epilepsy, Hypochondriacal Affection, Hysteric Passion, and Nervous Disorders, Successfully Treated.* In this volume, Perfect takes the mystery out of psychology by elucidating his methods of treatment. The fact that it went on to be republished as *Select Cases in the Different Species of Insanity, Lunacy, or Madness, with the Modes of Practice as Adopted in the Treatment of Each* in 1787 – and was later complemented by *A Remarkable Case of Madness, With the Diet and Medicines, Used in the Cure* in 1791 – suggests that the volume sold so well that its audience could not have been limited to the select few who were medical practitioners.[33] Put simply, Perfect wrote pop-psychology, the prose complement to his verse.[34] In the preface to *Cases of Insanity*, Perfect declares that he writes out of 'anxious care to improve the most important branches of his profession, by the faithful communication of some practical truths, selected from cases successfully treated, with an earnest desire to disseminate whatever may be in his power to collect for the direction of assistance of others'.[35] His emphasis on accessibility and the dissemination of knowledge mark Perfect as a true inheritor and purveyor of Scottish Enlightenment principles.

In its accessibility to the wider public, Perfect's medical prose may be said to capitalize on a literary fashion for self-help medical texts inaugurated, in part, by George Cheyne with his bestselling text from 1733, *The English Malady: or, A Treatise of Nervous Diseases of All Kinds, as Spleen, Vapours, Lowness of Spirits, Hypochondriacal, and Hysterical Distempers &c.* This text put the identification of disease into the hands of the lay reader – and increased its prevalence, I contend, because it made nervous illness desirable for social reasons. *The English Malady* had a profound effect upon the cultural attitude regarding melancholy, the nervous illness upon which Cheyne focuses in this text. After the publication of Dr Cheyne's text, melancholy was regarded as indicating the sufferer's distinct Englishness – for melancholy is the 'English Malady' to which he refers in the title – as well as his superior sensibility and wealth, even while it rescued the subject from imputations of insanity.[36] Referring to England's naval and colonial exploits, Cheyne opines,

> Since our Wealth has increas'd, and our Navigation has been extended, we have
> ransack'd all parts of the *Globe* to bring together its whole Stock of Materials for *Riot,
> Luxury,* and *Excess.* The Tables of the Rich and Great ... are furnish'd with Provisions
> of Delicacy, Number and Plenty.[37]

Members of the aristocracy are particularly susceptible to the 'English Malady'
because of their habits of '*Idleness* and *Luxury*', both signs of English wealth (they
are 'idle' because they are rich enough not to work) and colonial success (rich
foreign foods crowd their tables and distended stomachs).[38] Such habits strain
their delicate nerves, which he compares to the luxurious and foreign material
'Silk'.[39] In other words, if a person is so rich that she can afford all the fine foods
the world has to offer, can idle around instead of working and is so high class
that her very body takes on the qualities of fine, exotic fabric, then she may, upon
perusal of Cheyne's text, decide that she is plagued with the 'English Malady'.

While some critics have identified a moral judgment behind Cheyne's identification of the 'English Malady' as the product of gluttony and luxurious living,[40]
a closer examination of Cheyne's text reveals that his definition of the disorder
practically made it a compliment to be diagnosed with melancholy. Further-
more, by distinguishing between melancholy and madness, Cheyne attempted
to protect his rich patients from any accusations of insanity. He declared that
only the coarse and ignorant would mistake one for the other: '*nervous* Distempers ... are under some Kind of *Disgrace* and *Imputation*, in the Opinion of
the *Vulgar* and *Unlearned*; they pass among the Multitude for a lower Degree
of *Lunacy*, and the first Step towards a *distemper'd Brain*'.[41] Cheyne's declaration that nervous illness was categorically different from madness – and, in that
sense, any undesirable, permanent, or uncontrollable disease – was seized upon
by members of the upper classes who wished to steer clear of a diagnosis of their
ills that would undermine their social positions and honour. In what is perhaps
the most famous instance of this phenomenon, King George III attempted to
convince his court, when he fell into his first fits of insanity, '"I'm nervous, I'm
not ill, but I'm nervous"'.[42]

However, as Perfect's prose and verse shows, some later nerve theorists maintained that melancholy was, indeed, a type of madness. We may even surmise that
these psychologist-poets wrote at such length about the mentally harmful effects
of an immodest lifestyle in order to protest against the popular Cheynian definition of melancholy as a disease of which one should be proud.[43] Perfect agreed
with Cheyne that bad nerves were a sign of wealth, but, while Cheyne added
that nervous illness was a sign of the sufferers' greater emotional sensitivity and
sympathy, thereby protecting them from imputations of insanity, Perfect framed
bad nerves as the result of greed, decadence and mental instability.[44] Cheyne's
diagnosis actually fostered histrionics, not moderation, for one displayed one's
wealth and aristocratic sensitivity through fits of fainting and weeping. Cheyne's

supposed finger-wagging about luxury and gluttony are actually incentives for both, since the nervous patient is more English and superior to others in sensibility and class. By contrast, Perfect made nervous illness undesirable by associating it with madness, he made wealth and rich food truly dangerous and he made himself, not the rich patient and patron, the ultimate moral authority. His related pronouncements in verse and prose mark Perfect as one of the new breed of hygienists, who taught mental and bodily health through self-governance, maintenance and the avoidance of external deleterious influences.

To say the least, Perfect did not wholeheartedly agree with the esteemed Cheyne when the latter opposed nervous complaints, or melancholy, to madness. Perfect makes his dissent clear in the preface to *Cases of Insanity*:

> The cure of maniacal patients must ever be esteemed an object of the last importance to individuals, as well as to society in general; Hypochondriacal, Hysterical, and Nervous Complaints have ... engrossed much of the writer's time and attention, as in numberless cases some one or other of those diseases has apparently been the leading principle to the various species of madness.[45]

The same 'Nervous Complaints' that Cheyne would identify as a mark of his patients' superiority are here presented as the first steps towards insanity. Perfect must certainly have been familiar with Cheyne's famous text, but he seems unconcerned that, in the above passage, he marks himself out as one of the '*Unlearned* ... Multitude' according to Cheyne's pronouncement concerning all who associate nervous illness with madness.[46] In this statement, Perfect also shows his theoretical kinship with Beddoes, who similarly argues that nervous illness is the root cause of all other types of mental ailments in *Hygëia*. By framing his identification of nervous illness with insanity in a social context ('The cure of maniacal patients must ever be esteemed an object of the last importance to individuals, as well as to society in general'), Perfect defines himself as a governor of social ills – a true hygienist – as much as he is healer of the individual mind and body.

In *Cases of Insanity ... and Nervous Disorders, Successfully Treated*, Perfect sometimes illustrates his sympathy with earlier nerve theorists like Cheyne, even while he indicates how his differences posit him and the subject defined by his psychological theories in a unique light. Of the non-hereditary causes of madness, Perfect lists 'Anxiety, excessive Grief, Frights, Intenseness of Study, irregular Living, or strong and ungoverned Passions', as well as 'chronical congestions, occasioned by gluttony or idleness'; earlier nerve theorists attributed nervous disease to precisely the same factors.[47] Moreover, Perfect implicitly urges control over 'strong ... Passions', that scourge of the sensitive, and 'gluttony or idleness', the downfall of the wealthy, in order to maintain a healthy balance in mind and body.[48] Yet, the fact that Perfect links what would be commonly understood as the causes of nervous illness to 'madness' constitutes his major difference from earlier nerve theorists, especially Cheyne. While James Boswell could confess, '"We hypochondriacks ... may console ourselves in the hour of gloomy distress, by thinking that our sufferings make our superiority"',[49] no patient or reader of Perfect could be so self-congratulatory over his diagnosis, which Perfect further defines in this preface as '"Reason buried in the Body's Grave"'.[50] This definition of madness shows its roots in nerve theory by linking the body and mind, as well as its existential consequences by betokening the death of the healthy mind in the tomb of the body. This warning speaks to the utter necessity of adopting the nerve theorist's strictures, the psychologist's definition of healthy subjectivity: refusal to do so is to be non-existent.

The personal effects of adopting the tenets of nerve theory are as crucial for the individual who is called upon to define herself in accordance with them as with any psychological discourse, but Perfect, like Beddoes and Trotter, illustrates the broadly social scope of his form of mental and bodily governance through some of his specific treatments, as well as in his poetry. In the above preface, Perfect notes that one of the forms of treatment in his asylum is to refuse visitors to the patients, presumably to control the social influences upon them as he does other external factors, like food and drink.[51] All of these aspects of his therapeutic approach point to his role as a hygienist, one who advises individuals with reference to their place in wider society and vice versa, and whose approach focuses on the dangers of external influences. Thus, when Perfect writes in the preface to *The Laurel-Wreath* that his poems 'were written as the recreation of some *solitary*, many *pensive*, and some *leisure* hours, when disengaged from the weightier concerns of my *avocation* in life', he does not assert that the topics that form the lessons of his poetry are frivolous.[52] Rather, he presents his poems as dramatic illustrations of the benefits of isolation and meditation, not only for the poet, but also for wider society, which benefits from reading the verse. The theme of isolation as therapeutic through its limitation of the subject's exposure to external influences, represented by society and phenomena related to it, becomes an organizing principle in Perfect's poetry. His verse may therefore be regarded as an attempt to encourage his reader to accept his medical advice by presenting attractive images and scenes that depict the felicity attendant upon its adoption.

In *The Bavin of Bays: Containing Various Original Essays in Poetry* and *The Laurel-Wreath; Being a Collection of Original Miscellaneous Poems, On Subjects Moral, Comic, and Divine*, Perfect carries out his promise in the preface to the latter volume 'to *amuse*, if not *improve*' the reader in these 'poetical Essays'.[53] In this statement of purpose, Perfect – like Ferriar, as I mention in Chapter 2 and, on some level, all of the psychologist-poets – surely responds to Horace's famous formulation about the purpose of poetry as, ideally, both '*dulce et utile*', or 'pleasing and useful'.[54] Similarly, in 'Essay on Akenside's Poem on the *Pleasures of Imagination*', Anna Letitia Barbauld describes Erasmus Darwin's verse as exemplary of what she calls 'Didactic, or prescriptive Poetry', and, in the following quotation, she singles out poetry about medicine to discuss the relative merits of didactic poetry:

> Allured perhaps too much ... by the hopes of novelty, hardly any branch of knowledge has been so abstruse, or so barren of delight as not to have afforded a subject to the Didactic Poet. Even the loathsomeness of disease and the dry maxims of medical knowledge have been decorated with the charms of Poetry.[55]

Barbauld's comment upon the 'charms of Poetry' as capable of mitigating the less enchanting qualities of didacticism and medical subject matter expresses Perfect's purpose aptly. His prose documents about mental illness are composed mostly of case histories of insanity with brief introductory sections that delineate his theory of disease, neither of which seem designed to engage the lay reader in the fashion of, for example, Bakewell's *The Domestic Guide*. His poetry, however, is replete with appealing *vignettes* of meditative isolation, the very kinds of scenes that his psychological therapy was intended to produce.

Perfect hones his role as a governor of health whose concern for social relations forms a major aspect of his therapeutic approach to mental health in many of his poems. The poet's advice to lead a humble, rural lifestyle in 'Solitude: An Ode' from *The Laurel-Wreath* is clearly linked to his theory that removal from society can calm the nervous, or mad, mind, which he also hoped to address by establishing his asylum in the countryside. In the first two stanzas, the psychologist-poet illustrates that 'contentment', a word he uses often as shorthand for mental health, derives from the solitary contemplation associated with rural life. Moreover, the 'mind' and 'soul' are described as privy to the same influences, which emphasizes the spiritual side of nerve theory, as well as Perfect's commonalities with Cotton and Beattie:

> Hail, blest retreat, where Solitude
> With calmness fills my breast!
> Where worldly tumults ne'er intrude,
> To interupt my rest.
>   Where Sleep refreshing holds the night,
> And lulls the easy mind:
> No empty fears the soul affright,
> To Providence resign'd.[56]

He goes on to note that 'Contemplation' brings these boons and later hints that he made this discovery in his work as a doctor:

> *Here* solid pleasures ever flow,
> And Science's glories rife,
> To teach my heart this truth to know,
> "From Riches' Perils rise".[57]

In the next two stanzas, Perfect confirms our suspicion that his advice is derived from his profession as a psychologist by asserting that 'Reason is ... [his] faithful guide' to the contemplative 'retreat' of which he writes and which provides protection from 'Folly' and 'madness'.[58] He ends the poem by characterizing this retreat as being opposed to city life and high society:

> The Court and Play, as pompous wiles,
> I from my breast repel:
> And banish Fortune's jilting smiles,
> In Solitude to dwell.[59]

Because it is associated with 'Pride' and 'pompous wiles', which are opposed to humility, luxurious living does not allow for the quiet contemplation in nature that Perfect establishes as essential to mental health. While Cheyne's nerve theory seems more intent on helping his readers to perform their social standing and worth, Perfect advises Rousseauvian retreat.

Indeed, throughout his poetry, Perfect establishes himself as an early hygienist; that is to say, he is a doctor-cum-social governor devoted to providing rules for the maintenance of original health through the avoidance of external dangers. Perfect's most direct encomium to hygiene appears in a poem that summarizes his major concerns as a nerve theorist. In 'To Solitude', Perfect celebrates 'Content[ment]', 'Science' and 'Hygeia' (the goddess of health) as associated with a modest diet:

> Divested of trouble and strife,
> Let Science and Peace with me dwell;
> Thy whispers, Content, soothe my life,
> And Solitude sanction my cell.
> Though plain my repast be, yet there should I find
> Hygeia most bland and Minerva most kind.[60]

By linking 'plain' food to the attainment of 'Content', Perfect shows the important role it plays in his overall plan for poetic therapy: he uses verse to encourage his reader to imbibe his rules for the maintenance of health and avoidance of that which can destroy efforts to maintain good health, like rich food.

In another poem from this volume, Perfect confirms that joint mental and bodily health can only be attained by following his rules for the avoidance of external dangers, such as foreign luxuries. 'Contentment, An Ode' establishes that, for Perfect, 'contentment' or 'content' denotes a peaceful state of mind that is equally identifiable with emotional and spiritual wellbeing, a holistic concept that speaks to Perfect's identity as a hygienist and nerve theorist. Just as Cotton describes the personification of that quality with reference to humble living in the poem called 'Content' ('CONTENT shuns Courts, and oft'ner dwells/ With modest Worth in humble Cells'), Perfect devotes an entire poem to the topic and provides similar instructions regarding how to gain contentment, that is, through a humble lifestyle.[61] 'Contentment, An Ode' begins,

> Content! Thou balm of human life,
> In whom we ever find
>
> ....
>
>   Thy blest effects can riches bring,
> And such as safe endure,
> Beyond the charms of India's gold,
> More permanent and sure.
>   For, tho' thou may'st not always heal
> Disquietude of mind:
> Thy contribution yields the pow'r
> To keep the soul resign'd.[62]

In eliding the soul and mind again, Perfect indicates that the same type of therapy might be expected to have an effect on both, as can be expected from a psychologist studying the etherial fluids coursing through those superfine, almost immaterial, fibres, the nerves. The poet also clearly opposes 'contentment' to having wealth and thereby suggests that the rich cannot have mental peace. Perfect's role as a hygienist is, moreover, confirmed in his particular description of the external influences that threaten mental and bodily health: by referring to luxury metonymically in the phrase 'India's gold', Perfect underlines the foreignness of this dangerous external influence, a colonial trope that both Trotter and Beddoes develop, as well. Only by maintaining the sanctity of our bodies through his advice may we escape 'disquietude of mind'.[63] As I will explain further with reference to Trotter below, the foreignness of the luxury item signifies the culpability accrued in the way that it was obtained, such as through colonialism. It is as though the moral stain associated with the procurement of foreign luxury items manifests itself through the body as diseased nerves, which themselves occupy a liminal position between the spiritual and physical.

    In other poems, Perfect provides several reasons why contentment eludes the rich, all of which echo the factors that predispose one to nervous illness. In 'Ode to Poverty', Perfect echoes Cheyne, Trotter and Beddoes, all of whom trace nervous debility to overindulgence in foreign food:

> Contented Poverty's his lot;
> Security attends

> The narrow limits of his power,
> And Health his days befriends.
>   He fears no thieves – (the miser's dread);
> His morsel can enjoy
> With one true unmolested taste;
> His food will never cloy.
>   Not so with those, whose tables spread
> With meats luxuriously,
> Prepar'd and dress'd with Gallic art,
> Where thick diseases lie.
>   His fate, tho' poor, ne'er wounds his mind
> Or moves to rage his breast.[64]

Again, Perfect attests that the external influence of food is dangerous not just because it threatens the boundaries of the body, but because of its foreignness, to which he gestures with the adjective 'Gallic'. In this case, though, the moral danger presented to the nervous body is not the product of cruel colonialism, not the booty from 'ransack[ing] the glob' as Cheyne puts it in *The English Malady*. However, this food is, nevertheless, an external danger twice over: all food is a threat to the sanctity of the human body and its French foreignness further marks it out as threat to the autonomy of the body politic.[65] In 1766, the concept of French food would not have set off Revolutionary alarm bells, but rather associations with decadence and dissipation, positing it as a moral threat in physical form. Just as the modern-day hygienist teaches us to avoid the dangers external to the body, like germs and viruses, partly by advising each person in society to care for her own personal sanitation, Perfect teaches his reader how to 'befriend' 'Health' and avoid 'wound[ing] his mind' by shunning the external influence of rich foreign food.[66] While his meditation on the dangers of foreign food may show his adoption of some aspects of Cheynian nerve theory, though Perfect states clearly the disparity between their approaches by identifying insanity as a danger of insufficient self-regulation.

In 'To Health', Perfect rounds out the contours of his identity as a hygienist through the trope of excessive food as a dangerous luxury that can spoil the purity of the body and soul. Although he fixes his eye firmly on the general concept identified as the addressee of this apostrophe, his carefully chosen vocabulary suggests that he refers to mental health as surely as he refers to bodily health, thereby underlining his holistic approach as a nerve theorist. Perfect discusses the high life, again depicted through an image of gluttony, in terms of its psychological effects. I give the poem in its entirety:

>   Rich Buxom bliss, that Wealth exceeds.
> Whose blessing none excels:
> Oh! say, where thou has fixt thy seat,
> Where unmolested dwells?

Do palaces, or gilded roofs,
Thy balmy joys secure?
Do crowns of gold, or purple state,
Enjoy thee blithe and pure?
    What say'st thou, foul intemperance
With glutton grandeur lives,
And dire Pandora's anguish'd train
Of foul distempers gives?
    Which to the cot, and humble cell,
Is rare if ever known:
'Tis there, you chuse in peace to dwell,
And fix your blooming throne.

Such phrases as 'foul intemperance', 'anguish'd train' and 'foul distempers' present physical health as intricately connected to mental effects. Perfect thereby echoes his prose assertion, so typical of a nerve theorist, that bodily health and mental health are connected. Crucially, the moralistic celebration of a humble lifestyle reveals the wider cultural effect of the nerve theorist's holistic approach to health: by yoking together social and ethical action with mental health, the nerve theorist becomes, truly, a governor in wider social terms. As I will show with reference to Trotter, this holistic approach also alters the identity of the subject, whose body becomes a public site that may or may not display his capacity to relate to his community in a healthy way, mentally and physically.

III. Thomas Trotter: Ingestion, Colonization and Enervation

Trotter's identity as a nerve theorist is evident from his attention to the negative effects of irresponsible ingestion, but, while Cheyne and Perfect, amongst others, focus on the deleterious effects of rich – especially foreign food – Trotter (1760–1832) established his fame in the annals of medical writing by penning the first text on alcoholism as a psychological ailment. The focus of nerve theorists upon consumption of all sorts reveals its roots in traditional humouralism, in which food and drink were sometimes identified as the culprits responsible for upsetting bodily balances of bile, blood and other vital fluids.[67] Similarly, nerve theorists maintained that the dangers of food and drink lay in their ability to upset the delicate physical make-up of the nerves and the fluids that flowed through them but, unlike humouralists, nerve theorists added a greater social dimension to their discussion of the effects of consumption upon nerves by attributing the increased access to rich food to greater class and wealth, while their discussion of foreign foods implicitly reflects the moral dangers posed by England's colonial exploits. Since later nerve theorists, like Trotter and Beddoes, also associate nerves with mental illness, this newly social context also became the context within which the concept of subjectivity – the healthy, reflective mind – was formed. Thus, the need for self-regulation with reference to the consumption of food and drink becomes the physical, social and generally external expression of self-reflection.[68] Trotter, for his part, was apparently well aware that his object of study was not simply the individual, but the whole of society and the relations within it: in the preface to *A View of the Nervous Temperament*, he writes that his examination of 'The inhabitants of a large town ... may be construed into a kind of medical analysis of society'.[69] This baker's son from Melrose, Roxburghshire, born the same year as Beddoes (1760), may with great justice be called an early expert on 'social pathology'.[70]

Trotter is best known for *A View of the Nervous Temperament*, which resumed the in-depth study of nerves that had previously been accomplished by his mentor, Cullen. In this work, Trotter argues that England had by his time become decadent, too luxurious and recommended 'recurring to simplicity of living and manners, so as to check the increasing prevalence of nervous disorders; which, if not restrained soon, must inevitably sap our physical strength of constitution; make us an easy conquest to our invader; and ultimately convert us into a nation of slaves and idiots'.[71] Given that the situation he describes here is connected to England's 'commercial greatness' at sea, Trotter seems to fear that the country would fall prey to the very threats that it was itself imposing on others, in a kind of uncanny reversal of fortune that would make the colonialists – those great purveyors of slaves – themselves the slaves, but of success.[72] Trotter confirms this suggestion later in the study, where he bemoans,

> The East and West Indies at this moment, are a theatre of oppression and slavery, to gorge her with commercial wealth; and a district of Africa, larger than Europe, is made a field of blood, to purchase the natives for cultivating her colonies, whose produce only tends to weaken her manly character, and overwhelm her with nervous infirmities![73]

The 'produce' to which Trotter refers here might certainly be tropical and unusual foods, but, given his special interest in alcoholism, Trotter probably has in mind the most potent new import of the East and West Indies: rum. In this passage, Trotter paints a picture of mass degeneration, linking the demise of the slaves directly to the enervation of the English. Having acted in 1783 as a naval surgeon aboard a slave-ship sailing from Liverpool to the West Indies, Trotter knew well the horrors of slave-trading: he lobbied hard for fresh and varied food for the cargo of slaves, but the owner refused his demands because of the extra cost – and a violent outbreak of scurvy amongst the slaves resulted.[74] Trotter's treatment of nervous illness in his best-known text gestures to the damage done when the English body politic expands her borders through colonial exploits and opens herself to the deleterious influences of the products of other nations.

Trotter's attention, so common in nerve theory, to the dangers of foreign 'produce' is a powerful confirmation of the nerve theorist's social role as a hygienist: his target is a external danger twice over – foreign comestibles cross the boundary of the body in being consumed, as well as the nation's proper bounds – and it threatens the natural balance of the inviolable, healthy English subject. The fact that colonial exploits entailed slave-trading and other morally fraught endeavours underlines why the foreignness of the produce was associated with nervous illness, which, I have shown, was defined as manifesting moral and ethical transgressions in the body. To use Trotter's terms, England's 'manly character' leads her to success in the trying conditions on a ship at sea and in the colonies, but this very success weakens her with the 'nervous infirmities' brought about by strong drink, a gendered diagnosis that Logan identifies as characteristic of discussions of nervous illness in *Nerves and Narratives*.[75] Later in the same text, Trotter gestures to the contagious quality of nervous illness that is acquired by making the borders of the body politic too porous when he traces the explosion in new cases to 'Persons returned from the colonies'.[76] As a hygienist, Trotter advises how to maintain and preserve the original character of 'manliness' that England loses to such external forces. Perfect connected such dangers to English cities and Trotter, too, warns against the dangers of the city ('The remote causes of nervous diseases are chiefly to be sought in populous towns; and increase in proportion to the deviation from simplicity of living'), but his focus on colonial exploits illutrate his belief that locales beyond England's borders harbour the worst dangers of all.[77]

Trotter's writings and orientation in the medical community reflect his liberal politics as a Scot who completed his medical degree at Edinburgh University.[78] For example, his pronouncements upon the dangers of the uncontrolled consumption of food in *A View of the Nervous Temperament* echo similar calls for the subject's attention to medical rules for the maintenance of health – which may be summarized as the avoidance of the lifestyle of the rich and famous – in an earlier text Trotter called *An Essay ... on Drunkenness*. Porter elucidates the links between the texts thus: 'Chemical stimuli such as alcohol excited the senses; this action in turn eroded the nervous system, producing the "nervous temperament"; this disposition affected the psyche; and, finally, the imagination begat fresh desires, triggering chain reactions of cravings'.[79] *An Essay ... on Drunkenness* is Trotter's most original contribution to psychiatric theory, as it is among the first treatments of alcoholism as a disease of the mind, a sympathetic position that also reveals his humane politics. In Trotter's view, the alcoholic is not a sinner, but the victim of a mental affliction. 'In medical language', Trotter states early in the text, 'I consider drunkenness, strictly speaking, to be a disease' and, later in the work, he develops this concept in a way that illustrates the boundary-straddling quality of nerve theory, which brings together the study of society and the individual, the body and mind, the physical and spiritual: 'It is to be remembered that a bodily infirmity is not the only thing to be corrected. *The habit of drunkenness is a disease of the mind.* The soul itself has received impressions that are incompatible with its reasoning powers'.[80] He contends that the 'soul' and the body depend upon each other for proper balance, as well as that the soul and the mind, as the seat of reason, are the same faculty.[81]

Trotter depended on his extensive practical experience to support these daring claims, since he had many opportunities to observe the effects of 'drunkenness', as he calls it, in his duties as physician to the Channel Fleet and the Royal Naval Hospital. These experiences made him an active proponent of sobriety: he was responsible for the closure of 200 gin shops in Plymouth alone.[82] In *An Essay ... on Drunkenness*, Trotter distinguishes himself from most other writers who treated the subject before his time by refusing to preach at and judge his patients for an ailment that many in English society, medical professionals and laymen alike, saw as shameful. Sympathetically, he advises the physician who wishes to treat the alcoholic to 'consult his own experience of human nature, and what he has learned in the school of the world'.[83] By suggesting that the doctor may find the rules for proper treatment in his own experience, Trotter reminds his fellow psychologists that they are not essentially different from these unfortunate sufferers. His earnest desire to treat all who were ill illustrates Trotter's intellectual heritage as a pupil of the Whiggish medical schools of the Scottish Enlightenment.

Trotter's holistic approach also illustrates his intellectual heritage: just as the Scottish Enlightenment doctor was expected to be an active contributor to the literary culture of his time as much as the scientific, the patient's social circumstances were understood to be linked to his bodily and mental state. Through the social realm, Trotter's texts on 'drunkenness' and nervousness are related. Trotter states clearly in *Nervous Temperament* that advances in civilization are responsible for what he saw as the great rise in nervous illnesses in English society. Calling nervous complaints 'the progeny of wealth, luxury, indolence, and intemperance', the bane in disguise of the colonially and commercially successful English society of the Romantic period, Trotter muses,

> Where the earth is thinly peopled, and when commerce has made no progress, mankind live chiefly in families; and their habits and employments uniformly inculcate temperance and sobriety. Society and population must be far advanced, before luxurious living, and vicious customs, attain such growth as to enervate the human frame.[84]

With its focus on the benefits of 'temperance' and 'sobriety', this comment illustrates how closely related are his studies of nervous illness and drunkenness, but it also shows his belief that both physico-mental ailments are the products of social – and colonial – advancement.

Trotter's particular approach to the social aspect of mental illness distinguishes him from his forbears in nerve theory, such as Cheyne, and motivated his decision to write accessible verse and prose as a means of illustrating his psychological insights. In the first pages of *Nervous Temperament*, Trotter reforms the longstanding link between nervous illness and class. After quoting from *The English Malady*, he comments that the passage illustrates Cheyne's position that nervous disorders affect 'people of condition in England: from which we are led to believe they were then little known among the inferiour orders'; however, he continues, 'we shall find that nervous ailments are no longer confined to the better ranks in life, but rapidly expanding to the poorer classes', thanks to Britain's recent acquisition of 'vast wealth, so diffused among all ranks of people'.[85] He does not deny that Cheyne's proclamations about the link between class and nervous illness is true in some situations and he even confirms the link between nervous illness and the aristocratic woman of sensibility when he writes, 'the genteel lady is stretched on her couch, often a prey to some nervous affection, but always slow in convalescence', but he attempts to expand the popular notion of who may be afflicted by nervous illness when he asserts, 'Women of very moderate fortune, and the wives and daughters of all reputable tradesmen, in this country, may be said to indulge in most of the follies of their superiors'.[86] Trotter's reformation of Cheyne's proclamations about the cultural effects of nerves illustrates his democratic politics, so different from Cheyne's aristocratic aspirations. Trotter shows that he is concerned for the health of all classes of Britons and refuses to flatter and coddle the upper classes.

Most importantly for the development of the cultural identity of the nerve theorist in the Romantic period, Trotter shows in this unpopular definition of nervous illness that he, not the patient, is the 'master of madness'. As such, his warnings and recommended therapies for the treatment of nervous illness manifest his role as a governor and regulator, a true hygienist, for he recommends the preservation of the body (politic) through the avoidance of deleterious influences brought to an English society bastardized and weakened by the proceeds of colonialism. Trotter's reformation of the relationship between the nerve theorist and subject allies him with Perfect, whose identification of nervous illness as madness had many of the same effects. In *An Essay ... on Drunkenness*, Trotter warns:

> when apprehensions of danger, ill-grounded fears, and low spirits, accompany impaired digestions, the disease may then be named *hypochondriasis*. And when both these affections are present, while at the same time the mental disquietudes arise to derangement of intellect, or delirium, then only would I call the disease *melancholy*.[87]

By linking 'hypochondriasis' and 'melancholy' – those illnesses that Cheyne identified as belonging to the class of 'nervous diseases' in the long title of his major text (*The English Malady: or, A Treatise of Nervous Diseases of All Kinds, as Spleen, Vapours, Lowness of Spirits, Hypochondriacal, and Hysterical Distempers &c.*) – with 'derangement of intellect, or delirium', Trotter identifies nervous illness as a form of insanity.[88] Thus, when Trotter celebrates moderation, rural living and, ultimately, humility in his verse and prose, he is not using popular literary topics only for the sake of garnering applause from a reading public that had shown their appetite for such fare. Through these themes, Trotter presents his therapeutic approach to good mental health and, through the pleasing form of verse, he attempts to produce his reader's approval and adoption of his advice. Poetry thereby becomes a tool for the dissemination of advice for good mental hygiene.

That Trotter used his poetry to present his psychological theories to a wide reading public is suggested by the prose texts. '[H]e was not primarily, or at least not solely, targeting the *Essay* [... *on Drunkenness*] at a professional, medical readership', Porter insists, adding,

> Written in an entertaining and often personal style, and laced with anecdotes and asides, the work is far from being a dry handbook or technical treatise on habitual drunkenness, methodically detailing its diagnosis and treatment, and listing clinical case histories and therapeutics ... [H]e was clearly putting himself through his paces as a man of letters – an ambition eventually manifesting itself in his plays and verse.[89]

Trotter marries his identities of doctor and poet through the theme of humility and prepares his audience to recognize this elision by gesturing to his literary identity in his psychological writings. He begins several chapters in *The Essay ... on Drunkenness* with epigraphs from Shakespeare, while 'extracts from Horace, Virgil, James Thomson, Robert Burton and other literary lions are spliced into the text'.[90] He also shows his awareness of, and perhaps his desire to identify himself with, the tradition of psychologist-poets by discussing the verse of Erasmus Darwin, whom he calls 'A modern British physician of great eminence, himself a poet, far above mediocrity, both in his medical and metrical works'.[91] Most notably, though, Trotter indicates his view that writing poetry – the very act of versifying – is historically and intrinsically aligned with plain living, a lifestyle free of decadence and intoxication, thereby hinting that his psychological advice and his own versifying go hand in hand:

> Poetry, the first of the fine arts, took its rise among shepherds in the early ages of society, when the manners of mankind, as well as their diet, were simple; when the fermentation of the juice of the grape was unknown, and when the vine itself, either sprung up spontaneously, or was only cultivated as a fruit-tree.[92]

Shepherds, the original poets, Trotter claims, were the great purveyors of the glories of the simple life. The writing of poetry and the right way to live are historically bound, he asserts. Trotter, physician to slaves, mariners and alcoholics, replicates the same egalitarian principles that led him to care for those members of society that the aristocratic Cheyne would have shuddered to touch by dramatically illustrating his advice in both his medical prose and his poetry. His treatise on alcoholism not only anticipates his call for a return to simplicity in *A View of the Nervous Temperament*, but it also prepares his audience to recognize the significance of his references to humble subject-matter in *Sea-Weeds: Poems, Written on Various Occasions, Chiefly During a Naval Life*, the collected book of poetry from 1829 that brings together some of the verse he had written over a quarter of a century and resurrects, in its naval theme, his earlier long poem, *Suspiria Oceani*.[93] The kind of simplicity that Trotter lauds in *Sea-Weeds* is of the Rousseauvian sort that influenced the canonical Romantic poets so profoundly, but the difference between Trotter and these more popular poets is that Trotter's praise of simplicity has the weight of his considerable medical education and practice behind it, as well as the urgency of a doctor's orders regarding mental health.

In Trotter's poetry and prose, the established literary fashion of celebrating rural life and simple living takes on a psychological dimension because it is integrally related to his particular approach as a nerve theorist. While many of the poems in *Sea-Weeds* – such as 'The Cruize', 'The Life-Boat', 'Looks and Eyes', and 'The Furze Blossom' – are typically eighteenth-century style treatments in pairs of rhyming lines about such subjects as seafaring, heroism, love, pretty natural scenes, patriotism and nostalgia, a few remind us of Trotter's medical pedigree and prepare us to recall the medical advice for which he was best known.[94] He announces himself as a doctor on the title page of the book and, to whet our appetite for medical topics, he includes a poem called 'Vaccination', the first lines of which are as follows:

> See where yon sportful cherub lies,
> And feasts the fondest mother's eyes,
> While smiles responsive glow;
> There science, led by [Dr] Jenner's art,
> From fell disease has pluck'd the dart,
> And lightens human woe.[95]

In this way, Trotter locates the inspiration for his poems in his medical practice.[96] There are also a few poems in this volume that show a degree of humanity and meditative reflection that may be thought to reflect Trotter's day job as a psychologist.

The subject of Trotter's meditation in 'The Beggar's Bush (Cut Down by a Maniac about Forty-Eight Years Ago)' illustrates to the reader that the humblest objects around us – accessible to the rich and poor alike – are themselves the texts, in a sense, of what he calls 'the school of the world' in his treatise on alcoholism.[97] The bush is a vehicle for Trotter to demonstrate his wisdom about the working of the human mind, which he garnered from his deep researches as a psychologist. With its initial focus on a wild and common form of vegetation, 'The Beggar's Bush' soon reveals itself to be a remarkably Wordsworthian treatment of a lowly, natural subject that inspires a meditation on the speaker's perception of change, memory and the passing of time. In this poem from 1802, the poet reports that, besides himself, beggars, gypsies and war-scarred veterans have sought refuge and comfort under the bush. Trotter may gesture to his experience with such downtrodden types during his medical career and he certainly intimates his alliance with them, just as Wordsworth does when he became their imaginative historian in *Lyrical Ballads*. Despite the poem's title, the subject of humility and the human mind soon assert themselves as the real subjects of 'The Beggar's Bush', while the bush recedes as a mere servant of memory and meditation. The bush is only mentioned in detail in the first of the poem's six stanzas, after which it becomes simply a locale for the speaker's more detailed rumination on the lives of the downtrodden of society. Trotter emphasizes his human subjects' states of mind, including his own, when he writes, 'There ... have I witness'd the weather-beat gypsy, / All wrinkled and wan, yet so merry and gay' and 'How oft to its bower, when its top was all flowery, / Have I paus'd from my sports to contemplate the scene'.[98] Later, the bush appears to be an elusive representative of the speaker's own changing life in the lines,

> But where are my comrades in frolic and pleasure,
> That led up the dance on the new-shaven green;
> When school and employment gave pastime and leisure,
> Ah! where are the village delights to be seen.[99]

Trotter's lines mirror closely Blake's 'The Ecchoing Green' in both diction and rhythm and they may therefore show that his interest in the world of poetry even extended to its (then) lesser-known representatives, like Blake.[100] (Trotter may have known Blake's work through his interest in other poets published by Joseph Johnson, such as Erasmus Darwin). In a more general way, though, this stanza recalls the typically Romantic glorification of childhood that Wordsworth and Coleridge enact in such poems as 'Ode ("There Was a Time")' and 'Frost at Midnight', wherein childhood represents simplicity through its unspoiled nature and its freedom from the taint of the ennui and cynicism that drives us to seek the debauched pleasures of the city against which Trotter warns in his medical texts.[101] In 'The Beggar's Bush', youthful innocence is represented in the 'village delights' of the humble environment. Trotter ends the poem with the lines, 'Each streamlet and river, each spring and each fountain, / They speak revolution from time and from years'.[102] The course of a man's life is mirrored in the humblest manifestations of the natural environment, which also foster his meditative and philosophical abilities. Trotter reiterates here what he asserts in his psychological prose: the simple life fosters poetry and mental stability.

In the collection's next poem, entitled 'The Ass: An Ode, On the Melioration of the Species', Trotter's goal is, again, twofold: upon a casual reading, he appears to try to inspire a re-evaluation of a humble representative of the animal world, but a more focused reading reveals Trotter's desire to engage the reader in a re-assessment of the value of humility itself. [103] Like 'The Beggar's Bush', the poem focuses on a sight common to the lower-classes, which would, for most readers, indicate its unworthiness. However, Trotter explores such acts of evaluation – how we assign value to a thing – by choosing the ode form for his depiction of a donkey, since this type of poem is usually used to praise already exalted subjects. Trotter's ass, as it were, is anything but exalted:

> Once I beheld thee by the stable door,
> And down thy face the showers of hunger flew;
> While the stall'd horse had oats and hay in store,
> A thistle's top was all thou hadst to chew.[104]

Yet, the donkey is dignified simply by being the subject of praise in an ode, as well as through the selective history that the poet provides about the animal, including when he 'bore a God, / While all around Hosannas loud did ring'.[105] He then goes on to give the donkey some helpful advice: 'But cease, thou gentle ass, to fret and whine, / Nor envious be to view the well-fed steed', for, Trotter reasons, the horse often meets a brutal death on the battlefield.[106] 'Then tell thy kind their case might still be worse', he admonishes, 'Nor glory seek beside the slaughter'd horse'.[107] Trotter's reference to the unmistakably human goal of 'glory' reveals that the donkey is our own stand-in. Trotter advises not only the donkey to be thankful for and accept his humble station, but aims this advice at his readers, as well. Again, Trotter prescribes the simple life and, by advising against the hunger for glory through battle, seems to reiterate his prose condemnation of England's colonial exploits. Finally, at the end of the poem, the speaker looks forward to a time when, thanks to Lord Thomas Erskine's 'bill in the peers, to prevent cruelty to domestic animals', 'pity for the ass o'er all the world [will] prevail'.[108] Trotter's interest in animal rights shows the humanitarian attitude that made him one of the most innovative nerve theorists of his time, for it afforded him the ability to see alcoholism as a disease to be pitied and cured, rather than a vice to be disparaged.

Trotter illustrates throughout his poetry and prose the benefits of humility and the dangers, physical and spiritual, of greed, which he posits as the motivation for Britain's colonial project. In his versified prologue to his play called *Noble Foundling; or, The Hermit of the Tweed. A Tragedy, in Five Acts*, set in Scotland,

Trotter joins the concepts of humility with a love of country and patriotism by lamenting the dearth of attention contemporary tragedians give to local tales:

> Too oft the tragic muse, inclin'd to roam,
> Stretch'd her wide flight, disdaining scenes at home:
> Proud to expand on Greek and Roman name,
> Thought all beneath her but a foreign fame –
> Our humbler bard in unambitious strains,
> Invokes the buskin'd dame to native plains:
> O'er stubborn glebes his careful culture wields:
> And reaps his harvest in paternal fields.[109]

His choice of setting speaks to his desire to inculcate a love of homegrown topics in his reading audience, much as Wordsworth does in 'Michael', for example, in which the poet presents an unknown shepherd's loss of familial peace and unity as a tragedy all the more heartwrenching for the noble simplicity of his desires: to inscribe on his ancestral lands a testament of paternal love. In short, the tragedy may be told by 'the humbler bard in unambitious strains', in keeping with Trotter's poetic and psychological programme of developing in his readers an appreciation of simplicity, in this case the homely stories of their native land.[110] Contrarily, to pierce the borders of one's country through colonial voyages has the effect of sullying the simple, uniform purity of home, a project and result that is evidenced on the body of each Briton, the microcosm on which Trotter's nervous theory focuses. He illustrates this connection in his poetry, such as in 'Verses Written in the Ladies' Walk at Liverpool, in January, 1783', where he implores,

> Behold yon dome, where oft the massy bowl
> Pours riot staggering from a midnight flood;
> Each drop that glads the haughty owner's soul,
> Cost Afric's sons a torrent of their blood.[111]

Indeed, the cost of colonialism is not only written upon the nervous body of the drunkard, as Trotter illustrates in his psychological prose. Here, he confirms a position about colonialism that Beddoes would develop throughout his work: the supposed gains of colonialism are, in effect, losses to the British soul, or mind. The moral component of the nerve theorist's project is part of his heritage as a psychologist, as I have indicated in my discussion of moral philosophy and moral management. Trotter himself confirms this characteristic of his psychological theorizing when he states, to quote a key passage from his psychological prose again, '*The habit of drunkenness is a disease of the mind.* The soul itself has received impressions that are incompatible with its reasoning powers'.[112] The doctor-as-hygienist, to which Foucault gestures, is more than an advisor on proper sanitation. He prescribes rules for the maintenance of the body's balances, the country's borders and the soundness of the national mind and soul.

IV. Thomas Beddoes, British Ambition and the 'Middling Classes'

Of all the nerve theorists I discuss in this chapter, the most complex and certainly the best known is Beddoes (1760–1808).[113] He presents himself as a hygienist concerned with the means of the preservation of health, rather than cure, and the holistic approach to mind, body and soul. 'Beddoes's vision of the doctor as intellectual guru parallels Coleridge's ideal of the new intelligentsia, the clerisy, called to serve as moral leaders of the future', Porter writes, adding, 'the Beddoesian doctor would be the humanist physician become priest and preceptor to humanity'.[114] Beddoes's use of verse to express his cultural opinions is a dramatic illustration of his multifaceted social role not only because it presents him as both poet and scientist, but also because he uses his verse to comment upon and give moral guidance regarding social issues, such as the effects of colonialism. This hygienist's approach to maintaining the health of the individual body and body politic through revised relations with external forces was different from that of Perfect and Trotter, however; instead of finding the poisonous influence in the outside and modern world and advising retreat into the lifestyle of old-fashioned English country life, Beddoes warned that the danger resides within, although contact with foreign and modern influences offer the perverted inner nature more scope for action. The solution lay in a method of maintenance of a unique kind: treat the moral soil while it is still virtuous through proper education and preserve the health – ethical and physical, for they are intimately related in his theory – of the nation. Beddoes's diverse prose and poetry may be helpfully studied from this unifying perspective, best encapsulated in a declaration he makes in *Essay on the Causes, Early Signs, and Prevention of Pulmonary Consumption* that could double as the motto for the Scottish Enlightenment: 'The seeds of science will at times fructify more abundantly in many minds than in one. They cannot therefore, in such cases, be too soon cast abroad'.[115] Beddoes considered the literature of the imagination, including poetry, as essential to this educational task.

As much as the above quotation illustrates Beddoes's fulfilment of his role as a hygienist in accordance with the egalitarian politics that he learned while attending the Edinburgh University, it also gives rise to further meditation upon this figure's complexities, since several other comments he wrote seem to contradict this democratic gesture. Born in Shropshire in 1760, this son of a successful and liberal tanner was exposed early in his post-secondary education to the tenets of nervous theory when he attended the classes of Cullen.[116] He taught himself French, German and Latin, mastered chemistry – and became a Reader of it at Oxford, where he earned his MD – and became a leading literary and scientific figure in Bristol, where he settled with his wife, Anna (daughter of Richard Lovell Edgeworth and sister of the novelist Maria Edgeworth). His great influence is manifest in his successful founding of the Institute for Preventive

Medicine, where he employed his future biographer, John Edmonds Stock, and the Pneumatic Institute at Bristol, where he hoped to find a cure for tuberculosis through experimentation with gases.[117] Beddoes's influence is also literary: recent critics have claimed for him the title of 'father-figure' to Coleridge and 'central player, even a kind of actor-manager, in the early political history and fortunes of English Romanticism'.[118] His education, and professional and literary influence, are consistent with his reputation as a physician according to some commentators on Beddoes's life: Michael Neve, author of the *ODNB* entry for Beddoes, describes him as a 'patrician revolutionary', while, in 'Thomas Beddoes and the Physiology of Romantic Medicine', George Grinnell cites Beddoes's attention to the increasingly rich bourgeoisie as the doctor's major influence on Romantic medicine.[119] I argue that Beddoes's relation to class in his medical therapy showcases his complexities as a historical figure, for plenty of evidence suggests that he – as a good hygienist and holistic practitioner, interested in treating society as a whole – was at least as concerned with treating the lower-classes.

Although the title of Beddoes's major text on nervous illness, *Hygëia: or Essays Moral and Medical on the Causes Affecting the Personal State of our Middling and Affluent Classes*, suggests that it is intended for the 'middling and affluent classes' alone – as do such comments within the text that he limits his audience to this arena because 'There only do we find leisure for study; there only the necessary degree of intelligence; and the means of carrying good counsel fully into effect' – he adds that the lower classes will learn of his counsel from 'their superiors', thereby suggesting that he does retain a concern for the 'indigent', as he rather unsympathetically calls them.[120] Moreover, by gesturing to the need of the poor for his counsel on nervous illness, Beddoes also implies that they may suffer from the effects of nervous illness as surely as do the rich. Beddoes's concern for the health of the poor is most evident in several other works he penned, such as *A Guide for Self-Preservation, and Parental Affection* and *The History of Isaac Jenkins, and Sarah His Wife, and Their Three Children*, both of which include medical advice tailored especially to the needs of the lower-classes.[121] In the former work, Beddoes writes, 'I have endeavoured to write in a style so familiar as to be intelligible to all readers and all hearers. My purpose is to give the poor, in particular, some ideas on the art of rearing children', while, in the latter work, the subject matter – specifically, the dangers presented by the alehouse to the families of the working-class fathers who visit them – is adapted to the experience of the poor.[122] *Extract of a Letter on Early Instruction, Particularly that of the Poor* is addressed to a lady, but, as the title indicates, Beddoes devotes himself again to the service of the lower classes in writing it.[123] Beddoes indicates that he would take particular offence at Neve's description of him as 'patrician', since he dubs himself a 'plebeian' in *Alternatives Compared: or, What Shall the Rich Do to be Safe?*; in the relevant passage, Beddoes also asserts that the factors commonly identified as predisposing one for nervous illness are similarly capable of crossing class lines: 'Idleness and vanity are not purely Patrician qualities. We of Plebeian origin have wherewithal to appreciate the convenience of being honourable, independently of merit'.[124] Perhaps to distinguish himself from the famous eighteenth-century nerve-doctors to the aristocracy and yet careful not to alienate any class of reader, Beddoes offers therapy to the poor, as well as to the rich. In *City of Health, Fields of Disease: Revolutions in the Poetry, Medicine, and Philosophy of Romanticism*, Martin Wallen comments upon Beddoes's unifying medical approach: 'Romantic physicians, like Thomas Beddoes, began to reconsider the body as a system of interrelated parts, each of which had to be understood on its own as well as in terms of its contribution to the whole person'.[125] His class-encompassing socio-medical theory is an expression of his holistic approach.[126]

V. Learning Self-Help: Always a Pupil

Beddoes's complex attitude regarding class divisions are echoed in terms of knowledge-sharing, which underscores his identity as a product of the medical education of the Scottish Enlightenment. In the democratic fashion that we may expect of a former student of Cullen, Beddoes states over and again his desire to educate as many Britons as possible so that they may have a degree of control over their own health. For example, in *A Lecture Introductory to a Course of Popular Instruction on the Constitution and Management of the Human Body*, Beddoes proclaims, 'To furnish individuals with so much knowledge of themselves as should enable them to guard against habitual sickliness, and a variety of serious disorders, had been long an object of contemplation with me', and he states elsewhere in the text, '*The more widely any species of knowledge is disseminated, the more rapidly may we expect that it will make advances*'.[127] This 'observation', he maintains, is 'applicable to the science of the affections of the human body and to every other science', showing, again, that psychology and physiology are united in his holistic approach.[128] Yet, this very text also contains comments that complicate our view of Beddoes as an egalitarian disseminator of medical knowledge, in the style of his hero and friend, Erasmus Darwin. He asserts, 'I must, indeed, have expressed myself ill, if you do not understand that I think books inadequate to the foundation of either species of medical knowledge; the professional or the popular' and, in case we insist on missing his point, he adds, 'To several medical writings for the people, it has, probably with great justice, been objected, that they tempt all the world to set up for doctors'.[129] Five years later in *Hygëia*, he would continue his attack on books about 'domestic medicine' for the popular purpose of treating illnesses at home, such as in his comment upon John Wesley's *Primitive Physick*, published only fifty years before in 1747, as 'fit only for a primitive age'.[130] Naturally, one wonders what distinguishes Beddoes's many medical texts intended for the use of the masses from the likes of Wesley's. In answer, Beddoes provides a mantra for his reader, which he seems to hope we will repeat to ourselves (and the booksellers) until it becomes a cultural fact: 'We want not to be taught how to prescribe, but how to avoid the necessity of prescriptions'.[131] As a hygienist, Beddoes provides in his popular medical texts rules for the maintenance and preservation of original health, rather than advice for cure and treatment with external correctives. These rules, he reasons, are empowering enough for the common person, since medicine 'cannot be safe in any but the most expert hands', as he maintains in the *Hygëia* chapter headings. If we adopt these rules for self-preservation, which Beddoes imparts through both poetry and prose, we accept our new definition as subjects of psychological power.

Essential to an understanding of Beddoes's role as a 'doctor of society', as Porter has so aptly dubbed him, is the significance of nerve theory in his medical writings. Because the nerve theorist's cultural role throughout the eighteenth and into the nineteenth century was as a social moderator and governor of health and because nerve theory involves an element of esotericism that affords the expert in it a kind of secret of knowledge (one of the defining features of power in Foucault's memorable definition),[132] we cannot appreciate fully Beddoes's contribution to the development of disciplinary power – and, especially, how his poetry functions in the cultural identity he worked so hard to form – by viewing him as an associationist alone.[133] Vickers shows convincingly that Beddoes was an associationist of such dedication and originality that he replaced David Hartley's associationist theory with one that accounted for the important links between emotions and ideas, instead of only how ideas lead to inevitably successive ideas, a reinterpretation of the tenets of associationism that echoes through the thought of Thomas Brown, as I will show in the next chapter.[134] However, other critics, such as Wallen, Paul Youngquist and Grinnell, have treated Beddoes, by and large, as a nerve theorist, even if they have not applied this label to him, by focusing almost solely on *Hygëia*, which treats those illnesses, such as hypochondria (in men) and hysteria (in women) that have traditionally been classed as the purview of nerve theorists.[135] In their entry on Beddoes in *Three Hundred Years of Psychiatry*, Hunter and Macalpine comment that his interest in insanity 'explains why he gave so much attention in his writings to nervous diseases', a comment that also gestures to Beddoes's particular handling of nervous illness as madness (and, in turn, this interpretation illustrates the essential difference between his approach and Cheynian theory, as I have argued).[136] Beddoes himself gives us good reason to view him as a nerve theorist: in 'Essay on the Nature and Prevention of Some of the Disorders Commonly Called Nervous' in *Hygëia*, Beddoes announces, 'There are certainly no diseases of whatever name, in which the nerves are not affected'.[137] If, indeed, all diseases are nervous on some level, then any treatment he offers posits him as a nerve-doctor. I contend that, in addition to treating Beddoes as an associationist, we must also consider the ramifications of his contributions to nerve theory.

Elsewhere in *Hygëia*, Beddoes shows himself to be a new kind of nerve theorist, one of the same stamp as Perfect and Trotter: 'All diseases, nay, every sort of injury, will, on strict consideration, be found to affect the mind'; he later adds, 'nervous complaints ... bring on mental incapacity of every degree. – Sometimes bland idiotism, sometimes idiotism with intervening accessions of frenzy. Of the last variety, there stands upon record no example, equal in celebrity to that of the great Dr Jonathan Swift'.[138] Unlike Cheyne, Beddoes maintains that nervous illness affects the proper function of the mental powers, instead of being a sign of one's superior intelligence, feeling and education – in short, a sign of one's sensibility. By exemplifying his point with a literary giant, Beddoes indicates that no claim to genius or celebrity could exonerate one from his damning diagnosis of nervous illness as insanity itself. In this way, he also illustrates his agreement with Perfect and Trotter, who likewise shun the traditional role of the nerve theorist as a panderer to high society and the literati through such a redefinition of nervous illness. The power to define nervous illness belonged to the expert nerve theorist, these psychologist-poets imply, not the patient.

Beddoes's revised form of nerve theory establishes a new power dynamic with the patient and wider public (as the source of potential patients) and reinforces the esoteric aspect of nerve theory that had always characterized it because of its emphasis on imponderable fluids and invisible fibres perceptible only to the trained expert. Beddoes's repeated injunctions that the public learn from his texts the rules for the maintenance of health and not the 'methods of cure', to quote an alternate title for Perfect's *Cases of Insanity*, illustrates that he actively developed his role as the possessor of special knowledge, a 'daemonic secret'.[139] For instance, in *Hygëia* Beddoes states about nerve theory:

> the parts concerned in many diseases have been so often examined by dissection, that the physician can read the state of the interior as plainly as if the body were a book, the alteration in organs accessible to the sense, and the patient's account of his feelings, serving him for letters. In nervous complaints, everything is different.[140]

Beddoes presents the subject's body as a text that is offered up to and read easily by the physiologist, especially the pathologist, who searches only for physical evidence of disease, but, where nervous illness is concerned, the subject's body becomes a bastion of recondite information, illegible to all but those initiated into the mysteries of nerve theory. Beddoes writes the subject's body – and mind, for the ephemeral quality of the nerves served as a kind of metaphor for the intangible reality that is the mind – into existence as an esoteric text. He constructs the body as a book through his own engagement with language in prose and verse. In so doing, Beddoes presents himself as a master of language as the writer through which information about the nervous subject is passed down and, by implication, the master of the body that is here constituted as an illegible text. To put a finer point on it, Beddoes becomes the master and maker of the subject's body that is defined through and as a textual expression of the discipline of psychology.

Disciplinary power and the subject are defined in a single move. Bernbauer and Mahon's summary of Foucault's approach to the subject as a product of disciplinary power is worth repeating here, for they might as well have been speaking of Beddoes's above description of the nerve theorist and subject: 'The self is constituted as a hermeneutical reality, as an obscure text requiring permanent decipherment'.[141] Crucially, Beddoes also constructs the poet as an inductee into these mysteries in a statement from *Hygëia* that provides insight into his vision regarding how his own literary identity as a poet relates to his role as a definer of disciplinary power through his prose. Here, he concedes that stimulating the imagination may lead to madness and has done so for a 'small number of poets', adding

> as from the nature of their favourite pursuit, they must often purposely stimulate their imaginations, and exact them almost to an ideal phrenzy ... They have [, however,] ... a practical knowledge, at least, of the way in which imagination is affected. They are therefore in the secret,

which saves them from going insane.[142] Indeed, information regarding the composition of the mind is a 'secret' and only those who are privy to it may escape madness; most poets and psychologists may rest secure in their knowledge of this secret, but everyone else who does not possess this knowledge is hereby defined as potentially mad, which is partly why all lay readers are identifiable as subjects (and potential patients) in psychological texts. In most of his writings, Beddoes does not state his position as a definer of disciplinary power and the subject so directly, but our understanding of his literary goals – to construct the reader as a socially oriented subject who will interiorize his rules for the maintenance of health – helps us to recognize the wider psychological ramifications of his writing.

Beddoes means to govern through education, a point that he enacts through his poetry and elucidates in several prose documents specifically tailored to this purpose. He often begins these prose works by stating that he wishes to educate children, which contributes towards his goal of providing the tools necessary for the maintenance of a healthy foundation so that later invasive methods of cure are not needed (i.e. in order 'to avoid the necessity of prescriptions'). However, in a move that further underlines the similarities between the cultural role of the moral manager and that of the Romantic-era nerve theorist, it soon becomes clear that his broader target is society, particularly the poorest classes, now infantilized and subjectified as a helpless, uneducated lot in need of a governor. For instance, in *Extract of a Letter on Early Instruction, Particularly that of the Poor*, Beddoes moves quickly from his stated specific subject to one that is more highly politicized: 'Oppression, I am aware, such as is practised upon slaves and what is generally taught for religion, together with the time and manner of teaching it, stifle ... benevolent tendencies: both indeed so far brutalize the mind and so entirely pervert our sympathy as to make us feel pleasure from the pain of our fellow-creatures'.[143] His abolitionist line would have been familiar in 1792, for similar sentiments were expressed by Whigs and Tories alike.[144] However, because Beddoes's comments are accompanied by a condemnation of the tyran-nical nature of religion, they identified him as the sympathizer with the French Revolution that he was in those days.[145] His plan for the *preservation* of natural 'benevolent tendencies' demands that citizens are taught his method of main-tenance as children. The same plan to maintain originary virtue in society can only be effected if it is built anew in accordance with the Revolutionary plan to renovate society by tearing it down first. Without such early education, Beddoes implies, society becomes cruel.

Indeed, the broadly social educative purpose of *Extract of a Letter on Early Instruction, Particularly that of the Poor* is evident from the title itself, which quickly moves from a focus on children to class. In an argument that establishes him as a hygienist devoted to providing advice for the maintenance of originary health and virtue, Beddoes advances the argument, *á la* Jean-Jacques Rousseau, that humankind is naturally benevolent in the first few pages of the work. The good doctor augments this familiar premise – replete with Revolutionary *frisson*, thanks to its connections with one of the contributors to the great *Encyclopae-dia*[146] – with his own theory of education, informed by associationist principles that reflect his reading of Hartley's psycho-philosophical work:[147]

> Nature has made us very early sensible to kindness ... Such is the mechanism of human nature at all ages; and it may easily be matured into an habitual affection for those who serve and are kind to us – into ... benevolence. Now proper stories exhibiting these feelings in action, would render the conception of them more distinct and more agreeable: and the child would be gradually habituated to that harmony of mind which so much contributes to render a person not only good but amiable.[148]

Several elements of Beddoes's theory are worth noting, as they illustrate his conception of the purpose of his own literary offerings. Firstly, he implies here and elsewhere in the same text that retaining one's natural benevolence does not depend upon retiring from destructive influences and environment (like the city in Rousseau, Trotter and Perfect), but, rather, upon active and early intervention to maintain such benevolence through the educational principles presented by Beddoes.[149] This difference is notable because it posits the developer of these educational principles as essential to the formation of the health of the individual and society. Secondly, Beddoes's emphasis upon the need for 'proper stories exhibiting' benevolence shows clearly his attempt to develop an audience for his own works of education, such as *The History of Isaac Jenkins*, a story about the moral reformation of a father who spends his poor family's meagre savings on alcohol. Beddoes concludes this short tract with the comment that it was 'intended as a specimen of compositions for the ... purpose' of educating 'poor children, and indeed for the grown poor', which again illustrates that his theories for children's education are of a piece with his plan to govern wider society's morals.[150] As I will show, *Alexander's Expedition* may also be considered in this light. Finally, the above comment hints broadly at the associationist principle upon which Beddoes formed many of his psychological theories: he suggests that the physical structure of one's mind will come to reflect certain ideas through their reinforcement. In a gesture reminiscent of Alex's re-education into society's norms through Ludovico's Technique in Anthony Burgess's *A Clockwork Orange*, Beddoes suggests here that children's minds must be moulded actively to reflect ideas and mores that are socially desirable; instead of using eye-clamps and other negative reinforcements to achieve these ends, however, Beddoes suggests that proper sentiments in works of literature may suffice.[151] By authoring several works of literature that fit the bill, Beddoes asserts his role as the master of language and the definer of the properly constituted subject – one that is, through the strength of education, impervious to the forces that may twist its originally benevolent nature.

In the section immediately following this one, Beddoes laments the result of inadequate education in a passage that supports his previous warning about the possibility of cruelty – a perversion of the primary benevolence of human nature – and that also hints at a hitherto unnoticed goal of *Alexander's Expedition*. Beddoes writes,

> Cruelty to animals is one among the earliest and most pernicious acquisitions of ill-educated children; and yet the same constitution of their nature, disposes them to acquire the habitual sentiment of compassion for both men and animals; for the cry of distress pierces the bosom of the child, and by exciting a painful sensation, prompts him to attempt the relief of the sufferer! You see then how nature has laid the foundation of virtue in our earliest feelings, and how easy the transition from these feelings to good habits and principles.[152]

The lack of proper training, of the literary sort that Beddoes himself provides and recommends for children's education, may lead to a cruel nature in a child. As that child and many others like him grow up, society as a whole becomes characterized by this perversity. Beddoes's plan for children's education goes further than the work by authors like Barbauld, which he mentions in *Extract of a Letter on Early Instruction*.[153] Indeed, he builds upon this previous work by emphasizing that his focus is society as a whole and his recommendations for education are, therefore, nothing less than his pedagogical plan for Britain itself. In this social focus, his emphasis on the maintenance of originary health and deflection of pernicious influences, and the moral basis of his approach, Beddoes manifests his fellowship with other nerve theorists and vocation as a hygienist.

Beddoes's comments upon the potential of literary works to educate society reveal a purpose of *Alexander's Expedition* that has not been noticed: this poem about curbing colonial practice recommends the avoidance of the pernicious foreign influences that stimulate negative inner change. The long poem – which Beddoes himself calls an imitation of Erasmus Darwin's work – has been described accurately by several critics as 'anti-colonial', but it is more than a criticism of acquisitive governmental foreign practices.[154] Early in the preface to the long poem, Beddoes prepares his reader to recognize it as educational through a passage that echoes his above comments on the educational capacity of imaginative literature. The writer of such works, he insists,

> may entitle himself to public gratitude, by offering to those, who feel oppressed by the burden of life, some engaging pursuit ... It is Fancy that has worked so many miracles in art and science; and one may lament, both for the sake of knowledge and humanity, that some attention is not paid to this truth in education.[155]

Beddoes repeats a sentiment he proffers in *Extract of a Letter on Early Instruction*: people learn best when their imaginations are engaged, as the pleasure attendant upon such reading predisposes them to accept the teachings of such works, a sentiment that underscores Beddoes's associationist influences and shows his similarities with Thomas Brown, as I will explain in the next chapter. Beddoes's message appears to be that, in the present poem, he attempts to teach his reader something about colonialism through the entertaining form of literature. However, what he attempts to teach society through this poem is not simply a disinclination to war and colonial practices by presenting everything connected to it as appalling. After all, his portrayal of Alexander is far from the 'standard, Augustan view of Alexander the Great as a power-crazed tyrant and author of "mad misrule"' that Porter suggests it is.[156] Beddoes openly scoffs at this construction of Alexander when he writes, 'Several of the most popular modern writers, as Pope in England ... have amused themselves with representing Alexander as a mere madman. And without doubt it was much more obvious, considering only his military expeditions and passionate excesses, to bring the matter to this simple issue, than to enter into his extensive schemes'.[157] Beddoes wishes to do more, later calling the hero 'honourably distinguished among Conquerors by his eager thirst as well as liberal encouragement of science; and in his character', Beddoes adds, '"the romantic traveller is blended with the adventurous soldier"'.[158] If the pre-eminent representative of colonialism for the eighteenth century, Alexander the Great, is presented in a positive light, then we must ask: How can this poem be an anti-colonial one? The answer lies in its unique form and in the presentation of the colonized people of Asia.

Beddoes's comment about the danger of martial poetry in his preface to *Alexander's Expedition* shows that he was aware of the fine line he walked in penning a poem about 'the conqueror of Asia' that was not wholly deprecating of its subject:

> The spirit of antient poetry must undoubtedly have contributed to pervert the moral sentiments of mankind, by establishing a false standard of excellence ... It may be worth while to consider whether, in consequence of the present absurd mode of education, a similar pernicious influence is not still exerted upon the ardour of the youthful mind ... Whenever, therefore, it shall become the business of instruction to inculcate just sentiments, the spirit of a great part of the antient poetry will become disgusting.[159]

We can expect, therefore, that the sentiments in the poem to which these comments are appended may replace the 'disgusting' ones of yore and that they will do so through 'The art of humanizing the mind ... [to make] it feel the full force of moral obligation'.[160] Beddoes attempts to reach these goals by avoiding graphic descriptions of the martial efforts of Alexander which may glorify the latter's deeds by presenting them in the attractive means afforded by the literature of 'Fancy', as he notes above, and, instead, glorifying the conquered Indians and describing the horrors of colonialism, partly in the prose footnotes. In these footnotes, which Beddoes rightly describes as 'a profusion' (roughly 70 per cent of the volume is devoted to footnotes), the poet attempts 'to diffuse more widely a knowledge of old and new Hindoo literature' and claims that Alexander himself regarded 'the natives ... [as] a brave and hardy race'.[161] Beddoes also uses the attractive form of verse to entice his audience into agreement with his sentiments about the damnable project of colonialism:

> Mourn, India, mourn – the womb of future Time
> Teems with the fruit of each portentous crime.
> The Crescent onward leads consuming hosts,
> And Carnage dogs the Cross along thy coasts;
> From Christian strands, the Rage accursed of gain
> Wafts all the Furies in her baleful train:
> Their eye-ball strained, impatient of the way,
> They snuff, with nostril broad, the distant prey.
> – And now, the Rout pollutes the hallowed shore,
> That nursed young Art, and infant Science bore.
> Fierce, in the van, her firebrand Warfare waves,
> Dire, at her heels, the cry of hell-hounds raves;
> Roused by the yell, the Greedy and the Bold
> Start to the savage chace of blood and gold.[162]

Significantly, Beddoes does not suggest that outside forces such as those found in colonized countries are deleterious influences unto themselves, as Cheyne, Perfect and Trotter do when they locate in foreign food the source of nervous illness and social incapacity. Rather, Beddoes maintains that the source of social ills originates within the individual, although they may be stimulated by exposure to outside forces. Perhaps because they were never educated to prize foreign cultures through texts that would concretize the originary benevolence of their natures – a fault that this poem intends to correct in its reader by teaching about India's early claims to 'young Art, and infant Science' – the conquerors' 'savage' natures are stimulated into greater cruelty through exposure to foreign situations that promise to gratify their antisocial desires.[163] In this way, Beddoes uses some principles of education derived from associationism to augment his role as a hygienist and nerve theorist devoted to the maintenance of the nation's originary virtue and health.

In two footnotes, one following the other and unified by theme, Beddoes attempts to convince his audience that contact with foreign influences is dangerous not because of the essence of the foreign object, but because of the ill-formed nature of the subject himself. Thus, Beddoes chooses a theme that, despite its originality, underlines the similarities between his approach and that of his fellow nerve theorists. The first footnote begins by illustrating that contact with difference or foreignness contributes greatly to the social and moral malady upon which he focuses: 'In consequence of the difference of colour, customs, religious creed or rather title of their religion, the European Soldiers have little or no fellow-feeling with the natives of these regions; and they will, of course, take every opportunity of giving loose to their rapacity, cruelty and caprice'.[164] Never having read of the courage of the Indian race, the beauty of their literature, or even their scientific prowess – a sorry fate that the readers of *Alexander's Expedition* escape – these soldiers lack the sympathy that is inspired through the kind of education that Beddoes provides. They are, therefore, at liberty to give full reign to the cruelty of their now perverted, but originally benevolent, natures.[165] Like the brutal children who torture animals in the vignette from *Extract of a Letter on Early Instruction*, the English soldiers in question, similarly untaught to sympathize with their victims, 'Plunder[ed] the women and children of defenceless villages' while their Indian defenders were away helping the English fight their common enemy – a circumstance that should have encouraged the colonists to identify with the Indians in question.[166] This footnote is followed by one that describes a very similar situation and raises the (by then) familiar metaphor of food as the vehicle of foreign danger. What establishes this passage as distinct from others of a similar nature in texts about nervous illness, however, is that the food itself does not convey moral and physical contagion through its foreign spiciness or richness. Rather, the food only presents the occasion for the innate cruelty of the colonists to express itself: 'On the meek race each plague of guilt is poured; / Gaunt famine gleans the relics of the sword/ For food their fruitless cries thy infants raise'.[167] The appended footnote to these lines relates that, in the historical episode that inspired them, the English soldiers ate all of the food from a region of India until the 'natives' starved to death in the thousands.[168] As in the foregoing note, Beddoes's real focus is the 'rapacity' of the colonists, a specific type of cruelty born of greed and indulged by the license of being in a foreign land where there are no claims on the sympathy of the conquerors. Here, as in the work of the other nerve-theorists-cum-hygienists that I describe in this chapter, food acts as a metaphor for the external dangers that threaten the social and individual body. Beddoes's underlying message is that Britain, having been raised on martial poetry that augments cruelty in the subject, is not prepared by education to sympathize with the foreign elements it encounters through colonialism. As such, such forces prove deleterious to the moral and physical health of the nation, for it offers greater scope for the satiation of its cruel nature. This message not only confirms Beddoes's associationist dedication to education, but also his unique identity as a Romantic-era nerve theorist, as I will show with reference to *Hygëia*.

External forces like food and other pleasures offered by colonial success – and on offer in the city – alienate us from our original, healthy and virtuous selves. In his educational works for children and *Alexander's Expedition*, Beddoes invokes cruelty as the most common manifestation of this perversity of character, but, in *Hygëia*, he clarifies his holistic position as a nerve theorist by showing that such perversion shows itself in the body, particularly the nervous body of the bourgeoisie, which expresses its twisted nature through indigestion, drunkenness, insanity and, ultimately, male effeminacy. The opportunity for Romantic-era Britain to express its cruel nature is one of the dangers of colonialism, which is an aspect of modern life against which nerve theorists since Cheyne warned. Cruelty is a perversity because humans are naturally benevolent, Beddoes claims in *Extract of a Letter on Early Instruction* and elsewhere. Other perversities produced through a lack of proper social and bodily maintenance manifest themselves as the symptoms of nervous illness. He censures the fashion for excessive sensibility, citing the 'drooping, blighted creatures, frequently half-insane', who 'abused their animal powers [i.e. natural sensory functions] till their sensibility acquired the unnatural property of deriving pain from the slightest impression'.[169] In 'Essay on the Preservation of the Physical Power of Enjoyment; with Remarks on Food and Indigestion', in which Beddoes warns against the dangers of 'hypochondriasis', he invokes food again as a danger to the maintenance of health, remarking, 'Our danger arises from untutored appetite'.[170] The popularity of the metaphor of overindulgence in food as representative of all external dangers against which nerve theorists warn speaks to its aptness. The example of food was particularly illustrative because one of the most immediate ways in which the readers of Beddoes's texts experienced the effects of colonialism was through the change in their diets, such as the introduction of Indian curries, chutneys and other previously unknown comestibles.[171] Moreover, through the trope of gluttony – a moral failing – such discussions of food as ruinous to the physical health of the body illustrates such advice by nerve-theorists to be directed at a subject whose moral and physical essences are inseparable. The moral ills of greed and overindulgence cause hypochondriasis, although indirectly: excessive eating leads to indigestion, which, together with low spirits, is the very definition of hypochondriasis, according to Beddoes.[172] Beddoes recommends temperance in *Hygëia*, despite once being an enthusiastic supporter and promulgator of John Brown's theories – even going so far as to translate Brown's work from the Latin in *The Elements of Medicine of John Brown, MD* – in which alcohol and opium are sometimes prescribed for their salubrious effects on the 'excitability' of the patient, to use a term from Brunonian theory.[173] Like Perfect and Trotter, Beddoes also locates in alcohol one of the deleterious external influences that can impede the preservation of good health.[174] To put his advice in light of his educational theories, the original virtue of the body may be corrupted through a lack of preservation, the means of which are the focus of Beddoes's prose and verse lessons. Since Beddoes proposes to teach the subject how to avoid perverting her original – healthy and virtuous – nature, he posits himself as essential to the maintenance of selfhood, the real identity of the subject, whose very essence may be lost, perverted, without his intervention.

Despite his similarities with his fellow nerve-theorists, Beddoes's recommendations for the preservation of health in the face of dangerous outside forces also reveals his difference from Trotter and Perfect, at least upon a casual perusal of his comments. On one hand, in a commentary on the 'forms of misery' called nervous illness or excessive sensibility, Beddoes mentions that Rousseau recommends the rejection of 'social refinement' and retreat 'from the institutions of polished society' into isolation in order to counteract the source of such dis-ease, like the luxuries found in the city, a solution that Beddoes and Perfect also proffer.[175] It is also true that Beddoes's complaint that 'Every circumstance of modern life conspires to soothe a man into the excess of effeminacy' and 'unmanly delicacy' allies him with Trotter, who celebrates the macho lifestyle of pre-civilized Germanic peoples as the model for maintaining nervous fortitude.[176] The same may be said of Beddoes's recommendation that one may avoid nervous illness if one performs manual labour, which likewise implies that the reader should aspire to be like Trotter's pre-civilized, hale and hearty Germans.[177] And, yet, on the other hand, Beddoes does not advise retreat from the city, however much he despises its ill effects upon the physical and moral health of the nation; nor does he recommend a Rousseauvian retreat from social advance. He states clearly his belief that 'To accelerate the progress of civilization, is probably our only practicable plan'.[178] As contradictory as these comments may seem, though, Beddoes shows his real dedication to his role as a governor of society in them. He insists on remaining actively involved with British society by writing a variety of educational texts about the maintenance of health – social, moral and physical – that everyone could understand. He adopted his own advice by remaining in the city and continuing to work for the scientific and social advancement of society. Beddoes ultimately died in Bristol, writing socio-medical texts to his last days.[179]

The question remains: how can one remain in the city, exposed to the perverting influences of excess and rich (often foreign) food, not to mention its soft rugs and bad air in unventilated rooms, and yet maintain one's moral and physical health?[180] The answer lies in Beddoes's many educational texts for children: the proper course of education will ensure the subject's mental and physical fortitude, thereby increasing her ability to withstand such dangerous external forces. Armed with the Beddoesian mantra, 'We want not to be taught how to prescribe, but how to avoid the necessity of prescriptions', society can renovate itself with each succeeding and increasingly strong generation.[181] The grown poor, also the focus of these texts, can learn how to raise their children upon these salutary principles. Is there any hope for the adults whose natures are already perverted into cruelty and whose bodies manifest their unhealthy state in nervous illness and its subsidiary symptoms, like drunkenness, indigestion, madness and male effeminacy? The conclusion of *Isaac Jenkins* suggests that, with the protracted and personal treatment of a doctor, like Dr Josiah Langford (the stand-in for Beddoes, who narrates the tale), even the gluttonous alcoholic, whose broken body manifests his moral failing to resist overindulgence, may reform himself. However, as Beddoes asserts over and again, no one can expect to correct themselves through the texts they read. Even *Hygëia* can only delineate the need for cure, instead of providing the means for it, for a personal consultation with a proven expert is the only way the nervous subject may be healed. In this way, Beddoes defines his reader as a subject defined by psychological writing as surely as he does when he describes the nervous body as a text, illegible to all except the expert nerve theorist.[182] The British subject defined in Beddoes's socio-medical texts is forever ill, always in need of healing and untreatable by any but those with the most specialized training. This textual subject is, thus, defined, weakened and truly subjectified: he is made an object of study and, because he is inaccessible even to himself, who remains without the esoteric psychological knowledge he needs to treat himself, he is never on the side of disciplinary power. Beddoes's egalitarian wish to provide educational texts for all classes of society only spreads the net of disciplinary power wider, making modern subjects of the entire society and a powerful governor of Beddoes.

VI. Verse as a Tool of Governance

Beddoes's approach was clearly influenced by associationism, particularly in his ideas about education, but I focus on how associationism relates to his nerve theory because this approach defines his role as a hygienist, doctor of society and medical governor whose main goal is the preservation of health and prevention of the effects of deleterious external influences upon the body and mind. As part of the deeply social nature of the hygienist's role, these nerve-theorists depend upon poetry in order to express their unique identities and train the reader to adopt a socially moderated subjectivity in an attractive form. The purpose of their verse was very much like that of Thomas Brown, as I will explain in the following chapter. Indeed, in both, the attractive and entertaining qualities of verse are essential for the psychologist-poet's effort to entice the reader into accepting the social rules he presents. The social function of the discipline of psychology is integral to the creation of modern society, Foucault asserts:

> Modern society, then, from the nineteenth century up to our own day, has been characterised on the one hand, by a legislation, a discourse, an organisation based on public right, whose principle of articulation is the social body and the delegative status of each citizen; and, on the other hand, by a closely linked grid of disciplinary coercions whose purpose is in fact to assure the cohesion of this same social body.[183]

Because each citizen has the right to accept or reject the 'disciplinary coercions' that are presented by the psychologist to govern society, they must be offered in an attractive form, such as through poetry. Just as important as the effect of this verse upon the reader is the literary identity of the psychologist-poet that it creates. The writing of poetry solidifies the hygienist's role as a master of holistic care, body and mind, society and the individual – and the definer of rules for ethical and physical health – because, by writing poetry, he defines himself as a cultural commentator. The modern subject is thereby defined through the disciplinary power expressed in the psychological definitions of nerve theory and other educational texts that disseminate the rules for moral and physical health to the Romantic reader, as well as through the poetry that illustrates these rules and entices the reader into accepting them through attractive imagery.

The reason why these nerve theorists wrote poetry may be traced to their very identities as nerve theorists: since they believed that nervous illness encompassed the social, moral, emotional and physical aspects of the subject, they used several kinds of writing to appeal to the reader/subject on a variety of levels. Beddoes expresses the multifaceted nature of nerve theory best when he proclaims, in *Contributions to Physical and Medical Knowledge, Principally from the West of England,*

> The science of human nature is altogether incapable of division into independent branches. Books may profess to treat separately of the rules of conduct, or the mental faculties and the personal condition. But the moralist and the metaphysician will each to a certain point encroach upon the province of the physiologist,

adding, 'Without reference to the body, it is ... impossible to unfold the nature of the mind. Physiology, therefore ... appears to be the foundation of ethics and pneumatology [or psychology]'.[184] Indeed, the nerve theorist treats the subject's body and mind as one, an approach that Trotter, Perfect and Beddoes apply to the literary expression of their work, where the prose definition of their social, physical and psychological theories may be traced in their verse. By using verse to disseminate, dramatize and advertise their psychological theory, these governors of social health and morals redefine themselves as masters of language on several levels and literature as one of the many means through which modern power is dispersed.

4. THE UNELECTED LEGISLATOR: ASSOCIATIONISM AND THOMAS BROWN'S SUBLIMINAL POETIC LESSONS

Brown's poetry is so voluminous – he published seven volumes of verse[1] – and his psychological approach is so complex and influential that he warrants a chapter of his own. He also stands out from the other psychologist-poets described in this study because he states most clearly how and why he uses verse for associationist purposes. In *Lectures on the Philosophy of the Human Mind*, the Professor of Moral Philosophy at Edinburgh University delineated his associationist psychological theories, which many viewed as threatening to the Christian concept of free will. Significantly, he also applied associationist principles to his literary theorizing and attempted to practise versified psychology that appears, frighteningly, to be a kind of mind-control. As his psychological prose and poetic prefaces reveal, Brown believed that the psychologist-poet understands the reader better than the reader understands herself, which enables him to use the special qualities of verse to implant his message into the reader's mind. This message is a moral one that confirms the socially governing and Christian roots of psychology and links Brown's verse to that of Cotton and Beattie, most obviously, but also to that of all of the psychologist-poets whom I have examined here, since I have shown that, in their ways, moral management and nerve theory also governed society by providing rules for morality. More specifically with reference to Brown's poetry, he shows that the associationist-poet can encourage the reader to follow his ethical directions without even appearing to give advice. Although this autocratic use of psychology in verse may be alarming, it is not a perversion of the principles of associationism. It is, rather, an apt application of its principles, as I will illustrate with reference to the writings of Hartley and Stewart, as well as Brown's own. Brown may seem to differ from his fellow psychologist-poets in his overtly tyrannical sentiments, but, as I will illustrate, he is the paramount example of the psychologist who leads society through verse because he seizes upon the unique qualities of poetry that are amenable to the deployment of his associationist programme. This psychologist-poet uses his understanding of and talents for both associationism and verse to effect a perfect amalgamation of the disciplines.

I. Associationism: Exemplary of or Anathema to Romanticism?

Associationism may be said to have inaugurated the interest in the links between approaches to the mind and literary writing in Romantic criticism. After all, the Romantic period, as Richardson recognizes in 'Of Heartache and Head Injury: Reading Minds in *Persuasion*', 'has long been viewed as dominated by an associationist account of mind'.[2] Studies on the associationist knowledge of the canonical Romantic poets are numerous and began to appear as early as the 1930s, while later critics researched how Shelley's, Coleridge's, Wordsworth's and other famous Romantic writers' reading of associationism – mostly that of Hartley, which was popularized by Joseph Priestley's revised publication of Hartley's *Observations on Man* – might have impacted their literary works.[3] Most of these critics outline evidence of associationist thinking in canonical Romantic writers' work, while a few, like Cairns Craig in *Associationism and the Literary Imagination*, go further to explain how associationism is integrally linked with the stated ideals of Romantic literature. For example, Craig argues that associationism was influential for Romanticism because psychologists since Hume had maintained that associations and therefore all thought, logical and otherwise, was generated by passion and emotion, a concept that was dear to the Romantics, many of whom celebrated subjective and inner experience over the logical and empirical: 'The priority that association gave to the imagination – since association itself is nothing other than an operation of the imagination – as well as to the passions made it rapidly appealing in discussions of the origin and effects of art'.[4] (I will argue that this feature of associationism also speaks to the aptness of Brown's use of verse, widely viewed as an emotional medium, for the promulgation of his associationist message). As is the case with all psychological inquiry, associationism's attention to the subjective motions of our inner selves further illustrates its philosophical links with Romanticism. Yet, specific features of associationist subjectivity also reveal how it is distinct from the prevailing literary ideal. Associationism had long been accused of denying our free will and power of volition, which would posit the resulting self-reflexive subject as an impotent assemblage of chance perceptions instead of the high-Romantic creator of her external world through the dominance of subjective perception.

In various ways, associationists and later commentators have attempted to deny that associationism constructs the subject as a passive receptor of external impressions. Their reasons for doing so are understandable, for the stakes are high: Hunter and Macalpine call Brown's theory of the mind one of the first genuine examples of psychology, while William Parry-Jones notes, 'the psychology

[of] association ... as propounded by Locke, Hume and Hartley, exerted considerable influence on contemporary psychiatric thought and formed the basis of new systems of classification of insanity'.[5] In other words, if we may justly accuse associationism of being autocratic and volition-denying, then we open the door to similar allegations against psychology as a whole.

Brown's well-known statements of associationist tenets complicate attempts to defend associationism against accusations that it denies free will by either damning or only weakly defending the psychological approach. *Lectures on the Philosophy of the Human Mind*, which is the record of the lessons Brown delivered as Professor of Moral Philosophy at Edinburgh University after he took over the post from his former teacher, Stewart, is a testament to the influence of Brown's views, since it went into nineteen editions by 1851. Indeed, despite – or perhaps because of – the immense popularity of Brown's theories, many people revolted against them, claiming that they 'left little room for the play of free will and self-determination'.[6] Even his assertion of the basic principles of associationism proclaim ominously against our prized notions of moral and emotional liberty: in *Lectures*, Brown claims

> That there is a tendency of ideas to suggest each other, without any renewed perception of the external object which originally excited them, and that the suggestion is not altogether loose and indefinite, but that certain ideas have a peculiar tendency to suggest certain other relative ideas in associated trains of thought.[7]

He later adds that these ideas 'form ... one complex and inseparable whole', or, in other words, that the network of ideas, which is identifiable as the subject, cannot be reformed in a significant way.[8] This 'whole' is 'inseparable' even to the subject herself, who is unaware when the connections are being made or how the associations are formed and who is therefore powerless over the whole network of resulting associations – a network that is the very structure of our minds and may, therefore, be understood as subjectivity itself. (Brown confirms, 'We are conscious of our present feeling whatever it may be; for this is, in truth, only another name for our consciousness itself').[9] Suggestion – another word that Brown uses for 'association' – occurs 'spontaneously', without our control.[10] Since later contemplation upon our own thoughts can only involve those that already exist – and have been formed 'spontaneously' – the notion that we can will our thoughts into being is nonsensical. Brown explains: 'The contradiction implied in this direct volition of any particular idea, is, indeed, so manifest, that the assertion of such a direct power over the course of our thought is now pretty generally abandoned'.[11] Brown's work was both widely known and abhorred for the very reasons implied by such statements, for they contribute to a notion of the self as passive and involuntary, a far cry from Romantic ideal of the world- and self-creating subject.

Brown attempts to soften the existential and spiritual consequences of his theory in various ways, but he does so only halfheartedly, it seems. He illustrates his educational heritage under Stewart at Edinburgh University through these weak refutations since Stewart claims in his *Elements of the Philosophy of the Human Mind* that we do have free will over our thoughts in so far as we can voluntarily organize them, only to add soon thereafter that the power of our will does not extend as far as we may think.[12] In this concession, Stewart seems to follow up, however grudgingly, on a statement he makes a few pages earlier: 'So completely ... is the mind in this particular [of the rules of association] subjected to physical laws, that it has been justly observed [footnote: 'By Lord Kaims and others'], we cannot, by an effort of our will, call up any one thought; and that the train of our ideas depends on causes which operate in a manner inexplicable by us'.[13] It is easy to see why Stewart offers this defence, as weak as it is. As J. C. Stewart-Robinson, author of the ODNB entry for Brown, maintains, 'The notion from Locke, thence [Étienne] Condillac, that higher mental operations might arise out of a "succession of feelings" which just happen to occur to the mind was anathema to the Scottish view of a fully constituted mind, active in its own self-cultivation'.[14] Associationism's apparent denial of free will was not only un-Scottish, it was also potentially unchristian. Hartley puts a finer point on the implications of the involuntary nature of our associations in a way that shows how heretical the psychological approach must have appeared to be at the time of his writing. In the preface of *Observations on Man, his Frame, his Duty, and his Expectations*, he asserts, 'I no where deny practical Freewill, or that voluntary Power over our Affections and Actions, by which we deliberate, suspend, and choose, and which makes an essential Part of our Ideas of Virtue and Vice, Reward and Punishment'.[15] The philosopher insists that his theory about the sensory perception of external phenomena as the creator of our inner associations and all of the ethical behaviour that follows upon them is not tantamount to saying that we are divested of inner responsibility for our moral decisions and our resultant behaviour and therefore spared the pains of hell or rewards of heaven. However, even Hartley's defence is unconvincing because, according to his own theory, the formation of our associations is doubly uncontrollable: first, because they are the result of sensing what is external to and therefore unmanageable by us and, second, because associations are formed unconsciously. If our associations guide our actions – and all of the associationists attest to this notion to some degree – and if we express our morals through action, which is undeniable, then associations do guide our morality. In this way, the associationist subject is truly formed by external and unmanageable forces. Brown echoes such defensive sentiments when he asserts, 'We not merely perceive objects, and conceive or remember them simply as they were, but we have the power of combining them in various new assemblages, – of forming at our will ... a new a varied universe, with every succession of our thought'.[16] (He was, no doubt, also concerned for his own good reputation as a good Christian and Scot, judging by his repeated references to God and morality throughout his psychological works and his passionate attachment to his native Scotland, having been 'born at Kirkmabreck, Kirkcudbrightshire, the youngest of thirteen children of the Rev. d Samuel Brown').[17]

Later commentators attempt to defend associationism through similar arguments. Most recently, Craig claims that associationism demands the active participation of the self in the world around it, which rescues the psychological approach from imputations that it denies free will.[18] However, the activity of the self in the combination of new experiences and formation of new associations does not alter the fact that the essential self is created haphazardly, involuntarily. The fact remains that the building blocks of associations are created by coincidence and circumstances beyond our control. Paths of association may be changed, but the original routes are necessarily laid down without our knowing. Moreover, since these irreducible and involuntary trains of thought are identifiable with consciousness and synonymous with the self, the serious implications of the debate regarding the involuntary nature of our associations for the creation of the subject are clear. In 'The Synthetic Imagination: Shelley and Associationism', Keith Shelley argues that eighteenth-century associationism was characterized by differing approaches to this matter of free will, with Hume approaching the mind as a passive instrument and Hartley portraying it as more active, but the critic also concedes that associationists phased out the will in the Romantic period, when Brown held sway: 'Associational patterns thus lead from voluntary to involuntary states ... as acts of the will are supplanted by precise custom-based responses'.[19] Historically and philosophically speaking, associationism leads to the notion of a self that is without control over its own construction. If the subject is a vast assemblage of ideas, ways of thinking and notions of the self, our ability to alter a few elements of it does not save it from being based on wayward chance and, at the worst, the cunning activity of those who wish to form it as they please through their knowledge of how associations are made, which describes Brown's poetic approach well.

It may seem paranoid to suggest that the associationist – an expert in the ways that the reader's perceptions, ideas, morals and, in short, her very subjectivity is created through different types of external phenomena – would attempt to shape that same subjectivity through his esoteric knowledge. And, yet, Brown gives his reader much to be suspicious about, since he states that he uses his verse to accomplish these very goals. Brown reveals in his psychological texts that our involuntarily formed associations and the mental processes that produce them are particularly amenable to the emotional and aesthetically pleasing qualities of verse and he applies this line of reasoning in the production of his poetry. In the preface to *The Paradise of Coquettes*, his most popular volume of verse, Brown describes the psychological consequences that poetry can have on its audience as 'that happy eloquence of verse, which in conveying to us moral truths, has impressed them on our hearts, in a manner that made it impossible for us to forget them'.[20] His phrase 'impressed them on our hearts' is a sure reference to the power of suggestion or the formation of associations in the subject's mind and, notably, it implies that the readers' 'hearts' are being acted upon by the poetry without the intervention of their will. Brown attempts to change his readers' moral views and, ultimately, to alter their behaviour through his poetry – and he means to do so without their knowledge that these internal changes are taking place.

I will return to *The Paradise of Coquettes* as Brown's most characteristic volume (indeed, in 1828, biographer David Welsh claims that it was upon this publication that 'the fame that he at present enjoys as a poet seems chiefly to rest'), but, first, it is essential to show how Brown's exceptional claims in the preface and even his decision to write associationist poetry in the first place are supported not only by his own psychological writings, but also by those of associationists before him, like Stewart and Hartley.[21] To begin with, these prose texts show that, far from being surprising, Brown's choice of the medium of poetry in which to present and practice his associationist theories was a logical extension of the psychological paradigm to which he contributed. Whether the associationist's intention is to produce new trains of thought in the reader or dramatize the principles of suggestion, poetry is the perfect medium for him because it works on the basis of passions and emotion – and, particularly in the Romantic period, poetry was regarded as having a particular facility for inspiring such subjective responses in the reader. In short, to reiterate Brown's contention from the preface to *The Paradise of Coquettes*, the special qualities of poetry enable it to 'impress' its principles 'on our hearts'.[22] Brown explains in *Lectures* that the emotional character of poetry is closely tied to the mechanics of verse, arguing that figurative language works on the basis of emotional association:

> In cases of the more shadowy resemblance of analogy, in like manner, – as in those comparisons of objects which constitute the similes and metaphors of poetry, ... there may have been a proximity of each to an emotion of some sort, which, as common to both, might render each capable indirectly of suggesting the other.[23]

Put otherwise, the emotional resonances inspired by poetic comparisons are produced not simply by the aptness of the comparison, which would only please us on a logical level. Rather, figurative language of this sort appeals to us because it reminds us of emotions that we have experienced with regard to each part of the comparison, which are compounded when the two are brought together. Poetry is an association-producing medium.

The link between poetry and associations derives from their mutual depend-ence upon emotions, as opposed to reason or logic. This link gestures to an aspect of the psychological approach as it developed throughout the eighteenth cen-tury that marked a sea-change in ideas about the basic character of the human mind and underlines the connection between associationism and the stated ide-als of Romanticism. Brown went so far as to claim that our very appreciation of beauty itself, whether poetic or otherwise, is both emotional and depend-ent upon associations: 'the chief part of beauty', he contends, 'is truly derived from that mental process which has been termed association – the suggestion of some feeling or feelings, not involved in the primary perception, nor necessarily flowing from it'.[24] The relationship between poetry and associations is therefore dynamic. Indeed, poetry creates associations because it is frequently beautiful, while our perception of poetry's beauty is, in part, a function of the associations that already exist in us. It is worth reiterating here what many critics before me have noted, specifically that Wordsworth makes this tenet of associationism a cornerstone of his poetic thought when he remarks in the preface to the *Lyrical Ballads* that his readers may appreciate his poems 'if he be in a healthful state of association'.[25]

That such a basic experience as the appreciation of poetry is intertwined with associations points to the power of this faculty, according to its proponents, who revised the original Lockean explanation of 'The mechanical association of ideas that have been frequently presented to the mind at the same time' into some-thing less 'mechanical', less logical and based on the passions.[26] As Craig puts it, Hume and Hartley argued that association is 'the foundation on which all mental activity, including reason, is built'.[27] This basic truth of associationism is essen-tial to understanding Hume's famous claim that the reason should always be a slave of the passions, which has so often been misinterpreted as his admittance of defeat.[28] The idea that emotions are the basic building blocks of the human mind gives associationism a Romantic *frisson* and the poetry that plays on our feelings an air of scientific rigour and importance. Nor was Brown the only associationist to afford poetry pride of place in his thinking about how the mind is structured upon the power of suggestions: Hartley's 'Proposition 82', penned 'To explain the Nature of figurative Words and Phrases, and of Analogy, from the foregoing Theory [of associationism]', reveals his view that the mind has a natural affinity for analogies and poetic comparisons because it is structured by a web of associa-tions.[29] Like Brown, then, Hartley believes that poetry is particularly suited to the emotional, associative mind, from which we may conclude that it is the most appropriate medium for the dissemination of associationist principles and the creation of new associations.

There exists yet another reason why Brown may have decided that writing poetry was consistent with his associationist task, a reason that simultaneously highlights the nature of the subject as it is created by this type of psychology and frames words, somewhat oddly, as external phenomena. According to associationism, the subject, the self, is a network of the learned associations (originally emotional with a strong dash of the logical later in life) of the subject in response to her sensory perception of the material world. As such, the subject is created from the outside in. The phenomenon of the self originates in and is oriented toward the external realm. Therefore, subjectivity is not a private, inner reality. What is true of the subject as defined through every psychological approach, then, is even more evident in associationist terms: whether through psychology's definition of the subject through the context of her relationship with the moral manager, one's society, or, in associationism, all that she senses in the external world, the subject is not a unique orchestration or expression of private, inner experience, nor a legitimate experience of self-reflection, until she learns how to understand and express her subjective reflections through psychology's language, a construct exterior to herself, defines her with reference to external forces. The definitions of psychology are always externally, socially oriented, but, as I will show, associationism presents this aspect of the discipline in particularly powerful terms.

Throughout the eighteenth century, associationism was distinguished and sometimes reviled for its external focus, which denied man's spiritual, non-material nature, its detractors declared. Priestley recognizes the religious fear that Hartleian psychology inspired even as he attempts to explain it away in his preface to *Hartley's Theory of the Human Mind*: he writes that Hartley's notably physical explanation about how the brain and vibrations create associations should not alarm the religious, 'except those who maintain that a future life depends upon the immateriality of the human soul. It will not at all alarm those who found all their hopes of a future existence on the Christian doctrine of *a resurrection from the dead*'.[30] Hartley's theory about what he called 'vibratuncles', those invisible tubes that he theorized could carry physical sensation to the brain through vibrations and form associations there, became outmoded by the Romantic period (and, indeed, Priestley's republication of Hartley's ideas was crucial to this development because he excised this part of the theory almost totally), but associationism retained its physical and sensational emphasis.[31] Brown's basic definition of association – which, he argues here, may also be termed 'suggestion' – illustrates that 'external cause[s]' are essential to the process:

> That, when two objects have been perceived by us in immediate succession, the presence of the one will often suggest the other, – though this second object, or a similar external cause, be not present, – is that great fact of association, or suggestion, which we must admit, whatever name we may give to it.[32]

Finally, because associationist theory presents words themselves not only as external objects, but the most suggestive of all association-creating external realities, the associationist subject is the linguistically defined social subject of psychology *par excellence*. In 'Proposition 79', Hartley argues that 'Words and Phrases must excite Ideas in us by Association, and they excite Ideas in us by no other means', in the course of which he asserts that words affect our physical senses – a step that is essential for the creation of associations – through speaking and hearing the spoken word, seeing the written word and touching it, as it were, during handwriting.[33] Moreover, Hartley later adds that some of us gain the strongest associations through reading, while all of us are particularly impressed through the aesthetically pleasing presentation of words, such as in poetry, I would venture to add:

> learned Men understand more readily by passing over the Words with the Eye only, since this Method, by being more expeditious, brings the Ideas closer together. However, all Men, both learned and unlearned, are peculiarly affected by Words pronounced in a manner suitable to their Sense and Design.[34]

Although Hartley does not clarify why 'Men, both learned and unlearned, are peculiarly affected by Words pronounced in a manner suitable to their Sense and Design', he seems to base his claim on the well-known associationist principle that we associate most strongly in response to the most vivid sensations, whether they are so by virtue of their beauty or some other characteristic.[35] In short, the pleasure provided to the reader through poetry's beauty is a major feature of its ability to create associations in her. Through his understanding of how to create a work of beauty, then, the poet has control over the reader's associations. Since poetic words are the most potent external causes that create associations, Brown does indeed choose his medium well when he uses verse to form the reader's associations. And if, as I have argued, the associationist subject is a compilation of associations, we may also conclude that Brown therefore attempts to form his reader's subjectivity through verse.

Crucially, the poet's ability to affect the reader in a particular way – his command over the reader's associations – stems from his command over his own associations. Stewart argues that poetry pleases us partly by inspiring us to appreciate the superior command that poets have over their associations. Asserting first that 'there is no instance in which the effect of habits of association is more remarkable, than in those men who possess a facility of rhyming', Stewart adds,

> The pleasure we receive from rhyme, seems also to arise, partly from our surprise at the command which the Poet must have acquired over the train of his ideas, in order to be able to express himself with elegance, and the appearance of ease, under the restraint which rhyme imposes ... [O]ur pleasure is heightened by our surprise at the author's habits of association when compared with our own.[36]

In other words, the poet may mould the reader's associations through his superior ability to manage his own 'train of ideas', which indicates his understanding of how they work. The pleasure of poetry is thoroughly associational in that we form associations more readily when we are impressed with the beauty of the manner in which ideas are presented to us and when we are impressed by the poet's mastery over his own associations. That the poet should have control over his own and the reader's associations seems to have been a well-known principle of associationism, judging by Wordsworth's preface to the *Lyrical Ballads*, to give a famous example to which I have already alluded. Here, Wordsworth clearly gestures to the notion that the poet's task, at least in part, is to engage the reader's associations in tandem with his own, which suggests that the poet maintains a level of control over and knowledge about his own associations. Additionally, Wordsworth's insistence that his poetry can only be appreciated properly by those who are in a 'healthful state of association' indicates that the poet claimed such a high level of expertise about associations that he could pass judgment on them in the manner of a trained psychologist.[37]

The associationists (and some poets, we may conclude) know something else about how the reader's associations work and how to manipulate them using verse: alliteration can 'influence ... the successions of our thought' without our knowledge that it does so, a concept about which Brown exclaims in *Lectures*, 'How readily suggestions of this kind occur, so as to modify indirectly the train of images and feelings in the mind, and what pleasure they can afford when they seem to have arisen without effort'.[38] Again, the poet must be artful enough to control the reader's associations – 'the trains of images and feelings in the mind' – without appearing to do so. Brown seems to have adopted this idea about the importance of apparent effortlessness in poetic thought-control from his master, Stewart, who asserts in *Elements of the Philosophy of the Human Mind*, 'When an idea ... is thus suggested by association, it produces a slighter impression ... than if it were presented more directly' and is thus more likely to please – or not to displease – the hearer, who will therefore be more likely to accept the idea.[39] In his article about Akenside's *Pleasures of Imagination* and associationism, Martin Kallich reveals that other poets besides Brown and Wordsworth were aware of the potentials offered by the combination of associationist principles and verse: 'the will of the poet is more powerful than the casual force of associations controlled by contiguity and can consciously employ 'the secret laws Which bring them to each other' in order to frame a work of art'.[40] The artful poet creates a symphony of special conditions through which he may engage or even implant suggestions in our minds, thanks to his knowledge of the 'secret laws' of the mind, a phrase that recalls strongly Beddoes's comment upon the 'secret' of the composition of the mind that prevents poets from going insane through the indulgence of their imaginations.[41] Armed with knowledge of and control over his own and the reader's associations, as well as linguistic mastery, the poet creates a work of beauty, balance or, to advance Brown's argument in the preface to *The Paradise of Coquettes*, humour that forms associations in the reader's mind through its apparent effortlessness. Moreover, precisely because the reader is unaware of being controlled, the poet may be 'a legislator still, fashioning our conduct, even when we are not conscious that we are obeying him'.[42] In the above ways, poetry is presented as the ideal medium for producing particular associations in the reader's mind, which, I will argue, is necessary for Brown's educational purposes as a psychologist-poet. This aspect of associationist poetry also positions the psychological approach as oppositional to the Romantic ideal of the self-created and world-creating subject. However, since several canonical poets, like Wordsworth and Coleridge, used their poetry to illustrate the veracity of associationist principles, we must reconsider our comfortable assumptions about such static and inherently unified Romantic ideals.

II. Brown's Associationist Verse and the Indirect Method of Moral Education

It is evident from an examination of Brown's, Wordsworth's and countless other poets' and associationists' writing that many Romantic-era thinkers regarded this psychological approach and verse to be complementary, but this opinion does not seem to have helped to popularize Brown's poetry. David Welsh, one of Brown's Romantic-era biographers, avers, 'That Dr Brown preferred poetry to philosophy, is certain', even though his official career would have indicated the opposite: he held the post as Professor of Moral Philosophy at Edinburgh University. Despite Brown's desire to gain prominence through his poetry, his dedication to verse seems only to have harmed his public image:

> The frequency with which the poetical works of Dr Brown succeeded each other began to excite remark. And while the devotion of his mind to poetry, to the neglect, as was supposed, of philosophy, was objected to him by his enemies almost as a moral defect in his character, even those were inclined to judge more favourably, regretted it as a weakness that materially injured his reputation.[43]

His attempts to become yet more involved in the literary life of Edinburgh led him to form, with Francis Jeffrey and other members of what was called 'The Academy of Physics', a better-known venture, namely the *Edinburgh Review*.[44] However, Brown eventually broke ties with the *Review*, apparently through some clash with Jeffrey (who seems to have had a great knack for starting rows).[45] Despite the dearth of appreciation for his verse, however, Brown persisted, penning by the end of his life several volumes of it. Given that he was not rewarded with the accolades he sought and was even accused of damaging his professional reputation by writing poetry, it is reasonable to suggest that he continued to pen verse in order to achieve some greater goal. The nature of this goal becomes apparent upon examination of Brown's statements about Christianity, morals and the ability of verse to educate.

Brown adopted the notion that verse could be used to educate the reader and encourage her to improve morally during his early university years as a student of moral philosophy under Stewart. The older philosopher writes, about the faculty to which all poetry appeals,

> The faculty of Imagination is the great spring of human activity, and the principal source of human improvement. As it delights in presenting to the mind scenes and characters more perfect than those which we are acquainted with, it prevents us from ever being completely satisfied with our present condition, or with our past attainments, and engages us continually in the pursuit of some untried enjoyment, or of some ideal excellence.[46]

Even before Stewart, associationism focused on reforming the morals of those whom it was thought to benefit. Indeed, Hartley comments on the educative properties of associationism and, crucially, he emphasizes that words are essential to this task in a statement that may have further influenced Brown to expand his linguistic mastery from psychological prose into the realm of verse; in a passage that illustrates why William Hatherell calls 'language ... the supreme associationist commodity' for Hartley, the philosopher asserts in *Observations on Man*,

> Since Words thus collect Ideas from various Quarters, unite them together, and transfer them both upon other Words, and upon foreign Objects, it is evident, that the Use of Words adds much to the Number and Complexness of our Ideas, and is the principal Means by which we make intellectual and moral Improvements.[47]

Brown concurs that association, morals and education are bound together in this manner when he comments, about the 'influence of peculiar directions of the suggesting principle on moral ... character', that 'what is commonly termed *education*, is nothing more than the art of skilfully guiding this ... [process], so as to form the intellectual and moral combinations in which wisdom and virtue exist'.[48] Brown considered verse to be particularly useful for guiding the reader's associations; therefore, poetry was, to him, the perfect medium 'to raise and refine the tone of the moral sentiments of his readers'.[49]

Although some of his readers seemed to think that poetry and psychology should not mix, Brown may have been encouraged to write associationist verse by reading other psychologist-poets' work.[50] In *Observations on the Zoönomia of Erasmus Darwin, MD* (which Brown wrote when he was only nineteen years old!), he shows that he considers the elder scientist's poetry worthy of serious consideration by discussing it early and analytically in the preface to this rigorous analysis of Darwin's mammoth study: 'The system of life, which forms the groundwork of *Zoönomia*, is marked by the same bold originality of thought, that distinguished the theoretical part of the *Botanic Garden*'.[51] By entitling one of his volumes *The Bower of Spring*, a title that is strongly reminiscent of Darwin's *Botanic Garden* or *The Temple of Nature*, Brown works on the reader's associative powers to ally himself with the tradition of psychologist-poets' verse, over which Darwin may be said to have presided.

Other evidence indicates that Brown was aware of Beddoes's poetry, which might well have been the case since he was *au courant* with the work of Darwin, Beddoes's great collaborator, friend and writer of the inspiration for Beddoes's poetic imitation, *Alexander's Expedition*. Apparent references to Beddoes's long poem exist throughout Brown's volume *The Renovation of India*. Brown notes that the subject matter for the volume was decided by the organizers of the competition for which he wrote it, a circumstance that would seem to obviate any assumptions about the influence Beddoes's colonial poem may have had on this long poem. However, some of the specific features of *The Renovation of India* are so like those in Beddoes's poem that it seems certain that Brown paid homage to his fellow psychologist-poet's work in his poem of a similar nature. For example, Brown complains about colonial attacks on India and recommends teaching religion and science to its inhabitants in his poem, while recognizing the ancient attainments in these fields of the Eastern nation, a feature that recalls Beddoes's poetic assertion, '– And now, the Rout pollutes the hallowed shore, / That nursed young Art, and infant Science bore'.[52] Also like Beddoes, who includes many references to Hindu culture in his voluminous notes to *Alexander's Expedition*, Brown attempts to kindle in his audience a desire to learn more about the holy books of India and he does so through a similar poetic technique: by appending an embarrassment of notes to the verse.[53] While Beddoes argues in the preface for the importance of his notes, Brown, similarly, declares in his own preface that he considers the notes to perform a function much like cod liver oil: to be salutary, if unpleasant, or 'a sort of tax, which the reader may very fairly be entreated to pay'.[54] The possible influence of Beddoes's work on that of Brown is most evident in the poem itself, particularly in the anti-colonial sentiments, which I outline with reference to *Alexander's Expedition* in Chapter 3. The democratic and Beddoesian echoes are unmistakable in *The Renovation of India*:

> India! – What thoughts of glory and of shame,
> What pride and sorrow, mingle at the name!
> – A realm of kings, by arts, and arms, and guile,
> Won to the little sceptre of our isle;
> Where merchant heroes, cold to nobler fire,
> Brib'd to be great, illustrious for hire,
> Even in the doubtful or victorious hour,

> *Gold* still in view, the single charm of power,
> With warrior's statesmen's sudden instinct wise,
> Achiev'd an empire for a plunderer's prize.[55]

Just as Brown implies that Britain depends on mercenaries to carry out their dirty colonial deeds, Beddoes compares the colonists of India, from the ancient Greeks to the English, to be far from honourable in their designs upon the Eastern nation:

> Fierce, in the van, her firebrand Warfare waves,
> Dire, at her heels, the cry of hell-hounds raves;
> Roused by the yell, the Greedy and the Bold
> Start to the savage chace of blood and gold.[56]

In sharing a bold, even dangerous, political stance with the firebrand and near-Revolutionary, Beddoes, Brown seems to ally himself very consciously with the Whiggish psychologist-poets who preceded him.

Finally, Brown's volume *The War-Fiend* provides evidence of the psychologist-poet's possible connections to Beddoes and Darwin, even while it illustrates Brown's unique desire to instill associationist principles in his reader's mind after the manner that he outlines in *Lectures*. Brown asserts his social connections with the world of Darwin and Beddoes not in the eponymous poem, but in those that immediately follow it, which are addressed to Thomas Wedgwood. Thomas Wedgwood was the younger brother of Josiah Wedgwood, with whom he shared an interest in associationism and who was a longtime member of Darwin's Lunar Society of Birmingham.[57] (Incidentally, Thomas Wedgwood was also friends with Coleridge at a time when Coleridge socialized with Beddoes and Darwin; in fact, in 1798, Coleridge stayed with the Wedgwoods at Bristol, where the elder psychologist-poets lived and where Beddoes ran his Pneumatic Institute).[58] Brown was inspired to write 'To Thomas Wedgwood, Esq.' and 'On the Death of Thomas Wedgwood, Esq.' when, as he notes in the prologue to the first poem, Wedgwood asked Brown to 'accompany him as his physician and friend' to the West Indies, to which Wedgwood fled in the hope that the warmer climate would cure his final illness.[59] Through such verses, Brown may have been trying to form his literary identity as a psychologist-poet. That is to say, by dropping the right names, Brown may have been trying to establish his poetic contributions in the context of the psychologist-poets tradition, of which Darwin and Beddoes were very visible members.[60]

Yet, Brown did not rely on such allusions to establish his identity as a psychologist-poet. Throughout his verse, he develops the poetic principles that he outlines in *Lectures*, one of the most influential associationist documents of the Romantic period. By presenting the dangers and suffering that result from inappropriate moral decisions through the attractive medium of poetry, Brown attempts to educate his reader through indirect, associationist means. Significantly, Brown rarely addresses his reader openly in these lines, as is common in the poetry of Christian psychologists, like Beattie and Cotton, or moral managers, like Ferriar, Bakewell and Duncan. In his effort to involve the reader's heart and mind without her awareness that the process is taking place – for he asserts that this method is most effective in changing the reader's paths of associations in the manner intended by the writer – Brown focuses almost all of the verse on fictional and non-fictional figures and their often extraordinary stories. He hopes to engage her feelings and form her associations by rousing her empathy in response to the poetic tale he relates, instead of by commanding the reader, 'Study the Science of your Heart', in the style of Cotton.[61] Thus, the subject that is formed through Brown's associationist poetry is, in several ways, externally created. Because she is the product of mental changes unbeknownst to herself and, borne of responses to lives, actions and an entire discourse not her own, she is a stranger to herself.

To return to *The War-Fiend*, Brown develops a moral position through the construction of an ethical quandary that is improperly handled in the poem, as he does in many other volumes. *The War-Fiend* describes the horrors of moral culpability, but his favourite theme – that of women's sexual morality – is replaced by the themes of war and revenge. Brown asserts that, because of 'his bloodthirsty and ambitious eagerness for combat', the 'war-fiend' accepts the help of an unseen and evil spirit to travel to the scene of war and, once there, gluts his desire for revenge in an atrocious manner:

> Swift pursue! The living ground
> Let thy panting courser spurn!
> Sweet as rise the groans around,
> Fiercer thirst of blood should burn.[62]

The poem goes on to detail the evils let loose by the 'war-fiend's' decision to ally with evil forces in his dedication to war, a theme that would have interested many Britons in this period because of the Napoleonic Wars. Here, as in several other volumes of poetry by Brown, the reader bears witness to the outcome of immorality. As such, Brown reveals in the *Lectures*, the reader will inevitably and, as it were, unconsciously refine her own ethical system in accordance with Brown's moral strictures. His lecture 'On the Influence of Particular Suggestions on the Intellectual and Moral Character' reveals how poetry, as a force of suggestion and external influence on our perceptions, may form the reader's moral character:

> In this tendency to mutual suggestion ... there is not a single perception or thought, or emotion of man, and consequently not an object around him, that is capable of acting on his senses, which may not have influence on the whole future character of

his mind, by modifying, for ever after, in some greater or less degree, those complex feelings of good and evil, by which his passions are excited or animated.[63]

Indeed, Brown's poetry is far from 'art for art's sake', in the style of Oscar Wilde and his fellow aesthetes during the *fin de siècle*. Like all of his fellow Romantic-era psychologist-poets – especially Beattie, whom he quotes often in his prose works about their mutual topic of expertise, moral philosophy[64] – Brown meant to educate his readers and form their ethics through his verse.

Brown establishes his public identity by emphasizing the psychological subject matter of much of his verse. For example, *Emily* is a series of short poems that, as Brown puts it in the preface to the volume, 'are an attempt to describe the feelings of a delicate mind, in its progress from one rash moral error, through different stages of vice'.[65] The nature of this 'rash moral error' may be guessed from the opening lines of 'Sonnet III' from the sequence:

> Come then, – come all my misery! – Let me sink
> Low as the thing I am! – Feign'st thou to mourn,
> Insulter? – No! Be proud, – for thou hast torn
> A heart that clung to thee![66]

This theme of a woman's decision to accept her lover's advances out of wedlock is one with which Brown seems to have been inordinately concerned, as is evident in his earlier long poem about Mary Wollstonecraft, *The Wanderer in Norway*, which, Brown asserts in the preface to the poem, 'is intended to be nothing more than the picture of an impassioned mind, in circumstances of strong and wild emotion'.[67] In this volume about the feminist author's experiences directly after she became pregnant and was jilted by Gilbert Imlay, thereafter following him to Norway, Brown means to present her as

> a memorable example of the infirmities which one great moral error may develope in a character, that, but for this single error, would, to the individual, as well as to others, have appeared incapable of looking on such feebleness but with contempt; and of the many miseries, in the endless unforeseen perplexities of distress.[68]

By using Wollstonecraft's biography to illustrate the suffering that 'followed the first great misery of having yielded to a guilty passion', Brown encourages his reader to make a different decision than she did and resist giving her lover 'all the rights of a husband without legitimate title'.[69] That Brown wants his reader to become personally engaged with the question of sexual morality that the poem raises is clear in an unusually direct address to the reader, in which he pleads for Wollstonecraft's cause:

> She seeks no pure esteem of honour born:–
> Yet let compassion mingle with thy scorn!

. . . .

In thee is pity safe. – Thy soul sublime
Can mourn the agony, and hate the crime.[70]

It may appear that Brown provides further evidence of his apparently liberal politics in this poem, which enjoins the audience to 'pity' Wollstonecraft at a time when public denunciation of her sexual immorality had reached an all-time high, thanks to the publication of William Godwin's *Memoirs of the Author of A Vindication of the Rights of Woman*, in which Wollstonecraft's widower revealed not only that she had borne Fanny, her first child, to Imlay out of wedlock, but also that she had attempted suicide several times.[71] However, the above lines capture well the spirit of the entire poem, in which Brown encourages his audience to denounce Wollstonecraft's 'moral errors' and even to develop a kind of personal horror for them. These poems exemplify Brown's attempts to inculcate his notions of proper morality in his reader through the passionate and illustrative medium of poetry.

Yet, the volume of poetry that most powerfully illustrates Brown's associationist method of versifying is *The Paradise of Coquettes*. Here, the psychologist-poet describes his approach in a detailed preface in which he illustrates that even the most apparently innocuous feature of the poem, its humorousness, is an associationist technique for conveying what he calls 'moral truths'.[72] In a statement to which I claim Percy Bysshe Shelley pays homage in the famous final sentence of 'A Defence of Poetry', in which he calls poets 'the unacknowledged legislators of the world', Brown asserts that the 'bard' in his day 'is a legislator still, fashioning our conduct, even when we are not conscious that we are obeying him'.[73] In other words, the poet can brainwash his audience into accepting his moral lessons through the distinct charm and memorable qualities of verse to which he gestures in *Lectures*. Besides the pleasing aesthetic qualities that, he claims in the psychological text, are particularly effective in impressing poetic suggestions upon the reader's mind, Brown notes in this preface that humour creates associations efficiently in the reader's mind because the pleasure it affords makes the sentiments it expresses memorable. Liveliness of all sorts can be used by the poet to form associations in the reader's mind, whether it involves imagistic beauty, aural balance and eloquence, or, amongst other features, a comic quality: 'The livelier the emotion may be, the longer must it continue to coexist with objects, and the quicker and surer, therefore, must it be to recal such objects as have at any time co-existed with it'.[74] In the preface to *Paradise*, Brown even claims that his comedic associationist poetry is superior to that of more popular Romantic poetry, explaining, 'The great evil of our serious poetry' is that 'by the very circumstance of its stately gravity, it has necessarily a didactic air, which lessens the force of its persuasion. It is an original sin of our nature, to be not very willing to admit reproof', while, he adds, 'a playful hand' can do much more to combat vice in its audience.[75] He implies that, thanks to his training as a psychologist, he has gained an understanding of human nature's propensity to accept the advice of a jocular master, which, in turn, has inspired him to write a humorous poem. Importantly, he does not suggest that didactic poetry is undesirable. On the contrary, he implies that verse with the 'force of ... persuasion' is optimal, but that it should not appear to be educative. Again, Brown suggests that his poetry aims to teach the reader without her being aware of the process, to trick her into adopting the content of his instruction. If successful, Brown establishes himself as the ultimate figure of psychological authority, for he thereby changes the mind of the reader – he forms her subjectivity – without her consent.

To be sure, the title of the volume – *The Paradise of Coquettes* – is a good indicator of its lighthearted tone, but this volume was not the only one in which Brown uses humour. For example, in *The Bower of Spring*, the eponymous poem is meant to be humorous, as becomes clear upon a perusal of Brown's atypically short preface to it. Here, Brown illustrates that he can laugh at his signature method of amalgamating poetry and scientific philosophy when he declares, with mock seriousness, '"The Bower of Spring", though in verse, is destined to unfold one of the most profound discoveries that have been made in the Philosophy of Nature', which is, as the pages thereafter indicate, that fine ladies' love of going to parties while wintering in the city has, by some mysterious force of sympathy between the ladies and the seasons, caused an unnatural extension of the winter months.[76] He later adds, 'there is as much sound philosophy in my short poem, as in many of the most subtile disquisitions that are addressed to the scientific ears of Royal Societies, or in hundreds and thousands of the pages of larger Treatises'.[77] In *Paradise*, too, Brown uses scientific discovery to augment the poem; after all, its humorous quality is a result of the poet's desire to teach the reader new morals through associationist techniques. The potential for success of his cunningly humorous and slyly didactic verse is evident even in the genuinely funny prose preface to *Paradise*. For example, he praises the ballad form on the score that it presents action immediately, unlike the epic, 'Which', he laments, 'often ... prepares the reader so fully for what is about to be presented to him, that the picture itself is in a great measure anticipated, and ... seems scarcely to have the charm of novelty'.[78] He goes on to surmise,

> How dull would a tragedy appear, if, at every shifting of the scene, during its first representation, some very kind friend at our elbow were to be unwearied in telling us, – Now the Princess is gone, to prepare the poison, which is afterwards to be slily mixed in the bowl for her rival, – Now the Prince is to discover, that he has been made the instrument of presenting death to his mistress, and is to swallow what remains in the goblet.[79]

Brown's talent for humorous writing is palpable. However, when the reader sees that he intends to inculcate his own notions of right and wrong in the reader, she chokes on her laughter because it becomes an expression of her compliance with his autocratic plans for her. Notably, though, just as all of the psychologist-poets express the beneficence of their seemingly despotic intentions, Brown did not see his morally coercive verse as such, but as an expression of his obligation to mankind: 'It is the duty of the poet', he urges in this preface, 'to avail himself, as much as his subject allows, of all the sources of pleasure in our mental frame, that lies within the compass of his art' in order to establish what he believed were the proper moral values in the reader.[80]

Brown's contention that circumlocutory education is the most effective means of forming powerful associations in the reader builds on Stewart's ideas about indirection, delineated above. Brown states his agreement with Stewart most powerfully in the preface to *Paradise* when he asserts, 'The notion of vice and virtue, that are truly effective, are not those which we call up, in our grave enquiries into the principles of morals and the practical duties of man, but those which float among the mind spontaneously, in the very hour or moment of action'.[81] Very subtly, indeed, does Brown attempt to inculcate his notions of moral action in the reader, for the poem itself appears to be nothing more than a (frankly lame) imitation of Alexander Pope's *The Rape of the Lock*, replete with beaux, ladies at their toilets, coquettes who are the recipients of divine revelation and scenes of love described in the language of war. The following lines are sufficient to illustrate the nature of the poem throughout its nine parts:

> Poet of Woman, – for that proudest name,
> I leave the contest of all meaner fame.
>
> . . . .
>
> Where Beaux, with more than love's short blindness dark,
> Lose, with their eyes, the power all eyes to mark;
> And heroes, graceful in the mazy strife,
> Lopt of their limbs and glory, limp for life:
> While Bards, twice butchering, every wound rehearse,
> And softly teach anatomy in verse.[82]

Brown's intention was not to capitalize on Pope's success through a close imitation of the style and subject matter of his most famous poem, he claims, but to 'represent the manners which are living around us, – to trace to the heart many of those little passions which are suffered to appear to the eye only in the smile or the frown' for the express purpose of teaching us the dangers of such behaviour. We may surmise from his assurance, elsewhere in the preface, that he intends to educate the reader regarding proper moral behaviour through his comedic poetry.[83]

III. A Daemonic Doctor and Impressionable Identity

By using verse to popularize the relatively new discipline of psychology and his identity as an associationist, Brown exemplifies the figure of the psychologist-poet. When Stewart-Robinson declares that Brown 'imagined his work [and especially his poetry] to be a "Georgics" of the mind, a culturing of its very science', he expresses eloquently the objective of all of the psychologist-poets: to marry the realms of psychology and literature, which were rapidly becoming more distinct as the disciplines became increasingly reified and their members professionalized.[84] Brown amalgamates psychology and verse more completely than does any other psychologist-poet because he identifies the unique qualities of verse, such as its beauty, elegance and subtlety, as the best means of employing the indirect method of education that the associationist needs in order to implant suggestions and, ultimately, moral values in the reader's mind. Finally, the fact that this psychologist-poet reveals his classist and snobbish attitudes towards many of his uneducated readers (as in the *Agnes* preface, quoted above)[85] – even while he admits that the reader must remain 'unconscious' that the poet-legislator is leading her to form certain ideas and moral values – indicates that the seemingly accidental tyranny that, I have argued, was always a feature of psychologist-poets' verse has become shameless authoritarianism by the second decade of the nineteenth century.[86] It may be too presumptuous to claim an absolute chronological pattern for the development of this tradition of poetry, but it does seem significant that this latter-day master of it would shun even lip-service to democracy and egalitarianism, even though Brown seems to echo the liberal sentiments of his fellow psychologist-poets in some other ways, as I hope I have established. That he was mistaken for having republican politics by his contemporaries corroborates further that Brown was received as a member of the tradition I have been describing, while his genuinely authoritarian attitude suggests that all such verse by psychologists is inherently reifying for their profession because it teaches its readers the language of their discipline and encourages the adoption of its principles.[87]

Through the proliferation of psychological concepts in wider society via the attractive medium of poetry, the reader is subjectified. This verse makes a subject of her by teaching her to consider herself as a subject, the 'I' who must be understood through self-reflection, or, in other words, psychological means. It also subjects her in the sense of restricting her freedom by limiting the definition of her identity to the confines of a particular psychological approach, that is to say, to its conception and attendant linguistic expression of what a self may be and how it is formed. What kind of subject is defined by associationism? The associationist subject is externally formed, defined by her relations with the outside world, since her paths of association – which Brown and others elide with their idea of the mind, consciousness, or, as Foucault would say, subjectivity –are constructed through the sensory perception of the material world. As such, this subject exemplifies the transformation of private experience and identity into something that is externally mediated, which is the process that every subject endures in response to psychological definition and is another aspect of its subjectification. If psychological texts had continued to be written only by the likes of Hume, Locke and Hartley, then the average reader might not be exposed to various psychological approaches' conceptualizations of who they are as subjects and might have escaped this form of subjectification. Indeed, earlier – and, truly, many late – psychological texts were written for specialist audiences and were all but inaccessible to a broad audience. But the trajectory that made psychology available to a wider range of readers and was exemplified in prose for Romantic readers by Priestley's rewriting of Hartley's *Observations on Man* was also manifested throughout the Romantic period in verse, as well, as I hope I have proven in this study. However much this contention may be true, it does not necessarily follow that these liberal educators were autocrats. For example, when Priestley reveals in the preface to *Hartley's Theory of the Human Mind* that he wants to make Hartley's '*theory of the mind* more intelligible, and the study of it more inviting', we need not counter that he deceitfully positions himself as our beneficiary even as he provides the means of our mental enslavement.[88] Like most of the psychologist-poets, who were motivated by the egalitarian and often republican political principles of Scottish medical schools whence much of British psychology developed, Hartley's intentions may have been entirely admirable. The ultimate and long-range effect of the dispersal of psychological knowledge throughout society was unknown. Despite their stated intentions, though, psychologists' poetry helped to establish their discipline and, simultaneously, it enlisted the otherwise anti-authoritarian field of literature as a servant of psychology.

CONCLUSION: THOMAS FORSTER, PHRENOLOGY AND THE REIFICATION OF THE DISCIPLINES

I. Phrenology, Cranial Bumps and the Text of the Soul

> When — — is drunken, and talks like a fool,
> 'Tis not at all strange; for by a known rule,
> (As people of learning will judge of a book,
> If but at its title and index they look,)
> You may swear by his forehead, his mouth, nose, and chin,
> That if he was sober, he's no sense within.[1]

The above poem by Bakewell about the features of a face as expressive of a person's inner character introduces the topic of phrenology, which, in turn, concludes this study in several important ways. I contend that phrenology is exemplary of psychology's tendency to define subjectivity in external terms, a process that unites all of the various psychological approaches I have been describing throughout this study and, as such, all of the discrete arguments I have developed in each chapter, as well. I will show that phrenology, especially as expressed in the verse and prose of Thomas Forster (1789–1860), defined the subject through its discourse in an ineluctable way that positioned the phrenologist as the master of the subject's personal identity and the subject as utterly circumscribed by disciplinary power.

As the science of reading cranial bumps and facial features as an index to personal identity, phrenology was 'designed to reveal the inner man from outer signs'.[2] The 'more empirical offspring' of the physiognomy of Johann Caspar Lavater (1741–1801), which studied the whole body to discover how the psychological and spiritual make-up of the subject expressed itself in the body, phrenology focused more specifically on the head and less stringently on the role of the spirit in forming the outer person.[3] These distinguishing characteristics gave the approach the reputation of being overly positivistic and deterministic.

Lavater's student, Franz Joseph Gall (1758–1828), broke away from his teacher in order to focus on the head and lectured and published around Europe and the United States with a student of his own, Johann Gaspar Spurzheim (1776–1832).[4] Gall and Spurzheim's new science of the mind proposed that one's psychological character – such as one's emotions, inclinations and basic personality – was reflected by various 'organs' or areas of the brain, which were larger or smaller according to their preponderance in the personality of the subject. Thanks to a particularly subtle and sensitive skull, as the phrenologists saw it, the size of these organs and aspects of one's individual psychology were expressed through the bumps and facial features of the subject's head.

Therefore, when Bakewell claims in 'On a Stupid Looking Fellow, When Drunk' to be able to judge his inebriated subject's intelligence by studying 'his forehead, his mouth, nose, and chin', he indicates that he subscribes to the tenets of phrenology.[5] However, as I maintain in Chapter 2, Bakewell used a moral management approach in his asylum, which illustrates his belief that the diseased mind is an emotional and ethical construct that can be cured through personal interaction with the patient. Moral management is therefore the quintessential 'Romantic' psychology, as Shorter defines the term, because it focuses on morals, emotions and even spirituality as basic to mental disease and cure, while, on the other hand, phrenology was exemplary of the empirical approach.[6] As such, Bakewell's phrenologically suggestive lines confirm what I have argued throughout this study: that in the time of the psychologist-poets, when the disciplinary boundaries were so fluid that psychologists could express their ideas through poetry and vice versa, these doctors of the mind often subscribed simultaneously to several different psychological approaches, like nerve theory, moral management, associationism and phrenology. By the end of this period of fluid boundaries between the disciplines, to reiterate Richardson's suggestive phrase for the situation, when psychology became increasingly reified, its definitions of subjectivity more concretized and its practitioners more professionalized (and wary of sharing their professional knowledge), doctors were encouraged to choose a distinct approach to the definition of the mind and use a single psychological discourse exclusively.[7] During the Romantic period, however, writers like Bakewell celebrated a variety of psychological approaches in both poetry and prose. Near the end of the period, psychologist-poets' works are peppered with an increasing number of caveats and apologias to defend their all-encompassing interests and diversity of media, but it was only in the latter half of the nineteenth century that the 'dialogue' between the humanities and medicine was decidedly 'disrupted', as Veatch so evocatively speaks of the break.

Bakewell's short poem, which appears above in its entirety, also emphasizes how a once-egalitarian project of the Scottish Enlightenment transformed into an increasingly authoritarian discipline with a broadly social focus. By chastising his subject for indulging too freely in alcohol, which marks the imbiber as irresponsible and insufficiently serious, Bakewell manifests the socially regulating function of psychology at the same time that he reveals his sympathy with Christian psychologists like Cotton and Beattie, who stress the ethical good of shunning bodily indulgence as key to mental health, as well as nerve theorists, who, as I have illustrated, make overindulgence in alcohol one of the key ways in which the subject 'sins' against the rules for the maintenance of good personal and social health set out by this governor and 'hygienist', as I have dubbed him. Significantly, by presenting the body as a 'book', Bakewell reiterates a comparison that Beddoes devises to represent the subject of medicine when, as I note in Chapter 3, he writes in *Hygëia* that 'the physician can read the state of the interior as plainly as if the body were a book, the alteration in organs accessible to the sense, and the patient's account of his feelings, serving him for letters. In nervous complaints, everything is different.'[8] Beddoes presents the subject's body as a text to stress the esotericism and unique authority of the nerve theorist. By comparing the drunk's face to a book, Bakewell echoes Beddoes by asserting that the facial features of the subject may be interpreted by the 'rule[s]' of phrenology.[9] In his use of the word 'rule', Bakewell confirms that the phrenologist's definitions of the facial and cranial features of the subject's head are an organized chart and hard evidence of what is, in fact, chaotic, immaterial and therefore not amenable to such an empirical treatment. In phrenology, human motivation, desires, character and emotions are treated as though they express themselves in the material world in no uncertain terms, which is the ultimate objectification of the private, indefinable inner self, the final transformation of this chaos – which was so feared because of its lack of structure, as I argue in Chapter 1 – into that which is regulated and not mysterious to the phrenologist.

In these lines, Bakewell also emphasizes the phrenologist's unique knowledge and authority and the subject's relative powerlessness with respect to psychological discourse. By commenting that this method of interpreting cranial features is only 'known' to 'people of learning', Bakewell implies that only those who have been inducted into the language of phrenology through a unique course of training are able to 'read' the text that is the subject's body.[10] The terms of this comparison imply that whoever is not a phrenologist – like the patient of the individual psychologist, the reader of the poem, the subject that is defined by psychology, all of whom I have treated as identifiable with one another throughout this study – is, like a book that is 'read' by the phrenologist and thereby transformed in an essential way into the *discourse* of psychology. In phrenology, the sign of the self is written indelibly on the head. Every innate characteristic is printed there and interpreted in a way that is defined entirely by the phrenologist. In fact, as Thomas Forster shows in his poetry, the head's bumps are the only true text of the self and assurance against deception about the subject's genuine character.

II. Thomas Forster and Phrenological Discourse

Forster is the last of the psychologist-poets I will explore in this study, but this study is one of the first to discuss his work.[11] This latter fact is surprising, since he is credited with coining the word 'phrenology' in *Philosophical Magazine*, which he later republished as *Sketch of the New Anatomy and Physiology of the Brain and Nervous System of Drs Gall and Spurzheim, Considered as Comprehending a Complete System of Zoonomy, With Observations on its Tendency to the Improvement of Education, of Punishment, and of the Treatment of Insanity*, from which the celebrated Spurzheim adopted it.[12] The dearth of criticism that accounts for the influence of Forster's contributions is even more mystifying when one considers the great number of works of literary criticism that discuss the influence of phrenology, in general, and Spurzheim's theory, in particular, upon the most famous Romantic writers. For instance, in 'Physiognomy, Phrenology, and Blake's Visionary Heads', Anne Mellor maintains that Blake was well acquainted with the principles of phrenology, while Jason Hall's fascinating and informative article, 'Gall's Phrenology: A Romantic Psychology', very helpfully considers this approach in terms of such accepted Romantic ideals as individualism and concludes that phrenology was in this way utterly Romantic, despite its materialistic bias. No doubt similarly aware of the broadly popular appeal of phrenology during the Romantic period, which was manifested in the crush of people in attendance upon Gall's 1825 lectures in London, a few other critics have examined Romanticism in light of phrenology, such as Rothman Salazar, who explores intersections between phrenology and Wordsworth's work in 'Historicizing Phrenology: Wordsworth, Pynchon, and the Discursive Economy of the Cranial Text', Burton Pollin in 'Nicholson's Lost Portrait of William Godwin: A Study in Phrenology' and Eric C. Walker in 'Reading Proof, Aids to Reflection, and Phrenology: A New Coleridge Letter'.[13] The greatest number of literary critical studies that consider the cultural influence of phrenology – and there are many – are devoted to Victorian works; these I will therefore pass over as beyond the scope of this study. Despite the plain interest of literary critics in phrenology, however, the figure who invented the word has escaped notice – until now.

Forster's contribution to phrenology went beyond giving a catchy name to a discipline that was sometimes also called 'cranioscopy'.[14] Born and educated in London, Forster made a huge impact on the medical community in Scotland by delivering a paper on phrenology to the Wernerian Society of Edinburgh, which was, according to Janet Browne, the first time anyone had done so before a learned society in Scotland.[15] (Forster also showed his admiration for his neighbours to the north by writing several poems in Scottish dialect, such as 'Address to Twa Tumbler Pidgeons' and 'On a Mouse Accidentally Killed', which begins, very derivatively of Robert Burns's 'To a Mouse', 'Alas! wee cow'ring donsie mouse').[16] Forster attempted to expand the scope of phrenological inquiry by showing how such concepts could intersect with other avenues of psychological inquiry in, for example, *Observations on Some Curious and Hitherto Unnoticed Abnormal Affections of the Organs of Sense and Intellect. And on Other Subjects of Physiology*, in which he writes, 'All our organs of sense and of intellect have their appropriate objects in the external world, of whose existence they give us notice, by representing them in corresponding actions of the sensorium'.[17] Here, Forster suggests that the external world, to which he attributed psychological health and illness in his most famous text, *Observations on the Casual and Periodical Influence of the Particular State of the Atmosphere on Human Health and Diseases, Particularly Insanity*, may shape the various 'organs' of our brain, which are thereafter studied by the phrenologist. He reiterates this link and explains how it may lead to psychological therapy later in the same text when he writes that 'the hallucinations of the madman and hypochondriac' are often due to 'the morbid action of the organ of cautiousness', adding, 'Like other affections of the brain too, this is influenced by atmospherical changes, and is worse about the new and full moon'.[18] Perhaps Forster is clearest about how his trademark theory about atmospheric influences on mental health works with phrenological concepts in a text that he published between the two above-mentioned works, called *Illustrations of the Atmospherical Origin of Epidemic Disorders of Health ... and Of the Twofold Means of Prevention, Mitigation, and Cure, by Change of Air, and by Diet, Regularity, and Simple Medicines*. He comments,

> The brain is the instrument of mental power, as the other nerves are of what is called automatic life. It is a complicated assemblage of the organs of the different sentiments, propensities, and intellectual faculties; and any one of these may have a morbid action, in proportion as its particular organ be disordered. And further, the organs of the brain are subject to disease similar to other parts of the body; – to inflammation, – to morbid irritability, – to loss of tone, – to paralytic affections. They suffer, also, in common with other parts, from atmospherical causes. Hence the weather can affect the mind through the medium of the brain.[19]

The brain guides the mind's formation and has a great effect on its constitution. In this assertion, Forster turns Lavater's approach to the relationship between the two faculties on its head, so to speak, since Lavater emphasized the body of man as the product of the 'spirit within man which shapes the body, and individual uniqueness'.[20] Given these original speculations and his close relationship with Spurzheim, it becomes clear that Forster's contributions to phrenology are worth exploring in greater detail.

As much as Forster made his unique mark on phrenological theory by combining it with his research into atmospherical influences upon psychological states, the homogeneity of his thought with that of many other psychologists in this study is apparent in his assertions about the link between the mind and the soul. Crucially, Forster identifies the mind with the soul in *Somatopsychonoologia Showing that the Proofs of Body Life and Mind Considered as Distinct Essences Cannot be Deduced from Physiology but Depend on a Distinct Sort of Evidence being an Examination of the Controversy Concerning Life Carried on by Mm. Laurence, Abernathy, Rennell, & Others* (signed 'Philostratus' because, Forster claims in the introduction, 'he wishes the argument of the Essay to stand on its own merits or demerits unprejudiced').[21] Forster identifies the 'soul', or the faculty that allows us to have a relationship with God, with the 'mind' in a way that at once gestures to his similarities with Cotton and Beattie, who also elided these concepts, and offers insights into the raging debates about animal rights during the period, to which I allude in Chapter 3: 'If the animals have minds', Forster quite reasonably and daringly asks, 'have they also souls; that is, are their minds to be everlasting?'[22] The 'everlasting' 'soul' is the equivalent of the 'mind' in this sentence. Since Forster states that the brain through which the mind or soul functions can be affected by the atmosphere – such as the position of the moon (in recognition of the popular notion of 'lunacy') and the weather – we may also deduce that the state of our souls, with which we relate to God and hope to enter heaven, can be damaged by a thunderstorm and thereafter change the course of our eternal lives. Yet, Forster has devised a loophole to save his theories from being ensnared in such irreligious conclusions by asserting that, however connected are the soul and the brain, they are, nevertheless, distinct. In *Epistolarium or Fasciculi of Curious Letters, Together With a Few Familiar Poems and Some Account of the Writers as Preserved Among the MSS of the Forster Family*, he exclaims, 'the brain is merely the instrument of the mind, it is not the mind itself!'.[23] This philosophical *deus ex machina* is weak, not to mention slightly misleading, since Forster claims elsewhere that the material organ can alter the spiritual one (e.g. Forster gestures to 'the inevitable conclusion, that every vital action, as well as every propensity, every intellectual and reflective faculty, and every sentiment of the mind, is the necessary consequence of the active state of an appropriate material organ'), instead of implying, as he does here that it is a mere 'instrument' or tool of the mind – this important caveat establishes Forster's orthodoxy in religious matters and his interest in the health of the soul and morals of the phrenological subject.[24]

In the same vein and text, Forster offers convincing argumentation to rescue his phrenological theories from imputations of being irredeemably materialistic, which was a matter of great concern to him as a believer in the eternity of the human (and animal) soul and, later in life, a staunch Roman Catholic. He exclaims, 'in reply to Locke; personal identity cannot consist in memory which is only one of its accidents: otherwise we must come to the absurd conclusion that loss of memory would cause a man not to be the same person as he was five seconds before he received a blow on the head!'.[25] He makes a similar claim in the volume that contains many of his poems, *Epistolarium or Fasciculi of Curious Letters*, where Forster reasons about

> the body, every particle of which is changed in a few years; while the mind, spiritual and identical and distinct from its constantly changing and perishable fabric, retains in old age a full memory of events that must have happened in childhood at a period when not one particle of its present flesh could have belonged to it. Thus then is the individual mind spiritual and superior to the body, which it is perpetually surviving and which it will continue to out live even when the external form of its present body is turned to dust.[26]

This reasonable and surprisingly contemporary argument maintains the psychologist-poet's identity as a keeper of society's soul, as he was in all other manifestations, but we must not conclude from his orthodoxy that Forster was backward or cowardly with respect to scientific advances. Indeed, in a manner that would impress even his atheistic Enlightenment forebears, Forster proclaims, 'The author is desirous of showing the completely distinct nature of physiology, and its harmlessness as far as respects any religious dogmas', adding,

> there is an ardent spirit of persecution in the mode of the attack and conduct adopted by persons who have joined in the cry against the supporters of materialism, which every lover of science must hold in abhorrence, convinced that truth is never brought to light by any safer means than a free and unrestrained examination of its evidences.[27]

Forster defends with equal vigour the most recent researches in neuroscience and the religious view that human life is also composed of spirit, soul, or mind.

Several literary critics have considered the question of why phrenology was so popular in the Romantic period, especially in consideration of its materialism, which seems to be anathema to the Romantic valorization of emotionalism and spirituality; its systematized nature, which seems to oppose the Romantic ideal of individuality and uniqueness; and its apparent determinism, which seems to challenge the Romantic conception of the self-creating subject. Mellor argues that even Spurzheim's materialistic phrenological theory recognizes the shaping role of the spirit upon the whole person, so much so that even Blake, the ultimate champion of the concept that man is an essentially spiritual being, could have accepted its principles.[28] Meanwhile, Hall maintains that phrenology emphasized the inevitable construction of unique individuals out of the twenty-seven faculties, or different dispositional 'organs', that compose the human brain, since they combine in an infinite variety of degrees to make a person.[29] 'Individual uniqueness is a central idea in Gall's psychology', Hall asserts, adding, 'He returns to the older idea of genetic innateness of character, which provides greater assurance of a persistent individuality, independent of environmental influences, but at the price of hints of determinism'.[30] The deterministic character of phrenology is evident in its four basic principles, as stated by Gall, which both Mellor and Hall cite; the first three are most relevant to this discussion: "1. Moral and intellectual faculties are innate, not acquired. 2. Their exercise depends on material organs. 3. The brain is the organ of all moral and intellectual faculties".[31] In other words, our psychological make-up is set from birth and imprinted on our brains. It follows that the only way to change our moral and intellectual identities is by altering the brain, since 'Their exercise depends on material organs', not vice versa. Forster might seem to avoid this dangerous conflation of principles by blurring their causal relationship, as I note above. However, in the 'Prolegomena in Philosophiam Musarum' in his volume of poetry, *Philosophia Musarum Containing the Songs and Romances of the Pipers [sic] Wallet, Pan, the Harmonia Musarum, and other Miscellaneous Poems*, Forster illustrates his ability to work through his own precepts and arrive at a logical, as opposed to emotional and defensive, conclusion by asserting that he himself

> had always been the selfsame being; and [was] confirmed [in] the opinion, which phrenology teaches us to entertain, of the predominance of cerebral configuration over all other causes of character; which shines constantly in essence, throught [sic] all the varieties in species produced by diversified education and the influence of external impressions.[32]

Since he asserts elsewhere that humans are a combination of spirit and matter, brain and soul, we may deduce that the 'selfsame being' of which he writes is comprised, in part, of soul. Thus, his soul, mind, or principle or organ of self-reflection is roughly determined from birth. Indeed, despite his occasional claims to the opposite, Forster indicates that he, like Gall and Spurzheim, believed that people have little control over the formation of their psychological beings.

In fact, Forster goes even further than do other phrenologists in denying to the subject the possibility of self-determination by laying explicit claim to linguistic power, which, as I will show, negates the subject's power to define her own identity. In a reiteration of his above comment, Forster leaves no doubt that, as a phrenologist, he was engaged in the business of defining and divining his subjects' very consciousnesses, their identities – what I have been calling their subjectivities – when he muses,

> This consciousness ... is an intuitive feeling, and resolves itself, after all the vain attempts of philosophers to explain it, into a conditional principle of existence. I believe that this very consciousness of a distinct being is itself dependent on the activity of some material and cerebral instrument ... For, strange as it may appear to those who are unacquainted with forms of insanity, this belief of our individual existence, this very power of discriminating between ourselves and the surrounding world, is weakened and nearly destroyed in particular cases of hepatic irritation and cerebral disorder, just as other powers of the Mind are.[33]

Identity is produced by 'the activity of some material and cerebral instrument' that is not only determined from birth, but also by phrenology. Forster and other phrenologists define 'consciousness' by reading the cranial bumps and facial features of the subject in accordance with their own definitions of the significance of these bumps. The phrenological system that ascertains the meaning of these cranial features is the equivalent of a dictionary or grammar for a language invented, read and spoken by phrenologists. As I have noted, other critics have objected that phrenology threatens the prized Romantic notion of self-determination because the 'organs' of personality and psychological characteristics are innate and therefore unchangeable. I agree that phrenology denies free-will and self-determination, but for an additional reason, as well: since the phrenologist alone decides upon the significance of these cranial manifestations, he truly defines the identity of the subject. By devising the discourse of phrenology – the dictionary, if you will, of human character – the psychologist makes himself the master of the subject and speaks her into being. Moreover, Forster maintains in his poetry and prose that these bumps provide the only reliable narrative of the subject's self.

III. 'Verses Inscribed on a Skull'

Of all the poems by the psychologists of the Romantic period, perhaps none is more perfectly expressive of the writer's psychological approach than Forster's 'Verses Inscribed on a Skull'. The entirety of the poem in description and overall message celebrates phrenology, while the very title provides an evocative image of the linguistic nature of the phrenologically defined modern subject: this skull is, literally, a phrenological document 'inscribed' with the signs of the self, which are further characterized as textual by being expressed in these 'verses'. The opening lines introduce the skull in question as a narrative that 'tells' of the person to which it belonged:

> O empty vault of former glory;
> Whate'er thou wert in time of old,
> Thy surface tells thy living store,
> Though now so hollow, dead, and cold!
> For in thy form is yet descry'd
> The traces left of young Desire;
> The painter's art, the statesman's pride,
> The Muse's song, the Poet's fire;
> But these, forsooth, now seem to be
> Mere bumps on thy pèriphery.[34]

These 'bumps' in the skull form around the 'organs' in the brain next to which they lay in life and are more pronounced when the organ and related character are more pronounced, rendering the dome of bone a narrative of the subject's character. Or, as Forster himself explains in *Sketch of the New Anatomy*, 'The size and figure of the skull are conformable to that of the brain; hence the organs are indicated on the outside of the head ... Dissection has proved a determined relation between the external form and the development of the organs within the cranium'.[35] Other lines from the poem provide even greater detail about the type of information the phrenologist may learn about the subject by reading his skull:

> These various organs show the place
> Where Friendschip [sic] loved where Passion glow'd
> Where Veneration grew in grace,
> Where Justice swayed, where many was proud –
> Whence Wit its slippery sallies threw
> On Vanity, thereby defeated;
> Where Hope's imaginary view
> Of things to come, fond fool, is seated;
> Where Circumspection made us fear,
> 'Mid gleams of joy some danger near,
> Here fair Benevolence doth grow
> In forehead high – here Imitation
> Adorns the stage, here on the brow
> Are Sound's and Colour's legislation.[36]

Certainly, 'Vanity' and 'Benevolence' are enduring characteristics and would seem to the lay reader to fall easily within the purview of the phrenologist, but Forster reveals in these lines that even apparently momentary traits can be imprinted in the skull, such as 'Hope' and 'Imitation'. These passages imply that the skull reflects not only innate and permanent character traits, but also acquired ones. Forster confirms and further complicates this implication in *Sketch of the New Anatomy*, where he writes, 'Though the relative bigness of the different organs, which is innate ... [personal character] is usually preserved through life; yet their activity is greatly to be increased or diminished by exercise', like muscles.[37] So, too, the poem suggests, may these muscle-like organs grow through use, for 'Hope' and 'Theft' seem to gesture to life experiences, rather than permanent and innate characteristics.[38] Meanwhile, by referring to organs of 'Sound[ ]' and 'Colour[ ]', Forster suggests that the subject's aptitude, sensitivity and perceptiveness are also on display in the skull's bumps. As an observer and regulator of so many aspects of the subject's character, the phrenologist presents his total mastery over the subject in this poem.

I suggest that Forster wrote this verse to proselytize about phrenology in a manner that would emphasize the scope of the phrenologist's knowledge and power over the reader – who is also the potential subject of phrenology. That this is Forster's goal becomes clear upon perusal of the following lines:

> Dear Nature, constant in her laws,
> Hath mark'd each mental operation,
> She every feeling's limit draws
> On all the heads throughout the nation,
> That there might no deception be;
> And he who kens her tokens well,
> Hears tongues which every where agree
> In language that no lies can tell –
> Courage, Deceit, Destruction, Theft,
> Have outlines on the skullcap left.[39]

Here, Forster underscores his role as a kind of social governor – like all of the other psychologists I describe in this study – when he casts his attention over 'all the heads throughout the nation'.[40] Truly, the phrenologist was not a detached observer of the apparent relationship between the skull's bumps and the subject's character, but, as his emphasis on such moral matters as 'Courage, Deceit, Destruction, [and] Theft' shows, he was concerned with ferreting out any socially undesirable traits and devising means of treating the blighted creatures that manifest them. In *Sketch of the New Anatomy*, Forster laments, 'There are cases, in which particular organs are so strong, in proportion to the rest, that certain propensities can hardly be controlled by the Will, and there are others, in which important organs are wanting', such that some people cannot control their inclinations, which, he adds, inclines us to pity them.[41] However, as a social governor, Forster is quick to add that this knowledge about human nature also emphasizes 'how important a duty it is to endeavour to counteract by education in infancy the original defects of organization'.[42] Again, the phrenologist is not content to study correlations between physical appearance and character. He offers his psychological knowledge as the basis for more effective social control, even going so far as to recommend a Nazi-style system of eugenics formed on the basis of phrenological information: 'It also shows the importance of a judicious selection of partners in marriage, since ... the first conditions of characters, are hereditary ... [and] defective organization may be handed down to posterity'.[43] Forster couches this discussion in the rhetoric of sympathy and humanity, but his conclusion that phrenology not only enables but actually necessitates control over even the sexual habits of 'all the ... [subjects] throughout the nation', to paraphrase 'Verses Inscribed on a Skull' loosely, posits this psychological governor as frighteningly dictatorial.[44] It also underscores his claim in 'Prolegomena in Philosophiam Musarum' from *Philosophia Musarum* that 'Phrenology is in fact the clue to the history of animated nature in every department: on its indication, in time to come, all government, legislation and indeed every function of the social compact must depend'.[45] With the induction of the doctor into the discipline of phrenology, the most powerful manifestation of the medical governor was born.

The above lines also show how tyrannical is the discourse of phrenology and that its mastery is linguistic. My argument here develops what I have contended throughout this study: that the authoritarian quality of psychology is as much a feature of how it develops and disperses its definitions, or its language, as is any tenet or claim inherent to the psychological approach itself. Therefore, its versified presentation of itself – with all of poetry's associations of beauty, attractiveness and wit – is vital to our understanding of how psychology has attempted to position itself in wider British culture. In 'Verses Inscribed on a Skull', Forster underscores the finality of phrenology's definition of the subject through its interpretation of the bumps on her head, a practice of reading that draws upon the authority associated with the written word, or, as Sander Gilman puts it, 'the special significance of words, of the act of writing as the sign of the rational in our society'.[46] Forster declares that the phrenologist has access to a text of absolute truth and can divine the psychological reality of his subject with absolute certainty, for the skull's bumps speak a 'language that no lies can tell'.[47] Clearly, not everyone can understand this language; it is only comprehensible to the learned few who 'ken ... [the] tokens well', a feature of phrenology that underscores its esotericism and denies access to its 'truths' to the vast number of those who are not inculcated into its definitions. The arcane quality of phrenological knowledge is a holdover from its roots in physiognomy, which, in Lavater's imagining, involved a 'new physiognomical gaze – using what he called 'an additional eye', his mind's eye, to peer behind transient, fleeting expressions and catch the hidden, secret soul'.[48] Just as the moral manager saw himself as blessed with special vision that afforded him a glimpse of the truth of insanity, as I note in Chapter 2, the physiognomist or phrenologist saw himself as an extraordinary man with an ability to see what was invisible to others, negating the egalitarianism established by the empirical project of the Enlightenment, in which all people had equal access to the truth. The phrenologist was an inductee into recondite knowledge, which facilitated his increased separation from the unknowing subject.

Forster goes further in the above lines to establish his linguistic power as a phrenologist. Significantly, he confirms that this 'language' of bumps on the skull, legible only to him and a few chosen others, is not the creation of the phrenologist; nor is phrenology itself devised by humans. Rather, 'Nature' has printed this truth-telling text on the skull of each person for one express purpose: 'That there might no deception be'.[49] In this assertion, Forster is actively engaged in creating ideology, or the cultural belief that the 'truths' he promotes are 'natural', divinely ordained, eternal. He also negates any possibility that the subject defined by phrenology could tell a tale of identity that differs from its claims about her and, in fact, he implies that she is likely to attempt to deceive others, since 'Nature' relates the truth about her character through the bumps on her skull precisely so 'That there might no deception be'.[50] The corollary of this statement is that, if there were no possibility of deception, 'Nature' would not have devised a way of narrating the tale of personal character through bumps on the subject's skull. As such, any objection she might have regarding phrenology's definition of her character must be taken as a lie designed to con others into an undeservedly generous opinion of her. Moreover, anything she claims about herself that is not spoken in the discourse of phrenology must be understood as patently false. In no uncertain terms, then, phrenology presented the discourse of psychology at apex of its power to define the modern subject and subjectify her completely.

In this way, Forster uses verse to confirm his linguistic mastery as a phrenologist and, in the utterly autocratic nature of his pronouncements about the language of phrenology, he provides a kind of conclusion to my narrative about how the psychologist-poets' verse developed throughout the Romantic period in tandem with various psychological approaches. Forster's example provides an apt conclusion to this exploration about why Romantic-era psychologists wrote poetry in other ways, as well. Indeed, it seems only fitting that this late psychologist-poet published some of his poetry for his family alone (the subtitle of *Epistolarium, or The Correspondence of the Forster Family, Letters and Essays* declares that it was *Printed for Private Circulation Only*) and that he expresses his love of linguistic obscurity by peppering his verse and even the titles of entire volumes with abstruse Latin phrases, in a reversal of Cullen's late eighteenth-century democratization of medical knowledge at Edinburgh University, which I describe in Chapter 1. After all, the division between the fields of science and the humanities – what Veatch has called the 'disruption' of the 'dialogue' between them – would manifest itself in psychology's development of an increasingly alien and esoteric discourse that shunned the principle of linguistic democracy that so many of the psychologist-poets celebrate in their work. Similarly, in *Sketch of the New Anatomy*, Forster defends phrenology against detractors who apparently recognized and resented this development in the field: 'Some persons have objected to our use of the newly formed names, instead of those before in popular use. But these old terms were used in various meanings and did not define so precisely the primitive faculties of the mind, as they were capable of being defined by a new set of terms'.[51] In his enthusiastic defence of phrenology's terminology, Forster seems to show his understanding that phrenology's authority relies upon the esotericism of its language.

Perhaps most revelatory of the ideological break between the two fields are Forster's comments about the practical application of the phrenological method to the study of poetry. In the preface of 'Prolegomena in Philosophiam Musarum',

Forster theorizes that verse 'exhibits the real character of the writer in his least suspicious colours', which posits poems as 'the genuine portraits of the writer's mind'.[52] He suggests that he reads poems in the same way that he reads skulls: to discover the true character of the subject, who is now the writer, as opposed to the reader. Forster validates our suspicions about this new approach to literary criticism when he continues,

> Phrenology, too, seemed to demand the perusal of such productions in order to complete our researches into the causes and varieties of the characters of different individuals. And in the zeal with which in 1815 I pursued this science, I sought, in the poetical works of our most renowned authours, the means of bringing to a successful issue the enquiries in which Dr Spurzheim, Dr Leach and myself were then engaged, as disciples of the celebrated Dr Gall.[53]

In these statements, Forster posits himself as a literary critic and, more importantly, he posits poets as the subjects, rather than the masters, of psychological discourse. I have identified the subject with the reader throughout this study because most of these psychologists address a lay reader who is not a master of the discourse that the psychologists develop in their verse. By situating himself as phrenologist and critic simultaneously, Forster not only reproduces the psycho-critical positions claimed by Lockhart and Jeffrey, as I discuss them in the introduction to this study, but he also introduces poets into the assemblage of those who are examined by the gaze – defined by David Shumway as 'a matter of applying a language or a mathematics to the thing seen so that it is constituted by the observer in his terms'[54] – rather than those who are the masters of it, an approach to literary criticism that would be taken up with great fervour in the twentieth century with critics proficient in the discourse of psychoanalysis. Notably, this way of reading poetry affords to the phrenological critic the same access to truth as do the bumps on the skull, since, Forster insists, poetry is spontaneous and less a product of the writer's volition than is, for example, scientific prose. The scientist's

> works afford to the phrenologist much fewer materials for comparing the character of the mind with the organization of the brain than do those of the poet. With him the imagination let loose upon all the objects of nature, takes its flights according to the bias of his individual genius; and fearless of criticism, because only engaged in the operations of fancy ... poetry exhibit[s] ... the actual state of the composer's feelings.[55]

By contrasting scientific prose with poetry, Forster helps to establish the divide between the two fields that would characterize the period following his own. By insisting that poetry tells the truth about the writer's character precisely because the poet has little control over how psychologically revelatory his work is, Forster again confirms that the poet-subject is powerless in comparison with the phrenologist. Intriguingly, in *Epistolarium or Fasciculi of Curious Letters*, Forster enlists other poets to support his claims: 'Poetry, as Wharton observes, in his note on Pope, offers the most correct picture of the human mind; being penned in moments when we are off our guard, and generally impressed with strong ideas and deeply felt ... emotions'.[56] As a poet himself, Forster thus appears rather divided in his sympathies. He is, at once, master and subject, a situation that is expressed most poignantly in his confession that he has even phrenologized himself by applying its principles to his own poetry.[57] He is truly, then, a border figure at the edge of the tradition of psychologist-poets.

IV. Rigid Boundaries, Disciplinarity and Subjectivity

I have endeavoured to establish in this exploration of the psychologist-poets of the Romantic period that their forgotten verse is important because it enhances our accepted notion of how psychology worked to establish itself in its earliest days and shows how disciplinary power uses a variety of unexpected methods to inculcate individuals into its discourse. Thus, to understand the formation of the modern subject fully, we must cast an eye over these long-silenced voices. It is vitally important that the psychologist-poets shared their ideas in verse because poetry thereby became another medium through which the discipline proselytized – another linguistic tool psychology used to inculcate the modern subject into its discourse and disperse its power, regardless of how democratic were the intentions of these early doctors of the mind. Influenced by the liberal politics of the Scottish Enlightenment, Romantic-era psychologists used an attractive textual medium to teach the masses, attract readers to their message, and define their cultural identities. Yet, they also thereby restricted the subject by providing her with a foreign system of self-reflection and identity-making. In *The Man Who Mistook His Wife for a Hat*, Oliver Sacks writes, 'We have, each of us, a life-story, an inner-narrative – whose continuity, whose sense, *is* our lives. It might be said that each of us constructs and lives, a "narrative", and that this narrative *is* us, our identities'.[58] Language and identity are not only related issues but, in this sense, they are inseparable. This concept overlaps closely with Foucault's contention that the discourse of psychology created the modern subject after the Classical period, which serves as the theoretical basis of this exploration. The modern subject is the individual who has learned to define her identity in terms defined by the disciplines, such as psychology. Thus, the subject's 'narrative' or 'identity', to use Sacks's words, is delineated by a discipline that has a regulating social function, as I have emphasized throughout this work, and which must perforce subject the subject, or oppress her in the interest of producing a member of society that falls in line with this new governor's ethical demands.

I do not imply that there could have been a free and self-determined subject that exists outside of language, psychological or otherwise. Nor does the scope of this project afford a discussion of the related and equally thorny issue of whether the modern subject could have ever resisted disciplinary power as I have described it.[59] My project here has been to illustrate one aspect of the development of psychology that has been overlooked hitherto, an absence in intellectual history about the connections between literature and psychology, as well as literature and science, more generally. I am not interested in questioning the truth-value of psychology in its past or present manifestations. I have simply examined the cultural motivations that inspire its discourse and the resultant effects upon modern subjectivity. At the very least, I hope I have illustrated that the forgotten verse of Romantic-era psychologists is a rich field of inquiry for students of literature and psychology alike.

NOTES

Introduction: Romantic-Era Psychologist-Poets and the Historical Context Of Early British Psychology

1. T. Bakewell, *The Domestic Guide, In Cases of Insanity. Pointing out the Causes, Means of Preventing, and Proper Treatment, of that Disorder. Recommended to Private Families, and the Notice of the Clergy* (Hanley: T. Allbut, 1805). All oddities of formatting, punctuation, spelling or grammar in the historical texts quoted in this study are the original author's own, unless otherwise noted. I only draw attention to anomalies that appear to be outright errors with the note 'sic'.

2. T. Bakewell, 'Lines, On Being Told that the Volitions of the Mind Would Overcome the Sense of Bodily Pain', in *The Moorland Bard; or, Poetical Recollections of a Weaver, in the Moorlands of Staffordshire*, 2 vols (London: T. Allbut, 1807), vol. 2, pp. 87–9. ll. 1–14, 27–38.

3. R. Porter, *Mind Forg'd Manacles: A History of Madness in England from the Restoration to the Regency* (London: Athalone Press, 1987), p. 115.

4. Committee on Madhouses, *First Report. Minutes of Evidence Taken Before the Select Committee Appointed to Consider of Provisions Being Made for the Better Regulation of Madhouses, in England* (1815), in R. Hunter and I. Macalpine (eds), *Three Hundred Years of Psychiatry 1535–1860* (London: Oxford University Press, 1963), pp. 698–703, on p. 698.

5. T. Arnold, *Observations on the Nature, Kinds, Causes and Prevention of Insanity*, 2 vols (London: Richard Phillips, 1806); J. Haslam, *Observations on Madness and Melancholy: Including Practical Remarks on those Diseases; Together with Cases: and An Account of the Morbid Appearances on Dissection* (London: G. Hayden, 1809), p. v.

6. P. W. Martin, *Mad Women in Romantic Writing* (New York: St Martin's Press, 1987); F. Burwick, *Poetic Madness and the Romantic Imagination* (University Park, PA: Pennsylvania State University Press, 1996).

7. A. Richardson, *British Romanticism and the Science of the Mind* (New York: Cambridge University Press, 2001).

8. J. Tambling, *Blake's Night Thoughts* (New York: Palgrave Macmillan, 2005); W. Brewer, *The Mental Anatomies of William Godwin and Mary Shelley* (Cranbury: Associated University Presses, 2001); N. Vickers, *Coleridge and the Doctors* (Oxford: Clarendon Press, 2004).

9. J. Faflak, *Romantic Psychoanalysis: The Burden of the Mystery* (Albany, NY: State University of New York Press, 2008).

10. N. Cotton, *Visions in Verse, For the Entertainment and Instruction of Younger Minds*, 3rd edn, revised (London: R. Dodsley, 1752); Hunter and Macalpine, *Three Hundred Years of*

Psychiatry, p. 426; T. I. M. Forster, *Epistolarium, or The Correspondence of the Forster Family, Letters and Essays. Printed for Private Circulation Only* (Bruges: C. De Moor, 1850), vol. 2.

11. M. Foucault, *Madness and Civilization: A History of Insanity in the Age of Reason*, trans. R. Howard (New York: Pantheon, 1965), pp. 269, 274.

12. M. Foucault, 'Two Lectures: Lecture Two: 14 January 1976', in C. Gordon (ed.), *Power/ Knowledge: Selected Interviews and Other Writings, 1972-1977*, trans. C. Gordon, L. Marshall, J. Mepham and K. Soper (New York: Pantheon Books, 1972), pp. 92–108, on p. 93.

13. J. Beattie, *Elements of Moral Science* (1790–3) (Philadelphia, PA: Hopkins and Earle, 1809); W. Perfect, *Select Cases in the Different Species of Insanity, Lunacy, or Madness, with the Modes of Practice as Adopted in the Treatment of Each* (Rochester, NY: W. Gillman, 1787), in *The Eighteenth Century* (ESTC reel (MICR) 6018, no. 7); A. Duncan, Sr, *Observations on the Structure of Hospitals for the Treatment of Lunatics, and on the General Principles on Which the Cure of Insanity May Be Most Successfully Conducted. To Which is Annexed, An Account of the Intended Establishment of a Lunatic Asylum at Edibnurgh* [*sic*] (Edinburgh: Archibald Constable & Co., 1809); T. Beddoes, *Hygëia: or, Essays Moral and Medical on the Causes Affecting the Personal State of our Middling and Affluent Classes*, 3 vols (Bristol: R. Phillips, 1802), vol. 1; T. Trotter, *A View of the Nervous Temperament; Being a Practical Inquiry into the Increasing Prevalence, Prevention, and Treatment of Those Diseases Commonly Called Nervous, Bilious, Stomach, Liver Complaints, Indigestion, Low Spirits, Gout, &c.* (Troy: Wright, Goodenow & Stockwell, 1808); J. Ferriar, *An Essay Towards a Theory of Apparitions* (London: Cadell and Davies, 1813); Bakewell, *The Domestic Guide*; T. Brown, *Lectures on the Philosophy of the Human Mind* (1820; Edinburgh: William Tait, 1828); T. Forster, *Observations on the Casual and Periodical Influence of the Particular State of the Atmosphere on Human Health and Diseases, Particularly Insanity*, 2nd edn (London: n.p., 1819).

14. Almost no critical discussion has been devoted to the poetry of the many physician-poets of the Romantic period, such as Hugh Downman (1740–1809), who wrote a poem full of paediatric advice called *Infancy; or, The Management of Children. A Didactic Poem, in Three Books* (Edinburgh: John Bell, 1776), http://galenet.galegroup.com. proxy1.lib.umanitoba.ca/servlet/ECCO, accessed 9 September 2008), Robert Couper (1750–1818), John Matthews (bap. 1755, d. 1826), William Drennan (1754–1820) (who was the first to call Ireland the 'emerald isle'), Thomas Lyle (1792–1859), John Mason (1764–1827), Nathan Drake (1766–1836), Thomas Lyle (1792–1859) and William Beattie (1793–1875) (biographer and doctor of the poet Thomas Campbell and friend and physician to the poet Samuel Rogers). Better known are the poems of the physician-poets John Armstrong (1708/9–79), (who wrote *The Art of Preserving Health* (1744) (in *Poems of Established Reputation* (Baltimore, MA: Warner and Hanna, 1803), pp. 4–55), Peter Pindar (whose real name was John Wolcot) (bap. 1738, d. 1819) and Mark Akenside (1721–70) but, again, the significance of their knowledge of medicine for their poetry has not been studied thoroughly.

15. Porter, *Mind Forg'd Manacles*, p. ix; Thiher, *Revels in Madness*, p. 167.

16. E. Shorter, *A Historical Dictionary of Psychiatry* (Oxford: Oxford University Press, 2005), pp. 232–3.

17. G. Bryson, *Man and Society: The Scottish Inquiry of the Eighteenth-Century* (Princeton, NJ: Princeton University Press, 1945), pp. 250, n. 47.

18. 'Psychology', *The Oxford English Dictionary* (Online) (Oxford: Oxford University Press, 2008), http://dictionary.oed.com.proxy1.lib.umanitoba.ca/cgi/entry/50191636? (accessed 12 April 2008). The *Oxford English Dictionary* recognizes the difficulty in

establishing the precise etymology and use of the word 'psychology' in its definition. Our contemporary use of the word is listed as its second definition ('The scientific study of the nature, functioning and development of the human mind, including the faculties of reason, emotion, perception, communication, etc.; the branch of science that deals with the (human or animal) mind as an entity and in its relationship to the body and to the environmental or social context') and appended to it is the note, 'it is difficult to determine when it began to be used in sense 2'. This caveat is followed by examples of the word's use in German and English eighteenth-century literature, but, in both cases, the *OED* suggests that these instances seem to use the word in the sense of the first defini- tion ('The study or consideration of the soul or spirit. Cf. PNEUMATOLOGY n. 1. Now rare') as much as in the second, contemporary definition. Please see note 54, on pp. 202–3, below, for a discussion of 'pneumatology'.

19. N. Vickers, 'Coleridge, Thomas Beddoes and Brunonian Medicine', *European Romantic Review*, 8:1 (1997), pp. 47–94, on p. 74; T. Forster, *Facts and Enquiries Respecting the Source of Epidemia, with an Historical Catalogue of the Numerous Visitations of Plague, Pestilence, and Famine*, 3rd edn (London: Keating and Brown, 1832), p. 77.

20. T. Bakewell, 'The Author's Dream: Addressed to the Reviewers', *The Moorland Bard; or, Poetical Recollections of a Weaver, in the Moorlands of Staffordshire*, 2 vols (London: T. Allbut, 1807), vol. 2, pp. 165–8. ll. 5–10.

21. R. Bloomfield, *The Farmer's Boy: A Rural Poem* (London: Vernor and Hood, 1800).

22. T. Beddoes, *Alexander's Expedition Down the Hydaspes and the Indus to the Indian Ocean* (London: J. Edmunds, 1792), in *The Eighteenth-Century* (ESTC reel (MICR) 3938, no. 3).

23. Ibid., p. iv.

24. In *Wordsworth and the Enlightenment: Nature, Man, and Society in the Experimental Poetry* (New Haven, CT: Yale University Press, 1989), Alan Bewell argues convincingly that the Enlightenment influenced Romanticism but he focuses instead on how Enlightenment interest in anthropology contributed to both Wordsworth's major poetry and his self-understanding. It is also important to note that many historians of psychology maintain that Locke's thought was a great influence on the formation of modern psychology, although I invoke him here for his more commonly recognized associations with empiricism.

25. D. Stewart, *Elements of the Philosophy of the Human Mind*, 3 vols (A. Strahan, and T. Cadell: London, 1792–1827), in *English Short Title Catalogue, Eighteenth Century Collections Online*, http://galenet.galegroup.com.proxy2.lib.umanitoba.ca/servlet/ECCO (accessed 7 July 2008); K. A. Webb, 'Ferriar, John (1761–1815)', *Oxford Dictionary of National Biography*, hereafter *ODNB* (Oxford: Oxford University Press, 2004), http://www.oxforddnb.com.myaccess.library.utoronto.ca/view/article/9368 (accessed 11 July 2005); G. T. Bettany and L. Rosner, 'Duncan, Andrew, the elder (1744-1828)', *ODNB* http://www.oxforddnb.com.myaccess.library.utoronto.ca/view/article/8212 (accessed 11 July 2005); M. Neve, 'Beddoes, Thomas (1760–1808)', *ODNB*, http://www.oxforddnb.com.myaccess.library.utoronto.ca/view/article/1919 (accessed 11 July, 2005); J. Wallace, 'Trotter, Thomas (bap. 1760, d. 1832)', *ODNB*, http://www.oxforddnb.com.myaccess.library.utoronto.ca/view/article/27763 (accessed 11 July 2005).

26. M. McNeil, 'Darwin, Erasmus (1731–1802)', *ODNB*, http://www.oxforddnb.com.myaccess.library.utoronto.ca/view/article/7177 (accessed 11 July 2005).

27. Bettany and Rosner, 'Duncan, Andrew, the elder'; S. B. Black, 'Perfect, William (1731/2–1809)', *ODNB*, http://www.oxforddnb.com.myaccess.library.utoronto.ca/view/article/58530 (accessed 11 July 2005).

28. R. J. Robinson, 'Beattie, James (1735-1803)', *ODNB*, http://www.oxforddnb.com. myaccess.library.utoronto.ca/view/article/1831 (accessed 2 August 2005).

29. J. Browne, 'Forster, Thomas Ignatius Maria (1789–1860)', *ODNB*, http://www. oxforddnb.com.myaccess.library.utoronto.ca/view/article/9920 (accessed 11 July, 2005).

30. G. Graham, 'Introduction', in G. Graham (ed.), *Scottish Philosophy: Selected Readings 1690-1960* (Exeter: Imprint Academic, 2004), pp. 1–11, on pp. 1–2.

31. Ibid., p. 3.

32. D. Hamilton, 'The Scottish Enlightenment and Clinical Medicine', in D. Dow (ed.), *The Influence of Scottish Medicine: An Historical Assessment of its International Impact* (Carnforth: The Parthenon Publishing Group, 1988), pp. 103–11, on p.105.

33. L. Rosner, *Medical Education in the Age of Improvement: Edinburgh Students and Apprentices, 1760–1826* (Edinburgh: Edinburgh University Press, 1991), pp. 120, 118.

34. Richardson, *British Romanticism and the Science of the Mind*, p. 7.

35. J. Christie and S. Shuttleworth, 'Introduction: Between Literature and Science', in J. Christie and S. Shuttleworth (eds), *Nature Transfigured: Science and Literature, 1700–1900* (Manchester: Manchester University Press, 1989), pp. 1–12, on p. 2.

36. Bryson, *Man and Society*, p. 14.

37. L. S. Jacyna, *Philosophic Whigs: Medicine, Science, and Citizenship in Edinburgh, 1789–1848* (London: Routledge, 1994), p. 52.

38. Ibid., p. 10.

39. Bryson, *Man and Society*, p. 10.

40. Jacyna, *Philosophic Whigs*, p. 1.

41. J. G. Crowther, *Scientists of the Industrial Revolution* (Philadelphia, PA: Dufour Editions, 1963), p. 149.

42. Jacyna, *Philosophic Whigs*, p. 11.

43. Ibid., p. 7.

44. Ibid., p. 3.

45. Ibid., p. 5.

46. Ibid., pp. 36–7, 17, 48.

47. Ibid., pp. 49, 40.

48. C. D. Waterston, 'Late Enlightenment Science and Generalism: The Case of Sir George Steuart Mackenzie of Coul, 1780–1848', in C. W. J. Withers and P. Wood (eds), *Sciences and Medicine in the Scottish Enlightenment* (East Linton: Tuckwell Press, 2002), pp. 301–26, on p. 314.

49. D. Hume, *A Treatise of Human Nature: A Critical Edition* (1739), ed. D. F. Norton and M. J. Norton (Oxford: Clarendon Press, 2007).

50. G. Graham, 'The Nineteenth-Century Aftermath', in A. Broadie (ed.), *The Cambridge Companion to the Scottish Enlightenment* (Cambridge: Cambridge University Press, 2003), pp. 338–50, on p. 344.

51. P. Flynn, 'General Introduction', in P. Flynn (ed.), *Enlightened Scotland: A Study and Selection of Scottish Philosophical Prose from the Eighteenth and Early Nineteenth Centuries* (Edinburgh: Scottish Academic Press, 1992), pp. ix–xxii, on p. 1.

52. M. N. McLane, *Romanticism and the Human Sciences: Poetry, Population, and the Discourse of the Species* (Cambridge: Cambridge University Press, 2000), pp. 36–7.

53. Bewell, *Wordsworth and the Enlightenment*, pp. 13, 14.

54. I call this field 'mysterious' because it seems not to be closely related to the study of 'pneumatics', despite the clear relation between 'pneumatics' and 'pneumatology' on

an etymological level. 'Pneumatics', the great interest of Humphrey Davy, involved the study of gasses and air, as is evident from Joseph Priestley's article on pneumatic chemistry, entitled 'Observations on Different Kinds of Air' (S. J. Burr, 'Inspiring Lunatics: Biographical Portraits of the Lunar Society's Erasmus Darwin, Thomas Day, and Joseph Priestley', *Eighteenth-Century Life*, 24:2 (2000), pp. 111–27, on p. 121). Moreover, the use of pneumatics seems to be have been centered on physical treatment: Darwin encouraged Beddoes to set up a pneumatic institute at Bristol for the cure of consumption (D. King-Hele, *Erasmus Darwin and the Romantic Poets* (New York: St Martin's Press, 1986), p. 91). 'Pneumatology', on the other hand, was almost synonymous with 'psychology'. According to Hunter and Macalpine, Beddoes used the term 'pneumatology' to refer to psychology, but some have identified it as referring to 'the nature of spirits, divine, angelic and human' (A. Broadie, 'The Human Mind and its Powers', in A. Broadie (ed.), *The Cambridge Companion to the Scottish Enlightenment* (Cambridge: Cambridge University Press, 2003), pp. 60–78, on p. 60). As I note in note 18, above (p. 201), the *OED* also defines 'pneumatology' as the study of 'the soul or spirit'. This definition of the term draws attention to the theological roots of psychology, which I will discuss in Chapter 1.

55. Beattie, *Elements of Moral Science*, p. xvi.
56. R. L. Emerson, 'Science and Moral Philosophy in the Scottish Enlightenment', in M. A. Stewart (ed.), *Studies in the Philosophy of the Scottish Enlightenment* (Oxford: Clarendon Press, 1990), pp. 11–36, on pp. 17, 18.
57. E. S. Reed, *From Soul to Mind: The Emergence of Psychology from Erasmus Darwin to William James* (New Haven, CT: Yale University Press, 1997), p. 3.
58. Graham, 'Introduction', p. 2.
59. Historian Alexander Broadie introduces Thomas Reid as the father of Common Sense philosophy and in opposition to Dugald Stewart, who developed the concept of unconscious thought. Reid maintained that all arguments to prove the existence of unconscious thought (as Stewart presents it) must be based on hypothesis alone, with no empirical basis or conviction, and that such arguments are therefore untrustworthy. However suspicious Reid was of Stewart's model of the unconscious, he remained devoted to the study of the mind. Richardson calls Reid's area of expertise Scottish '"common sense" psychology', which posited the mind as an 'active processor ... of experience' and not a 'passive register' (Richardson, *British Romanticism and the Science of the Mind*, p. 66).
60. Bryson, *Man and Society*, p. 11.
61. Ibid., p. 142.
62. Vickers, 'Coleridge, Thomas Beddoes and Brunonian Medicine', p. 59.
63. Bryson, *Man and Society*, p. 14.
64. Ibid., p. 124.
65. J. C. Stewart-Robertson, 'Brown, Thomas (1778–1820)', *ODNB*, http://www.oxforddnb.com.myaccess.library.utoronto.ca/view/article/3655 (accessed 11 July 2005); Flynn, 'General Introduction', (ed.), *Enlightened Scotland: A Study and Selection of Scottish Philosophical Prose from the Eighteenth and Early Nineteenth Centuries* (Edinburgh: Scottish Academic Press, 1992), pp. ix–xxii p. xi.
66. Ibid.
67. [F. Jeffrey], Unsigned review, *Edinburgh Review* (24 November 1814), in R. Woof (ed.), *William Wordsworth: The Critical Heritage* (London: Routledge, 2001), vol. 1, pp. 381–404, on p. 383.

68. J. G. Lockhart, 'Cockney School of Poetry', in *Blackwood's Edinburgh Magazine* (1818), in A. K. Mellor and R. E. Matlak (eds), *British Literature 1780–1830* (Fort Worth, TX: Harcourt Brace, 1996), pp. 159–61, on p. 159.

69. Writing more generally about the canonical Romantic poets' knowledge of science and specifically about Wordsworth's reaction to the success of Davy, Ross makes a similar claim about the influence of the man of science on the literary realm:

    > Evidence of Davy's fame in the Romantic public sphere, as well as similarities in the language, rhetoric, aims, and experience (both public and private) of the scientist and the poet, help to clarify why Wordsworth emphasized experiment, expertise, reason, and 'system' in his poetics and claimed that poetry is 'the breath and finer spirit of all knowledge ... the impassioned expression which is the countenance of all science'. I argue that both poetry and science required an affirming audience, addressed virtually the same polymathic public, and vied for the same jurisdiction (that of philosopher and sage).
    > (C. E. Ross, '"Twin Labourers and Heirs of the Same Hopes": The Professional Rivalry of Humphrey Davy and William Wordsworth', in N. Heringman (ed.), *Romantic Science: The Literary Forms of Natural History* (New York: State University of New York Press, 2003), pp. 23–52, on p. 24).

    As I do, Ross suggests that the literary realm was shaped, in part, by the scientific realm.

70. J. Bernauer and M. Mahon, 'Michel Foucault's Ethical Imagination', in G. Gutting (ed.), *The Cambridge Companion to Foucault*, 2nd edn (Cambridge: Cambridge University Press, 2005), pp. 149–75, on p. 154.

71. B. Taylor and R. Bain, Introduction to B. Taylor and R. Bain (eds), *The Cast of Consciousness: Concepts of the Mind in British and American Romanticism* (New York: Greenwood Press, 1987), pp. ix–xv, on p. ix.

72. Wordsworth, subtitle to *The Prelude*, p. 375; S. T. Coleridge, 'Kubla Khan: Or, A Vision in a Dream' (1816), in *The Major Works*, ed. H. J. Jackson (Oxford: Oxford University Press, 1985), pp. 102–4.

73. W. Wordsworth, 'Preface', *Lyrical Ballads* (1800, 1850), *The Prose Works of William Wordsworth*, ed. W. J. B. Owen and J. W. Smyser (Oxford: Clarendon Press, 1974), vol. 1, pp. 119–59, on p. 126. I will develop the associationist context of Wordsworth's comment further in Chapter 4.

74. Ibid., p. 139.

75. Ibid., p. 140.

76. Ibid., p. 141. With respect to Wordsworth's use of the general term 'science', it is notable that one of the most influential nerve-theorists of the eighteenth century, William Cullen, considered all science to be psychological at its base: '"if by Metaphysics we understand as I think we should the Operations of the human Mind in thinking, that is, the History of the human Mind, then I say Metaphysics are unavoidable not only in Physick, but perhaps in every Science if a man goes deep"' (quoted in J. P. Wright, 'Metaphysics and Physiology: Mind, Body, and the Animal Economy in Eighteenth-Century Scotland', in M. A. Stewart (ed.), *Studies in the Philosophy of the Scottish Enlightenment* (Oxford: Clarendon Press, 1990), pp. 251–301, on p. 251).

77. S. T. Coleridge, *Biographia Literaria or, Biographical Sketches of My Literary Life and Opinions* (1817), in *The Collected Works of Samuel Taylor Coleridge*, gen. ed. K. Coburn, 16 vols (London: Routledge and Kegan Paul, 1969–2001), vol. 7, ed. J. Engell and W. J. Bate, p. 6.

78. T. H. Levere, '"The Lovely Shapes and Sounds Intelligible": Samuel Taylor Coleridge, Humphrey Davy, Science and Poetry', in J. Christie and S. Shuttleworth (eds), *Nature Transfigured: Science and Literature, 1700–1900* (Manchester: Manchester University Press, 1989), pp. 85–101, on p. 88.

79. Coleridge, *Biographia Literaria*, p. 13, Coleridge's emphasis.

80. McLane, *Romanticism and the Human Sciences*, p. 65. Because his basic definition of a poem includes its opposition to science in *Biographia Literaria*, we can assume that Coleridge understood moral philosophy to constitute a science when he maintains that Wordsworth's project was not poetic on the grounds of its adherence to the principles of moral philosophy.

81. Richardson, *British Romanticism and the Science of the Mind*, p. 7.

82. A. Lovejoy, 'On the Discrimination of Romanticisms', *PMLA: Publications of the Modern Language Association of America*, 39:2 (1924), pp. 229–53.

83. M. Donnelly, *Managing the Mind: A Study of Medical Psychology in Early Nineteenth-Century Britain* (London: Tavistock, 1983), p. 41.

84. H. Bloom, Commentary to *Milton*, in *The Complete Poetry and Prose of William Blake*, rev. and ed. D. Erdman (New York: Anchor Books, 1988), p. 909–28; W. Blake, 'Milton' (1804), in D. Erdman (ed. and rev.) and H. Bloom (commentary), *The Complete Poetry and Prose of William Blake* (New York: Anchor Books, 1988), pp. 95–144. ll. 13–16.

85. W. Wordsworth, *The Prelude* (1805), *William Wordsworth: A Critical Edition of the Major Works*, ed. S. Gill (Oxford: Oxford University Press, 1984), pp. 375–590. ll. 431–41.

86. P. B. Shelley, 'A Defence of Poetry' (1840; composed 1821), in D. H. Reiman and N. Fraistat (eds), *Shelley's Prose and Poetry* (New York: W. W. Norton, 2002), pp. 509–35, on p. 535. Please see page 177 for my argument that Shelley lifted this phrase from Brown's prose.

87. Ibid., p. 517.

88. Ibid., p. 530.

89. Ibid., p. 517.

90. Quoted in McLane, *Romanticism and the Human Sciences*, p. 41.

91. Coleridge, S. T., *On the Constitution of the Church and State*, vol. 10, ed. J. Colmer, p. 43.

92. Ibid., p. 46.

93. Porter concurs that these psychologist-poets may be considered to be examples of the Coleridgean clerisy. In *Doctor of Society: Thomas Beddoes and the Sick Trade in Late-Enlightenment England*, he writes, 'Beddoes's vision of the doctor as intellectual guru parallels Coleridge's ideal of the new intelligentsia, the clerisy, called to serve as moral leaders of the future' ((London: Routledge, 1992), p. 190).

94. As I illustrate with regard to Beattie's prose and poetry in Chapter 1, the Professor of Moral Philosophy at Marischal College observed that the religious component of moral philosophy, or psychology, was already under threat in the 1760s. Beattie tried to prevent a positive break between the fields by teaching a form of spiritual psychology that was aimed at destroying what he saw as the source of the threat, Humean scepticism. It is also worth noting here that, in opposition to my above claim, one of the main contentions Reed makes in *From Soul to Mind* is that psychology did not attain its goal of being recognized as a science in the nineteenth century.

95. In one of the most famous statements of the Romantic period that defines reason as that which divides us from animals, Philippe Pinel writes in his seminal work, *A Treatise on Insanity*, 'Of all the afflictions to which human nature is subject, the loss of reason is at once the most calamitous and interesting. Deprived of this faculty, by which man is

principally distinguished from the beasts that perish, the human form is frequently the most remarkable attribute that he retains of his proud distinction' (trans. D. D. Davis (Sheffield: Cadell & Davies, 1806), p. xv).

96. Coleridge, *On the Constitution of the Church and State*, p. 44.

97. Emerson, 'Science and Moral Philosophy in the Scottish Enlightenment', pp. 33, 36.

98. Quoted in McLane, *Romanticism and the Human Sciences*, p. 66.

99. Byron and Keats are two major exceptions to the contention that Romantic poets saw themselves as cultural leaders. While it is true that Byron was, in a sense, the most socially engaged of the Romantics through the satirical nature of his verse and involvement in politics, he does not seem to be interested in guiding his readers to social improvement. Rather than providing answers to the problems he discerns, his cynical and nihilistic poetry may be viewed as simply criticizing society. Keats is another great exception to the notion that the Romantic poets understood poetry and the poet as having distinct cultural functions necessary to the proper guidance of society. In a series of proto-Decadent moments that surely made Oscar Wilde swoon some decades later, Keats pined in one letter, 'O for a Life of Sensations rather than of Thoughts!', identified 'The excellence of every Art' as a function of its relation to 'Beauty and Truth' and declared, 'We hate poetry that has a palpable design upon us' – such as, we can surmise, to improve us morally, socially and politically, as the poetry of the psychologist-poets attempts to do (J. Keats, *Letters of John Keats*, ed. R. Gittings (Oxford: Oxford University Press, 1970), pp. 37, 42, 61). For Keats, as for Wilde and the other aesthetes, art should serve no function.

100. M. McLuhan, *Understanding Media: The Extensions of Man*, intro. L. H. Lapham (Cambridge, MA: MIT Press, 1994).

101. M. Foucault, 'The Politics of Health in the Eighteenth Century', in C. Gordon (ed.), *Power/Knowledge: Selected Interviews and Other Writings, 1972–1977*, trans. C. Gordon, L. Marshall, J. Mepham and K. Soper (New York: Pantheon Books, 1972), pp. 166–82, on p. 177.

102. M. Foucault, A. Fontana and P. Pasquino, 'Truth and Power', in C. Gordon (ed.), *Power/Knowledge: Selected Interviews and Other Writings, 1972-1977*, trans. C. Gordon, L. Marshall, J. Mepham, K. Soper (New York: Pantheon Books, 1972), pp. 109–33, on p. 115. In this interview with Alessandro Fontana and Pasquale Pasquino, Foucault claims, 'When I think back now, I ask myself what else it was that I was talking about, in *Madness and Civilization* or *The Birth of the Clinic*, but power? Yet I'm perfectly aware that I scarcely ever used the word' (p. 115).

103. Veatch, *Disrupted Dialogue: Medical Ethics and the Collapse of Physician–Humanist Communication (1770–1980)* (Oxford: Oxford University Press, 2004), p. 9.

104. Ibid., pp. 35, 21.

1. Erasmus Darwin, James Beattie and Nathaniel Cotton as Pre-Romantic Psychologist-Poets

1. For example, Thomas Beddoes may be said to have been an associationist as much as he was a nerve theorist, as my discussion of his views on children's education illustrates in Chapter 3.

2. D. King-Hele, 'Disenchanted Darwinians: Wordsworth, Coleridge and Blake', *The Wordsworth Circle*, 25:2 (1994), pp. 114–18, on p. 118.

3.   Reed, *From Soul to Mind*, p. xi.
4.   Quoted in S. Harris, 'Introduction and Apologia', S. Harris (ed.) *Cosmologia* (Sheffield: Stuart Harris, 2002), pp. viii–x, xi–xiii, on p. xi.
5.   Crowther, *Scientists of the Industrial Revolution*, p. 259.
6.   A. L. Barbauld, 'Essay on Akenside's Poem on *The Pleasures of Imagination*', in M. Akenside, *The Pleasures of Imagination* (London: T. Cadell, Junior, and W. Davies, 1794) p. 4, in *Eighteenth Century Collections Online* http://galenet.galegroup.com.proxy1.lib. umanitoba.ca/servlet/ECCO (accessed 17 August 2007).
7.   E. Darwin, 'Advertisement', *The Botanic Garden*, 4th edn (Dudlin [*sic*]: J. Moore, 1796), pp. v–vi, on p. v.
8.   To be sure, interest in Darwin's influence on English Romanticism has grown in the last twenty years, as is evident in King-Hele's various works on Darwin, such as the above-mentioned book-length study and article. Other important critical works on Darwin are David Ullrich's 'Distinctions in Poetic and Intellectual Influence: Coleridge's Use of Erasmus Darwin' (*The Wordsworth Circle*, 15:2 (1984), pp. 74–80), James Holt McGavran Jr's 'Darwin, Coleridge, and "The Thorn"' (*The Wordsworth Circle*, 25:2 (1994), pp. 118–22), Maureen McNeil's 'The Scientific Muse: The Poetry of Erasmus Darwin' (in L. J. Jordanova (ed.), *Languages of Nature: Critical Essays on Science and Literature* (New Brunswick, NJ: Rutgers University Press, 1986), pp. 163–203), Sandra Burr's 'Inspiring Lunatics: Biographical Portraits of the Lunar Society's Erasmus Darwin, Thomas Day, and Joseph Priestley' (*Eighteenth-Century Life*, 24:2 (2000), pp. 111–27), and Nelson Hilton's 'The Spectre of Darwin' (*Blake: An Illustrated Quarterly*, 15:1 (1981), pp. 36–48), which outlines the Darwin's influence on Blake's work. The earliest work of modern criticism devoted to Darwin's verse is James Venable Logan's *The Poetry and Aesthetics of Erasmus Darwin* (Princeton, NJ: Princeton University Press, 1936), while Donald M. Hassler seems to have attempted a revival of interest in Darwin as early as 1973 with a critical biography that is entitled simply *Erasmus Darwin* (New York: Twayne Publishers, Inc., 1973). Finally, Stuart Harris compiled and edited Darwin's verse in *Cosmologia*.
9.   King-Hele, 'Disenchanted Darwinians', p. 118.
10. Ibid., pp. 114, 115.
11. Hilton, 'The Spectre of Darwin', p. 36.
12. Ullrich, 'Distinctions in Poetic and Intellectual Influence', p. 74.
13. Coburn quoted in King-Hele, 'Disenchanted Darwinians', p. 117.
14. McGavran, 'Darwin, Coleridge, and "The Thorn"', p. 120.
15. McNeil, 'The Scientific Muse', p. 164; Burr, 'Inspiring Lunatics', p. 113.
16. C. Darwin, *The Origin of Species: A Variorum Text* (1859), ed. M. Peckham (Philadelphia, PA: University of Pennsylvania Press, 2006); E. Darwin, *Zoönomia, or, The Laws of Organic Life* (New York: T. & J. Swords, 1796), vol. 1, in *Early American Imprints*, first series, no. 30312 http://infoweb.newsbank.com.myaccess.library.utoronto.ca/ (accessed 12 July 2005); Burr, 'Inspiring Lunatics', p. 114.
17. Reed, *From Soul to Mind*, p. 39.
18. Quoted in Burr, 'Inspiring Lunatics', p. 114; E. Darwin, *The Temple of Nature* (1803), ed. D. King-Hele (London: A Scolar Press Facsimile, 1973), ll. 233–4.
19. Logan, *The Poetry and Aesthetics of Erasmus Darwin*, p. 17; Darwin, E., *The Economy of Vegetation* (1792), in S. Harris (ed.), *Cosmologia* (Sheffield: Stuart Harris, 2002).
20. McNeil, 'Darwin, Erasmus (1731–1802)'; J. Brown, *The Elements of Medicine of John Brown, MD*, 2 vols, trans., rev. edn (London: J. Johnson, 1795), in *Eighteenth Century*

Collections Online, http://galenet.galegroup.com.proxy2.lib.umanitoba.ca/servlet/ ECCO (accessed 12 September 2008).

21. McNeil, 'Darwin, Erasmus (1731–1802)'.

22. Hunter and Macalpine, *Three Hundred Years of Psychiatry*, p. 547. Darwin outlines some of his opinions on madness in *Zoönomia*, which includes long discussions of 'pleasurable' delirium, the difference between madness and delirium and what we would today call psychosomatic reactions, as in the following quotation: 'I once saw a partial insanity, which might be called a voluntary diabetes, which was occasioned by the fear (and consequent aversion) of not being able to make water at all' (quoted in Hunter and Macalpine, *Three Hundred Years of Psychiatry*, pp. 305, 308). Assuredly, Darwin's theories were forward-looking not only for evolutionary science and literature, but for psychology, as well.

23. Logan, *The Poetry and Aesthetics of Erasmus Darwin*, p. 41.

24. L. J. Jordanova, Introduction to M. McNeil, 'The Scientific Muse', in L. J. Jordanova (ed.), *Languages of Nature: Critical Essays on Science and Literature* (New Brunswick, NJ: Rutgers University Press, 1986), pp. 159–63, p. 160.

25. J. Harris, 'Introduction', in J. Beattie, *James Beattie: Selected Philosophical Writings*, ed. J. A. Harris (Exeter: Imprint Academic, 2004), pp. 1–14, p. xii.

26. Ullrich, 'Distinctions in Poetic and Intellectual Influence', p. 76.

27. Richardson, *British Romanticism and the Science of the Mind*, p. 15.

28. King-Hele, 'Disenchanted Darwinians', p. 118.

29. Darwin, *Zoönomia*, unpag. Darwin's emphasis.

30. Ibid.

31. Darwin, *The Temple of Nature*, pp. 425–8.

32. Jordanova, Introduction to 'The Scientific Muse', p. 160.

33. Darwin, Preface to *Zoönomia*, unpag.

34. Ibid.

35. Ibid., Darwin's Emphasis.

36. Ibid.

37. Wordsworth, 'Preface', p. 130.

38. Darwin, *Zoönomia*, p. 305.

39. Burr, 'Inspiring Lunatics', p. 115.

40. Darwin, footnote in *The Temple of Nature*, p. 122.

41. Darwin, *The Temple of Nature*, p. 383.

42. Darwin, *The Temple of Nature*, pp. 352–9.

43. Jacyna, *Philosophic Whigs*, pp. 17, 47.

44. J. Beattie, 'The Minstrel, or Progress of Genius' (1771–4), *Poems of Established Reputation* (Baltimore, MA: Warner and Hanna, 1803), pp. 57–92, in *Early American Imprints*, http://link.library.utoronto.ca/eir/EIRdetail.cfm?Resources__ID=394581&T=F (accessed 11 July 2005).

45. L. Ritchie, 'Cotton, Nathaniel (1705–1788)', *ODNB*, http://www.oxforddnb.com.myaccess.library.utoronto.ca/view/article/6422 (accessed 11 July 2005).

46. M. Byrd, *Visits to Bedlam: Madness and Literature in the Eighteenth Century* (South Carolina, SC: University of South Carolina Press, 1974), p. 118.

47. Ibid., p. 116.

48. M. V. DePorte, *Nightmares and Hobbyhorses: Swift, Sterne and Augustan Ideas of Madness* (San Marino: The Huntington Library, 1974), p. 31.

49. Porter, *Mind Forg'd Manacles*, p. 102.

50. Wordsworth, subtitle to *The Prelude*, p. 375.
51. Byrd, *Visits to Bedlam*, p. 100
52. Ibid., p. 21; Porter, *Mind Forg'd Manacles*, p. 58.
53. Donnelly, *Managing the Mind*, p. 113.
54. S. Schaffer, 'States of Mind: Enlightenment and Natural Philosophy', in G. S. Rousseau (ed.), *The Languages of Psyche: Mind and Body in Enlightenment Thought*, (Berkeley, CA: University of California Press, 1990), pp. 233–90, on pp. 274–5.
55. Byrd, *Visits to Bedlam*, p. 18.
56. DePorte, *Nightmares and Hobbyhorses*, p. 34; Quoted in M. A. Rabb, 'Psychology and Politics in William Godwin's *Caleb Williams*: Double Bond or Double Bind?', in C. Fox (ed.), *Psychology in the Eighteenth Century* (New York: AMS Press, 1987), pp. 51–67, on p. 56.
57. This principle of Protestantism was especially important to nationalistic Scots in the eighteenth century because political developments divested Presbyterianism of much of its political power, leaving the likes of David Deans from Sir Walter Scott's *The Heart of Midlothian* in great inner turmoil about 'how far the government which succeeded the Revolution could be, without sin, acknowledged by true presbyterians, seeing that it did not recognize' the power of their church (ed. C. Lamont (1830; Oxford: Oxford University Press, 1982), p. 194). The question of the potential sinfulness of following society's rules, rather than the dictates of faith, grew still more after the 1701 Act of Union, since the increasing power of the English government lessened Presbyterian influence on Scottish culture.
58. S. Kierkegaard, *Fear and Trembling* (1843), trans. and intro. A. Hannay (London: Penguin, 1985).
59. S. Kierkegaard, *Concluding Unscientific Postscript to the Philosophical Fragments* (1846), trans. D. Swenson (New Jersey, NJ: Princeton University Press, 1941), p. 92. In *From Soul to Mind*, Reed classifies Kierkegaard as a contributor to the discipline of psychology, a position that I share.
60. Ibid., p. 3.
61. Beattie, *Elements of Moral Science*, p. 79.
62. N. T. Phillipson, 'James Beattie and the Defence of Common Sense', in B. Fabian (ed.), *Festschrift Für Rainer Gruenter* (Heidelberg: Carl Winter, 1978), pp. 145–54, on p. 147.
63. J. Beattie, *Evidences of the Christian Religion; Briefly and Plainly Stated* (Edinburgh: W. Creech, 1786), p. 38, http://galenet.galegroup.com.proxy2.lib.umanitoba.ca/servlet/ECCO (accessed 23 July 2008).
64. N. Cotton, *Observations on a Particular Kind of Scarlet Fever that Lately Prevailed in and about St Alban's. In a Letter to Dr Mead* (London: R. Mansby and H. S. Cox, 1749). This is the only medical text by Cotton that I can find; it is very short (twenty-two pages), it does not concern psychological matters and the spelling of Cotton's first name is unlike that of any other text I have seen. However, since it concerns the vicinity of St Alban's, the location of Cotton's insane asylum, I am certain it is his and, since it is the only medical prose he wrote, it is worth mentioning: Nathaneal Cotton, MD, *Observations on a Particular Kind of Scarlet Fever, that Lately Prevailed in and about St Alban's, In a Letter to Dr Mead* (London: R. Manby and H. S. Cox, 1749); Ritchie, 'Cotton, Nathaniel (1705–1788)'.
65. Ibid.
66. R. Walsh, 'The Life of Dr Cotton', *The Works of the British Poets, with Lives of the Authors* (Boston, MA: Charles Ewer and Timothy Bedlington, 1822), vol. 35, pp. 313–17, on pp. 315–16.

67. Porter, *Mind-Forg'd Manacles*, p. 17.

68. Quoted in Walsh, 'The Life of Dr Cotton', p. 316.

69. V. Skultans, *English Madness: Ideas on Insanity, 1580–1890* (London: Routledge, 1979), p. 3.

70. S. L. Gilman, *Disease and Representation: Images of Illness from Madness to AIDS* (Ithaca, NY: Cornell University Press, 1988), p. 9.

71. Burwick declares, 'Madness … is recognized by its very peculiarity, its deviation from social norms', adding that 'its boundaries are [therefore] renegotiated from age to age as norms change' (*Poetic Madness and the Romantic Imagination*, p. 3). In *Madness and Society in Eighteenth-Century Scotland*, Houston echoes this assertion: 'Because madness … is a quintessentially social illness rather than a mere biological fact, it must be understood in social terms relevant to the period in which the person lived' (Oxford: Clarendon Press, 2000), p. 20.

72. Foucault, *Madness and Civilization*, pp. 256, 64; T. S. Szasz, *The Myth of Mental Illness: Foundations of a Theory of Personal Conduct* (New York: Hoeber-Harper Inc., 1961), p. xv; R. D. Laing, *The Divided Self: An Existential Study in Sanity and Madness* (London: Tavistock Publications Limited, 1960), p. 38. Szasz also maintains in *The Myth of Mental Illness* that 'psychiatry' is the 'transformation of a religious ideology for a scientific one: medicine replaced theology; the alienist, the inquisitor' (p. xx), which, I admit, sounds very like my own argument in this chapter. However, again, the difference between our views lies in the extremity of the conclusions at which we arrive. I do not view 'religious ideology' as synonymous with the Inquisition, as Szasz does. Rather, my point is that a self-reflexive subject familiar to Christianity was eventually transformed into the psychological subject, the context for whom was social, rather than Divine.

73. E. Shorter, *A History of Psychiatry: From the Era of the Asylum to the Age of Prozac* (New York: John Wiley and Sons, Inc., 1997), pp. 30, 29.

74. N. Cotton, 'An Epistle to the Reader', *Visions in Verse, For the Entertainment and Instruction of Younger Minds*, 3rd edn, rev. (London: R. Dodsley, 1752), pp. 1–7. ll. 11–20.

75. Ibid., l. 15.

76. J. Mullan, *Sentiment and Sociability: The Language of Feeling in the Eighteenth Century* (Oxford: Clarendon Press, 1988), p. 203.

77. DePorte, *Nightmares and Hobbyhorses*, p. 12.

78. Except for the apothecaries, most of the traditional, non-academic healthcare workers were women, either 'gossips' or midwives. As such, the division that physicians were attempting to establish was, simultaneously, the initiation of a masculinist medical authority over a feminine and domestic medical authority.

79. Anon., *Pharmacopolae Justificati: or, Apothecaries Vindicated From the Imputation of Ignorance. Wherein is Shewn, That an Academical Education is No Way Necessary to Qualify a Man for the Practice of Physick* (J. Roberts: London, 1724), p. 1, in *The Eighteenth-Century* (ESTC reel (MICR) 13297).

80. Ibid., p. 5.

81. Ibid., p. 4.

82. This distinction would seem to divide, rather than unify, the approaches of Cotton, the practical apothecary, and Beattie, the professor of moral philosophy. As I will explain, though, Beattie complains about the undemocratic sophistries of academia and seeks to remedy them through accessible language, thereby showing his allegiance with Cotton and the anonymous author of *Pharmacopolae Justificati*.

83. Foucault, *Madness and Civilization*, p. 269.

84. Ritchie, 'Cotton, Nathaniel (1705–1788)'.
85. W. Cowper, 'Hope', *Poems by William Cowper, of the Inner Temple, Esq.* (London: J. Johnson, 1782), pp. 141–79, ll. 191–200, in *Eighteenth Century Collections Online*, http://galenet.galegroup.com.proxy1.lib.umanitoba.ca/servlet/ECCO (accessed 1 June 1 2008).
86. Ritchie, 'Cotton, Nathaniel (1705–1788)'.
87. As Edward W. Pitcher points out in 'Nathaniel Cotton, the Elder: An Anonymous Contributor to Dodsley's Museum (1746–7) and Wm Dodd's *Visitor* (1760)' (*American Notes and Queries*, 17:8 (1979), pp. 124–5)', 'Detraction A Vision' is another of Cotton's allegorical visions that, for some reason, did not appear in the original *Visions in Verse*. However, the poem was included in the posthumous *Various Pieces in Verse and Prose*, published by Cotton's son, (2 vols (London: J. Dodsley, 1791).
88. Watts's *Divine Songs for the Use of Children* was a best-selling phenomenon throughout the century, despite the fear it must have inspired in its young reader with lines like the following:

    God quickly stopped their wicked breath;
    And sent two raging bears,
    That tore them limb from limb to death,
    With blood, and groans, and tears.
    Great God! How terrible art thou
    To sinners e'er so young:
    Grant us thy grace, and teach us how
    To tame and rule our tongue.
    ('Against Scoffing and Calling Names', in *Divine Songs for the Use of Children*
    (1720) (Whitefish: Kessinger Publishing, 2003), pp. 44–6. ll. 17–24).

    By contrast, Cotton's moral poems 'for the entertainment and instruction of younger minds' appeal to the reader – both young and old, for, indeed, these poems are in no way simplistic and childish – through the gentle power of persuasion.
89. N. Cotton, 'Pleasure. Vision II', in *Visions in Verse, For the Entertainment and Instruction of Younger Minds*, 3rd edn, rev. (London: R. Dodsley, 1752), pp. 19–28. ll. 83–8.
90. The first definition for the noun 'vision' in the *OED* confirms the supernatural associations of the word: 'Something which is apparently seen otherwise than by ordinary sight; *esp.* an appearance of a prophetic or mystical character, or having the nature of a revelation, supernaturally presented to the mind either in sleep or in an abnormal state', *OED* online (Oxford: Oxford University Press, 2008), http://dictionary.oed.com.proxy1.lib.umanitoba.ca/ (accessed 25 July 2008).)
91. J. Bunyan, *The Pilgrim's Progress* (1678), ed. W. R. Owens (Oxford: Oxford University Press, 2003). Arguably, Cotton is indebted to Bunyan in more ways than one, since Bunyan's speaker is also a dreamer and Bunyan, like Cotton, wrote books for children. However, since the poets shared the same broad theme of faith, and since Bunyan published over sixty works of literature, some overlap is to be expected.
92. Although it is true that many Christian values are oriented towards the social, faith often concerns only the individual and her relationship with God. Did you attend to the priest's sermon at mass? Did an evil thought cross your mind? Did you say your prayers last night? Many duties of the faithful are purely private and subjective, not social.
93. Cotton, 'An Epistle to the Reader', ll. 27–32.
94. Books could reach very high prices in the eighteenth century. William St Clair confirms that, even by the Romantic period, many books that we now consider to be part of the

canon were prohibitively expensive to most readers, despite what has been called the explosion in literacy at the time. However, religious and conduct books – both of which categories *Visions in Verse* might be said to occupy – were mass-produced, cheaper and not nearly so exclusive as volumes written for a select class of more educated people. See W. St Clair, 'Who Read What in the Romantic Period', University of Toronto, Toronto, Ontario, 7 March 2005. As such, Cotton's volume might well be described as 'humbler' art.

95. N. Cotton, 'Content. Vision IV', in *Visions in Verse, For the Entertainment and Instruction of Younger Minds*, 3rd edn, rev. (London: R. Dodsley, 1752), pp. 43–51. ll. 71–6.

96. Cotton, 'An Epistle to the Reader', ll. 99–102, 109–12.

97. Ibid., ll. 125–8.

98. Cotton, 'Pleasure. Vision II', ll. 17–26. Cotton's emphasis.

99. Ibid., ll. 173, 175–80.

100. N. Cotton, 'Health. Vision III', in *Visions in Verse, For the Entertainment and Instruction of Younger Minds*, 3rd edn, rev. (London: R. Dodsley, 1752), pp. 29–39. ll. 49–58.

101. Thomas Brown makes a similar argument regarding his use of humour in his poetry, as I will explain in Chapter 4. In the preface to his volume of verse, *The Paradise of Coquettes*, Brown explains that, because human nature rejects didacticism, he inculcates his moral lessons in the reader indirectly through humour (London: John Murray, 1814), pp. xxxvi–vii.

102. Cotton, 'Health. Vision III', ll. 7–14.

103. Cotton, 'Pleasure. Vision II', ll. 99–112.

104. Ibid., ll. 135, 137.

105. Coleridge, 'Kubla Khan', ll. 2, 9, 16, 39, 20, 28.

106. Wordsworth, *The Prelude*, l. 49.

107. Ibid., ll. 141, 140, 142–3, 152.

108. M. Akenside, 'The Pleasures of Imagination; A Poem in Three Books' (1744), in *Poems of Established Reputation* (Baltimore, MA: Warner and Hanna, 1803).

109. Coleridge, 'Kubla Khan', l. 51.

110. Cotton, 'An Epistle to the Reader', l. 127.

111. Ibid., l. 15.

112. One of the great exceptions here is George Crabbe, who made similar use of the mysteries of the mind for very clearly instructive purposes in such poems as 'Sir Eustace Grey', 'Peter Grimes', and 'The Voluntary Insane'. See G. Crabbe, 'Sir Eustace Grey', in N. Dalrymple-Champneys (ed.), *The Complete Poetical Works* (Oxford: Clarendon Press, 1988), vol. 1, pp. 298–310; Crabbe, G., 'Peter Grimes' from 'The Borough', in ibid., pp. 567–74; G. Crabbe, 'The Voluntary Insane', in F. Pryor (ed.), *The Voluntary Insane* (London: Richard Cohen Books, 1995), pp. 47–90.

113. Given Cotton's special treatment of the poem, it is a mystery why it was not included in the first two editions of *Visions in Verse* (C. Buchanan, 'Preface', in N. Cotton, *Visions in Verse* (1752) (Bern: Herbert Lang, 1973), unpag).

114. N. Cotton, 'Death. Vision the Last', in *Visions in Verse, For the Entertainment and Instruction of Younger Minds*, 3rd edn, rev. (London: R. Dodsley, 1752), pp. 111–32. l. 316, 337–8.

115. J. Donne, 'Holy Sonnet 10', in M. H. Abrams (ed.), *The Norton Anthology of English Literature*, 5th edn (New York: W. W. Norton & Co., 1986), p. 1099, l. 13.

116. Cotton, 'Death. Vision the Last', ll. 335–6.

117. Ibid., ll. 135–6, 143–4.

118. Ibid., ll. 381–4, 389–90, 407–14.

119. Ibid., ll. 301–7, 315–16.

120. Cotton, 'An Epistle to the Reader', l. 127.

121. Cotton, 'Death. Vision the Last', ll. 320–6, 330.

122. J. Beattie, *An Essay on the Nature and Immutability of Truth, in Opposition to Sophistry and Scepticism* (1770) (Philadelphia, PA: Solomon Wieatt, 1809).

123. W. Forbes, *An Account of the Life and Writings of James Beattie, LLD* (New York: Isaac Riley and Co, 1806), p. 9.

124. Ibid., p. 10.

125. Ibid., p. 11.

126. Ibid., p. 13.

127. Monboddo asserted that humans and primates were close relatives in *Of the Origin and Progress of Language* (Preece, R., *Animals and Nature: Cultural Myths, Cultural Realities* (Vancouver, BC: University of British Columbia Press, 1999), p. 156. J. B. M. Burnett, Of the Origin and Progress of Language (1773–92) (Menston: Scolar Press, 1967).

128. Robinson, 'Beattie, James (1735–1803)'.

129. Phillipson, 'James Beattie and the Defence of Common Sense', p. 151.

130. Robinson 'Beattie, James (1735–1803)'.

131. Forbes, *An Account of the Life and Writings of James Beattie, LLD*, p. 25.

132. As abstract as Beattie's professional experience of psychology was, the insight into depression and madness that appears in his verse indicates his familiarity with the practical side of the subject. Such insight may be attributed to Beattie's own 'crippling bouts of anxiety and depression, exacerbated by what was clearly paranoia' (Phillipson, 'James Beattie and the Defence of Common Sense', p. 151) and his wife's mental illness, characterized by 'bizarre behaviour and paranoid delusions' (Robinson, 'Beattie, James (1735–1803)').

133. Beattie, *An Essay on the Nature and Immutability of Truth*, p. 9. All references to Beattie's *An Essay on ... Truth* are to the 1809 edition.

134. Ibid., pp. 13–14.

135. Ibid., pp. 57–8.

136. Ibid., p. 50.

137. Ibid., pp. 57–8.

138. Phillipson, 'James Beattie and the Defence of Common Sense', p. 152.

139. Beattie's moral philosophy is strongly linked to the literature of sensibility through a shared focus on morals and subjective feeling as authoritative. As R. F. Brissenden argues with respect to sensibility, 'the spontaneous moral responses of the individual and possess some special and general authority'. See *Virtue in Distress: Studies in the Novel of Sentiment from Richardson to Sade* (London: The Macmillan Press, Ltd., 1974), p. 54. I will discuss sentiment in greater detail in Chapter 2.

140. J. Harris, 'Introduction', p. 3.

141. Beattie, *Elements of Moral Science*, p. 48.

142. Ibid., p. 50.

143. Beattie, *An Essay on the Nature and Immutability of Truth*, p. 5.

144. Ibid., p. 6.

145. Ibid., p. 24.

146. E. H. King, *James Beattie* (Boston, MA: Twayne Publishers, 1977), p. 40; Robinson, 'Beattie, James (1735–1803)'; Phillipson, 'James Beattie and the Defence of Common Sense', p. 151.

147. King, *James Beattie*, p. 16.

148. Ibid., p. 47.

149. Phillipson, 'James Beattie and the Defence of Common Sense', pp. 145, 151.

150. Ibid., p. 152.

151. F. J. [full surname not given], 'Sketch of the Life of James Beattie, LLD', *The Minstrel: or, The Progress of Genius. Also, The Shipwreck. By William Falconer. With a Sketch of the Life of Each Author* (New York: Collins and Perkins, 1808), pp. iii–ix, on p. v.

152. H. Chisick, 'David Hume and the Common People', in P. Jones (ed.), *The 'Science of Man' in the Scottish Enlightenment: Hume, Reid and their Contemporaries* (Edinburgh: Edinburgh University Press, 1989), pp. 13, 12.

153. Ibid., pp. 12, 15.

154. Ibid., p. 14.

155. Phillipson, 'James Beattie and the Defence of Common Sense', p. 152.

156. Beattie, *An Essay on the Nature and Immutability of Truth*, p. 15.

157. Beattie, *Elements of Moral Science*, p. 64.

158. Quoted in Forbes, M., *Beattie and his Friends* (Westminster: Archibald Constable & Co. Ltd., 1904), p. 59.

159. King, *James Beattie*, p. 97.

160. Edwin may have been modelled after Beattie himself, but many other poets identified with the character; King notes that John Thelwall saw himself in Edwin, and that, more generally, the minstrel 'became for the Romantic poets a useful model of the poetic life' (King, *James Beattie*, p. 107).

161. J., 'Sketch of the Life of James Beattie, LLD', p. vi.

162. Beattie, 'The Minstrel, or Progress of Genius', unpag. Beattie's ellipsis.

163. Robinson and King have noted the links between Beattie's *The Minstrel* and Wordsworth's *The Prelude* (Robinson, 'Beattie, James (1735–1803)'; E. King, *James Beattie's The Minstrel and the Origins of Romantic Autobiography* (Lewiston, NY: The Edwin Mellen Press, 1992), p. 107.

164. Cotton, 'Death. Vision the Last', l. 316.

165. Beattie, 'The Minstrel, or Progress of Genius', ll. 136–44.

166. R. Goldsmith, 'The Selfless Self of Self: Hopkins' Late Sonnets', *Hopkins Quarterly*, 3 (1976), pp. 67–75, on p. 67.

167. Beattie confirms in his essay 'On Poetry and Music, As They Affect the Mind' that he reveals details of his own personal and subjective experience not for egotistical ends, but because he hopes to provide a new experience for the reader through these descriptions:

> the compositions of an ingenious author may operate upon the heart, whatever be the subject because ... The affections that prevail in the author himself direct his attention to objects congenial, and give a peculiar bias to his inventive powers, and a peculiar colour to his language. Hence his work, as well as face, if nature is permitted to exert herself freely in it, will exhibit a picture of his mind, and awaken correspondent sympathies with the reader.
>
> (*An Essay on the Nature and Immutability of Truth, in Opposition to Sophistry and Scepticism; On Poetry and Music, As They Affect the Mind; On Laughter, and Ludicrous Composition; On the Utility of Classical Learning* (Edinburgh: William Creech, 1776), pp. 347–580, on pp. 387–8)

The reader's subjectivity may be altered through his indirect experience of the writer's subjective life as it is reported in his work.

168. Beattie, 'The Minstrel, or Progress of Genius', ll. 20–7.

169. Ibid., ll. 28–36.

170. Ibid., ll. 55–63.

171. Ibid., ll. 64–7.

172. Ibid., ll. 82–6.

173. Ibid., ll. 443–51.

174. Beattie, *An Essay on the Nature and Immutability of Truth*, p. 57.

175. E. Burke, *A Philosophical Enquiry into the Origin of Our Ideas of the Sublime and Beautiful* (1757), intro. and notes A. Phillip (Oxford: Oxford University Press, 1990).

176. Beattie, *Elements of Moral Science*, pp. 88, 90.

177. King, *James Beattie's* The Minstrel *and the Origins of Romantic Autobiography*, p. 107; Robinson, 'Beattie, James (1735–1803)', unpag.

178. Beattie, 'The Minstrel, or Progress of Genius', ll. 181–9.

179. Wordsworth, *The Prelude*, ll. 42–7, 58–9.

180. In her discussion of Akenside's medical education, Barbauld recognizes that the culture that prized dialogue between scientific philosophy and literature was a product of Scottish medical schools:

Educated in the university of Edinburgh, he joined to his classic literature, the keen discriminating spirit of metaphysic inquiry, and the taste for moral beauty which has so much distinguished our northern seminaries, and which the celebrity of their professors and the genius of the place has never failed of communicating to their disciples.

('Essay on Akenside's Poem on *The Pleasures of Imagination*', pp. 8–9)

181. Cotton, 'Death. Vision the Last', l. 316.

182. Ibid., ll. 358, 359, 367–70.

183. Ibid., ll. 451–2.

184. J. Beattie, 'The Hermit', *Poems on Several Occasions* (Edinburgh: W. Creech, 1776), pp. 122–4. ll. 37–40.

185. Ibid., l. 34.

186. William Perfect, who I will discuss in Chapter 2 for his contributions to moral management, also shared with Cotton and Beattie a dedication to religio-psychological poetry, a fact that gestures to the overlap between many early psychologists' theoretical approaches. Perfect's poem 'Extempore, on Seeing a Scull' expresses the physician's Christian belief that we must relate all of our efforts, earthly or spiritual, back to God, who sees all and will exact his due:

Sure instance, *this*, of Life's contracted span,
Which bounds the days of immaterial man:

. . . .

Ye great, ye sordid, folish [sic], and ye vain,
Behold this object, and your vice restrain!
Tho' now it looks defil'd with earthy hue,
Despise it not – but your own picture view!
In time, weak man, thou creature of a day,
Renounce your sin, and bounden duty pay
To Heav'n's Supreme! On him infix your eye:
This hour defer not, for the next you die!

(in *The Laurel-Wreath; Being a Collection of Original Miscellaneous Poems, On Subjects Moral, Comic, and Divine*, 2 vols (London: Printed for the Author, 1766), vol. 1, pp. 156–7, ll. 1–2; 10–17), in *The Eighteenth Century* (ESTC reel (MICR) 1883, no. 8.)

The image of the skull expresses succinctly Perfect's dual focus on physical and mental reality, which was at the basis of his nerve theory. As is the case throughout his poetry, Perfect uses the material world to point to a greater spiritual reality here ('thou creature of a day, / Renounce your sin'), but he is more pointed in this poem about the real purpose of self-reflection ('your own picture view!') when he advises us to 'pay' our 'bounden duty' to 'Heav'n's Supreme', or God. You (the subject of his psychological approach) are to look within in order to 'infix your eye' on God who, it seems, is looking back. The speaker's action of contemplating a skull with reference to mortality is a clear reference to Shakespeare's *Hamlet*, which also inspired Perfect to pen 'A Parody from Hamlet', which opens memorably with the lines, 'To bleed, or not to bleed? – that is the question: / Whether it is better in the blood to bear / The load and pain a pleth'ric habit brings, / Or take advice from Hippocratic lore, / And by complying 'scape them?' ('A Parody from Hamlet, Wrote When Indisposed and in Doubt about Bleeding', in *A Bavin of Bays: Containing Various Original Essays in Poetry* (London: Printed for the author, 1763), pp. 156–7, ll. 1–5), in *The Eighteenth-Century* (ESTC reel (MICR) 8358, no. 1).

187. Harris, *Cosmologia*, p. xii.

2. The Human Touch: Thomas Bakewell, Andrew Duncan Sr, John Ferriar and Moral Management

1.   T. Bakewell, *The Moorland Bard; or, Poetical Recollections of a Weaver, in the Moorlands of Staffordshire*, 2 vols (London: T. Allbut, 1807).

2.   A. Duncan, *Short Account of the Rise, Progress, and Present State of the Lunatic Asylum at Edinburgh* (Edinburgh: A. Constable & Co., 1812).

3.   A. Duncan, *Miscellaneous Poems, Extracted from the Records of the Circulation Club at Edinburgh* (Edinburgh: P. Hill & Co., 1818).

4.   J. Ferriar, *The Bibliomania, an Epistle, to Richard Heber, Esq.* (1812), ed. Marc Vaulbert de Chantilly (London: The Vanity Press of Bethnal Green, 2001).

5.   Porter, *Mind Forg'd Manacles*, p. 3.

6.   Hunter and Macalpine, *Three Hundred Years of Psychiatry*, p. 695.

7.   R. Porter, 'Introduction' in J. Haslam, *Illustrations of Madness* (1810) (London: Routledge, 1988), pp. xi–xl, on p. xv.

8.   Hunter and Macalpine, *Three Hundred Years of Psychiatry*, p. 603.

9.   Shorter, *A Historical Dictionary of Psychiatry*, pp.180, 181.

10. S. Tuke, *Description of the Retreat, an Institution Near York, For Insane Persons of the Society of Friends. Containing an Account of its Origin and Progress, the Modes of Treatment, and a Statement of Cases* (York: W. Alexander, 1813).

11. Tuke, *Description of the Retreat*, pp. 132, 131.

12. Tuke also makes frequent reference to John Haslam, apothecary to Bethlem Hospital, and praises his recommendations of mild treatment in *Observations on Madness*, but I do not detail his theories here because Haslam is not generally viewed as a moral manager.

13. R. G. Hill, *Total Abolition of Personal Restraint in the Treatment of the Insane* (1838; New York: Arno Press, 1976), p. 21. Hill's emphasis.

14. Hunter and Macalpine, *Three Hundred Years of Psychiatry*, p. 538.

15. Hill, *Total Abolition of Personal Restraint*, pp. 10–11.

16. Porter, *Mind Forg'd Manacles*, p. 207.

17. Dale Peterson confirms that Bethlem was the oldest asylum in the world, while Donnelly adds that, although Bethlem was originally built as a convent, it began to house the insane as early as the fourteenth century. See D. Peterson (ed.), *A Mad People's History of Madness* (Pittsburgh, PA: University of Pittsburgh Press, 1982), p. 75 and Donnelly, *Managing the Mind*, p. 5.
18. Quoted in Hunter and Macalpine, *Three Hundred Years of Psychiatry*, p. 702.
19. Tuke, *Description of the Retreat*, p. 133.
20. Shorter, *A History of Psychiatry*, pp. 19–20; M. Arieno, *Victorian Lunatics: A Social Epidemiology of Mental Illness in Mid-Nineteenth-Century England* (London: Associated University Presses, 1989), p. 67.
21. L. Gamwell and N. Tomes, *Madness in America: Cultural and Medical Perceptions of Mental Illness Before 1914* (New York: Cornell University Press, 1995), p. 37.
22. Skultans, *English Madness*, p. 11.
23. E. Showalter, *The Female Malady: Women, Madness, and English Culture, 1830–1980* (New York: Pantheon, 1985), p. 29.
24. Hunter and Macalpine, *Three Hundred Years of Psychiatry*, p. 837.
25. Foucault, *Madness and Civilization*, p. 257.
26. Tuke, *Description of the Retreat*, pp. 160–1.
27. Ibid., pp. 22–3.
28. Please see my article 'Cure, Classification, and John Clare' for a more in-depth exploration of the classificatory labours of early psychology; in *Victorian Literature and Culture*, 33 (2005), pp. 269–91.
29. Bakewell, p. xi.
30. Tuke, *Description of the Retreat*, p. 226.
31. Duncan, *A Short Account of the Rise, Progress, and Present State of the Lunatic Asylum at Edinburgh*, p. 15.
32. Quoted in Vickers, 'Coleridge, Thomas Beddoes and Brunonian Medicine', p. 74.
33. Porter, *Mind Forg'd Manacles*, pp. 224, 223, 206.
34. Tuke, *Description of the Retreat*, p. ix; Tuke quotes John Haslam here.
35. Tuke, *Description of the Retreat*, p. viii.
36. Porter, *Mind Forg'd Manacles*, pp. 226–7. Tuke presents the poems of mad patients in *A Description of The Retreat*. The 'hypochondriac's' verse, which I transcribe here in full, provides an intriguing glimpse into the perspective opposite to the one I delineate in this study. Helpfully, it shows that, while the moral managers did not see the insane in purely physical terms, the mad themselves may have done so and, while the moral managers thought that they constructed a welcoming 'Retreat' for the protection and care of lunatics, the inmates of such asylums prayed for their release:

    A miracle, my friends, come view,
    A man, admit his own words true,
    Who lives without a soul;
    Nor liver, lungs, nor heart has he,
    Yet, sometimes, can as cheerful be
    As if he had the whole.
    His head (take his own words along)
    Now hard as iron, yet ere long
    Is soft as any jelly;
    All burnt his sinews, and his lungs;
    Of his complaints, not fifty tongues

> Could find enough to tell ye.
> Yet he who paints his likeness here,
> Has just as much himself to fear,
> He's wrong from top to toe;
> Ah friends! pray help us, if you can,
> And make us each again a man,
> That we from hence may go.
>   (footnote in Tuke, *Description of the Retreat,* pp. 152–3)

The poet's feeling of alienation from his own body attests to the existential crisis into which patients may find themselves, whether through their illness or the definitions of psychology.

37. T. Ferriar, *Medical Histories and Reflections* (London: T. Cadell, 1792), vol. 1; Ferriar, T., *Medical Histories and Reflections* (London: Cadell and Davies, 1795), vol. 2.
38. Tuke, *Description of the Retreat,* p. v.
39. G. J. Barker-Benfield, *The Culture of Sensibility: Sex and Society in Eighteenth-Century Britain* (Chicago, IL: The University of Chicago Press, 1992), p. 7. Like Bakewell's poetry, Duncan's verse focuses on the need for charity, but this feature alone does not suggest its connections with the literature of sentiment. Arguably, even John Ferriar's exploration of the connections between his psychological theories and the Gothic in *An Essay Towards a Theory of Apparitions* may be said to be connected to the moral managers' rewriting of this psycho-literary relationship, as the Gothic has been shown to be the dark reflection of the novel of sentiment: the histrionics so integral to the Gothic genre may be seen as an extreme expression of sensibility's tears.
40. S. Richardson, *Clarissa; or, The History of a Young Lady* (1747–8), ed. A. Ross (Harmondsworth: Penguin, 1985); S. Richardson, *Pamela; or, Virtue Rewarded* (1740), intro. M. Kinkead-Weekes (London: Dent, 1962); H. Fielding, *Joseph Andrews* and *Shamela,* ed. and rev. T. Keymer (New York: Oxford World's Classics, 1999).
41. Barker-Benfield, *The Culture of Sensibility,* p. 7.
42. G. S. Rousseau, 'Nerves, Spirits, and Fibres: Towards Defining the Origins of Sensibility', *Blue Guitar,* 2 (1976), pp. 125–53. However, in *The English Malady: or, A Treatise of Nervous Diseases of All Kinds, as Spleen, Vapours, Lowness of Spirits, Hypochondriacal, and Hysterical Distempers &c.,* Cheyne does not consider animal spirits and nerves to be equally important principle actors (London: G. Strahan and J. Leake, 1733). Indeed, while he attributes to nerves many motions of the human frame, he discounts the concept of animal spirits: he complains about the 'Absurdity of attempting to account for nervous Diseases by the Existence of animal Spirits', finally adding, 'To conclude this dark Subject of animal Spirits, if they must be suppos'd, we may affirm they cannot be of the Nature of any Fluid we have a Notion of, from what we see or know' (pp. xxii, 88).
43. Rousseau, 'Nerves, Spirits, and Fibres', p. 135.
44. Vickers, *Coleridge and the Doctors,* p. ix.
45. J. Andrews and A. Scull, *Undertaker of the Mind: John Monro and Mad-Doctoring in Eighteenth-Century England* (Berkeley and Los Angeles, CA: University of California Press, 2000), pp. 80, 81.
46. W. F. Bynum, 'The Nervous Patient in Eighteenth- and Nineteenth-Century England: The Psychiatric Origins of British Neurology', in W. F. Bynum, R. Porter and M. Shepherd (eds), *The Anatomy of Madness* (London: Tavistock, 1985), vol. 1, pp. 89–102, on p. 91. My emphasis.
47. Shorter, *A History of Psychiatry,* p. 24; Mullan, *Sentiment and Sociability,* p. 214.

48. L. D. Smith, 'Bakewell, Thomas (1761–1835)', *ODNB*, http://www.oxforddnb.com. myaccess.library.utoronto.ca/view/article/56715 (accessed 11 July 2005).

49. Ibid.

50. Ibid.

51. Ibid.

52. T. Bakewell, *A Letter Addressed to the Chairman of the Select Committee of the House of Commons, Appointed to Enquire into the State of Mad-Houses: To Which is Subjoined, Remarks on the Nature, Causes, and Cure of Mental Derangement* (Stafford: C. Chester, 1815).

53. Ibid., p. 3.

54. Ibid., p. 32.

55. Bakewell, *The Domestic Guide*, p. 25.

56. Ibid., p. xi.

57. Ibid., pp. 3, xi.

58. Ibid., p. 27.

59. This is a particularly poignant instance of how the democratic principles of the psychologist-poets were inherently tied to the establishment of disciplinary power: by rejecting the impulse to linguistic esotericism, which is traditionally understood as identifiable with the 'demonic' knowledge of the psychologist, Bakewell unwittingly (it seems) disperses power more effectively because he makes psychological discourse – the discourse of subjectivity – available to more people.

60. Ibid., p. 57.

61. Bakewell, 'The Author's Dream', pp. 165–8.

62. Ibid., ll. 21–4.

63. In the preface, Bakewell makes only the following simple claim to expertise on insanity: 'His competence to write upon the subject of insanity arose from its having often employed his thoughts, from reading, and experience' ('Preface', *The Moorland Bard; or, Poetical Recollections of a Weaver, in the Moorlands of Staffordshire* 2 vols (London: T. Allbut, 1807), vol. 1, pp. vii–xiv, on p. xi).

64. Bakewell, 'The Author's Dream', l. 3.

65. Ibid., ll. 26, 28.

66. T. Bakewell, 'The Weaver's Request, That the Public Will Hear his Song', *The Moorland Bard; or, Poetical Recollections of a Weaver, in the Moorlands of Staffordshire*, 2 vols (London: T. Allbut, 1807), vol. 1, pp. 1–2. ll. 1–2, 5–6, 9–10.

67. Bakewell, *A Letter Addressed to the Chairman*, p. 28.

68. Bakewell, 'Preface', p. xii.

69. T. Bakewell, 'Epistle to a Neighbouring Gentleman, Complaining of the Want of Poetic Fame', *The Moorland Bard,* vol. 1, pp. 7–13. ll. 8–9, 15–17.

70. Bakewell, 'Preface', *The Moorland Bard*, p. x.

71. Bakewell, 'Epistle to a Neighbouring Gentleman', ll. 73–6, 97–100.

72. Bakewell, 'Preface', p. viii. After having married three times, Bakewell was finally outlived by his third wife when he died on 6 September 1835 at Spring Vale. See Smith, 'Bakewell, Thomas (1761–1835)'.

73. T. Bakewell, 'The Author's Advertisement for a Wife', *The Moorland Bard*, vol. 2, pp. 45–8. ll. 45–8.

74. Ibid., p. 48.

75. T. Bakewell, 'Lines Written on a Blank Leaf of My Domestic Guide, and Presented to a Young Lady', in *The Moorland Bard*, vol. 1, pp. 55–6. ll. 1–4, 11–12.

76. J. Andrews and A. Scull, *Customers and Patrons of the Mad-Trade: The Management of Lunacy in Eighteenth-Century London: With the Complete Text of John Monro's 1766 Case Book* (Berkeley, CA: University of California Press, 2003), p. 53.

77. Please see my chapter 'A Gendered Affliction' in *Cultural Constructions of Madness in Eighteenth Century Writing: Representing the Insane*, in A. Ingram with M. Faubert (New York: Palgrave Macmillan, 2005) pp. 136–69,, for a discussion of women and madness in the early Romantic period.

78. Bakewell, *The Domestic Guide*, p. 26.

79. T. Bakewell, 'Epistle to a Lady, Who had Requested Some Maxims of Health', in *The Moorland Bard*, vol. 2, pp. 90–8. ll. 35–8.

80. Ibid., ll. 11–14.

81. Bakewell, *A Letter Addressed to the Chairman of the Select Committee of the House of Commons*, p. 19.

82. Bakewell, 'Epistle to a Lady, Who had Requested Some Maxims of Health', ll. 51–4; 59–60.

83. Samuel Tuke explains that the keepers at The Retreat would welcome ladies from the nearby town to take tea with the inmates of the asylum, during which events 'All who attend, dress in their best clothes, and vie with each other in politeness and propriety' (Tuke, *A Description of The Retreat*, p. 178). Although this scene seems to me like paradise compared to most descriptions of late eighteenth-century madhouses, Foucault was particularly incensed by the thought of it and accused the supposed fiend, William Tuke, of creating 'an asylum where he substituted for the free terror of madness the stifling anguish of responsibility' (*Madness and Civilization*, p. 247). Regardless of one's personal opinion of how agonizing it is to suppress the urge to terrorize others, this description of teatime at The Retreat underlines that the focus on social responsibility was a distinguishing feature of moral management.

84. Bakewell, 'Epistle to a Lady, Who had Requested Some Maxims of Health', ll. 63–70.

85. Ibid., ll. 147–50.

86. Bakewell, T., 'Epistle to a Lady; Occasioned by Her Advertisement, in a London Paper, For Country Lodgings in a Family Where There Were None but Females, Complaining at the Same Time of Frequent Depression of Spirits', in *The Moorland Bard*, vol. 2, pp. 49–51. ll. 13–16; 20–4.

87. Tuke, *A Description of The Retreat*, pp. 157, 159.

88. Bakewell, 'Preface', *The Domestic Guide, In Cases of Insanity. Pointing out the Causes, Means of Preventing, and Proper Treatment, of that Disorder. Recommended to Private Families, and the Notice of the Clergy* (Hanley: T. Allbut, 1805), pp. vii–xi, on p. vi.

89. Ibid., and *The Domestic Guide, In Cases of Insanity*, pp. vi, 79.

90. Bakewell, *A Letter Addressed to the Chairman of the Select Committee of the House of Commons*, p. 18.

91. Bettany and Rosner, 'Duncan, Andrew, the elder (1744–1828)'.

92. Ibid.

93. Ibid.

94. Duncan, *A Short Account of the Rise, Progress, and Present State of the Lunatic Asylum at Edinburgh*, unpag.

95. Duncan, *A Short Account of the Rise, Progress, and Present State of the Lunatic Asylum at Edinburgh*, p. 5.

96. Foucault, 'The Politics of Health in the Eighteenth Century', p. 177.

97. Please see Chapter 1 of this study and R. M. Strozier, *Foucault, Subjectivity and Identity: Historical Constructions of Subject and Self* (Detroit, MI: Wayne State University Press, 2002), p. 19, for a discussion of psychology as the systematization of subjectivity; my article, 'Cure, Classification, and John Clare', develops the concept of psychology as a process of categorization and division, as well.

98. Duncan, *A Short Account of the Rise, Progress, and Present State of the Lunatic Asylum at Edinburgh*, p. 9. As the situation stood at the time of his writing this text, however, the 'mid-class' building alone was complete. Such attention to the separation of patients along the lines of social class does not necessarily denote Duncan's snobbery, though: decades before he published his prose psychological texts, he founded 'a public dispensary, an institution for giving free medicines and medical advice to the poor. This afterwards became the Royal Public Dispensary, incorporated by royal charter in 1818' (Bettany and Rosner, 'Duncan, Andrew, the elder (1744–1828)').

99. Duncan, *A Short Account of the Rise, Progress, and Present State of the Lunatic Asylum at Edinburgh*, pp. 14–15.

100. Duncan asserts his dedication to the gentle treatment of patients in his unreserved praise of The Retreat, which Tuke later quotes in his *Description of the Retreat*: 'The Retreat at York is at this moment the best regulated establishment in Europe, either for the recovery of the insane, or for their comfort, where they are in an incurable state', noting thereafter that that the Edinburgh asylum should be run in the same way: 'particularly that chains, stripes, and every other rough mode of treatment should be completely banished' (Duncan, *A Short Account of the Rise, Progress, and Present State of the Lunatic Asylum at Edinburgh*, pp. 15, 16). With these final words, Duncan illustrates his adherence to the practice of moral management in its most recognizable form: as a therapy for the insane based on gentle treatment.

101. A. Duncan, 'Advice Given to the Rich and Great, by a Physician, Who has Very Nearly Arrived at the Eightieth Year of his Age ... 1st of May, 1822' (no publishing information given; collected in volume entitled *Medical Tracts* no. 868 at the Wellcome Institute for the History of Medicine Library), ll. 1–10.

102. Bettany and Rosner, 'Duncan, Andrew, the elder (1744–1828)'.

103. A. Duncan, *Observations on the Office of Faithful Teacher, and on the Duty of an Attentive Student of Medicine, Delivered as an Introductory Lecture to the Institute of Medicine in the University of Edinburgh* (Edinburgh: Bell & Bradfute, 1823), pp. 40–1.

104. Arguably, Duncan's poems are more advisory than epistolary, since they instruct directly without the usual appendage of the address (i.e. 'Dear Jane'). However, he signs several of them in the style of a letter. For example, the poem entitled '1st May 1818' is signed, 'Medicus Septuagenarius' after the text of the poem, a signature that further establishes the poet's desire to relate to the reader personally by gesturing to his advanced age and profession.

105. Harris, 'Introduction', p. 3.

106. The *ODNB* entries for the following figures reveal their involvement with a wide variety of different societies, some medical, some more generally scientific and some political: in addition to the clubs listed above, Duncan founded the Caledonian Horticultural Society (Bettany and Rosner, 'Duncan, Andrew, the elder (1744–1828)'); Perfect was a member of the London Medical Society (Black, 'Perfect, William (1731/2–1809)'); Beattie was a member of the Aberdeen Philosophical Society (Robinson, 'Beattie, James (1735–1803)'); Erasmus Darwin was a fellow of the Royal Society, the Botanical Society at Lichfield, the Lunar Society based in Birmingham and the Derby Philosophical Society (McNeil, 'Darwin, Erasmus (1731–1802)'); Trotter belonged to the Literary and

Philosophical Society (Wallace, J., 'Trotter, Thomas (bap. 1760, d. 1832)', *ODNB*, http://www.oxforddnb.com.myaccess.library.utoronto.ca/view/article/27763 (accessed 11 July 2005)) and, finally, Forster was a member of the Linnean Society, the London Phrenological Society in 1825, the Royal Astronomical Society and the Animals' Friends Society, but he declined fellowship of the Royal Society because he disliked 'some of its rules' (Browne, J., 'Forster, Thomas Ignatius Maria (1789–1860)', *ODNB*, http://www.oxforddnb.com.myaccess.library.utoronto.ca/view/article/9920 (accessed 11 July 2005)).

107. Duncan's interest in such clubs started early: during his student days, he acted as the president of the Royal Medical Society. See Bettany and Rosner, 'Duncan, Andrew, the elder (1744–1828)'.

108. A. Duncan, *Miscellaneous Poems*. The Circulation Club was a social club attended by many Romantic-era doctors in Edinburgh. One of its most illustrious members was Dr Monro *Secundus*, a biography of whom appeared in the first edition of *Miscellaneous Poems* while Duncan was, as he describes himself in the preface, 'the Old Secretary, who, although he has officiated in that capacity for forty years, is still a young Fellow' (unpag.). The Circulation Club may be one and the same as the same as the 'Harveian Club', of which Duncan has been identified as a founding member by Bettany and Rosner, for Duncan also notes later in the volume that one 'Dr Harvey ... [was] the discoverer of the Circulation of the Blood', which hints at the origin of both clubs' names (Duncan, *Miscellaneous Poems, Extracted from the Records of the Circulation Club at Edinburgh*, p. 34. See also Bettany and Rosner, 'Duncan, Andrew, the elder (1744–1828)'.

109. Duncan, A., 'Diploma of Doctor of Mirth, Solemnly Conferred on Alexander Wood, Esq. April 12, 1813', in *Miscellaneous Poems, Extracted from the Records of the Circulation Club at Edinburgh* (Edinburgh: P. Hill & Co., 1818), pp. 33–5. ll. 1–5.

110. Erasmus Darwin also writes about the positive effects of alcohol in *Zoönomia*:

> Hence we become acquainted with that very curious circumstance, why the drunken vertigo is attended with an increase of pleasure; for the irritative ideas and motions occasioned by internal stimulus, that were not attended to in our sober hours, are now just so much increased as to be succeeded by pleasurable sensation, in the same manner as the more violent motions of our organs are succeeded by painful sensation. And hence a greater quantity of pleasurable sensation is introduced into the constitution; which is attended in some people with an increase of benevolence and good humour'
>
> (Darwin, *Zoönomia*, p. 181).

Notably, however, Darwin soon thereafter warns against the deadening effect of alcohol upon the nerves, which more closely allies his approach with that of Trotter and Beddoes.

111. A. Duncan 'Fragment of the Life of the *Scriba Praetorious* ... Written by Himself in Hudibrastic Rhyme', *Miscellaneous Poems*, pp. 9–26. ll. 53–6.

112. Duncan, 'Fragment of the Life of the *Scriba Praetorious*', pp. 41–2.

113. Duncan's explanation of Gregory's position on medical clubs and alcohol reveals as much about Gregory and Duncan's relationship as it does about their respective medical opinions. In what seems to be an out-of-character episode in Duncan's life, the two doctors at Edinburgh University carried on a very public dispute for decades, which is detailed, partly poetically, in *A Letter to Dr James Gregory of Edinburgh*. In the preface to this work, Duncan explains, 'Dr James Gregory, more than twelve months ago, distributed different printed papers, which clearly implied an accusation of Theft against me', and continues, 'Dr Gregory, I am well assured, has distributed far and wide, printed copies of his "Fables" and "Old Story", which gave rise to a *fama clamosa* highly injurious to

my character', in A. Duncan, *A Letter to Dr James Gregory of Edinburgh, In Consequence of Certain Printed Papers Intitled, – 'The Viper and File;' – 'There is Wisdom in Silence;' – 'An Old Story', &c. Which Have Lately Been Distributed by Him, and Which are Evidently Intended to Propagate and Support Groundless and Malevolent Calumnies Against Innocent Men* (Edinburgh. Edinburgh: A. Constable and Co., 1811), pp. vii, viii. These poems of Gregory, who was a physician and fellow professor, seem to accuse Duncan of stealing Gregory's ideas, no doubt of a medical nature. I do not detail this dispute in the present study because all of the poems at the heart of it are Gregory's and he was not a psychologist. However, the conflict suggests that poetry was regarded by doctors of all kinds in the Romantic period as a viable method in which to communicate their professional ideas, not to mention their complaints against each other.

114. A. Duncan, 'Untitled' [On the death of Princess Charlotte, written 1 May 1818], in *Miscellaneous Poems*, pp. 39–40. ll. 29–34.

115. A. Duncan, 'Untitled' [Written 1 May 1821], in *Tribute of Veneration, Addressed to the First Meeting of the Loyal Edinburgh Association, for Commemorating the Reign of George III* (Edinburgh: Archibald Constable & Co., 1821), p. 16. ll. 11–16.

116. Cotton, 'Death. Vision the Last', ll. 323–4. Another of Duncan's poems indicates his rightful place in the tradition of psychologist-poets. His poetic biography, 'Fragment of the Life of the *Scriba Praetorious*', suggests the influence of Beattie's *The Minstrel* in ambition, execution and plan, even if it delivers only fifty-six lines of the intended product. By describing his intended bio-epic as 'Hudibrastic', Duncan alerts us to its mock-heroic intent and verse structure (rhyming couplets of iambic tetrameter), since the descriptor recalls Samuel Butler's 'burlesque-heroic' poem, *Hudibras*, which has these characteristics (1663–8; Oxford: Clarendon Press, 1975). Duncan mocks all pedantic, footnote-laden writing by tiresome intellectuals (a party to which I dearly hope I do not belong) but, in particular, he seems to aim his humorous barbs at the most famous psychologist-poet of all, namely Erasmus Darwin. Every page of the seventeen devoted to Duncan's 'Fragment of the Life' includes so much footnoted material that the poem itself is relegated to a sliver of space at the top of the page, much like Darwin's poems, all epic in length, written in heroic style and so encumbered by footnotes that one often wonders if the poem itself is not just an organizational ploy for the author to publish a series of brief prose essays on various scientific subjects. Duncan hints at this view of Darwin's poems by providing mere doggerel as the introduction to his long and considerably more interesting prose footnotes. The poem begins, 'At Pinkerton I first drew my breath, / And breathe I must until my death' (Duncan, 'Fragment of the Life of the *Scriba Praetorious*, ll. 1–2). The first, massive footnote begins at the mention of the word 'Pinkerton'. Duncan's implicit criticism is that the verse of scientist-poets appears sometimes secondary to the information they wish to relate, making it, truly, a servant of science.

117. Webb, 'Ferriar, John (1761–1815)'.

118. Ferriar, *Medical Histories and Reflections*, vol. 2, pp. 108, 109.

119. Webb, 'Ferriar, John (1761–1815)'.

120. Ferriar, *Medical Histories and Reflections*, vol. 1, pp. 219, 242.

121. Ibid., p. 248.

122. This same egalitarian attitude inspired Ferriar to champion the medical rights of paupers, as it did Bakewell and Duncan, and to take up the cause of slaves. In the poetic 'Prologue' that introduces *The Prince of Angola*, Ferriar sums up the goal of his drama in a manner that confirms its egalitarian message:

> Hear Misery cry from yon blood-water'd Lands;
> Lo, suff'ring Crouds to you extend their Hands;
> Those ghastly Seams unmeasur'd Lashes tore,
> Those wasted Limbs the cleaving Fetters wore –
> See mangled Victims fill th' Oppressor's Den,
> *And hear Compassion tell you –* THESE ARE MEN.
> (Ferriar, J., *The Prince of Angola, A Tragedy, Altered from the Play of Oroonoko. And Adapted to the Circumstances of the Present Times* (Manchester: J. Harrop, 1788), ll. 27–32, Ferriar's formatting and spelling).

Here, Ferriar pleads with his audience to recognize their fellowship with the tortured slaves, just as his writings on moral management emphasized the humanity of the insane. Both beleaguered groups were classified as brutes by their oppressors.

123. Ferriar, *Medical Histories and Reflections*, vol. 1, p. 218.

124. Webb, 'Ferriar, John (1761–1815)'.

125. J. Ferriar, 'Illustrations of Sterne', *Illustrations of Sterne: With Other Essays and Verses*, 2nd edn, 2 vols (London: Cadell and Davies, 1812), vol. 1, pp. 17–193, vol. 2, pp. 9–63; L. Sterne, *Life and Opinions of Tristram Shandy, Gentleman* (1760–7; New York: Norton, 1980).

126. Ferriar, 'Illustrations of Sterne', e.g., p. 111.

127. Ferriar, J., 'Of Genius', *Illustrations of Sterne: With Other Essays and Verses*, 2nd edn, 2 vols (London: Cadell and Davies, 1812), vol. 2, pp. 161–81, on pp. 164–5.

128. Ibid., pp. 175–9.

129. J. Ferriar, 'Of Certain Varieties of Man, Described by Authors', *Illustrations of Sterne*, vol. 2, pp. 65–97, on pp. 96–7.

130. Ibid., p. 97.

131. Horace, selections from *Ars Poetica*, in V. B. Leitch (gen. ed.), *The Norton Anthology of Theory and Criticism* (New York: W. W. Norton, 2001), pp. 124–35, on p. 123 (unsigned introduction to Horace).

132. J. Ferriar, *The Bibliomania*; Hunter and Macalpine, *Three Hundred Years of Psychiatry*, p. 543; M. Vaulbert de Chantilly, 'Introduction', in J. Ferriar, *The Bibliomania*, pp. 3–21, on p. 8. Although Ferriar published another version of *The Bibliomania* in 1809, I refer to the second, longer version of 1812. All references to the text are to the modern Vaulbert de Chantilly transcription.

133. Ferriar, *The Bibliomania*, ll. 1–6.

134. Ibid., ll. 34–43, 259–64.

135. Ibid., ll. 278–81.

136. J. Ferriar [also attributed to Ferrier, J. and Grey in Wellcome Catalogue], *The Theory of Dreams in which an Inquiry is Made into the Powers and Faculties of the Human Mind, as they are Illustrated in the Most Remarkable Dreams Recorded in Sacred and Profane History*, 2 vols (London: F. C. and J. Rivington, 1808), vol. 1, pp. 52–3.

137. Ferriar, *The Theory of Dreams*, p. 3. Ferriar's identity as a possible influence on psychoanalytic theory is also suggested by the fact that he introduced the term 'hysterical conversion', which was later adopted by Sigmund Freud and became a hallmark of his theories about neuroses (Hunter and Macalpine, *Three Hundred Years of Psychiatry*, p. 543).

138. Ferriar, *An Essay Towards a Theory of Apparitions*, e.g. p. 102.

139. Ibid., p. viii.

140. Ibid., pp. 14, ix.

141. Ferriar, *The Theory of Dreams*, p. 54.
142. Showalter, *The Female Malady*, p. 27; Porter, *Mind Forg'd Manacles*, p. 223; Smith, 'Bakewell, Thomas (1761–1835)'.
143. Bakewell, *A Letter Addressed to the Chairman of the Select Committee of the House of Commons*, p. 16; Hunter and Macalpine, *Three Hundred Years of Psychiatry*, p. 705.
144. Tuke, *Description of the Retreat*, pp. 150, 141.
145. Tuke, *Description of the Retreat*, pp. 139, 141.
146. Ferriar, *The Prince of Angola*, l. 26; Duncan, *A Short Account of the Rise, Progress, and Present State of the Lunatic Asylum at Edinburgh*, p. 5; Bakewell, 'Epistle to a Neighbouring Gentleman', ll. 8–9.
147. Porter, 'Introduction', in J. Haslam, *Illustrations of Madness*, p. xiv; Porter, *Mind-Forg'd Manacles*, p. 282.
148. M. Foucault, *Ethics: Subjectivity and Truth*, ed. P. Rabinow, trans. R. Hurley et al (New York: The New Press, 1994), vol. 1, p. 43.
149. Cooper, A. M., 'Blake and Madness: The World Turned Inside Out', *English Literary History (ELH)*, 57 (1990), pp. 585–642, on p. 619; Porter, *Mind Forg'd Manacles*, pp. 217–18.
150. Ibid., pp. 209; 210.
151. In Hunter and Macalpine, *Three Hundred Years of Psychiatry*, pp. 538–9.
152. Tuke, *Description of the Retreat*, pp. 172–3.
153. Hunter and Macalpine, *Three Hundred Years of Psychiatry*, p. 538.
154. In Hunter and Macalpine, *Three Hundred Years of Psychiatry*, pp. 539–40.
155. Foucault, *Ethics*, p. 39.

3. Thomas Trotter, William Perfect and Thomas Beddoes: Nervous Illness And Social Hygiene

1. The fact that nerve theory plays a major role in this chapter and the last may be understood as my recognition of the major role that the approach played in forming the psycho-literary culture of Britain in the Romantic period. Indeed, by the end of the eighteenth century, all sickness was considered the result of nerves because of Cheyne's popularity. See J. Oppenheim, *'Shattered Nerves': Doctors, Patients, and Depression in Victorian England* (New York: Oxford University Press, 1991), p. 13.
2. Anon., *A Treatise on the Dismal Effects of Low-spiritedness. In which is Contained, Many Useful Hints for Preventing that Disagreeable and Destructive Disorder from Taking Root in the Human System* (London: Printed for W. Owen, 1750); quoted in Mullan, *Sentiment and Sociability*, p. 214.
3. Porter, *Doctor of Society*, p. 190.
4. Foucault, 'The Politics of Health in the Eighteenth Century', p. 284. My emphasis.
5. Nerve-theorist Thomas Willis was the 'first scientist unassailably to posit that the seat of the soul is strictly limited to the brain, nowhere else' (Rousseau, 'Nerves, Spirits, and Fibres', pp. 135, 134).
6. Porter, *Doctor of Society*, p. 189.
7. E. Shorter, *From Paralysis to Fatigue: A History of Psychosomatic Illness in the Modern Era* (New York: The Free Press, 1992), p. 1.
8. Shorter, *A Historical Dictionary of Psychiatry*, p. 5.

9. Oppenheim, *'Shattered Nerves'*, p. 80; R. Porter, 'Barely Touching: A Social Perspective on Mind and Body', in G. S. Rousseau (ed.), *The Languages of Psyche: Mind and Body in Enlightenment Thought* (Berkeley, CA: University of California Press, 1990), pp. 45–80, on p. 66.

10. Janice Caldwell explains the raging debate in the following way: 'In part, the vitalist movement was a reaction against eighteenth-century mechanism, protesting that life could not be adequately accounted for by mechanical physics alone' (*Literature and Medicine in Nineteenth-Century Britain: From Mary Shelley to George Eliot* (Cambridge: Cambridge University Press, 2004), p. 26). However, atheistic nerve theorists like Beddoes could not have pleased the most religious of the vitalists.

11. As Porter puts it, 'Mediating between the body and the soul, [were] the nerves' ('The Rage of Party: A Glorious Revolution in English Psychiatry?', *Medical History: A Quarterly Journal Devoted to the History of Medicine and Related Sciences*, 27 (1983), pp. 35–50, on p. 47). This interconnectedness of soul or mind and body crossed over into the doctor's role, Charles Rosenberg affirms: 'There were no categorical boundaries between the realms of body and mind in late eighteenth- and early nineteenth-century medical theory. Nor was there a parallel boundary between doctors of the body and mind' (C. E. Rosenberg, 'Body and Mind in Nineteenth-Century Medicine: Some Clinical Origins of the Neurosis Construct', *Bulletin of the History of Medicine*, 63 (1989), pp. 185–97, on p. 188).

12. Mullan, *Sentiment and Sociability*, p. 236.

13. Shorter's identification of nervous illness and psychosomatic illness is borne out by Romantic-era medical theory: Sayer Walker writes in *A Treatise on Nervous Diseases* (1796) that his method of treatment can help to 'determine whether the state of the body is to be attributed to that of the mind, or the latter to the former' (from *A Treatise on Nervous Diseases* (1796), in R. Hunter and I. Macalpine (eds), *Three Hundred Years of Psychiatry*, pp. 552–3, on p. 552); Shorter, *From Paralysis to Fatigue*, p. 1.

14. Bynum, 'The Nervous Patient in Eighteenth- and Nineteenth-Century England', p. 90.

15. P. M. Logan, *Nerves and Narratives: A Cultural History of Hysteria in Nineteenth-Century British Prose* (London: University of California Press, 1997), p. 139; quoting Trotter's *A View of the Nervous Temperament*.

16. 'Hygiene', *OED* online, http://dictionary.oed.com.proxy2.lib.umanitoba.ca/cgi/entry/50110112 (accessed 7 February 2008).

17. Ibid.

18. Ibid.

19. 'Hygienic', *OED* online, http://dictionary.oed.com.proxy2.lib.umanitoba.ca/cgi/entry/50110113 (accessed 7 February 2008).

20. These themes also suggest overlap and possible influence between these psychologist-poets' work and that of others in the tradition, such as Cotton and Beattie, not to mention a shared interest in bringing about egalitarian principles through the celebration of modest living that gestures to their roots in the Scottish Enlightenment.

21. Vickers, 'Coleridge, Thomas Beddoes and Brunonian Medicine', p. 55; Porter, *Doctor of Society*, pp. 15, 167.

22. W. Perfect, *Cases of Insanity, the Epilepsy, Hypochondriacal Affection, Hysteric Passion, and Nervous Disorders, Successfully Treated* ([probably Rochester], NY: n.p., c. 1785), in *The Eighteenth-Century* (ESTC reel (MICR) 99, no. 14).

23. Foucault, 'The Politics of Health in the Eighteenth Century', p. 176.

24. The valorization of a humble and rural lifestyle in Romantic poetry is one of its most widely noted ideals. Not only did Wordsworth and Coleridge live as neighbours in the

rural surroundings of Grasmere, but they mention this lifestyle often in their poetry, such as in Coleridge's mention of his rural 'cottage' in 'Frost at Midnight', or in Wordsworth's contrast between the moral goodness of the rural life in 'Michael', as opposed to the perverting influences of the city, which eventually ruin Michael's son, Luke (S. T. Coleridge, 'Frost at Midnight', *The Major Works*, ed. and intro. H. J. Jackson (Oxford: Oxford University Press, 1985), pp. 87–9. l. 4); W. Wordsworth, 'Michael: A Pastoral Poem' (1798), *William Wordsworth: A Critical Edition of the Major Works*, ed. S. Gill (Oxford: Oxford University Press, 1984), p. 224–36). The number of references to the ideal of rural and humble living in Romantic poetry are too numerous to mention and too well-established to require more evidence.

25. Perfect, *Cases of Insanity*, unpag.
26. Perfect, 'A Parody from Hamlet', l. 29.
27. Black, *An Eighteenth[-]Century Mad-Doctor*, p. 64.
28. Ibid., p. 41.
29. W. Perfect, *Cases in Midwifery: Principally Founded on the Correspondence of ... Dr Colin Mackenzie, with References, Quotations, and Remarks, by William Perfect*, 3rd edn, 2 vols (Rochester, NY: W. Gillman, 1789), in *The Eighteenth Century* (ESTC reel 6925, no. 6); Black, *An Eighteenth[-]Century Mad-Doctor*, p. 65. Perfect clearly endeavoured to appeal to a wide audience by developing a democratic approach to medical writing and care, but he maintained his claim to formal education and experience in other contexts, such as in the advertisement that he placed in the *Kentish Gazette* in November of 1784: "'Lunatic Asylum. – Ladies and gentlemen continue to be accommodated with board, lodging, washing, etc. under the immediate inspection of Doctor Perfect, the sole proprietor and medical professor (an advantage of the utmost consequence, and which too seldom occurs!) whose approved medicines need no other comment than the reputation they have for many years gained in insanity ... His patients are treated with tenderness, delicacy, sympathizing humanity, and a well-regulated diet'" (quoted in Black, *An Eighteenth[-]Century Mad-Doctor*, p. 65). Perfect's claim of being a 'medical professor' shows his wish to be identified as formally involved with medical education, while his reference to a 'well-regulated diet' as part of his therapeutic approach illustrates his roots in nerve theory, in which food takes a central role.
30. Black, *An Eighteenth[-]Century Mad-Doctor*, p. 55. Black also notes that Perfect 'deplored the custom of denying a decent interment to the corpses of hanged men, stripped and flung into a common burial pit', and adds that he sought to protect those living in incarceration, too, by receiving donations for them (Black, *An Eighteenth[-]Century Mad-Doctor*, p. 42). If Perfect's anti-establishment rebelliousness seems to be undermined by his eventual attainment of an MD, which might be taken as bowing to the pressure of physicians who did not recognize his qualifications as an apothecary, surgeon and man-midwife, then surely he shows his unconventional and liberal sympathies by taking up the cause of convicted criminals.
31. Quoted in Black, *An Eighteenth[-]Century Mad-Doctor*, p. 54.
32. Perfect does not forget his characteristic humility as he accuses his fellow asylum-keepers of having too much in common with their charges. Tongue firmly in cheek, he shows that he considers his own commonalities with the insane in the preface to *The Laurel-Wreath*, where he writes 'that I have casually thought myself happy in enjoying the lucid intervals of a harmless Muse' (Preface to *The Laurel-Wreath; Being a Collection of Original Miscellaneous Poems, On Subjects Moral, Comic, and Divine*, 2 vols (London: Printed for the Author, 1766), vol. 1, pp. iii–iv, on p. iii, in *The Eighteenth Century* (ESTC reel (MICR)

1883, no. 8)). His carefully chosen words imply that, familiar as he is with his muse's 'lucid intervals', he has also experienced her periods of madness.

33. W. Perfect, *A Remarkable Case of Madness, With the Diet and Medicines, Used in the Cure* (Rochester, NY: For the author, 1791), in *The Eighteenth-Century* (ESTC reel (MICR) 13297. no. 5); Perfect, *Select Cases in the Different Species of Insanity.*

34. We need not only look to Perfect's efforts in medical prose to establish his democratic attitude towards his readers. While some people in eighteenth-century England – such as Edmund Massey, author of *A Sermon Against the Dangerous and Sinful Practice of Inoculation*, 3rd edn (London: William Meadows, 1722) – thought that inoculation was immoral, Perfect fought hard to establish the public's right to be inoculated against smallpox and he appeals to the public through the accessible medium of verse. In an untitled poem that appeared in the *Westminster Journal* for 30 August 1766, Perfect establishes his identity as a doctor of the people, over and against the opinions of physicians:

> Attend to my theme, every rank and degree!
> Ye lasses so lovely, come listen to me!
> Oh, how you'll caress me on knowing my skill,
> Who love in the cause for to flourish my quill!
> All marks on your bosoms or scars on your face
> My art shall prevent your dear forms to disgrace,
>
> . . . .
>
> By my potent art that disease is defied
> I've cured near a million when one has not died;
>
> . . . .
>
> The Doctor may shake his unfortunate head,
> And say with a sneer, "He can raise from the dead!"
> At my miracles rare let the Faculty brawl:
> My practice shall show that I outdo them all!
>
> (ll. 1–6, 13–14, 17–20; quoted in Black, *An Eighteenth[-]Century Mad-Doctor*, p. 43)

The humorous tone of this verse reveals Perfect's humility, for it shows that he does not take himself too seriously, while his warm appeal to people of 'every rank and degree' shows his egalitarian impulse. He notes that he takes up his 'quill' as a means of expressing his 'love' for his potential patients and thereby underlines the concept that writing, especially poetry, was the psychologist-poet's way of showing his sympathy with the wider public and educating them on a broad scale. Finally, Perfect emphasizes that his democratic attitude contrasts with that of the 'sneer[ing]' doctors of the 'Faculty', those 'college boys' who are so unfamiliar with his homely practice that they call his methods 'miracles'. Perfect's democratic principles bear witness to his education at St Andrews, a typically Whig Scottish university.

35. Perfect, *Cases of Insanity*, pp. v–vi.

36. George Grinnell points out that Cheyne's text also focuses on the treatment of 'hypochondria', which was linked with 'melancholia'. See 'Thomas Beddoes and the Physiology of Romantic Medicine', *Studies in Romanticism*, 45:2 (2006), pp. 223–50, on p. 226.

37. Cheyne, *The English Malady*, p. 49.

38. Ibid., p. 59.

39. Ibid., p. 61.

40. e. g., Mullan, *Sentiment and Sociability*, p. 236.

41. Cheyne, *The English Malady*, p. 260.
42. Porter, *Mind Forg'd Manacles*, p. 13.
43. If these psychologist-poets' lengthy verses in celebration of humble living did influence the early Romantics, then we may claim that Cheyne's work inspired indirectly the Romantic celebration of rural living. That is, we may surmise that the psychologist-poets associated wealth with melancholy because of Cheyne's vastly influential text, but – because they disagreed that melancholy was unrelated to madness – they responded by preaching the mental health benefits of a humble lifestyle in verse, which, in turn, may have contributed to the popularity of the same concept in the most popular Romantic works.
44. Perhaps the most famous declaration of the link between insanity and sensibility in Romantic-era literature is by Mary Wollstonecraft. Despite (or perhaps in order to compensate for) her own early authorship of a novel of sensibility, called *Mary, A Fiction* ((1788) and *The Wrongs of Woman* (1798), ed. G. Kelly (London: Oxford University Press, 1976)), Wollstonecraft declares in *A Vindication of the Rights of Men* ((1790), *Mary Wollstonecraft: Political Writings*, ed. J. Todd (Toronto, ON: University of Toronto Press, 1993)) (the influence of which may be attributed to its being the first response to Edmund Burke's *Reflections on the French Revolution* (1790)), 'Sensibility is the *manie* of the day' (*A Vindication of the Rights of Men*, p. 6). In her follow-up work on the social status of women, *A Vindication of the Rights of Woman with Strictures on Political and Moral Subjects*, Wollstonecraft expands by asserting that women's 'senses are inflamed, and their understanding neglected, consequently they become the prey of their senses, delicately termed sensibility, and are blown about my every momentary gust of feeling' (1792), ed. A. Tauchert (London: J. M. Dent, 1995), p. 69. Here, Wollstonecraft figures the woman of sensibility as driven to insanity through overindulgence in sensual pleasure, which presents her as quite the opposite of the ephemeral, delicate and fainting heroines of such novels of sensibility as Richardson's *Clarissa*.
45. Perfect, *Cases of Insanity*, p. vi.
46. Cheyne, *The English Malady*, p. 260. To be sure, Cheyne had an illustrious roster of patients, amongst whom he could list David Hume. Skultans describes this relationship in a way that emphasizes the positive associations with melancholy that Cheyne encouraged: 'David Hume thought he was suffering from the spleen or vapours but was pleased to learn through his correspondence with Dr Cheyne that he had, in fact, contracted "the disease of the learned"' (*English Madness*, p. 4).
47. Perfect, *Cases of Insanity*, pp. 2, 3.
48. Ibid., p. 3.
49. Bynum, 'The Nervous Patient in Eighteenth- and Nineteenth-Century England', p. 91. Samuel Johnson, however, was highly sceptical of Boswell's interpretation of melancholy. According to Allan Ingram, he warned his friend 'off the popular association of melancholy with genius', saying, with reference to Cheyne's approach, '"Do not let him teach you a foolish notion that melancholy is a proof of acuteness"' (Ingram, A. (ed.), *Patterns of Madness in the Eighteenth Century* (Liverpool: Liverpool University Press, 1998), p. 123); Johnson quoted in Porter, 'The Rage of Party', p. 44).
50. Perfect, *Cases of Insanity*, p. 1.
51. Ibid., p. 3.
52. Preface to *The Laurel-Wreath*, pp. iii–iv. Perfect's emphasis.
53. Ibid., p. iv. Perfect, *A Bavin of Bays*, pp. 156–7, in *The Eighteenth-Century* (ESTC reel (MICR) 8358, no. 1). In *Wordsworth and the Enlightenment*, Bewell notes that Wordsworth called the *Lyrical Ballads* '"short essays" [,] ... showing the blurred boundary

between scientific writing and literature proper' (Bewell, *Wordsworth and the Enlighten-ment*, p. 15). I would add that Perfect blurred this boundary almost thirty years earlier by calling his own poems 'essays'. While the fact that *The Bavin of Bays* and *The Laurel-Wreath* were published by Perfect himself might lead one to the hasty conclusion that he did not find much public support for his poetic efforts, the subscription list reveals that a number of medical practitioners – amongst them 'Doctor Bartholomew', 'Mr Burt, Surgeon', and six other 'surgeons' – were eager to acquire the volume, while a greater number of formally educated medical practitioners appear in the subscription list of *The Laurel-Wreath*, such as 'Richard Frewen, MD', 'Edward Bull, MD', and 'William Hervey, MD'. We may surmise that the success of Perfect's first volume made his second volume attractive to a more educated class of medical practitioners, or that he was gaining friends and correspondents in the medical community, a possibility that his membership in the London Medical Society in 1795 confirms (Black, *An Eighteenth[-]Century Mad-Doc-tor*, p. 66). Perfect's reputation reached into the Romantic period, as is evident from the republication of his poems in 1796 in a volume called *Poetic Effusions: Pastoral, Moral, Amatory and Descriptive* (London: A. Milne, 1796).

54. Horace, *Ars Poetica*, p. 123.

55. Barbauld, 'Essay on Akenside's Poem on *The Pleasures of Imagination*', p. 4. How true Barbauld's words appear in consideration of Perfect's poem, 'To Health' from *Poetic Effu-sions*, in which he even goes so far as to describe the aesthetically displeasing topic of the sick bed:

> Dispel distemper's shade;
> Her roses see in sickness pale,
> The lilies too in whiteness fail,
> Support the sinking Maid.
> Thy lenient balm propitious shed,
> Thy blossoms round her temples spread,
> And mitigate her pain;
> Smooth the pillow of disease,
> Descend bright messenger of ease!
> Resume thy smiling reign.
> ('To Health', *The Laurel-Wreath; Being a Collection of Original Miscellaneous Poems, On Subjects Moral, Comic, and Divine*, 2 vols (London: Printed for the Author, 1766), vol. 1, pp. 162–3. ll. 33–42, in *The Eighteenth Century* (ESTC reel (MICR) 1883, no. 8)).

56. W. Perfect, 'Solitude: An Ode', *The Laurel-Wreath; Being a Collection of Original Miscel-laneous Poems, On Subjects Moral, Comic, and Divine*, 2 vols (London: Printed for the Author, 1766), vol. 1, pp. 87–9, ll. 1–8, in *The Eighteenth Century* (ESTC reel (MICR) 1883, no. 8).

57. Ibid., ll. 13–16.

58. Ibid., ll. 25, 18, 22.

59. Ibid., ll. 29–32.

60. Perfect, 'To Solitude', pp. 153–6. ll. 9–14.

61. Cotton, 'Content. Vision IV', ll. 71–2.

62. W. Perfect, 'Contentment, An Ode', *The Laurel-Wreath; Being a Collection of Original Miscellaneous Poems, On Subjects Moral, Comic, and Divine*, 2 vols (London: Printed for the Author, 1766), vol. 1, pp. 60–3, ll. 1–2, 13–20, in *The Eighteenth Century* (ESTC reel (MICR) 1883, no. 8).

63. Here, I am thinking of the boundaries of the body in relationship to food in the way that Julia Kristeva describes them in *The Powers of Horror: An Essay on Abjection,* trans. L. S. Roudiez (New York: Columbia University Press, 1982): food is one of the sources of 'abjection' against which the psyche must struggle to maintain its sanctity, autonomy and health.

64. W. Perfect, 'An Ode to Poverty', *The Laurel Wreath,* vol. 2, pp. 77–80, ll. 29–42, in *The Eighteenth Century.*

65. Cheyne, *The English Malady,* p. 49.

66. Perfect, 'An Ode to Poverty ', ll. 32, 41.

67. Porter, *Mind-Forg'd Manacles,* p. 13.

68. Notably, although Perfect and Trotter were in agreement about the dangers posed by excessive libations, the former advises abstemiousness, not total deprivation, in 'The Social Thought; or The Tea-Pot Resign'd' from *The Laurel-Wreath*:

> Thou genial bowl, whose gladsome juice
> Invit'st to frolic joy and mirth:
> Soft happiness thou canst produce,
> And give to gayest pleasures birth!
> Oh! let us in those pleasures roll,
> Bacchus, power of Wine and Love,
> 'Tis thou canst elevate the soul,
> And make our sluggish senses move!

>> Perfect, *The Laurel-Wreath,* vol. 1, pp. 173–4, ll. 1–8.

69. Trotter, *A View of the Nervous Temperament,* p. viii.

70. Porter, *Doctor of* Society, p. 94.

71. Trotter, *A View of the Nervous Temperament,* p. vii.

72. Ibid., p. vii.

73. Ibid., p. 145.

74. Wallace, 'Trotter, Thomas (bap. 1760, d. 1832)'. J. Wallace goes on to explain that Trotter's early experiences on this voyage led him to publish *Observations on the Scurvy* in 1786 with a second edition in 1792; Trotter is credited with being amongst the first physicians 'responsible for introducing universal distribution of lemon juice throughout the navy in 1795, an action which effectively abolished the problem of scurvy' (unpag.). He also 'became an ardent abolitionist' as a result of his experience on the Liverpool slave-ship: Wallace comments, 'The Society in Newcastle for the Abolition of the Slave Trade records how he gave evidence to the House of Commons on their [i.e. the slaves'] behalf in 1791' (unpag.).

75. Logan, *Nerves and Narratives,* p. xiii.

76. Trotter, *A View of the Nervous Temperament,* p. 45.

77. Ibid., p. 52.

78. Wallace, 'Trotter, Thomas (bap. 1760, d. 1832)'.

79. Porter, *Doctor of Society,* p. 99.

80. T. Trotter, *An Essay Medical, Philosophical, and Chemical on Drunkenness and its Effects on the Human Body* (1804), ed. R. Porter (London: Routledge, 1988), pp. 8, 172. Trotter's emphasis.

81. A review of *An Essay ... on Drunkenness* in the *Edinburgh Medical and Surgical Journal* from 1805 indicates that Trotter's work challenged his audience to contend with questions regarding the relationship between the body and mind: 'Whatever may be the nature of mind, whatever the connexion between body and mind, it is certain that

the intellectual faculties may be affected and deranged by disease, and by other changes induced on the material organs of our system' (Anon., Review of *An Essay, Medical, Philosophical and Chemical, on Drunkenness and its Effects on the Human Body, Edinburgh Medical and Surgical Journal*, 1:1 (1805), pp. 73–81, on p. 73). That this review appears in the first ever volume of this long-standing journal suggests the influence of and interest in Trotter's work for the medical community in Scotland.

82. T. Trotter, 'Preface', *Sea-Weeds: Poems, Written on Various Occasions, Chiefly During a Naval Life* (Newcastle: Longman and Co., 1829), pp. xii–xxv, on p. xvii. Today we often associate such calls for temperance with Puritanism and moral rigidity, but Porter's snapshot of the period reveals why Trotter was so concerned about drunkenness: 'In certain regions of Europe, advances in capitalist agriculture were by then producing occasional huge grain supplies. The upshot was that great towns became flooded with really cheap spirits; during the 'gin craze' in London between the 1730s and the 1750s there were at one point 8,000 dram shops in the capital, and one could notoriously get drunk for a penny and dead drunk for twopence' (Introduction to T. Trotter, *An Essay Medical, Philosophical, and Chemical on Drunkenness and its Effects on the Human Body* (1804), ed. R. Porter (London: Routledge, 1988), pp. ix–xl, on p. x).

83. Trotter, *An Essay Medical, Philosophical, and Chemical on Drunkenness*, p. 172.

84. Trotter, *A View of the Nervous Temperament*, pp. 19, 21.

85. Ibid., pp. xiii–iv.

86. Ibid., pp. 32, 49.

87. Trotter, *An Essay Medical, Philosophical, and Chemical on Drunkenness*, p. 130.

88. Trotter's comment earlier in the same text details in more specific terms the link between nervous illness and insanity, even while it serves as valuable historical proof of the state of the argument regarding the body's relationship to the mind to which nerve theorists had contributed for decades:

> It would be an endless digression ... to detail the various theories and conjectures of physicians and metaphysicians on the connection between body and mind. That our intellectual part can be disturbed, and so completely deranged, by bodily diseases, as to be incapable of using its reasoning powers, is a fact sufficiently established to be universally admitted.
>
> (Trotter, *An Essay Medical, Philosophical, and Chemical on Drunkenness*, p. 41)

Here, Trotter suggests that a disorder that originates in the body may affect the mind because the health of one is intricately bound to the other.

89. Porter, 'Introduction', *Drunkenness*, pp. xxii–xxiii.

90. Ibid., p. xxiii.

91. Trotter, *An Essay Medical, Philosophical, and Chemical on Drunkenness*, p. 162.

92. Ibid., p. 162.

93. T. Trotter, *Suspiria Oceani: A Monody on the Death of Richard Earl Howe, K. G. Admiral of the Fleet and General of his Majesty's Forces* (London: T. Hatchard, 1800).

94. T. Bakewell, 'The Cruize', 'The Life-Boat', 'Looks and Eyes', and 'The Furze Blossom', *Sea-Weeds*, pp. 50–1, 85–7, 111–12, 69–71.

95. 'Vaccination', *Sea-Weeds*, pp. 117–20. ll. 1–6.

96. After these hints about his vocation, you might expect the poem entitled 'The Swallow' to be about a successfully administered draught of medicine; alas, it is about a bird – but the bird does swoop around the infirmary of the ship ('The Swallow', *Sea-Weeds*, pp. 61–3).

97. T. Trotter, 'The Beggar's Bush (Cut Down by a Maniac about Forty-eight Years Ago)', *Sea-Weeds,* pp. 103–4.
98. Ibid., ll. 7–8, 3–4.
99. Ibid., ll. 17–20.
100. W. Blake, 'The Ecchoing Green', *The Complete Poetry and Prose of William Blake,* rev. and ed. D. Erdman (New York: Anchor Books, 1988), p. 8.
101. Coleridge, 'Frost at Midnight'; W. Wordsworth, 'Ode ("There was a Time")' (1807), *William Wordsworth,* ed. S. Gill, pp. 297–302.
102. Trotter, 'The Beggar's Bush', ll. 23–4.
103. Trotter again shows his unique contribution to a popular literary theme in this poem about animal rights, upon which several prominent Romantic-era poets composed. Recent critical attention to this theme includes the work of David Perkins, such as his articles 'Religion and Animal Rights in the Romantic Era', in R. J. Barth (ed.), *The Fountain Light: Studies in Romanticism and Religion in Honor of John L. Mahoney* (New York: Fordham University Press, 2002), pp. 1–21, 'Compassion for Animals and Radical Politics: Coleridge's "To a Young Ass"' (*ELH* (*English Literary History*), 65:4 (1998), pp. 929–44) and, most notably, *Romanticism and Animal Rights* (Cambridge: Cambridge University Press, 2003), a highly informative work that details many aspects of the animal rights movement during the period, including the subject of the keeping of pets. In addition to the work of critics like Stephanie Rowe ('Listen to Me': *Frankenstein* as an Appeal to Mercy and Justice, on Behalf of the Persecuted Animals', in F. Palmeri (ed.), *Humans and Other Animals in Eighteenth-Century British Culture: Representation, Hybridity, Ethics* (Burlington: Ashgate, 2006), pp. 137–52), Nadita Batra explores, more specifically, the formal cultural changes that reflect the movement in 'Animal Rights in the Romantic Period: Legal Jurisdiction in England and the Intellectual Milieu' (*Atenea,* 16:1–2 (1996), pp. 99–113), Barbara Seeber investigates the subject of sport hunting in 'The Hunting Ideal, Animal Rights, and Feminism in *Northanger Abbey* and *Sense and Sensibility*', in T. Belleguic (ed.), *Lumen: Selected Proceedings from the Canadian Society for Eighteenth-Century Studies* (Kelowna: Academic, 2004), pp. 295–308, and Timothy Morton shows that P. B. Shelley's vegetarianism is linked to this movement in 'Joseph Ritson, Percy Shelley and the Making of Romantic Vegetarianism', *Romanticism: The Journal of Romantic Culture and Criticism,* 2:1 (2006), pp. 52–61.
104. T. Trotter, 'The Ass: An Ode, On the Melioration of the Species', *Sea-Weeds,* pp. 105–10. ll. 59–62.
105. Ibid., ll. 30–1.
106. Ibid., ll. 67–8.
107. Ibid., ll. 77–78. Trotter also takes this seemingly innocuous topic as an opportunity to advance his radical political opinions by accusing 'free-born Britons' of slaying 'English chargers', as well as 'the noblest host of loyal Gauls' (Ibid., ll. 49, 54, 52). This volume was published in 1829, some time after the worst of the English paranoia over the French Revolution had passed, but Trotter informs the reader in a footnote that these lines refer to a battle at Cape Quiberon in 1795 (*Sea-Weeds,* p. 108), at which time his anti-English and pro-French comments could well have earned him a stay in the Tower. The poem may have been penned at this time.
108. Ibid., footnote on p.110, and l. 106.
109. T. Trotter, *Noble Foundling; or, The Hermit of the Tweed. A Tragedy, in Five Act*s (London: Longman, Hurst, Rees, Orme, and Brown, 1812), ll. 1–8.
110. Ibid., l. 5.

111. T. Trotter, 'Verses Written in the Ladies' Walk at Liverpool, in January, 1783', *Sea-Weeds*, pp. 43–4. ll. 13–16.

112. Trotter, *An Essay Medical, Philosophical, and Chemical on Drunkenness*, p. 172.

113. Beddoes seems to have been very influential in his own day, as well: Porter suggests that Beddoes influenced Trotter's thinking about the chemical basis of alcohol addiction (Porter, Introduction to *Drunkenness*, p. xxvi).

114. Porter, *Doctor of Society*, p. 190.

115. T. Beddoes, *Essay on the Causes, Early Signs, and Prevention of Pulmonary Consumption for the Use Parents and Preceptors* (Bristol: T. N. Longman and O. Rees, 1799), p. 16, in *The Eighteenth-Century* (ESTC reel 99, no. 14)).

116. Neve, 'Beddoes, Thomas (1760–1808)'. Unless otherwise noted, all biographical information about Beddoes in this paragraph is from Michael Neve's entry in the online *ODNB*.

117. Vickers, 'Coleridge, Thomas Beddoes and Brunonian Medicine', p. 47.

118. King-Hele, *Erasmus Darwin and the Romantic Poets*, p. 92. Neve, 'Beddoes, Thomas (1760–1808)'.

119. Ibid.; Grinnell, 'Thomas Beddoes and the Physiology of Romantic Medicine'.

120. Beddoes, *Hygëia*, pp. 8–9,

121. T. Beddoes, *A Guide for Self-Preservation, and Parental Affection* (London: Bulgin and Rosser, 1793), in *The Eighteenth-Century* (ESTC reel (MICR) 4409. No. 14); T. Beddoes, *The History of Isaac Jenkins, and Sarah His Wife, and Their Three Children* (Bristol: n.p., 1796), in *The Eighteenth-Century* (ESTC reel (MICR) 4409, no. 15).

122. Beddoes, *A Guide for Self-Preservation*, p. iv.

123. T. Beddoes, *Extract of a Letter on Early Instruction, Particularly that of the Poor* (1792), in *Eighteenth Century Collections Online*, http://galenet.galegroup.com.proxy1.lib.umanitoba.ca/servlet/ECCO (accessed 22 May 2008).

124. T. Beddoes, *Alternatives Compared: or, What Shall the Rich Do to be Safe?* (London: J. Debrett, 1797), p. 3.

125. M. Wallen, *City of Health, Fields of Disease: Revolutions in the Poetry, Medicine, and Philosophy of Romanticism* (Aldershot: Ashgate, 2004), p. 4.

126. Neve suggests that Beddoes's 'patrician' character and 'elitist disappointments' were expressed in his degrading comments on the 'idiocies of the poor' ('Beddoes, Thomas (1760–1808)'), but I would hasten to add that he also questions the character and wisdom of the aristocracy in his writing: 'Those who know any thing of the higher order in society, know their general impatience of continued attention. Have they serious business? It must be brought before them prepared for instant dispatch: – it would be too troublesome to disentangle its perplexities. They cannot be put out of their lazy, picktooth mood' (Beddoes, *Alternatives Compared*, p. 10). Beddoes appears not to have been classist; he hated everyone equally.

127. T. Beddoes, *A Lecture Introductory to a Course of Popular Instruction on the Constitution and Management of the Human Body* (Bristol: Joseph Cottle, 1797), pp. 5, 23. Beddoes's emphasis.

128. Ibid., p. 23.

129. Ibid., pp. 62, 63.

130. Beddoes, *Hygëia*, p. 7; Wesley, J., *Primitive Physick: or, An Easy and Natural Method of Curing Most Diseases* (1747) (Bristol: John Grabham, 1759).

131. Beddoes, *A Lecture Introductory to a Course of Popular Instruction*, p. 62.

132. Here, I refer to the afore-quoted text, 'it was in the esotericism of his knowledge, in some almost daemonic secret of knowledge, that the doctor had found the power to unravel insanity' (Foucault, *Madness and Civilization*, p. 274).

133. Like many doctors of this period, Beddoes may be classified as representative of any number of scientific approaches. His founding of the Pneumatic Institute in Bristol, as well as his personal meeting with Lavoisier in France, may seem to identify him principally as a chemist. In his excellent article on the Brunonian connections between Beddoes and Coleridge, Vickers has shown that Beddoes had a palpable interest in psychology, so much so that Coleridge analysed dreams with him and called in Beddoes to treat poet Charles Lloyd when the latter was suffering from delirium and hallucinations (Vickers, 'Coleridge, Thomas Beddoes and Brunonian Medicine', p. 52). (Lloyd was later an inmate at the madhouse of Beddoes's good friend, Erasmus Darwin. See Burwick, *Poetic Madness and the Romantic Imagination*, p. 6). If Beddoes may be categorized as an early psychologist, the question remains: What kind of psychologist was he? Vickers identifies him as an associationist, while Grinnell treats him as a nerve theorist. He was neither to the exclusion of the other, but I side with Grinnell in this matter because Beddoes's major text, *Hygëia*, was about nervous illness.

134. Vickers, 'Coleridge, Thomas Beddoes and Brunonian Medicine', p. 51.

135. P. Youngquist, *Monstrosities: Bodies and British Romanticism* (Minneapolis, MN: University of Minneapolis Press, 2003).

136. Hunter and Macalpine, *Three Hundred Years of Psychiatry*, p. 579.

137. Beddoes, *Hygëia*, p. 9.

138. Ibid., pp. 12, 186.

139. Foucault, *Madness and Civilization*, p. 274.

140. Beddoes, *Hygëia*, vol. 3, p. 13.

141. Bernauer and Mahon, 'Michel Foucault's Ethical Imagination', p. 154.

142. From Beddoes's *Hygëia* as quoted in J. E. Stock, *Memoirs of the Life of Thomas Beddoes, MD, with an Analytical Account of his Writings* (1811) (Bristol: Thoemmes Press, 2003), p. 265.

143. Beddoes, *Extract of a Letter on Early Instruction*, p. 6.

144. Lord Mansfield had worked to abolish slavery in England two decades before. However, the slave-trade was still alive and well in the English colonies and would not be outlawed until 1808, when the government finally bowed to the pressure of the many tracts, poems and protests written in favour of total abolition. Hannah More's 'Slavery: A Poem' (1788), in A. K. Mellor and R. E. Matlak (eds), *British Literature 1780–1830* (Fort Worth, TX: Harcourt Brace, 1996), pp. 206–9 and William Roscoe's 'The Wrongs of Africa, A Poem' (London: R. Faulder, 1787–8), http://galenet.galegroup.com. proxy2.lib.umanitoba.ca/servlet/ECCO (accessed 11 August 2008), the title of which attempted to capitalize on the success of Thomas Paine's *Rights of Man: Being an Answer to Mr Burke's Attack on the French Revolution* (1791) (London: J. M. Dent & Sons, Ltd., 1915) and Mary Wollstonecraft's *The Rights of Woman*, are only two of the countless verses written in favour of abolition during the Revolutionary period.

145. Beddoes's darkly threatening text, *Alternatives Compared: or, What Shall the Rich Do to be Safe?*, published in 1797, seems to warn that the continuation of unsympathetic behaviour amongst the 'rich' and influential will result in 'danger' of the sort that was met with in France: "'How are the possessors of influence to exert it for their own and the public security? Shall they continue, reckless and passive, in their leadingstrings? adopt a temporising system? or endeavour, in union with their inferiors, to obtain a change

of men and measures?"' (Beddoes, *Alternatives Compared*, p. 6). The figure of the scientist-sage had an important role in the French Revolution. Porter argues, 'The *ancien régime* was sick: mentally (the diseases of poverty, hunger, violence), and psychologically (ignorance and folly, superstition and enthusiasm). *Philosophes*-physicians were needed to diagnose social pathology and prescribe reformed regimens' (*Doctor of Society*, p. 87). Beddoes appears to present himself as a candidate for a parallel role in England.

146. The *Encyclopædia* (1751–1772) to which Rousseau, Voltaire, Charles-Louis Montesquieu and Denis Diderot contributed, amongst others, is widely recognized for its influence on the philosophy and language of the French Revolution. In *Discourse on the Origin of Inequality*, Rousseau argues that inequality between people – the great evil that inspired the French Revolution – is 'scarcely noticeable in the state of nature' and that civilization 'made man wicked while making him sociable' (trans. F. Philip, ed. P. Colman (Oxford: Oxford University Press, 1994), p. 53). According to Rousseau, humankind is most authentic and morally superior in nature, which, he argued, stood in glorious opposition to the perverting, manmade structures of the class system and religion.

147. Beddoes also mentions Adam Smith's conception of sympathy as it appears in his *Theory of Moral Sentiments* as an important influence upon his thinking in this section. See Beddoes, *Extract of a Letter on Early Instruction*, p. 7 and A. Smith, *Theory of Moral Sentiments* (1790), ed. K. Haakonssen (Cambridge: Cambridge University Press, 2002).

148. Beddoes, *Extract of a Letter on Early Instruction*, pp. 5–6.

149. Ibid., e.g., p. 3.

150. Beddoes, *The History of Isaac Jenkins*, p. 43.

151. A. Burgess, *A Clockwork Orange* (1962) (New York: W. W. Norton, 1987).

152. Beddoes, *The History of Isaac Jenkins*, p. 6.

153. Beddoes, *Extract of a Letter on Early Instruction*, p. 5.

154. Beddoes, *Alexander's Expedition*, p. iv; Porter, *Doctor of Society*, p. 167; Vickers, 'Coleridge, Thomas Beddoes and Brunonian Medicine', pp. 55–6.

155. Beddoes, *Alexander's Expedition*, p. iv.

156. Porter claims that 'Beddoes partly endorsed' this commonly accepted representation of Alexander, but this comment undermines the originality of Beddoes's depiction of the Macedonian hero (Porter, *Doctor of Society*, p. 166).

157. Beddoes, *Alexander's Expedition*, pp. 23–4.

158. Ibid., p. 4.

159. Ibid., pp. 4, 38.

160. Ibid., p. 12.

161. Ibid., pp. iv, 12.

162. Ibid., ll. 275–88.

163. Ibid., l. 284.

164. Ibid., pp. 33–4.

165. Ibid., p. 73.

166. Ibid., p. 34.

167. Ibid., ll. 303–5

168. Ibid., p. 35.

169. Beddoes, *Extract of a Letter on Early Instruction*, p. 87.

170. Beddoes, *Hygëia*, vol. 2, p. 5.

171. William Makepeace Thackeray (who, incidentally, was born in Calcutta) illustrates in his most famous novel that Indian food was only beginning to be introduced to English tables during the Romantic period. In *Vanity Fair* (1847–8), set around the time of

the Napoleonic Wars (indeed, Captain George Osborne dies in the Battle of Waterloo), Joseph Sedley tricks Rebecca Sharp into eating a chili pepper with her curry, knowing full well that the potency of both are unfamiliar to her, while he is relatively immune to their effects since he has just returned to England from being stationed in Bengal with the East India Company. The narrator confirms, 'Rebecca had never tasted the dish before' (W. M. Thackeray, *Vanity Fair* (1847-8), ed. J. Sutherland (Oxford: Oxford University Press, 1983), p. 29). Out of a desire to please the wealthy young bachelor, Becky gamely tries the food. Its heat cools her interest in him.

172. Beddoes, *Hygëia*, vol. 2, p. 77.
173. Brown, *The Elements of Medicine*.
174. Beddoes, *Hygëia*, vol. 3, p. 81.
175. Beddoes, *Hygëia*, vol. 1, p. 87.
176. Ibid., p. 2.
177. Ibid., p. 79.
178. Ibid., pp. 88, 89.
179. Neve, 'Beddoes, Thomas (1760–1808)'.
180. Beddoes, *Hygëia*, vol. 1, p. 2.
181. Beddoes, *A Lecture Introductory to a Course of Popular Instruction*, p. 62
182. Beddoes, *Hygëia*, vol. 3, p. 13.
183. Foucault, 'Two Lectures', p. 106.
184. T. Beddoes, 'Introduction', *Contributions*.

4. The Unelected Legislator: Associationism and Thomas Brown's Subliminal Poetic Lessons

1. These are: *The Renovation of India: a Poem. With the Prophecy of Ganges, an Ode* (Edinburgh: Mundell, Doig, & Stevenson, 1808); *The Paradise of Coquettes, a Poem in Nine Parts* (London: John Murray, 1814); *The Wanderer in Norway, with Other Poems*, 2nd edn (London, J. Murray, 1816); *The War-Fiend, with Other Poems*, 2nd edn (London: J. Murray, 1816); *The Bower of Spring, with Other Poems* (Philadelphia: M. Thomas, 1817); *Agnes a Poem in Four Parts* (Edinburgh: Archibald Constable and Co. 1818); *Emily, with Other Poems*, 2nd edn (Edinburgh: A. Constable and Co., 1819).

2. A. Richardson, 'Of Heartache and Head Injury: Reading Minds in *Persuasion*', *Poetics Today*, 23:1 (2002), pp. 141–60, on p. 142.

3. D. Hartley, *Observations on Man, his Frame, his Duty, and his Expectations*, 2 vols (London: James Leake and Wm. Frederick, 1749), vol. 1, http://galenet.galegroup. com.proxy2.lib.umanitoba.ca/servlet/ECCO (accessed 4 July 2008); J. Priestley, *Hartley's Theory of the Human Mind, on the Principle of the Association of Ideas; With Essays Relating to the Subject of It* (1775), 2nd edn (London: J. Johnson, 1790), http://galenet. galegroup.com.proxy2.lib.umanitoba.ca/servlet/ECCO (accessed 2 July 2008); C. Craig, *Associationism and the Literary Imagination: From the Phantasmal Chaos* (Edinburgh: Edinburgh University Press, 2007), p. 17. Besides Richardson's above-mentioned article, I refer here to Leon Howard's 'Thomas Odiorne: An American Predecessor of Wordsworth', *American Literature: A Journal of Literary History, Criticism, and Bibliography*, 10:4 (1939), pp. 417–36, in which the critic explores the two writers' interests in associationism; other more recent works of this nature include J. C. Sallé's article, 'Hazlitt the Associationist', *Review of English Studies: A Quarterly Journal of English Literature*

and the English Language, 15:57 (1964), pp. 38–51; Robert Brainard Pearsall's article 'Wordsworth Reworks His Hartley', *Bulletin of the Rocky Mountain Modern Language Association*, 24:2 (1970), pp. 75–83; Jonathan Lamb's articles 'Language and Hartleian Associationism in *A Sentimental Journey*', *Eighteenth-Century Studies*, 13 (1980), pp. 285–312 and 'Hartley and Wordsworth: Philosophical Language and Figures of the Sublime', *Modern Language Notes*, 97:5 (1982), pp. 1064–85; Bryan Keith Shelley's 'The Synthetic Imagination: Shelley and Associationism', *Wordsworth Circle*, 14:1 (1983), pp. 68–73; Joseph E. Reihl's 'Keats's "Ode on a Grecian Urn" and Eighteenth-Century Associationism' (*Publications of the Arkansas Philological Association*, 9:1 (1983), pp. 85–96); Beth Lau's 'Keats, Associationism, and "Ode to a Nightingale"', *Keats-Shelley Journal: Keats, Shelley, Byron, Hunt, and Their Circles*, 32 (1983), pp. 46–62; John Hayden's 'Wordsworth, Hartley, and the Revisionists', *Studies in Philology*, 81:1 (1984), pp. 94–118; Jerome Christensen's 'Philosophy/Literature: The Associationist Precedent for Coleridge's Late Poems', in W. E. Cain (ed.), *Philosophical Approaches to Literature: New Essays on Nineteenth- and Twentieth-Century Texts* (Lewisburg, NY: Bucknell University Press, 1984), pp. 27–50; W. H. Christie's 'Francis Jeffrey's Associationist Aesthetics', *British Journal of Aesthetics*, 33:3 (1993), pp. 257–70; Marjorie Garson's 'Associationism and the Dialogue in *Emma*', *Eighteenth-Century Fiction*, 10:1 (1997), pp. 79–100; Isabelle Bour's 'Epistemological Ambiguities: Reason, Sensibility and Association of Ideas in Mary Wollstonecraft's *Vindication of the Rights of Woman*', *Bulletin de la Société d'études Anglo-Américaines des XVIIe et XVIIIe Siècles*, 49 (1999), pp. 299–310; William Hatherell's '"Words and Things": Locke, Hartley and the Associationist Context for the Preface to *Lyrical Ballads*' (*Romanticism: The Journal of Romantic Culture and Criticism*, 12:3 (2006), pp. 223–35); and Malcolm Andrews's 'The English Cottage as Cultural Critique and Associationist Paradigm', in P. Brown (ed. and intro) and M. Irwin (ed.), *Literature and Place 1800–2000* (Oxford: Peter Lang, 2006), pp. 49–68.). Romantic critics by no means inaugurated such research into the links between associationism and literature, however. Quite possibly, Romantic critics took their cue from critics of eighteenth-century literature, who began publishing articles on the topic decades before with such works as Howard Anderson's 'Associationism and Wit in *Tristram Shandy*' (*Philological Quarterly*, 48 (1969), pp. 27–41) and Martin Kallich's 'The Association of Ideas and Akenside's *Pleasures of Imagination*', *Modern Language Notes*, 62:3 (1947), pp. 166–73, to mention only two of several.

4.   Craig, *Associationism and the Literary Imagination*, p. 11.
5.   Hunter and Macalpine, *Three Hundred Years of Psychiatry*, p. 753; W. L. Parry-Jones, *The Trade in Lunacy: A Study of Private Madhouses in England in the Eighteenth and Nineteenth Centuries* (London: Routledge & Kegan Paul, 1972), p. 10.
6.   Hunter and Macalpine, *Three Hundred Years of Psychiatry*, p. 753.
7.   Brown, *Lectures on the Philosophy of the Human Mind*, p. 219.
8.   Ibid., p. 253. In *Hartley's Theory of the Human Mind, on the Principle of the Association of Ideas*, in which Joseph Priestley outlines some of the most basic principles of associationism as they were handed down to Thomas Brown around the turn of the nineteenth century, the author confirms Hartley's contention that our associations make up a person's subjectivity, construct the self, or, as he puts it, 'make any man whatever he is': Hartley asserts

> not only that all our *intellectual pleasures and pains*, but that all the phaenom-
> ena of *memory, imagination, volition, reasoning*, and every other mental affection
> and operation, are only different modes, or cases, of the association of ideas: so

that nothing is requisite to make any man whatever he is, but a sentient principle [mind].

(Priestley, *Hartley's Theory of the Human Mind*, p. xxvii; Priestley's emphasis).

9. Brown, *Lectures on the Philosophy of the Human Mind*, p. 262.
10. Ibid., pp. 253, 256.
11. Ibid., p. 265.
12. D. Welsh, 'A Memoir of Dr Brown', in T. Brown, *Lectures on the Philosophy of the Human Mind* (1820) (William Tait: Edinburgh, 1828), pp. v–xxxi, on p. vii; Stewart, *Elements of the Philosophy of the Human Mind*, p. 291.
13. Ibid., p. 289.
14. Stewart-Robertson, 'Brown, Thomas (1778–1820)'.
15. Hartley, *Observations on Man*, pp. vii–viii.
16. Brown, *Lectures on the Philosophy of the Human Mind*, p. 269. However, such comments did not allay critics' accusations of Brown's 'metaphysical "*infidélité*"' against the principles of John Reid and Stewart, as one biographer claims: 'Even while Brown was inscribing *Agnes; a Poem* to Stewart in 1818 "with best regards", his mentor was scarcely able to restrain his ire at the liberties which his pupil now took of his philosophy' (Stewart-Robertson, 'Brown, Thomas (1778–1820)').
17. Welsh, 'A Memoir of Dr Brown', p. xxii; Stewart-Robertson, 'Brown, Thomas (1778–1820)'.
18. Craig, *Associationism and the Literary Imagination*, p. 19.
19. Shelley, 'The Synthetic Imagination: Shelley and Associationism', pp. 68, 70
20. Brown, *The Paradise of Coquettes,* p. xxxiv.
21. Welsh, 'A Memoir of Dr Brown', p. xv.
22. Brown, *The Paradise of Coquettes,* p. xxxiv.
23. Brown, *Lectures on the Philosophy of the Human Mind*, p. 255.
24. Ibid., p. 371.
25. Wordsworth, 'Preface', *Lyrical Ballads* (1800 edn), p. 126.
26. Priestley, *Hartley's Theory of the Human Mind,* p. xxv.
27. Craig, *Associationism and the Literary Imagination*, p. 10.
28. Ibid., p. 18.
29. Hartley, *Observations on Man*, pp. 291, 296.
30. Priestley, *Hartley's Theory of the Human Mind*, p. xxii.
31. Nor was Hartley the first to emphasize the physical basis of the human mind: Priestley notes that Locke also attributed thinking to mere matter (Priestley, *Hartley's Theory of the Human Mind,* p. xxiii). Meanwhile, as is illustrated in Beddoes's engagement with associationism, outlined in the previous chapter with reference to his discussion of education, others besides Brown maintained this focus in the nineteenth century. Vickers touches on this aspect of Beddoes's thought when he writes, 'To Beddoes, knowledge is simply the consciousness of sense perceptions, either directly, by sensory stimulus, or indirectly, through memory' in his article, 'Coleridge, Thomas Beddoes and Brunonian Medicine' (about John – not Thomas – Brown) (p. 54).
32. Brown, *Lectures on the Philosophy of the Human Mind*, p. 253.
33. Hartley, *Observations on Man*, p. 268.
34. Ibid., p. 288.
35. Brown, *Lectures on the Philosophy of the Human Mind*, p. 255.
36. Stewart, *Elements of the Philosophy of the Human Mind*, pp. 292, 299–300.

37. Wordsworth, 'Prelude', *Lyrical Ballads* (1800 edn), p. 126. Wordsworth's most direct and concise description of the *Lyrical Ballads* reveals that he wrote his reputation-making early verses as illustrations of associationist principles: 'the purpose' of 'each of these poems', he declares, is 'to illustrate the manner in which our feelings and ideas are associated in a state of excitement'. William Hatherell explores this aspect of the poems in 'Words and Things': Locke, *Hartley and the Associationist Context* for the Preface to *Lyrical Ballads*.

38. Brown, *Lectures on the Philosophy of the Human Mind*, p. 229.

39. Stewart, *Elements of the Philosophy of the Human Mind*, p. 279.

40. Kallich, 'The Association of Ideas and Akenside's *Pleasures of Imagination*', p. 171.

41. From Beddoes's *Hygëia* as quoted in Stock, *Memoirs of the Life of Thomas Beddoes*, p. 265. Please see Chapter 3, p. 150, for an in-depth discussion of Beddoes's comment.

42. Brown, *The Paradise of Coquettes,* p. xxxv.

43. Welsh, 'A Memoir of Dr Brown', p. xvii.

44. Ibid., p. viii.

45. Stewart-Robertson, 'Brown, Thomas (1778–1820)'; Welsh, 'A Memoir of Dr Brown', p. viii.

46. Stewart, *Elements of the Philosophy of the Human Mind*, p. 521.

47. Hatherell, 'Words and Things', p. 227; Hartley, *Observations on Man,* p. 287. That associationism has retained its links with moral education is evident in Cairns Craig's recent statement, '"Association" governs our emotions – our "passions" – as effectually as it does our ideas; it provides the building blocks of mind and society: understanding its operations will explain the workings of both and provide the resources to shape and organise them better' (Craig, *Associationism and the Literary Imagination*, p. 9).

48. Brown, *Lectures on the Philosophy of the Human Mind*, p. 287.

49. Welsh, 'A Memoir of Dr Brown', p. xvii.

50. Brown also indicates his indebtedness to the poetry of physician Mark Akenside, especially *The Pleasures of Imagination*, which has been described as exemplary of associationist verse by critic Martin Kallich. Brown quotes Akenside's poetry at length in *Lectures* (e.g. Brown, *Lectures on the Philosophy of the Human Mind*, p. 269) and, according to Stewart-Robinson, he wanted to become a second Akenside. (I do not study Akenside as a psychologist because he did not write any psychological prose and is almost uniformly classified as a physician by critics and historians). The same biographer asserts that Brown's friends found his poetic attempts embarrassing, adding, 'Dr James Gregory, with whom he entered into medical practice in 1806, regarded his amalgam of verse with philosophy as badly conceived' (Stewart-Robertson, 'Brown, Thomas (1778-1820)'). In response to this claim, I would add that, because Gregory, a physician and fellow professor at Edinburgh University, wrote poetry himself, we must take his criticism of Brown as, potentially, professional and avocational jealousy; See Gregory's *Epigrams and Poems* (Edinburgh: Printed by John Moir, 1810).

51. T. Brown, *Observations on the Zoönomia of Erasmus Darwin, MD* (Mundell & Son: Edinburgh: 1798), in *The Eighteenth-Century* (ESTC reel (MICR) 1619, no. 25), p. vii.

52. Brown, *The Renovation of India*, pp. 3–4; Beddoes, *Alexander's Expedition*, ll. 283–4.

53. Brown, *The Renovation of India*, p. 14. Of course, in this feature both Beddoes and Brown may be paying homage to Erasmus Darwin, the psychologist-poet extraordinaire whose great popularity inspired many scientific versifiers after him.

54. Ibid., p. 19.

55. Ibid., ll. 25–34.

56. Ibid., ll. 285–8.

57. F. Doherty, 'Tom Wedgwood, Coleridge and "Metaphysics"', *Neophilologus,* 71:2 (1987), pp. 305–15, on pp. 305, 311; McNeil, 'The Scientific Muse', p. 164.

58. Doherty, 'Tom Wedgwood, Coleridge and "Metaphysics"', p. 305.

59. Francis Doherty describes Wedgwood's interests in a way that suggests why he would have seen a sympathetic mind and friend in Brown: well-known for his 'constant self-scrutiny and self-analysis', Wedgwood achieved, as he put it in a letter to Godwin, the '"conceived discovery that Emotions were subject to all the admitted laws of Association"' (Ibid., p. 311).

60. Judging by Brown's inscription to Richard Heber on the flyleaf of edition of *The Renovation of India* in the Yale University library collection, Brown also appears to have moved in the same social circles as did Ferriar, who entitled his longest poem, *The Bibliomania, an Epistle, to Richard Heber, Esq.*

61. Cotton, 'Death. Vision the Last', l. 316.

62. Brown, *The War-Fiend*, p. 27, ll. 65–8.

63. Brown, *Lectures on the Philosophy of the Human Mind*, p. 281.

64. Brown paid the highest compliment to Beattie's work and dramatized his lifelong desire to amalgamate the interests of psychology and verse by quoting Beattie's poem 'The Hermit' (which is strongly linked to *The Minstrel*) in the last lecture he ever delivered. In a moving description, Welsh notes that 'those who recollect the manner in which he … recited the very affecting lines from Beattie's Hermit, will not wonder that some who attended his last course should conceive that the emotion he displayed arose from a foreboding of his own approaching dissolution' (Welsh, 'A Memoir of Dr Brown', p. xviii).

65. Brown, *Emily*, p. 5. The simple fact that Brown professes to describe poetically a 'mind' gestures to his psychological purpose in his poetry. For this reason, his poem *Agnes*, a poetic tale about the love and suffering endured by the chief of a clan and his dutiful daughter (much in the manner of Sir Walter Scott's *The Lay of the Last Minstrel* (1805), intro. F. T. Palgrave (Whitefish: Kessinger Publishing, 2007), may also be regarded as contributing materially to his associationist goals. Brown avers in the forty-four-page preface to *Agnes*, 'I have attempted chiefly to paint the feelings of gentle and delicate minds, in situations that derive their interest, not from the events that have led to them, but from the very gentleness and delicacy of the minds that are placed in them' (Brown, *Agnes*, p. 53). Indeed, as in *Emily*, Brown shows his interest in the subtleties of human psychology by choosing 'delicate' minds, rather than mad or passionate ones that can be painted in broad brushstrokes and with little subtle knowledge.

66. Brown, *Emily*, ll. 1–4.

67. Brown, *The Wanderer in Norway*, p. 9.

68. Ibid., p. 10.

69. Ibid., pp. 11, 17.

70. Ibid., ll. 41–2; 47–8.

71. W. Godwin, *Memoirs of the Author of A Vindication of the Rights of Woman* (1798), eds P. Clemit and G. L. Walker (Peterborough: Broadview Press, 2001).

72. Brown, *The Paradise of Coquettes*, p. xxxiv.

73. Shelley, 'A Defence of Poetry', p. 140; Brown, *The Paradise of Coquettes*, p. xxxv.

74. Brown, *Lectures on the Philosophy of the Human Mind*, p. 255.

75. Brown, *The Paradise of Coquettes*, p. xxxvi–vii.

76. Brown, *The Bower of Spring*, p. 3.

77. Ibid., p. 6.
78. Ibid., p. x.
79. Ibid., pp. x–xi.
80. Ibid., p. xviii. That Brown considered most readers to be ignorant and in need of a good education at the hands of the more learned members of British society, such as poets, is clear from his preface to *Agnes*, in which he complains at length that poetry descriptive of the workings of 'fine' minds, such as his, is little appreciated by contemporary audiences because most readers are hopelessly uneducated:

> how very few are there, in the wide number of those whose eyes are to glance rapidly over his pages, whom a poet would think worthy of taking to his council! The well-educated, and the ill-educated alike are readers; and ... the Wife or Daughter of the humble artisan ... are admitted to be present, as it were, at the sublime Mysteries of Literature, over which they may not be very well qualified to preside. (Brown, *Agnes*, pp. 29–30)

Such statements provide insight into Welsh's admittance – or defence – that, although Brown 'was often represented as of republican sentiments', doubtlessly because of his apparent contributions to and sympathies with the democratic tradition of psychologist-poets, such avowals were not true (Welsh, 'A Memoir of Dr Brown', p. xxiii).
81. Ibid., p. xxxiii.
82. Brown, *The Paradise of Coquettes*, ll. 9–10; 31–6.
83. Ibid., pp. xl–xli.
84. Stewart-Robertson, 'Brown, Thomas (1778–1820)'.
85. Brown, *Agnes*, pp. 29–30.
86. Brown, *The Paradise of Coquettes*, p. xxxv.
87. Welsh, 'A Memoir of Dr Brown', p. xxiii.
88. Priestley, *Hartley's Theory of the Human Mind*, p. v.

Conclusion: Thomas Forster, Phrenology and the Reification Of The Disciplines

1. T. Bakewell, 'On a Stupid Looking Fellow, When Drunk', *The Moorland Bard*, vol. 1, p. 66.
2. Hunter and Macalpine, *Three Hundred Years of Psychiatry*, p. 712.
3. A. K. Mellor, 'Physiognomy, Phrenology, and Blake's Visionary Heads', in R. N. Essick and D. R. Pearce (eds), *Blake in His Time* (Bloomington, IN: Indiana University Press, 1978), pp. 53–74, on p. 53.
4. J. Y. Hall, 'Gall's Phrenology: A Romantic Psychology', *Studies in Romanticism*, 16:3 (1977), pp. 305–17, on pp. 305–6.
5. Bakewell, 'On a Stupid Looking Fellow, When Drunk', l. 4.
6. Shorter, *A Historical Dictionary of Psychiatry*, p. 117.
7. Richardson, *British Romanticism and the Science of the Mind*, p. 7.
8. Beddoes, *Hygëia*, vol. 3, p. 13.
9. Bakewell, 'On a Stupid Looking Fellow, When Drunk', l. 2.
10. Ibid., ll. 2, 3.
11. The only discussions of Forster and his work that I have found are Janet Browne's entry on him in the *ODNB* and that of Hunter and Macalpine (*Three Hundred Years of Psychiatry*, p. 721).

12. Browne, 'Forster, Thomas Ignatius Maria (1789–1860)'; Hunter and Macalpine, *Three Hundred Years of Psychiatry*, p. 714; T. Forster, *Epistolarium or Fasciculi of Curious Letters, Together With a Few Familiar Poems and Some Account of the Writers as Preserved Among the MSS of the Forster Family* (Bruges: Vandecasteele-Werbroucke, 1845), p. 157; T. Forster, *Sketch of the New Anatomy and Physiology of the Brain and Nervous System of Drs Gall and Spurzheim, Considered as Comprehending a Complete System of Zoonomy, With Observations on its Tendency to the Improvement of Education, of Punishment, and of the Treatment of Insanity. Reprinted from The Pamphleteer, with Additions* (London: Messrs. Law and Whittaker, [1815]). Perhaps we should applaud Spurzheim for choosing amongst Forster's coinages judiciously upon considering some of his other linguistic offerings in this text, such as 'Organ of Believingness', or 'Organ of Mysterizingness', which he also called the 'Organ of Surnaturality' (Forster, *Epistolarium or Fasciculi of Curious Letters*, pp. 52, 156). The phrenologists would part company after a disagreement regarding the existence of the latter of these organs; one cannot help but wonder if Spurzheim might have been persuaded to believe in the 'Organ of Mysterizingness' if it did not have such a unconvincing name.
13. Mellor, 'Physiognomy, Phrenology, and Blake's Visionary Heads', p. 59; R. Salazar, 'Historicizing Phrenology: Wordsworth, Pynchon, and the Discursive Economy of the Cranial Text', *Raritan: A Quarterly Review*, 8:1 (1988), pp. 80–91; B. R. Pollin, 'Nicholson's Lost Portrait of William Godwin: A Study in Phrenology', *Keats-Shelley Journal: Keats, Shelley, Byron, Hunt, and Their Circles*, 16 (1967), pp. 51–60; E. C. Walker, 'Reading Proof, Aids to Reflection, and Phrenology: A New Coleridge Letter', *European Romantic Review*, 8:3 (1997), pp. 323–40.
14. Mellor, 'Physiognomy, Phrenology, and Blake's Visionary Heads', p. 58.
15. Browne, 'Forster, Thomas Ignatius Maria (1789–1860)'.
16. T. Forster, 'Address to Twa Tumbler Pidgeons', *Philosophia Musarum Containing the Songs and Romances of the Pipers [sic] Wallet, Pan, the Harmonia Musarum, and other Miscellaneous Poems* (Bruges: n.p., 1845), pp. 12–15. l. 1; T. Forster, 'On a Mouse Accidentally Killed', *Philosophia Musarum Containing the Songs and Romances of the Pipers [sic] Wallet, Pan, the Harmonia Musarum, and other Miscellaneous Poems* (Bruges: n.p., 1845), pp. 15–16; R. Burns, 'On a Mouse, On Turning Her Up in Her Nest, With the Plough, November 1785' (1785), in A. K. Mellor and R. E. Matlak (eds), *British Literature 1780–1830* (Fort Worth, TX: Harcourt Brace, 1996), p. 357.
17. T. Forster, *Observations on Some Curious and Hitherto Unnoticed Abnormal Affections of the Organs of Sense and Intellect. And on Other Subjects of Physiology* (Turnbridge Wells: John Coldbran, 1841), p. 3.
18. Forster, *Observations on the Casual and Periodical Influence of the Particular State of the Atmosphere on Human Health and Diseases*, pp. 11, 12.
19. T. Forster, *Illustrations of the Atmospherical Origin of Epidemic Disorders of Health ... and Of the Twofold Means of Prevention, Mitigation, and Cure, by Change of Air, and by Diet, Regularity, and Simple Medicines* (Chelmsford: Meggy and Chalk, 1829), p. 5.
20. Hall, 'Gall's Phrenology', p. 307.
21. T. Forster [signed Philostratus], *Somatopsychonoologia Showing that the Proofs of Body Life and Mind Considered as Distinct Essences Cannot be Deduced from Physiology but Depend on a Distinct Sort of Evidence being an Examination of the Controversy Concerning Life Carried on by Mm. Laurence, Abernathy, Rennell, & Others* (London: R. Hunter, 1823), p. vi.

22. Ibid., p. 41. Perhaps what this lifelong animal-lover, member of the Animals' Friends Society and writer of such poems as 'To my Auld Dog Shargs' (T. Forster, *Epistolarium or Fasciculi of Curious Letters*, p. 48) really wanted to know was whether he would meet his pets in heaven.

23. Ibid., p. 96.

24. Forster, *Somatopsychonoologia*, p. viii.

25. Ibid., p. 18.

26. Forster, *Epistolarium or Fasciculi of Curious Letters*, p. 96.

27. Forster, *Somatopsychonoologia*, pp. v–vi.

28. Mellor, 'Physiognomy, Phrenology, and Blake's Visionary Heads', pp. 57–8.

29. Hall, 'Gall's Phrenology', p. 312.

30. Ibid., p. 312.

31. Ibid., p. 309, quoting Gall.

32. T. Forster, 'Prolegomena in Philosophiam Musarum', *Philosophia Musarum Containing the Songs and Romances of the Pipers [sic] Wallet, Pan, the Harmonia Musarum, and other Miscellaneous Poems* (Bruges: n. p., 1845), pp. iii–xxxxvii [Forster's Roman numerals], on p. v.

33. Forster, *Somatopsychonoologia*, p. ix.

34. T. Forster, 'Verses Inscribed on a Skull', *Philosophia Musarum Containing the Songs and Romances of the Pipers [sic] Wallet, Pan, the Harmonia Musarum, and other Miscellaneous Poems* (Bruges: n.p., 1845), pp. 108–11. ll. 1–10.

35. Forster, *Sketch of the New Anatomy*, pp. 19–20.

36. Forster, 'Verses Inscribed on a Skull', ll. 51–64.

37. Forster, *Sketch of the New Anatomy*, p. 16.

38. Forster, 'Verses Inscribed on a Skull', l. 19.

39. Ibid., ll. 11–20.

40. Ibid., l. 14.

41. Forster, *Sketch of the New Anatomy*, p. 15.

42. Ibid., p. 16.

43. Ibid.

44. Forster, 'Verses Inscribed on a Skull', l. 14.

45. Forster, 'Prolegomena in Philosophiam Musarum', p. xxii.

46. Gilman, *Disease and Representation*, p. 63.

47. Forster, 'Verses Inscribed on a Skull', ll. 16, 18.

48. Porter, 'Barely Touching', p. 77.

49. Forster, 'Verses Inscribed on a Skull', ll. 11, 15.

50. Ibid., l. 15.

51. Forster, *Sketch of the New Anatomy*, p. 147.

52. Forster, 'Prolegomena in Philosophiam Musarum', p. iii.

53. Ibid., pp. iii–iv.

54. D. R. Shumway, *Michel Foucault* (Boston, MA: Twayne Publishers, 1989), p. 52. Jean Starobinski asserts that this observer/observed relationship lies at the very heart of psychology in *The Living Eye*: 'To show oneself; to see without being seen. Modern psychology has demonstrated that exhibitionism and voyeurism form a dual system of opposed yet complementary tendencies', J. Starobinski, *The Living Eye*, trans. A. Goldhammer (Cambridge, MA: Harvard University Press, 1989), p. 26.

55. Forster, 'Prolegomena in Philosophiam Musarum', p. iv.

56. Forster, *Epistolarium or Fasciculi of Curious Letters*, pp. 51–2.

57. Forster, 'Prolegomena in Philosophiam Musarum', p. v.

58. O. Sacks, *The Man Who Mistook His Wife for a Hat* (London: Gerald Duckworth & Co. Ltd., 1985), p. 105. Sacks's emphasis.

59. One of the most persistent complaints about Foucault's theorization of modern subjectivity as a product of disciplinary power is that it does not afford a space of resistance to the subjectified masses and that it denies even the possibility of defying power, an objection that stems from such remarks as the following: 'where there is power, there is resistance ... consequently, this resistance is never in a position of exteriority in relation to power' and 'one is always "inside" power, there is no "escaping" it' (Foucault, *The History of Sexuality*), p. 95.

WORKS CITED

Akenside, M., 'The Pleasures of Imagination; A Poem in Three Books' (1744), in *Poems of Established Reputation* (Baltimore, MA: Warner and Hanna, 1803).

Anderson, H., 'Associationism and Wit in *Tristram Shandy*', *Philological Quarterly*, 48 (1969), pp. 27–41.

Andrews, J. and A. Scull, *Customers and Patrons of the Mad-Trade: The Management of Lunacy in Eighteenth-Century London: With the Complete Text of John Monro's 1766 Case Book* (Berkeley, CA: University of California Press, 2003).

—, *Undertaker of the Mind: John Monro and Mad-Doctoring in Eighteenth-Century England* (Berkeley and Los Angeles: University of California Press, 2000).

Andrews, M., 'The English Cottage as Cultural Critique and Associationist Paradigm', in Brown, P. (ed. and intro.) and Irwin, M. (ed.), *Literature and Place 1800–2000* (Oxford: Peter Lang, 2006), pp. 49–68.

Anon., Review of *An Essay, Medical, Philosophical and Chemical, on Drunkenness and its Effects on the Human Body*, *Edinburgh Medical and Surgical Journal*, 1:1 (1805), pp. 73–81.

—, *A Treatise on the Dismal Effects of Low-spiritedness. In which is Contained, Many Useful Hints for Preventing that Disagreeable and Destructive Disorder from Taking Root in the Human System* (London: Printed for W. Owen, 1750).

—, *Pharmacopolae Justificati: or, Apothecaries Vindicated From the Imputation of Ignorance. Wherein is Shewn, That an Academical Education is No Way Necessary to Qualify a Man for the Practice of Physick* (Roberts, J: London, 1724), in *The Eighteenth-Century* (ESTC reel (MICR) 13297).

Arieno, M., *Victorian Lunatics: A Social Epidemiology of Mental Illness in Mid-Nineteenth-Century England* (London: Associated University Presses, 1989).

Armstrong, J., *The Art of Preserving Health*, in *Poems of Established Reputation* (Baltimore: Warner and Hanna, 1803), pp. 4–55.

Arnold, T., *Observations on the Nature, Kinds, Causes and Prevention of Insanity*, 2 vols (London: Richard Phillips, 1806).

Bakewell, T., *A Letter Addressed to the Chairman of the Select Committee of the House of Commons, Appointed to Enquire into the State of Mad-Houses: To Which is Subjoined, Remarks on the Nature, Causes, and Cure of Mental Derangement* (Stafford: C. Chester, 1815).

—, 'The Author's Dream: Addressed to the Reviewers', in *The Moorland Bard; or, Poetical Recollections of a Weaver, in the Moorlands of Staffordshire*, 2 vols (London: T. Allbut, 1807), vol. 2, pp. 165–8.

—, 'The Author's Advertisement for a Wife', in *The Moorland Bard; or, Poetical Recollections of a Weaver, in the Moorlands of Staffordshire*, 2 vols (London: T. Allbut, 1807), vol. 2, pp. 45–8.

—, 'Epistle to a Lady; Occasioned by Her Advertisement, in a London Paper, For Country Lodgings in a Family Where There Were None but Females, Complaining at the Same Time of Frequent Depression of Spirits', in *The Moorland Bard; or, Poetical Recollections of a Weaver, in the Moorlands of Staffordshire*, 2 vols (London: T. Allbut, 1807), vol. 2, pp. 49–51.

—, 'Epistle to a Lady, Who had Requested Some Maxims of Health', in *The Moorland Bard; or, Poetical Recollections of a Weaver, in the Moorlands of Staffordshire*, 2 vols (London: T. Allbut, 1807), vol. 2, pp. 90–8.

—, 'Epistle to a Neighbouring Gentleman, Complaining of the Want of Poetic Fame', in *The Moorland Bard; or, Poetical Recollections of a Weaver, in the Moorlands of Staffordshire*, 2 vols (London: T. Allbut, 1807), vol. 1, pp. 7–13.

—, 'Lines Written on a Blank Leaf of My Domestic Guide, and Presented to a Young Lady', in *The Moorland Bard; or, Poetical Recollections of a Weaver, in the Moorlands of Staffordshire*, 2 vols (London: T. Allbut, 1807), vol. 1, pp. 55–6.

—, 'Lines, On Being Told that the Volitions of the Mind Would Overcome the Sense of Bodily Pain', in *The Moorland Bard; or, Poetical Recollections of a Weaver, in the Moorlands of Staffordshire*, 2 vols (London: T. Allbut, 1807), vol. 2, pp. 87–9.

—, 'On a Stupid Looking Fellow, When Drunk', *The Moorland Bard; or, Poetical Recollections of a Weaver, in the Moorlands of Staffordshire*, 2 vols (London: T. Allbut, 1807), vol. 1, p. 66.

—, Preface to *The Moorland Bard; Or, Poetical Recollections of a Weaver, in the Moorlands of Staffordshire* 2 vols (London: T. Allbut, 1807), vol. 1, pp. vii–xiv.

—, 'The Weaver's Request, That the Public Will Hear his Song', in *The Moorland Bard; or, Poetical Recollections of a Weaver, in the Moorlands of Staffordshire*, 2 vols (London: T. Allbut, 1807), vol. 1, pp. 1–2.

—, Preface to *The Domestic Guide, In Cases of Insanity. Pointing out the Causes, Means of Preventing, and Proper Treatment, of that Disorder. Recommended to Private Families, and the Notice of the Clergy* (Hanley: T. Allbut, 1805), pp. vii–xi.

—, *The Domestic Guide, In Cases of Insanity. Pointing out the Causes, Means of Preventing, and Proper Treatment, of that Disorder. Recommended to Private Families, and the Notice of the Clergy* (Hanley: T. Allbut, 1805).

Barbauld, A. L., 'Essay on Akenside's Poem on *The Pleasures of Imagination*', in M. Akenside, *The Pleasures of Imagination* (London: T. Cadell, Junior, and W. Davies, 1794), in *Eighteenth Century Collections Online*, http://galenet.galegroup.com.proxy1.lib.umanitoba.ca/servlet/ECCO [accessed 17 August 2007].

Barker-Benfield, G. J., *The Culture of Sensibility: Sex and Society in Eighteenth-Century Britain* (Chicago, IL: The University of Chicago Press, 1992).

Batra, N., 'Animal Rights in the Romantic Period: Legal Jurisdiction in England and the Intellectual Milieu', *Atenea*, 16:1–2 (1996), pp. 99–113.

Beattie, J., *Elements of Moral Science* (1790–3) (Philadelphia, PA: Hopkins and Earle, 1809.)

—, *Evidences of the Christian Religion; Briefly and Plainly Stated* (Edinburgh: W. Creech, 1786), http://galenet.galegroup.com.proxy2.lib.umanitoba.ca/servlet/ECCO (accessed 23 July 2008).

—, 'The Hermit', *Poems on Several Occasions* (Edinburgh: W. Creech, 1776), pp. 122–4.

—, 'On Poetry and Music, As They Affect the Mind', *An Essay on the Nature and Immutability of Truth, in Opposition to Sophistry and Scepticism; On Poetry and Music, As They Affect the Mind; On Laughter, and Ludicrous Composition; On the Utility of Classical Learning* (Edinburgh: William Creech, 1776), pp. 347–580.

—, 'The Minstrel, or Progress of Genius' (1771–74), *Poems of Established Reputation* (Baltimore, MA: Warner and Hanna, 1803), pp. 57–92, in *Early American Imprints*, http://link.library.utoronto.ca/eir/EIRdetail.cfm?Resources__ID=394581&T=F (accessed 11 July 2005).

—, *An Essay on the Nature and Immutability of Truth, in Opposition to Sophistry and Scepticism* (1770) (Philadelphia, PA: Solomon Wieatt, 1809).

Beddoes, T., *Hygëia: or, Essays Moral and Medical on the Causes Affecting the Personal State of our Middling and Affluent Classes*, 3 vols (Bristol: R. Phillips, 1802), vol. 1.

—, 'Introduction', *Contributions to Physical and Medical Knowledge, Principally from the West of England*, ed. T. Beddoes (London: T. N. Longman and O. Rees, 1799), pp. 3–25, in *Eighteenth Century Collections Online*, http://galenet.galegroup.com.proxy1.lib.umanitoba.ca/servlet/ECCO [accessed 20 May 2008].

—, *Essay on the Causes, Early Signs, and Prevention of Pulmonary Consumption for the Use Parents and Preceptors* (Bristol: T. N. Longman and O. Rees, 1799), in *The Eighteenth-Century* (ESTC reel 99, no. 14).

—, *A Lecture Introductory to a Course of Popular Instruction on the Constitution and Management of the Human Body* (Bristol: Joseph Cottle, 1797).

—, *Alternatives Compared: or, What Shall the Rich Do to be Safe?* (London: J. Debrett, 1797).

—, *The History of Isaac Jenkins, and Sarah His Wife, and Their Three Children* (Bristol: n. p., 1796), in *The Eighteenth-Century* (ESTC reel (MICR) 4409, no. 15).

—, *A Guide for Self-Preservation, and Parental Affection* (London: Bulgin and Rosser, 1793), in *The Eighteenth-Century* (ESTC reel (MICR) 4409. No. 14).

—, *Alexander's Expedition down the Hydaspes and the Indus to the Indian Ocean* (London: J. Edmunds, 1792), in *The Eighteenth-Century* (ESTC reel (MICR) 3938, no. 3).

—, *Extract of a Letter on Early Instruction, Particularly that of the Poor* (n. p., 1792), in *Eighteenth Century Collections Online*, http://galenet.galegroup.com.proxy1.lib.umanitoba.ca/servlet/ECCO [accessed 22 May 2008].

Bernauer, J. and Mahon, M. 'Michel Foucault's Ethical Imagination', in G. Gutting (ed.), *The Cambridge Companion to Foucault*, 2nd edn (Cambridge: Cambridge University Press, 2005), pp. 149–75.

Bettany, G. T. and Rosner, L 'Duncan, Andrew, the elder (1744-1828)', *Oxford Dictionary of National Biography* (Oxford: Oxford University Press, 2004), http://www.oxforddnb. com.myaccess.library.utoronto.ca/view/article/8212 [accessed 11 July 2005].

Bewell, A., *Wordsworth and the Enlightenment: Nature, Man, and Society in the Experimental Poetry* (New Haven, CT: Yale University Press, 1989).

Black, S. B., 'Perfect, William (1731/2–1809)', *Oxford Dictionary of National Biography* (Oxford: Oxford University Press, 2004), http://www.oxforddnb.com.myaccess.library. utoronto.ca/view/article/58530 [accessed 11 July 2005].

—, *An Eighteenth[-]Century Mad-Doctor: William Perfect of West Malling* (Kent: Darenth Valley Publications, 1995).

Blake, W., 'Milton' (1804), in Erdman, D. (ed. and rev.) and Bloom, H. (commentary), *The Complete Poetry and Prose of William Blake* (New York: Anchor Books, 1988), pp. 95–144.

—, 'The Ecchoing Green', *The Complete Poetry and Prose of William Blake*, rev. and ed. Erdman, D. (New York: Anchor Books, 1988), p. 8.

Bloom, H., Commentary to *Milton*, in *The Complete Poetry and Prose of William Blake*, rev. and ed. D. Erdman (New York: Anchor Books, 1988), p. 909–28.

Bloomfield, R., *The Farmer's Boy: A Rural Poem* (London: Vernor and Hood, 1800).

Bour, I., 'Epistemological Ambiguities: Reason, Sensibility and Association of Ideas in Mary Wollstonecraft's *Vindication of the Rights of Woman*', *Bulletin de la Société d'études Anglo-Américaines des XVIIe et XVIIIe Siècles*, 49 (1999), pp. 299–310.

Brewer, W., *The Mental Anatomies of William Godwin and Mary Shelley* (Cranbury: Associated University Presses, 2001).

Brissenden, R. F., *Virtue in Distress: Studies in the Novel of Sentiment from Richardson to Sade* (London: The Macmillan Press, Ltd., 1974).

Broadie, A., 'The Human Mind and its Powers', in A. Broadie (ed.), *The Cambridge Companion to the Scottish Enlightenment.* (Cambridge: Cambridge University Press, 2003), pp. 60–78.

Brown, J., *The Elements of Medicine of John Brown, MD. Translated from the Latin, with Comments and Illustrations, by the Author. A New Edition, Revised and Corrected. With a Biographical Preface by Thomas Beddoes,* 2 vols (London: J. Johnson, 1795), in *Eighteenth Century Collections Online*, http://galenet.galegroup.com.proxy2.lib.umanitoba.ca/servlet/ECCO (accessed 12 September 2008).

Brown, T., *Lectures on the Philosophy of the Human Mind* (1820; Edinburgh: William Tait, 1828).

—, *Emily, with Other Poems*, 2nd edn (Edinburgh: Archibald Constable and Co., 1819).

—, *Agnes a Poem in Four Parts* (Edinburgh: Archibald Constable and Co. 1818).

—, *The Bower of Spring, with Other Poems* (Philadelphia: M. Thomas, 1817).

—, *The Wanderer in Norway, with Other Poems*, 2nd edn (London, J. Murray, 1816).

—, *The War-Fiend, with Other Poems*, 2nd edn (London: J. Murray, 1816).

—, *The Paradise of Coquettes, a Poem in Nine Parts* (London: John Murray, 1814).

—, *The Renovation of India: a Poem. With the Prophecy of Ganges, an Ode* (Edinburgh: Mundell, Doig, & Stevenson, 1808).

—, *Observations on the Zoönomia of Erasmus Darwin, MD* (Mundell & Son: Edinburgh: 1798), in *The Eighteenth-Century* (ESTC reel (MICR) 1619, no. 25).

Browne, J., 'Forster, Thomas Ignatius Maria (1789–1860)', *Oxford Dictionary of National Biography* (Oxford: Oxford University Press, 2004), http://www.oxforddnb.com.myaccess.library.utoronto.ca/view/article/9920 [accessed 11 July 2005].

Bryson, G., *Man and Society: The Scottish Inquiry of the Eighteenth-Century* (Princeton, NJ: Princeton University Press, 1945).

Buchanan, C., Preface to N. Cotton, *Visions in Verse* (1752) (Bern: Herbert Lang, 1973), unpag.

Bunyan, J., *The Pilgrim's Progress* (1678), ed. W. R. Owens (Oxford: Oxford University Press, 2003).

Burgess, A., *A Clockwork Orange* (1962; New York: W. W. Norton, 1987).

Burke, E., *A Philosophical Enquiry into the Origin of Our Ideas of the Sublime and Beautiful* (1757), intro. and notes Phillip, A. (Oxford: Oxford University Press, 1990).

Burnett, J. B. M., *Of the Origin and Progress of Language* (1773-92) (Menston: Scolar Press, 1967).

Burns, R., 'On a Mouse, On Turning Her Up in Her Nest, With the Plough, November 1785' (1785), in Mellor, A. K. and Matlak, R. E. (eds), *British Literature 1780-1830* (Fort Worth: Harcourt Brace, 1996), p. 357.

Burr, S. J., 'Inspiring Lunatics: Biographical Portraits of the Lunar Society's Erasmus Darwin, Thomas Day, and Joseph Priestley', *Eighteenth-Century Life*, 24:2 (2000), pp. 111–27.

Burton, R., *The Anatomy of Melancholy* (1621) (London: T. Tegg, 1845).

Burwick, F., *Poetic Madness and the Romantic Imagination* (University Park, PA: Pennsylvania State University Press, 1996).

Butler, S., *Hudibras* (1663–8 Oxford: Clarendon Press, 1975).

Bynum, W. F., 'The Nervous Patient in Eighteenth- and Nineteenth-Century England: The Psychiatric Origins of British Neurology', in W. F. Bynum, R. Porter and M. Shepherd (eds), *The Anatomy of Madness* (London: Tavistock, 1985), vol. 1, pp. 89–102.

Byrd, M., *Visits to Bedlam: Madness and Literature in the Eighteenth Century* (South Carolina: University of South Carolina Press, 1974).

Caldwell, J. M., *Literature and Medicine in Nineteenth-Century Britain: From Mary Shelley to George Eliot* (Cambridge: Cambridge University Press, 2004).

Cheyne, G., *The English Malady: or, A Treatise of Nervous Diseases of All Kinds, as Spleen, Vapours, Lowness of Spirits, Hypochondriacal, and Hysterical Distempers &c.* (London: G. Strahan and J. Leake, 1733).

Chisick, H., 'David Hume and the Common People', in P. Jones (ed.), *The 'Science of Man' in the Scottish Enlightenment: Hume, Reid and their Contemporaries* (Edinburgh: Edinburgh University Press, 1989).

Christensen, J., 'Philosophy/Literature: The Associationist Precedent for Coleridge's Late Poems', in Cain, W. E. (ed.), *Philosophical Approaches to Literature: New Essays on Nineteenth- and Twentieth-Century Texts* (Lewisburg: Bucknell University Press, 1984), pp. 27–50.

Christie, J. and S. Shuttleworth, 'Introduction: Between Literature and Science', in Christie, J. and Shuttleworth, S. (eds), *Nature Transfigured: Science and Literature, 1700-1900* (Manchester: Manchester University Press, 1989), pp. 1–12.

Christie, W. H., 'Francis Jeffrey's Associationist Aesthetics', *British Journal of Aesthetics*, 33:3 (1993), pp. 257–70.

Coleridge, S. T., *On the Constitution of the Church and State* (1830), in *The Collected Works of Samuel Taylor Coleridge*, gen. ed. K. Coburn, 16 vols (London: Routledge and Kegan Paul, 1969-2001), vol. 10, ed. J. Colmer.

—, *Biographia Literaria or, Biographical Sketches of My Literary Life and Opinions* (1817), in *The Collected Works of Samuel Taylor Coleridge*, gen. ed. K. Coburn, 16 vols (London: Routledge and Kegan Paul, 1969-2001), vol. 7, ed. J. Engell and W. J. Bate.

—, 'Kubla Khan: Or, A Vision in a Dream' (1816), in *The Major Works*, ed. H. J. Jackson, (Oxford: Oxford University Press, 1985), pp. 102–4.

—, 'Frost at Midnight' (1798), in *The Major Works*, ed. and intro. Jackson, H. J (Oxford: Oxford University Press, 1985), pp. 87–9.

Committee on Madhouses, *First Report. Minutes of Evidence Taken Before the Select Committee Appointed to Consider of Provisions Being Made for the Better Regulation of Madhouses, in England* (1815), in R. Hunter and I. Macalpine (eds), *Three Hundred Years of Psychiatry 1535-1860* (London: Oxford University Press, 1963), pp. 698–703.

Cooper, A. M., 'Blake and Madness: The World Turned Inside Out', *English Literary History (ELH)*, 57 (1990), pp. 585–642.

Cotton, N., *Various Pieces in Verse and Prose*, 2 vols. (London: J. Dodsley, 1791).

—, 'Content. Vision IV', in *Visions in Verse, For the Entertainment and Instruction of Younger Minds*, 3rd edn, rev. (London: R. Dodsley, 1752), pp. 43–51.

—, 'Death. Vision the Last', in *Visions in Verse, For the Entertainment and Instruction of Younger Minds*, 3rd edn, rev. (London: R. Dodsley, 1752), pp. 111–32.

—, 'An Epistle to the Reader', in *Visions in Verse, For the Entertainment and Instruction of Younger Minds*, 3rd edn, rev. (London: R. Dodsley, 1752), pp. 1–7.

—, 'Health. Vision III', in *Visions in Verse, For the Entertainment and Instruction of Younger Minds*, 3rd edn, rev. (London: R. Dodsley, 1752), pp. 29–39.

—, 'Pleasure. Vision II', in *Visions in Verse, For the Entertainment and Instruction of Younger Minds*, 3rd edn, rev. (London: R. Dodsley, 1752), pp. 19–28.

—, *Observations on a Particular Kind of Scarlet Fever that Lately Prevailed in and about St Alban's. In a Letter to Dr Mead* (London: R. Mansby and H. S. Cox, 1749).

Cowper, W., 'Hope', *Poems by William Cowper, of the Inner Temple, Esq.* (London: J. Johnson, 1782), pp. 141–79, in *Eighteenth Century Collections Online*, http://galenet.galegroup.com.proxy1.lib.umanitoba.ca/servlet/ECCO (accessed 1 June 1 2008).

Crabbe, G., 'The Voluntary Insane', in Pryor, F. (ed.), *The Voluntary Insane* (London: ichard Cohen Books, 1995), pp. 47–90.

—, 'Sir Eustace Grey', in N. Dalrymple-Champneys (ed.), *The Complete Poetical Works* (Oxford: Clarendon Press, 1988), vol. 1, pp. 298–310.

—, 'Peter Grimes' from 'The Borough', in N. Dalrymple-Champneys (ed.), *The Complete Poetical Works* (Oxford: Clarendon Press, 1988), vol. 1, pp. 567–74.

Craig, C., *Associationism and the Literary Imagination: From the Phantasmal Chaos* (Edinburgh: Edinburgh University Press, 2007).

Crowther, J. G., *Scientists of the Industrial Revolution* (Philadelphia, PA: Dufour Editions, 1963).

Darwin, C., *The Origin of Species: A Variorum Text* (1859), ed. Peckham, M. (Philadelphia, PA: University of Pennsylvania Press, 2006).

Darwin, E., *The Temple of Nature* (1803), ed. D. King-Hele (London: A Scolar Press Facsimile, 1973).

—, *Zoönomia, or, The Laws of Organic Life* (New York: T. & J. Swords, 1796), vol. 1, in *Early American Imprints*, first series, no. 30312, http://infoweb.newsbank.com.myaccess.library.utoronto.ca/ (accessed 12 July 2005).

—, 'Advertisement', *The Botanic Garden*, 4th edn (Dudlin [sic]: J. Moore, 1796), pp. v–vi.

—, *The Economy of Vegetation* (1792), in S. Harris (ed.), *Cosmologia* (Sheffield: Stuart Harris, 2002).

—, 'Introduction' and 'Apologia', in S. Harris (ed.), *Cosmologia* (Sheffield: Stuart Harris, 2002)

Davidson, A. I., 'Ethics as Aesthetics: Foucault, the History of Ethics, and Ancient Thought', in Gutting, G (ed.), *The Cambridge Companion to Foucault*, 2nd edn (Cambridge: Cambridge University Press, 2005), pp. 123–48.

DePorte, M. V., *Nightmares and Hobbyhorses: Swift, Sterne and Augustan Ideas of Madness* (San Marino, CA: The Huntington Library, 1974).

Doherty, F., 'Tom Wedgwood, Coleridge and "Metaphysics"', *Neophilologus,* 71:2 (1987), pp. 305–15.

Donne, J., 'Holy Sonnet 10', in Abrams, M. H. (ed.), *The Norton Anthology of English Literature*, 5th edn (New York: W. W. Norton & Co., 1986), p. 1099.

Donnelly, M., *Managing the Mind: A Study of Medical Psychology in Early Nineteenth-Century Britain* (London: Tavistock, 1983).

Downman, H., *Infancy; or, The Management of Children. A Didactic Poem, in Three Books* (Edinburgh: John Bell, 1776), http://galenet.galegroup.com.proxy1.lib.umanitoba.ca/servlet/ECCO [accessed 9 September 2008].

Duncan, Sr, A., *Observations on the Office of Faithful Teacher, and on the Duty of an Attentive Student of Medicine, Delivered as an Introductory Lecture to the Institute of Medicine in the University of Edinburgh* (Edinburgh: Bell & Bradfute, 1823).

—, 'Advice Given to the Rich and Great, by a Physician, Who has Very Nearly Arrived at the Eightieth Year of his Age ... 1st of May, 1822' (no publishing information given;

collected in volume entitled *Medical Tracts* no. 868 at the Wellcome Institute for the History of Medicine Library).

—, *Miscellaneous Poems, Extracted from the Records of the Circulation Club at Edinburgh* (Edinburgh: P. Hill & Co., 1818).

—, 'Fragment of the Life of the *Scriba Praetorious* ... Written by Himself in Hudibrastic Rhyme', in *Miscellaneous Poems, Extracted from the Records of the Circulation Club at Edinburgh* (Edinburgh: P. Hill & Co., 1818), pp. 9–26.

—, 'Diploma of Doctor of Mirth, Solemnly Conferred on Alexander Wood, Esq. April 12, 1813', in *Miscellaneous Poems, Extracted from the Records of the Circulation Club at Edinburgh* (Edinburgh: P. Hill & Co., 1818), pp. 33–5.

—, 'Untitled' [On the death of Princess Charlotte, written 1 May 1818], in *Miscellaneous Poems, Extracted from the Records of the Circulation Club at Edinburgh* (Edinburgh: P. Hill & Co., 1818), pp. 39–40.

—, 'Untitled' [Written 1 May 1821], in *Tribute of Veneration, Addressed to the First Meeting of the Loyal Edinburgh Association, for Commemorating the Reign of George III* (Edinburgh: Archibald Constable & Co., 1821), p. 16.

—, *A Short Account of the Rise, Progress, and Present State of the Lunatic Asylum at Edinburgh* (Edinburgh: Archibald Constable & Co., 1812).

—, *A Letter to Dr James Gregory of Edinburgh, In Consequence of Certain Printed Papers Intitled, – 'The Viper and File;' – 'There is Wisdom in Silence;' – 'An Old Story,' &c. Which Have Lately Been Distributed by Him, and Which are Evidently Intended to Propagate and Support Groundless and Malevolent Calumnies Against Innocent Men* (Edinburgh. Edinburgh: Archibald Constable and Co., 1811).

—, *Observations on the Structure of Hospitals for the Treatment of Lunatics, and on the General Principles on Which the Cure of Insanity May Be Most Successfully Conducted. To Which is Annexed, An Account of the Intended Establishment of a Lunatic Asylum at Edibnurgh* [sic] (Edinburgh: Archibald Constable & Co., 1809).

Emerson, R. L., 'Science and Moral Philosophy in the Scottish Enlightenment', in M. A. Stewart (ed.), *Studies in the Philosophy of the Scottish Enlightenment* (Oxford: Clarendon Press, 1990), pp. 11–36.

Faas, E., *Retreat into the Mind: Victorian Poetry and the Rise of Psychiatry* (Princeton: Princeton University Press, 1988).

Faflak, J., *Romantic Psychoanalysis: The Burden of the Mystery* (Albany, NY: State University of New York Press, 2008).

Faubert, M., 'Cure, Classification, and John Clare', *Victorian Literature and Culture*, 33 (2005), pp. 269–91.

—, 'A Gendered Affliction', in A. Ingram with M. Faubert, *Cultural Constructions of Madness in the Eighteenth Century: Representing the Insane* (Houndmills: Palgrave Macmillan, 2005), pp. 136-69.

Ferriar, J., *An Essay Towards a Theory of Apparitions* (London: Cadell and Davies, 1813).

—, *The Bibliomania, an Epistle, to Richard Heber, Esq.* (1812), ed. and intro. Vaulbert de Chantilly, M (London: The Vanity Press of Bethnal Green, 2001).

—, 'Illustrations of Sterne', *Illustrations of Sterne: With Other Essays and Verses*, 2nd edn, 2 vols (London: Cadell and Davies, 1812), vols 1–2, pp. 17–193 (vol. 1), pp. 9–63 (vol. 2).

—, 'Of Certain Varieties of Man, Described by Authors', *Illustrations of Sterne: With Other Essays and Verses*, 2nd edn, 2 vols (London: Cadell and Davies, 1812), vol. 2, pp. 65–97.

—, 'Of Genius', *Illustrations of Sterne: With Other Essays and Verses*, 2nd edn, 2 vols (London: Cadell and Davies, 1812), vol. 2, pp. 161–81.

— [also attributed to Ferrier, J. and Grey in Wellcome Catalogue], *The Theory of Dreams in which an Inquiry is Made into the Powers and Faculties of the Human Mind, as They are Illustrated in the Most Remarkable Dreams Recorded in Sacred and Profane History*, 2 vols (F. C. London: and J. Rivington, 1808), vol. 1.

—, *Medical Histories and Reflections* (London: Cadell and Davies, 1795), vol. 2.

—, *Medical Histories and Reflections* (London: T. Cadell, 1792), vol. 1.

—, *The Prince of Angola, A Tragedy, Altered from the Play of Oroonoko. And Adapted to the Circumstances of the Present Times* (Manchester: J. Harrop, 1788).

Fielding, H., *Joseph Andrews* and *Shamela*, ed. and rev. T. Keymer (New York: Oxford World's Classics, 1999).

Flynn, P., 'General Introduction', in P. Flynn (ed.), *Enlightened Scotland: A Study and Selection of Scottish Philosophical Prose from the Eighteenth and Early Nineteenth Centuries* (Edinburgh: Scottish Academic Press, 1992), pp. ix–xxii.

Forbes, W., *An Account of the Life and Writings of James Beattie, LLD* (New York: Isaac Riley and Co, 1806).

Forbes, M., *Beattie and his Friends* (Westminster: Archibald Constable & Co. Ltd., 1904).

Forster, T., *Facts and Enquiries Respecting the Source of Epidemia, with an Historical Catalogue of the Numerous Visitations of Plague, Pestilence, and Famine*, 3rd edn (London: Keating and Brown, 1832).

—, *Epistolarium, or The Correspondence of the Forster Family, Letters and Essays. Printed for Private Circulation Only*, 2 vols (Bruges: C. De Moor, 1850), vol. 2.

—, *Epistolarium or Fasciculi of Curious Letters, Together With a Few Familiar Poems and Some Account of the Writers as Preserved Among the MSS of the Forster Family* (Bruges: Vandecasteele-Werbroucke, 1845).

—, 'Address to Twa Tumbler Pidgeons', *Philosophia Musarum Containing the Songs and Romances of the Pipers [sic] Wallet, Pan, the Harmonia Musarum, and other Miscellaneous Poems* (Bruges: n.p., 1845), pp. 12–15.

—, 'On a Mouse Accidentally Killed', *Philosophia Musarum Containing the Songs and Romances of the Pipers [sic] Wallet, Pan, the Harmonia Musarum, and other Miscellaneous Poems* (Bruges: n. p., 1845), pp. 15–16.

—, 'Prolegomena in Philosophiam Musarum', *Philosophia Musarum Containing the Songs and Romances of the Pipers [sic] Wallet, Pan, the Harmonia Musarum, and other Miscellaneous Poems* (Bruges: n. p., 1845), pp. iii–xxxxvii [Forster's Roman numerals].

—, 'Verses Inscribed on a Skull', *Philosophia Musarum Containing the Songs and Romances of the Pipers [sic] Wallet, Pan, the Harmonia Musarum, and other Miscellaneous Poems* (Bruges: n. p., 1845), pp. 108–11.

—, *Observations on Some Curious and Hitherto Unnoticed Abnormal Affections of the Organs of Sense and Intellect. And on Other Subjects of Physiology* (Turnbridge Wells: John Coldbran, 1841).

—, *Illustrations of the Atmospherical Origin of Epidemic Disorders of Health ... and Of the Two-fold Means of Prevention, Mitigation, and Cure, by Change of Air, and by Diet, Regularity, and Simple Medicines* (Chelmsford: Meggy and Chalk, 1829).

— [signed Philostratus], *Somatopsychonoologia Showing that the Proofs of Body Life and Mind Considered as Distinct Essences Cannot be Deduced from Physiology but Depend on a Distinct Sort of Evidence being an Examination of the Controversy Concerning Life Carried on by Mm. Laurence, Abernathy, Rennell, & Others* (London: R. Hunter, 1823).

—, *Observations on the Casual and Periodical Influence of the Particular State of the Atmosphere on Human Health and Diseases, Particularly Insanity*, 2nd edn (London: n.p., 1819).

—, *Sketch of the New Anatomy and Physiology of the Brain and Nervous System of Drs Gall and Spurzheim, Considered as Comprehending a Complete System of Zoonomy, With Observations on its Tendency to the Improvement of Education, of Punishment, and of the Treatment of Insanity. Reprinted from The Pamphleteer, with Additions* (London: Messrs Law and Whittaker, [1815]).

Foucault, M., *Ethics: Subjectivity and Truth*, ed. P. Rabinow, trans. R. Hurley et al (New York: The New Press, 1994), vol. 1.

—, *The History of Sexuality*, trans. R. Hurley, 3 vols (New York: Vintage Books, 1980), vol. 1.

— (ed.), *I, Pierre Rivière, Having Slaughtered My Mother, My Sister and My Brother: A Case of Parricide in the Nineteenth Century* (New York: Pantheon Books, 1975).

—, Fontana A. and Pasquino, P. 'Truth and Power', in C. Gordon (ed.), *Power/Knowledge: Selected Interviews and Other Writings, 1972-1977*, trans. C. Gordon, L. Marshall, J. Mepham, K. Soper (New York: Pantheon Books, 1972), pp. 109–33.

—, and Brochier, J. J. 'Prison Talk', in Gordon C. (ed.), *Power/Knowledge: Selected Interviews and Other Writings, 1972-1977*, trans. C. Gordon, L. Marshall, J. Mepham, K. Soper (New York: Pantheon Books, 1972), pp. 37–54.

—, 'The Politics of Health in the Eighteenth Century', in Gordon C. (ed.), *Power/Knowledge: Selected Interviews and Other Writings, 1972-1977*, trans. C. Gordon, L. Marshall, J. Mepham and K. Soper (New York: Pantheon Books, 1972), pp. 166–82.

—, 'Two Lectures: Lecture Two: 14 January 1976', in Gordon, C. (ed.), *Power/Knowledge: Selected Interviews and Other Writings, 1972-1977*, trans. C. Gordon, L. Marshall, J. Mepham, K. Soper (New York: Pantheon Books, 1972), pp. 92–108.

—, *Madness and Civilization: A History of Insanity in the Age of Reason*, trans. R. Howard (New York: Pantheon, 1965).

—, 'What is an Author?', in Leitch, V. B. (gen. ed.), *The Norton Anthology of Theory and Criticism* (New York: W. W. Norton, 2001), pp. 1622–36.

Gamwell, L. and N. Tomes, *Madness in America: Cultural and Medical Perceptions of Mental Illness Before 1914* (New York: Cornell University Press, 1995).

Garson, M., 'Associationism and the Dialogue in *Emma*', *Eighteenth-Century Fiction*, 10:1 (1997), pp. 79–100.

Gilman, S. L., *Disease and Representation: Images of Illness from Madness to AIDS* (Ithaca, NY: Cornell University Press, 1988).

Godwin, W., *Memoirs of the Author of A Vindication of the Rights of Woman* (1798), eds Clemit, P. and Walker, G. L. (Peterborough: Broadview Press, 2001).

—, *Caleb Williams, or, Things as They Are* (1794), ed. and intro. D. M. McCracken (Oxford: Oxford University Press, 1970).

Goldsmith, R., 'The Selfless Self of Self: Hopkins' Late Sonnets', *Hopkins Quarterly*, 3 (1976), pp. 67–75.

Graham, G., 'Introduction' to G. Graham (ed.), *Scottish Philosophy: Selected Readings 1690–1960* (Exeter: Imprint Academic, 2004), pp. 1–11.

—, 'The Nineteenth-Century Aftermath', in A. Broadie (ed.), *The Cambridge Companion to the Scottish Enlightenment* (Cambridge: Cambridge University Press, 2003), pp. 338–50.

Gregory, J., *Epigrams and Poems* (Edinburgh: Printed by John Moir, 1810).

Grinnell, G., 'Thomas Beddoes and the Physiology of Romantic Medicine', *Studies in Romanticism*, 45:2 (2006), pp. 223–50.

Hall, J. Y., 'Gall's Phrenology: A Romantic Psychology', *Studies in Romanticism*, 16:3 (1977), pp. 305–17.

Hamilton, D., 'The Scottish Enlightenment and Clinical Medicine', in D. Dow (ed.), *The Influence of Scottish Medicine: An Historical Assessment of its International Impact* (Carnforth: The Parthenon Publishing Group, 1988), pp. 103–11.

Harris, J., 'Introduction', in J. Beattie, *James Beattie: Selected Philosophical Writings*, ed. J. A. Harris (Exeter: Imprint Academic, 2004), pp. 1–14.

Hartley, D., *Observations on Man, his Frame, his Duty, and his Expectations*, 2 vols (London: James Leake and Wm. Frederick, 1749), vol. 1, http://galenet.galegroup.com.proxy2.lib.umanitoba.ca/servlet/ECCO (accessed 4 July 2008).

Haslam, J., *Observations on Madness and Melancholy: Including Practical Remarks on those Diseases; Together with Cases: and An Account of the Morbid Appearances on Dissection* (London: G. Hayden, 1809).

Hassler, D. M., *Erasmus Darwin* (New York: Twayne Publishers, Inc., 1973).

Hatherell, W., '"Words and Things": Locke, Hartley and the Associationist Context for the Preface to *Lyrical Ballads*', *Romanticism: The Journal of Romantic Culture and Criticism*, 12:3 (2006), pp. 223–35.

Hayden, J., 'Wordsworth, Hartley, and the Revisionists', *Studies in Philology*, 81:1 (1984), pp. 94–118.

Hill, R. G., *Total Abolition of Personal Restraint in the Treatment of the Insane* (1838; New York: Arno Press, 1976).

Hilton, N., 'The Spectre of Darwin', *Blake: An Illustrated Quarterly*, 15:1 (1981), pp. 36–48.

Horace, selections from *Ars Poetica*, in V. B. Leitch (gen. ed.), *The Norton Anthology of Theory and Criticism* (New York: W. W. Norton, 2001), pp. 124–35.

Houston, R. A., *Madness and Society in Eighteenth-Century Scotland* (Oxford: Clarendon Press, 2000).

Howard, L., 'Thomas Odiorne: An American Predecessor of Wordsworth', *American Literature: A Journal of Literary History, Criticism, and Bibliography*, 10:4 (1939), pp. 417–36.

Hume, D., *A Treatise of Human Nature: A Critical Edition* (1739), eds D. F. Norton and M. J. Norton (Oxford: Clarendon Press, 2007).

Hunter, R. and I. Macalpine (eds), *Three Hundred Years of Psychiatry 1535–1860* (London: Oxford University Press, 1963).

Hunter, R. and Macalpine, I. (eds), Introductions to Nathaniel Cotton, Andrew Duncan, Thomas Forster, John Ferriar, Thomas Bakewell, Thomas Trotter, Thomas Beddoes, Thomas Brown, *Three Hundred Years of Psychiatry 1535-1860* (London: Oxford University Press, 1963), pp. 425–26; 631; 721; 543–4; 705–6; 587–8; 578–9; 752–3.

'Hygiene', *Oxford English Dictionary* (Online) (Oxford: Oxford University Press, 2008), http://dictionary.oed.com.proxy2.lib.umanitoba.ca/cgi/entry/50110112 [accessed 7 February 2008].

'Hygienic', *Oxford English Dictionary* (Online) (Oxford: Oxford University Press, 2008), http://dictionary.oed.com.proxy2.lib.umanitoba.ca/cgi/entry/50110113 [accessed 7 February 2008].

Ingram, A. with Faubert, M. *Cultural Constructions of Madness in Eighteenth Century Writing: Representing the Insane* (New York: Palgrave Macmillan, 2005).

Ingram, A. (ed.), *Patterns of Madness in the Eighteenth Century* (Liverpool: Liverpool University Press, 1998).

J., F. [full surname not given], 'Sketch of the Life of James Beattie, LLD', *The Minstrel: or, The Progress of Genius. Also, The Shipwreck. By William Falconer. With a Sketch of the Life of Each Author* (New York: Collins and Perkins, 1808), pp. iii–ix.

Jacyna, L. S., *Philosophic Whigs: Medicine, Science, and Citizenship in Edinburgh, 1789–1848* (London: Routledge, 1994).

[Jeffrey, F.], Unsigned review, *Edinburgh Review*, (November 24 1814), in R. Woof (ed.), *William Wordsworth: The Critical Heritage* (London: Routledge, 2001), vol. 1, pp. 381–404.

Jordanova, L. J., Introduction to M. McNeil, 'The Scientific Muse: The Poetry of Erasmus Darwin', in Jordanova, L. J. (ed.), *Languages of Nature: Critical Essays on Science and Literature* (New Brunswick, NJ: Rutgers University Press, 1986), pp. 159–63.

Kallich, M., 'The Association of Ideas and Akenside's *Pleasures of Imagination*', *Modern Language Notes*, 62:3 (1947), pp. 166–73.

Keats, J., *Letters of John Keats*, ed. Gittings, R. (Oxford: Oxford University Press, 1970).

Kierkegaard, S., *Concluding Unscientific Postscript to the Philosophical Fragments* (1846), trans. D. Swenson, (New Jersey: Princeton University Press, 1941).

—, *Fear and Trembling* (1843), trans. and intro. A. Hannay (London: Penguin, 1985).

King, E. H., *James Beattie's* The Minstrel *and the Origins of Romantic Autobiography* (Lewiston: The Edwin Mellen Press, 1992).

—, *James Beattie* (Boston, MA: Twayne Publishers, 1977).

King-Hele, D., 'Disenchanted Darwinians: Wordsworth, Coleridge and Blake', *The Wordsworth Circle*, 25:2 (1994), pp. 114–18.

—, *Erasmus Darwin and the Romantic Poets* (New York: St Martin's Press, 1986).

Kristeva, J., *Powers of Horror: An Essay on Abjection*, trans. L. S. Roudiez, (New York: Columbia University Press, 1982).

Laing, R. D., *The Divided Self: An Existential Study in Sanity and Madness* (London: Tavistock Publications Limited, 1960).

Lamb, J., 'Hartley and Wordsworth: Philosophical Language and Figures of the Sublime', *Modern Language Notes*, 97:5 (1982), pp. 1064–85.

—, 'Language and Hartleian Associationism in *A Sentimental Journey*', *Eighteenth-Century Studies*, 13 (1980), pp. 285–312.

Lau, B., 'Keats, Associationism, and "Ode to a Nightingale"', *Keats-Shelley Journal: Keats, Shelley, Byron, Hunt, and Their Circles*, 32 (1983), pp. 46–62.

Levere, T. H., '"The Lovely Shapes and Sounds Intelligible": Samuel Taylor Coleridge, Humphrey Davy, Science and Poetry', in Christie, J. and Shuttleworth, S. (eds), *Nature Transfigured: Science and Literature, 1700–1900* (Manchester: Manchester University Press, 1989), pp. 85–101.

Lockhart, J. G., 'Cockney School of Poetry', in *Blackwood's Edinburgh Magazine* (1818), in Mellor, A. K. and Matlak, R. E. (eds), *British Literature 1780–1830* (Fort Worth, TX: Harcourt Brace, 1996), pp. 159–61.

Logan, J. V., *The Poetry and Aesthetics of Erasmus Darwin* (Princeton, NJ: Princeton University Press, 1936).

Logan, P. M., *Nerves and Narratives: A Cultural History of Hysteria in Nineteenth-Century British Prose* (London: University of California Press, 1997).

Lovejoy, A., 'On the Discrimination of Romanticisms', *PMLA: Publications of the Modern Language Association of America*, 39:2 (1924), pp. 229–53.

Martin, P. W., *Mad Women in Romantic Writing* (New York: St Martin's Press, 1987).

Massey, E., *A Sermon Against the Dangerous and Sinful Practice of Inoculation*, 3rd edn (London: William Meadows, 1722).

McGavran, J. H., 'Darwin, Coleridge, and "The Thorn"', *The Wordsworth Circle*, 25:2 (1994), pp. 118–22.

McLane, M. N., *Romanticism and the Human Sciences: Poetry, Population, and the Discourse of the Species* (Cambridge: Cambridge University Press, 2000).

McLuhan, M., *Understanding Media: The Extensions of Man*, intro Lapham, L. H.(Cambridge: MIT Press, 1994).

McNeil, M., 'Darwin, Erasmus (1731-1802)', *Oxford Dictionary of National Biography*, (Oxford: Oxford University Press, 2004), http://www.oxforddnb.com.myaccess.library. utoronto.ca/view/article/7177 [accessed 11 July 2005].

—, 'The Scientific Muse: The Poetry of Erasmus Darwin', in Jordanova, L. J. (ed.),

Languages of Nature: Critical Essays on Science and Literature (New Brunswick, NJ: Rutgers University Press, 1986), pp. 163–203.

Mellor, A. K., 'Physiognomy, Phrenology, and Blake's Visionary Heads', in R. N. Essick and D. R. Pearce (eds), *Blake in His Time* (Bloomington, IN: Indiana University Press, 1978), pp. 53–74.

More, H., 'Slavery: A Poem' (1788), in Mellor, A. K. and Matlak, R. E. (eds), *British Literature 1780-1830* (Fort Worth: Harcourt Brace, 1996), pp. 206–9.

Morton, T., 'Joseph Ritson, Percy Shelley and the Making of Romantic Vegetarianism', *Romanticism: The Journal of Romantic Culture and Criticism*, 2:1 (2006), pp. 52–61.

Mullan, J., *Sentiment and Sociability: The Language of Feeling in the Eighteenth Century* (Oxford: Clarendon Press, 1988).

Neve, M., 'Beddoes, Thomas (1760–1808)', *Oxford Dictionary of National Biography* (Oxford: Oxford University Press, 2004), http://www.oxforddnb.com.myaccess.library.utoronto. ca/view/article/1919 [accessed 11 July, 2005].

Oppenheim, J., *'Shattered Nerves': Doctors, Patients, and Depression in Victorian England* (New York: Oxford University Press, 1991).

Paine, T., *Rights of Man: Being an Answer to Mr Burke's Attack on the French Revolution* (1791) (London: J. M. Dent & Sons, Ltd., 1915).

Parry-Jones, W. L., *The Trade in Lunacy: A Study of Private Madhouses in England in the Eighteenth and Nineteenth Centuries* (London: Routledge & Kegan Paul, 1972).

Pearsall, R. B., 'Wordsworth Reworks His Hartley', *Bulletin of the Rocky Mountain Modern Language Association*, 24:2 (1970), pp. 75–83.

Perfect, W., 'To Solitude', *Poetic Effusions: Pastoral, Moral, Amatory and Descriptive* (London: A. Milne, 1796), pp. 153–6.

—, *A Remarkable Case of Madness, With the Diet and Medicines, Used in the Cure* (Rochester, NY: For the author, 1791), in *The Eighteenth-Century* (ESTC reel (MICR) 13297. no. 5).

—, *Cases in Midwifery: Principally Founded on the Correspondence of ... Dr Colin Mackenzie, with References, Quotations, and Remarks, by William Perfect*, 3rd edn, 2 vols (W. Gillman: Rochester: 1789), in *The Eighteenth Century* (ESTC reel 6925, no. 6).

—, *Select Cases in the Different Species of Insanity, Lunacy, or Madness, with the Modes of Practice as Adopted in the Treatment of Each* (Rochester, NY: W. Gillman, 1787), in *The Eighteenth Century* (ESTC reel (MICR) 6018, no. 7).

—, *Cases of Insanity, the Epilepsy, Hypochondriacal Affection, Hysteric Passion, and Nervous Disorders, Successfully Treated* (Rochester?: n. p., *c.* 1785), in *The Eighteenth-Century* (ESTC reel (MICR) 99, no. 14).

—, 'Contentment, An Ode', *The Laurel-Wreath; Being a Collection of Original Miscellaneous Poems, On Subjects Moral, Comic, and Divine*, 2 vols (London: Printed for the Author, 1766), vol. 1, pp. 60–3, in *The Eighteenth Century* (ESTC reel (MICR) 1883, no. 8).

—, 'Extempore, on Seeing a Scull', in *The Laurel-Wreath; Being a Collection of Original Miscellaneous Poems, On Subjects Moral, Comic, and Divine*, 2 vols (London: Printed for the Author, 1766), vol. 1, pp. 156–7, in *The Eighteenth Century* (ESTC reel (MICR) 1883, no. 8).

—, 'An Ode to Poverty ', in *The Laurel-Wreath; Being a Collection of Original Miscellaneous Poems, On Subjects Moral, Comic, and Divine*, 2 vols (London: Printed for the Author, 1766), vol. 2, pp. 77–80, in *The Eighteenth Century* (ESTC reel (MICR) 1883, no. 8).

—, Preface to *The Laurel-Wreath; Being a Collection of Original Miscellaneous Poems, On Subjects Moral, Comic, and Divine*, 2 vols (London: Printed for the Author, 1766), vol. 1, pp. iii–iv, in *The Eighteenth Century* (ESTC reel (MICR) 1883, no. 8).

—, 'The Social Thought; or The Tea-Pot Resign'd', *The Laurel-Wreath; Being a ollection of Original Miscellaneous Poems, On Subjects Moral, Comic, and Divine*, 2 vols (London: Printed for the Author, 1766), vol. 1, pp. 173–4, in *The Eighteenth Century* (ESTC reel (MICR) 1883, no. 8).

—, 'Solitude: An Ode', *The Laurel-Wreath; Being a Collection of Original Miscellaneous Poems, On Subjects Moral, Comic, and Divine*, 2 vols (London: Printed for the Author, 1766), vol. 1, pp. 87–9, in *The Eighteenth Century* (ESTC reel (MICR) 1883, no. 8).

—, 'To Health', *The Laurel-Wreath; Being a Collection of Original Miscellaneous Poems, On Subjects Moral, Comic, and Divine*, 2 vols (London: Printed for the Author, 1766), vol. 1, pp. 162–3, in *The Eighteenth Century* (ESTC reel (MICR) 1883, no. 8).

—, 'A Parody from Hamlet, Wrote When Indisposed and in Doubt about Bleeding', in

A Bavin of Bays: Containing Various Original Essays in Poetry (London: Printed for the author, 1763), pp. 156–7, in *The Eighteenth-Century* (ESTC reel (MICR) 8358, no. 1).

Perkins, D., *Romanticism and Animal Rights* (Cambridge: Cambridge University Press, 2003).

—, 'Religion and Animal Rights in the Romantic Era', in. Barth, R. J. (ed.), *The Fountain Light: Studies in Romanticism and Religion in Honor of John L. Mahoney* (New York: Fordham University Press, 2002), pp. 1–21.

—, 'Compassion for Animals and Radical Politics: Coleridge's "To a Young Ass"', *ELH* (*English Literary History*), 65:4 (1998), pp. 929–44.

Peterson, D. (ed.), *A Mad People's History of Madness* (University of Pittsburgh Press, 1982).

Phillipson, N. T., 'James Beattie and the Defence of Common Sense', in B. Fabian (ed.), *Festschrift Für Rainer Gruenter* (Heidelberg: Carl Winter, 1978), pp. 145–54.

Pinel, P., *A Treatise on Insanity*, trans. D. D. Davis, (Sheffield: Cadell & Davies, 1806).

Pitcher, E. W., 'Nathaniel Cotton, the Elder: An Anonymous Contributor to Dodsley's *Museum* (1746-7) and Wm Dodd's *Visitor* (1760)', *American Notes and Queries*, 17:8 (1979), pp. 124-5.

Pollin, B. R., 'Nicholson's Lost Portrait of William Godwin: A Study in Phrenology', *Keats-Shelley Journal: Keats, Shelley, Byron, Hunt, and Their Circles*, 16 (1967), pp. 51–60.

Porter, R., *Doctor of Society: Thomas Beddoes and the Sick Trade in Late Enlightenment England* (London: Routledge, 1992).

—, 'Barely Touching: A Social Perspective on Mind and Body', in G. S. Rousseau (ed.), *The Languages of Psyche: Mind and Body in Enlightenment Thought* (Berkeley, CA: University of California Press, 1990), pp. 45–80.

—, 'Introduction', in J. Haslam, *Illustrations of Madness* (1810) (London: Routledge, 1988), pp. xi–xl.

—, 'Introduction' in T. Trotter, *An Essay Medical, Philosophical, and Chemical on Drunkenness and its Effects on the Human Body* (1804), ed. R. Porter (London:

Routledge, 1988), pp. ix–xl.

—, *Mind Forg'd Manacles: A History of Madness in England from the Restoration to*

the Regency (London: Athalone Press, 1987).

—, 'The Rage of Party: A Glorious Revolution in English Psychiatry?', *Medical History:*

A Quarterly Journal Devoted to the History of Medicine and Related Sciences, 27 (1983), pp. 35–50.

Preece, R., *Animals and Nature: Cultural Myths, Cultural Realities* (Vancouver: University of British Columbia Press, 1999).

Priestley, J., *Hartley's Theory of the Human Mind, on the Principle of the Association of Ideas; With Essays relating to the Subject of It* (1775), 2nd edn (London: J. Johnson, 1790), http://galenet.galegroup.com.proxy2.lib.umanitoba.ca/servlet/ECCO [accessed 2 July 2008].

'Psychology', *The Oxford English Dictionary* (Online) (Oxford: Oxford University Press, 2008), http://dictionary.oed.com.proxy1.lib.umanitoba.ca/cgi/entry/50191636? [accessed 12 April 2008].

Rabb, M. A., 'Psychology and Politics in William Godwin's *Caleb Williams*: Double Bond or Double Bind?', in C. Fox, (ed.), *Psychology in the Eighteenth Century* (New York: AMS Press, 1987), pp. 51–67.

Reed, E. S., *From Soul to Mind: The Emergence of Psychology from Erasmus Darwin to William James* (New Haven, CT: Yale University Press, 1997).

Reihl, J. E., 'Keats's "Ode on a Grecian Urn" and Eighteenth-Century Associationism', *Publications of the Arkansas Philological Association*, 9:1 (1983), pp. 85–96.

Richardson, A., 'Of Heartache and Head Injury: Reading Minds in *Persuasion*', *Poetics Today*, 23:1 (2002), pp. 141–60.

—, *British Romanticism and the Science of the Mind* (New York: Cambridge University Press, 2001).

Richardson, S., *Clarissa; or, The History of a Young Lady* (1747-8), ed., intro. and notes A. Ross (Harmondsworth: Penguin, 1985).

—, *Pamela; or, Virtue Rewarded* (1740), intro. M. Kinkead-Weekes (London: Dent, 1962).

Ritchie, L., 'Cotton, Nathaniel (1705-1788)', *Oxford Dictionary of National Biography* (Oxford: Oxford University Press, 2004), http://www.oxforddnb.com.myaccess.library.utoronto.ca/view/article/6422 [accessed 11 July 2005].

Robinson, R. J., 'Beattie, James (1735-1803)', *Oxford Dictionary of National Biography* (Oxford: Oxford University Press, 2004), http://www.oxforddnb.com.myaccess.library.utoronto.ca/view/article/1831 [accessed 2 August 2005].

Rorty, R., *Philosophy and the Mirror of Nature* (Princeton: Princeton University, 1979).

Roscoe, W., *The Wrongs of Africa, A Poem* (London: R. Faulder, 1787-8), http://galenet.galegroup.com.proxy2.lib.umanitoba.ca/servlet/ECCO [accessed 11 August 2008].

Rosenberg, C. E., 'Body and Mind in Nineteenth-Century Medicine: Some Clinical Origins of the Neurosis Construct', *Bulletin of the History of Medicine*, 63 (1989), pp. 185–97.

Rosner, L., *Medical Education in the Age of Improvement: Edinburgh Students and Apprentices, 1760–1826* (Edinburgh: Edinburgh University Press, 1991).

Ross, C. E., '"Twin Labourers and Heirs of the Same Hopes": The Professional Rivalry of Humphrey Davy and William Wordsworth', in Heringman, N. (ed.), *Romantic Science: The Literary Forms of Natural History* (New York: State University of New York Press, 2003), pp. 23–52.

Rousseau, J.-J., *Discourse on the Origin of Inequality*, trans. F. Philip, ed. Colman P. (Oxford: Oxford University Press, 1994).

Rousseau, G. S., 'Nerves, Spirits, and Fibres: Towards Defining the Origins of Sensibility', *Blue Guitar*, 2 (1976), pp. 125–53.

Rowe, S., '"Listen to Me": *Frankenstein* as an Appeal to Mercy and Justice, on Behalf of the Persecuted Animals', in F. Palmeri (ed. and intro.), *Humans and Other Animals in Eighteenth-Century British Culture: Representation, Hybridity, Ethics* (Burlington: Ashgate, 2006), pp. 137–52.

Sacks, O., *The Man Who Mistook His Wife for a Hat* (London: Gerald Duckworth & Co. Ltd., 1985).

Salazar, R., 'Historicizing Phrenology: Wordsworth, Pynchon, and the Discursive Economy of the Cranial Text', *Raritan: A Quarterly Review*, 8:1 (1988), pp. 80–91.

Sallé, J. C., 'Hazlitt the Associationist', *Review of English Studies: A Quarterly Journal of English Literature and the English Language*, 15:57 (1964), pp. 38–51.

Schaffer, S., 'States of Mind: Enlightenment and Natural Philosophy', in G. S. Rousseau (ed.), *The Languages of Psyche: Mind and Body in Enlightenment Thought* (Berkeley, CA: University of California Press, 1990), pp. 233–90.

Scott, W., *The Heart of Midlothian* (1830), ed. and intro. Lamont, C. (Oxford: Oxford University Press, 1982).

—, *The Lay of the Last Minstrel and The Lady of the Lake* (1805), intro. Palgrave, F. T. (Whitefish: Kessinger Publishing, 2007).

Seeber, B. K., 'The Hunting Ideal, Animal Rights, and Feminism in *Northanger Abbey* and *Sense and Sensibility*', in T. Belleguic (ed. and preface), *Lumen: Selected Proceedings from the Canadian Society for Eighteenth-Century Studies* (Kelowna: Academic, 2004), pp. 295–308.

Shelley, B. K., 'The Synthetic Imagination: Shelley and Associationism', *Wordsworth Circle*, 14:1 (1983), pp. 68–73.

Shelley, P. B., 'A Defence of Poetry', in D. H. Reiman and N. Fraistat (eds), *Shelley's Prose and Poetry* (New York: W. W. Norton, 2002), pp. 509–35.

Shorter, E., *A Historical Dictionary of Psychiatry* (Oxford: Oxford University Press, 2005).

—, *A History of Psychiatry: From the Era of the Asylum to the Age of Prozac* (New York: John Wiley and Sons, Inc., 1997).

—, *From Paralysis to Fatigue: A History of Psychosomatic Illness in the Modern Era* (New York: The Free Press, 1992).

Showalter, E., *The Female Malady: Women, Madness, and English Culture, 1830–1980* (New York: Pantheon, 1985).

Shumway, D. R., *Michel Foucault* (Boston: Twayne Publishers, 1989).

Skultans, V., *English Madness: Ideas on Insanity, 1580–1890* (London: Routledge, 1979).

Smith, A., *Theory of Moral Sentiments* (1790), ed. K. Haakonssen (Cambridge: Cambridge University Press, 2002).

Smith, L. D., 'Bakewell, Thomas (1761-1835)', *Oxford Dictionary of National Biography* (Oxford: Oxford University Press, 2004), http://www.oxforddnb.com.myaccess.library. utoronto.ca/view/article/56715 [accessed 11 July 2005].

St Clair, W., 'Who Read What in the Romantic Period', University of Toronto, Toronto, Ontario, 7 March 2005.

Starobinski, J., *The Living Eye*, trans. Goldhammer, A. (Cambridge, MA: Harvard University Press, 1989).

Sterne, L., *Life and Opinions of Tristram Shandy, Gentleman* (1760–7; New York: Norton, 1980).

Stewart, D., *Elements of the Philosophy of the Human Mind*, 3 vols (London: Strahan, A. and Cadell, T., 1792–1827), in *Eighteenth Century Collections Online*, http://galenet. galegroup.com.proxy2.lib.umanitoba.ca/servlet/ECCO (accessed 7 July 2008).

Stewart-Robertson, J. C., 'Brown, Thomas (1778-1820)', *Oxford Dictionary of National Biography* (Oxford: Oxford University Press, 2004), http://www.oxforddnb.com.myaccess. library.utoronto.ca/view/article/3655 [accessed 11 July 2005].

Stock, J. E., *Memoirs of the Life of Thomas Beddoes, MD, with an Analytical Account of his Writings* (1811) (Bristol: Thoemmes Press, 2003).

Strozier, R. M., *Foucault, Subjectivity and Identity: Historical Constructions of Subject and Self* (Detroit, MI: Wayne State University Press, 2002).

Szasz, T. S., *The Myth of Mental Illness: Foundations of a Theory of Personal Conduct* (New York: Hoeber-Harper Inc., 1961).

Tambling, J., *Blake's Night Thoughts* (New York: Palgrave Macmillan, 2005).

Taylor, B. and R. Bain, 'Introduction', in B. Taylor and R. Bain (eds), *The Cast of Consciousness: Concepts of the Mind in British and American Romanticism* (New York: Greenwood Press, 1987), pp. ix–xv.

Thackeray, W. M., *Vanity Fair* (1847–8), ed. J. Sutherland (Oxford: Oxford University Press, 1983).

Thiher, A., *Revels in Madness: Insanity in Medicine and Literature* (Ann Arbor: The University of Michigan Press, 1999).

Trotter, T., 'The Ass: An Ode, On the Melioration of the Species', *Sea-Weeds: Poems, Written on Various Occasions, Chiefly During a Naval Life* (Newcastle: Longman and Co., 1829), pp. 105–10.

—, 'The Beggar's Bush (Cut Down by a Maniac about Forty-eight Years Ago)', *Sea-Weeds: Poems, Written on Various Occasions, Chiefly During a Naval Life* (Newcastle: Longman and Co., 1829), pp. 103–4.

—, 'The Cruize', *Sea-Weeds: Poems, Written on Various Occasions, Chiefly During a Naval Life* (Newcastle: Longman and Co., 1829), pp. 50–1.

—, 'The Furze Blossom', *Sea-Weeds: Poems, Written on Various Occasions, Chiefly During a Naval Life* (Newcastle: Longman and Co., 1829), pp. 69–71.

—, 'The Life-Boat', *Sea-Weeds: Poems, Written on Various Occasions, Chiefly During a Naval Life* (Newcastle: Longman and Co., 1829), pp. 85–7.

—, 'Looks and Eyes', *Sea-Weeds: Poems, Written on Various Occasions, Chiefly During a Naval Life* (Newcastle: Longman and Co., 1829), pp. 111–12.

—, 'Preface', *Sea-Weeds: Poems, Written on Various Occasions, Chiefly During a Naval Life* (Newcastle: Longman and Co., 1829), pp. xii–xxv.

—, 'The Swallow', *Sea-Weeds: Poems, Written on Various Occasions, Chiefly During a Naval Life* (Newcastle: Longman and Co., 1829), pp. 61–3.

—, 'Vaccination', *Sea-Weeds: Poems, Written on Various Occasions, Chiefly During a Naval Life* (Newcastle: Longman and Co., 1829), pp. 117–20.

—, 'Verses Written in the Ladies' Walk at Liverpool, in January, 1783', *Sea-Weeds: Poems, Written on Various Occasions, Chiefly During a Naval Life* (Newcastle: Longman and Co., 1829), pp. 43–4.

—, *Noble Foundling; or, The Hermit of the Tweed. A Tragedy, in Five Acts* (London: Longman, Hurst, Rees, Orme, and Brown, 1812).

—, *A View of the Nervous Temperament; Being a Practical Inquiry into the Increasing Prevalence, Prevention, and Treatment of Those Diseases Commonly Called Nervous, Bilious, Stomach, Liver Complaints, Indigestion, Low Spirits, Gout, &c.* (Troy: Wright, Goodenow & Stockwell, 1808).

—, *An Essay Medical, Philosophical, and Chemical on Drunkenness and its Effects on the Human Body* (1804), ed. Porter, R. (London: Routledge, 1988).

—, *Suspiria Oceani: A Monody on the Death of Richard Earl Howe, K. G. Admiral of the Fleet and General of his Majesty's Forces* (London: T. Hatchard, 1800).

Tuke, S., *Description of the Retreat, an Institution Near York, For Insane Persons of the Society of Friends. Containing an Account of its Origin and Progress, the Modes of Treatment, and a Statement of Cases* (York: W. Alexander, 1813).

Ullrich, D. W., 'Distinctions in Poetic and Intellectual Influence: Coleridge's Use of Erasmus Darwin', *The Wordsworth Circle*, 15:2 (1984), pp. 74–80.

Vaulbert de Chantilly, M., 'Introduction', in J. Ferriar, *The Bibliomania*, (ed.) Vaulbert de Chantilly, M. (London: The Vanity Press of Bethnal Green, 2001), pp. 3–21.

Veatch, R. M., *Disrupted Dialogue: Medical Ethics and the Collapse of Physician-Humanist Communication (1770–1980)* (Oxford: Oxford University Press, 2004).

Vickers, N., *Coleridge and the Doctors* (Oxford: Clarendon Press, 2004).

—, 'Coleridge, Thomas Beddoes and Brunonian Medicine', *European Romantic Review*, 8:1 (1997), pp. 47–94.

'Vision', *Oxford English Dictionary* (Online) (Oxford: Oxford University Press, 2008), http://dictionary.oed.com.proxy1.lib.umanitoba.ca//cgi/entry/50278245 [accessed 25 July 2008].

Walker, E. C., 'Reading Proof, Aids to Reflection, and Phrenology: A New Coleridge Letter', *European Romantic Review*, 8:3 (1997), pp. 323–40.

Walker, S., from *A Treatise on Nervous Diseases* (1796), in Hunter, R. and Macalpine, I. (eds), *Three Hundred Years of Psychiatry 1535-1860* (London: Oxford University Press, 1963), pp. 552–3.

Wallace, J., 'Trotter, Thomas (bap. 1760, d. 1832)', *Oxford Dictionary of National Biography* (Oxford: Oxford University Press, 2004), http://www.oxforddnb.com.myaccess.library.utoronto.ca/view/article/27763 [accessed 11 July 2005].

Wallen, M., *City of Health, Fields of Disease: Revolutions in the Poetry, Medicine, and Philosophy of Romanticism* (Aldershot: Ashgate, 2004).

Walsh, R., 'The Life of Dr Cotton', *The Works of the British Poets, with Lives of the Authors* (Boston, MA: Charles Ewer and Timothy Bedlington, 1822), vol. 35, pp. 313–17.

Waterston, C. D., 'Late Enlightenment Science and Generalism: The Case of Sir George Steuart Mackenzie of Coul, 1780–1848', in C. W. J. Withers and P. Wood (eds), *Sciences and Medicine in the Scottish Enlightenment* (East Linton: Tuckwell Press, 2002), pp. 301–26.

Watts, I., 'Against Scoffing and Calling Names', in *Divine and Moral Songs for the Use of Children* (1720) (Whitefish: Kessinger Publishing, 2003), pp. 44–6.

Webb, K. A., 'Ferriar, John (1761–1815)', *Oxford Dictionary of National Biography* (Oxford: Oxford University Press, 2004), http://www.oxforddnb.com.myaccess.library.utoronto.ca/view/article/9368 (accessed 11 July 2005).

Welsh, D., 'A Memoir of Dr Brown', in Brown, T., *Lectures on the Philosophy of the Human Mind* (1820) (William Tait: Edinburgh, 1828), pp. v–xxxi.

Wesley, J., *Primitive Physick: or, An Easy and Natural Method of Curing Most Diseases* (1747) (Bristol: John Grabham, 1759).

Wollstonecraft, M., *Mary, A Fiction* (1788) and *The Wrongs of Woman* (1798), ed. G. Kelly (London: Oxford University Press, 1976).

—, *A Vindication of the Rights of Woman with Strictures on Political and Moral Subjects* (1792), ed. A. Tauchert (London: J. M. Dent, 1995).

—, *A Vindication of the Rights of Men* (1790), *Mary Wollstonecraft: Political Writings*, ed. Todd, J. (Toronto: University of Toronto Press, 1993).

Wordsworth, W., Preface to *Lyrical Ballads* (1800, 1850), *The Prose Works of William Wordsworth*, eds Owen, W. J. B. and Smyser, J. W. (Oxford: Clarendon Press, 1974), vol. 1, pp. 119–59.

—, *The Prelude* (1805), *William Wordsworth: A Critical Edition of the Major Works*, ed. S. Gill (Oxford: Oxford University Press, 1984), pp. 375–590.

—, 'Ode ("There was a Time")' (1807), *William Wordsworth: A Critical Edition of the Major Works*, ed. Gill, S. (Oxford: Oxford University Press, 1984), pp. 297–302.

—, 'Michael: A Pastoral Poem' (1798), *William Wordsworth: A Critical Edition of the Major Works*, ed. S. Gill (Oxford: Oxford University Press, 1984), p. 224–36.

Wright, J. P., 'Metaphysics and Physiology: Mind, Body, and the Animal Economy in Eighteenth-Century Scotland', in M. A. Stewart, (ed.), *Studies in the Philosophy of the Scottish Enlightenment* (Oxford: Clarendon Press, 1990), pp. 251–301.

Youngquist, P., *Monstrosities: Bodies and British Romanticism* (Minneapolis, MN: University of Minneapolis Press, 2003).

INDEX